INTRODUCTION TO MICROPROCESSORS

CHARLES M. GILMORE
PRESIDENT, ADVANCED COMPUTER CONCEPTS

Gregg Division
McGraw-Hill Book Company

New York	Madrid
Atlanta	Mexico
Dallas	Montreal
St. Louis	New Delhi
San Francisco	Panama
Auckland	Paris
Bogotá	San Juan
Guatemala	São Paulo
Hamburg	Singapore
Johannesburg	Sydney
Lisbon	Tokyo
London	Toronto

Library of Congress Cataloging in Publication Data

Gilmore, Charles Minot (date)
Introduction to microprocessors.

(Basic skills in electricity and electronics)
Includes index.
1. Microprocessors. I. Title. II. Series.
QA76.5.G5143   001.64   80-26115
ISBN 0-07-023304-7

Acknowledgments
Students, teachers, school administrators, and industrial trainers have contributed to the development of the *Basic Skills in Electricity and Electronics* series. Classroom testing of preliminary editions has been conducted at the following sites:

Burr D. Coe Vocational Technical High School (East Brunswick, New Jersey)
Chantilly Secondary School (Chantilly, Virginia)
Nashoba Valley Technical High School (Westford, Massachusetts)
Platt Regional Vocational Technical High School (Milford, Connecticut)
United States Steel Corporation: Edgar Thomson, Irvin Works (Dravosburg, Pennsylvania)

The publisher gratefully acknowledges the helpful comments and suggestions received from these participants.

Introduction to Microprocessors

1 2 3 4 5 6 7 8 9 0   VHVH   8 9 8 7 6 5 4 3 2

Sponsoring Editors: Gordon Rockmaker and Mark Haas
Editing Supervisors: Zaza Ziemba and Paul Berk
Design Supervisor: Nancy Axelrod
Production Supervisor: Kathleen Morrissey
Art Supervisor: George T. Resch

Cover Photography: Martin Bough/Studios, Inc.

ISBN   0-07-023304-7

Contents

Editor's Foreword

The Gregg/McGraw-Hill *Basic Skills in Electricity and Electronics* series has been designed to provide entry-level competencies in a wide range of occupations in the electrical and electronics fields. The series consists of instructional materials geared especially for the career-oriented student. Each major subject area covered in the series is supported by a textbook, an activities manual, and a teacher's manual. All the materials focus on the theory, applications, and experiences required for those just beginning their chosen vocations.

There are two basic considerations in the preparation of educational materials for such a series: the needs of the learner and the needs of the employer. The materials in the series have been designed to meet those needs. They are based on many years of experience in the classroom and with electricity and electronics. In addition, these books reflect the needs of industry and commerce as developed through questionnaires, surveys, interviews with employers, government occupational trend reports, and various field studies.

Further refinements both in pedagogy and technical content resulted from actual classroom experience with the materials. Preliminary editions of selected texts and manuals were field tested in schools and in-plant training programs throughout the country. The knowledge gained from this testing has enhanced the effectiveness and the validity of the materials.

Teachers will find the materials in each of the subject areas well coordinated and structured around a framework of modern objectives. Students will find the concepts clearly presented with many practical references and applications. In all, every effort has been made to prepare and refine the most effective learning tools possible.

The publisher and editor welcome comments from teachers and students using this book.

Charles A. Schuler
Project Editor

BASIC SKILLS IN ELECTRICITY AND ELECTRONICS

Charles A. Schuler, Project Editor

Books in this series

Introduction to Television Servicing by Wayne C. Brandenburg
Electricity: Principles and Applications by Richard J. Fowler
Instruments and Measurements by Charles M. Gilmore
Introduction to Microprocessors by Charles M. Gilmore
Small Appliance Repair by Phyllis Palmore and Nevin E. André
Electronics: Principles and Applications by Charles A. Schuler
Digital Electronics by Roger L. Tokheim

Preface

Introduction to Microprocessors is an introductory text on microprocessors and microcomputers. It is written for students who are relatively new to the field of electronics. The prerequisites are modest. A student should have an elementary background in solid-state electronics, digital circuits, and mathematics. In most cases, the only real requirement is for first-year algebra; a solid-state electronics and digital-circuit background will serve to reduce the amount the student must take on faith.

Students who have completed a course in microprocessors using this text can continue on a number of career paths. They will have sufficient background to enter the field of repair and maintenance of microprocessor-based products and systems. They will also be well-prepared to continue in a curriculum for technologists or design-engineering technicians.

This text uses a twofold approach to microprocessors: the students learn about the microprocessor by examining its microprograms and other firm ware and by examining the electrical and mechanical components (hardware). Considerable time is spent on learning the basic parts of an instruction set. However, a number of chapters are devoted to important hardware such as RAM, ROM, UARTs, I/O devices, and the like.

In addition, wherever possible, concepts are supported and reinforced with real-life examples. Usually these examples take the form of short programs such as a file-sort program, a clock program, and so on. Admittedly it is not always possible to use this approach, because some real-life examples are such small, intrinsic parts of the processor's whole program as to make a separate treatment meaningless.

The text has been organized into three sections. Chaps. 1 through 5 cover microprocessor fundamentals, including the basic concepts of processors, binary arithmetic, and programming; Chaps. 6 through 10 introduce the major instruction types of software and architecture used by most microprocessors; and Chaps. 11 through 14 examine the microprocessor and its peripheral devices as hardware. These chapters also discuss microprocessor test equipment.

This text is based on a nonexistent microprocessor. There are a number of reasons for doing this. A prime reason is that most commercially available microprocessors are too complex to use when introducing a student to the concepts. Once the fundamental concepts are mastered adapting them to fit a particular device is no problem. Also, it is not my objective to unduly emphasize a particular microprocessor or microprocessor family. It is difficult, if not impossible, to teach a course around a particular microprocessor and not have that device or family become the student's "processor for life." You will find that our hypothetical microprocessor does a few things that no one microprocessor does today. How it will compare to microprocessors of the future is beyond my ability to project in this rapidly changing field.

As always, the preparation of a text involves many people. Included in this text are ideas gathered from innumerable discussions with talented engineers and instructors currently using microprocessors and teaching about them. We have seen at first hand the shortcomings in the technical training of our support people. In essence, offering a solution to that problem became the rationale for this textbook.

Many thanks go to Barbara Tittle and Janice Brown, who typed the manuscript and contributed editorial help. Special thanks go to my wife, Polly, who put up with me while the text was in preparation and who provided editing and guidance. Thanks also to Josey, who provided elementary examples.

I look forward to suggestions and comments from students and teachers.

Charles M. Gilmore

Safety

Electric devices and circuits can be dangerous. Safe practices are necessary to prevent electric shock, fires, explosions, mechanical damage, and injuries resulting from the improper use of tools.

Perhaps the greatest hazard is electric shock. A current through the human body in excess of 10 milliamperes can paralyze the victim and make it impossible to let go of a "live" conductor. Ten milliamperes is a small amount of electrical flow: It is *ten one-thousandths* of an ampere. An ordinary flashlight uses more than 100 times that amount of current! If a shock victim is exposed to currents over 100 milliamperes, the shock is often *fatal*. This is still far less current than the flashlight uses.

A flashlight cell can deliver more than enough current to kill a human being. Yet it is safe to handle a flashlight cell because the resistance of human skin normally will be high enough to greatly limit the flow of electric current. Human skin usually has a resistance of several hundred thousand ohms. In low-voltage systems, a high resistance restricts current flow to very low values. Thus, there is little danger of an electric shock.

High voltage, on the other hand, can force enough current through the skin to produce a shock. The danger of harmful shock increases as the voltage increases. Those who work on very high-voltage circuits must use special equipment and procedures for protection.

When human skin is moist or cut, its resistance can drop to several hundred ohms. Much less voltage is then required to produce a shock. Potentials as low as 40 volts can produce a fatal shock if the skin is broken! Although most technicians and electrical workers refer to 40 volts as a *low voltage*, it does not necessarily mean *safe voltage*. You should, therefore, be very cautious even when working with so-called low voltages.

Safety is an attitude; safety is knowledge. Safe workers are not fooled by terms such as *low voltage*. They do not assume protective devices are working. They do not assume a circuit is off even though the switch is in the OFF position. They know that the switch could be defective.

As your knowledge of electricity and electronics grows, you will learn many specific safety rules and practices. In the meantime:

1. Investigate before you act
2. Follow procedures
3. When in doubt, *do not act*: Ask your instructor

GENERAL SAFETY RULES FOR ELECTRICITY AND ELECTRONICS

Safe practices will protect you and those around you. Study the following general safety rules. Discuss them with others. Ask your instructor about any that you do not understand.

1. Do not work when you are tired or taking medicine that makes you drowsy.
2. Do not work in poor light.
3. Do not work in damp areas.
4. Use approved tools, equipment, and protective devices.
5. Do not work if you or your clothing are wet.
6. Remove all rings, bracelets, and similar metal items.
7. Never assume that a circuit is off. Check it with a device or piece of equipment that you are sure is operating properly.

8. Do not tamper with safety devices. *Never* defeat an interlocking switch. Verify that all interlocks operate properly.

9. Keep your tools and equipment in good condition. Use the correct tool for the job.

10. Verify that capacitors have discharged. Some capacitors may store a lethal charge for a long time.

11. Do not remove equipment grounds. Verify that all grounds are intact.

12. Do not use adaptors that defeat ground connections.

13. Use only an approved fire extinguisher. Water can conduct electric current and increase the hazards and damage. Carbon dioxide (CO_2) and certain halogenated extinguishers are preferred for most electrical fires. Foam types may also be used in some cases.

14. Follow directions when using solvents and other chemicals. They may explode, ignite, or damage electric circuits.

15. Certain electronic components affect the safe performance of the equipment. Always use the correct replacement parts.

16. Use protective clothing and safety glasses when handling high-vacuum devices such as television picture tubes.

17. Do not attempt to work on complex equipment or circuits before you are ready. There may be many hidden dangers.

18. Some of the best safety information for electric and electronic equipment is in the literature prepared by the manufacturer. Find it and use it!

Any of the above rules could be expanded. As your study progresses, you will learn many of the details concerning proper procedure. Learn them well, because they are the most important information available.

Remember, always practice safety; your life depends on it.

What Is the Microprocessor?

■ In this chapter, we will first look briefly at the history of the microprocessor. We will see why advances in computer technology and in solid-state technology led to its development. We will then find out what the microprocessor is. We will learn about its two chief functions: control and processing. We will begin to learn the special vocabulary that has developed around microprocessors. Although much of this vocabulary lacks precise, scientifically defined meanings, we will clear up some of the basic terms.

We will learn the difference between a microprocessor and a microcomputer; and we will see that, although it is an exaggeration to call a microprocessor a "computer on a chip," nevertheless, the microprocessor does bear comparison with computers of the past. Finally, we will learn to measure the power of a microprocessor, through the size of its data word, its range of memory addressing, and its speed of operation.

1-1 A BRIEF HISTORY

To understand how the microprocessor came about, we must follow the growth of two major technologies: digital computers and solid-state circuits. How did these two technologies happen to come together in the early 1970s to produce the microprocessor?

The digital computer does computations under the control of a *program*. The general way in which the computations are done is called the digital computer's *architecture*. The microprocessor has architecture similar to the digital computer's. In other words, the microprocessor is like the digital computer because both do computations under program control. Consequently, the history of the digital computer will help us understand the microprocessor.

The history of solid-state circuits will also help, because the microprocessor *is* a solid-state circuit—a large-scale integrated microcircuit, to be more precise.

The chart in Fig. 1-1 shows the major events in these two technologies as they developed over the last four decades. Follow this chart as you read the following account of how the two technologies developed from the days of World War II.

During World War II, scientists developed computers especially for military use. After the war, in the latter half of the 1940s, digital computers were developed for scientific and civilian purposes.

Electronic circuit technology also advanced during World War II. Radar work increased the understanding of fast digital circuits called *pulse circuits*.

After the war, scientists made great progress in solid-state physics. Scientists at Bell Laboratories invented the transistor, a solid-state device, in 1948.

In the early 1950s, the first general-purpose digital computers appeared. They used vacuum tubes for the active electronic components. Vacuum-tube modules were used to build basic logic circuits such as gates and flip-flops. By assembling gate and flip-flop modules, scientists built the computer's calculating logic, control logic, and memory circuits. Vacuum tubes also formed part of the machines built to communicate with the computer.

From studying digital circuits, you know that building even a simple adder circuit takes quite a few gates. Most digital computers, of course, have a number of adders. Building a digital computer requires many circuits.

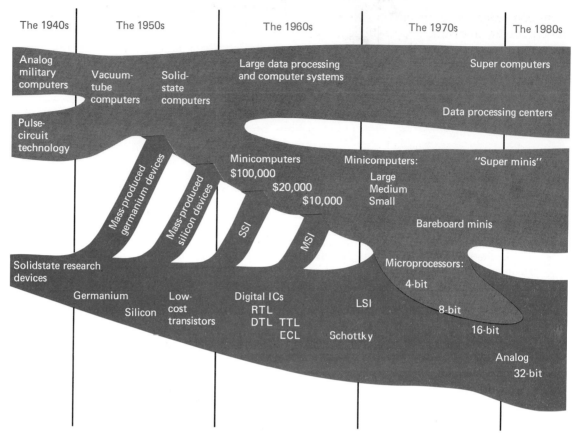

| The 1940s | The 1950s | The 1960s | The 1970s | The 1980s |

Fig. 1-1 The evolution of the microprocessor. The microprocessor is a product of computer and semiconductor technology.
Linked from the mid 1950s, these technologies merged in the
early 1970s in a product called the microprocessor.

Since all their circuits were made of bulky vacuum tubes, the early digital computers were huge. Because the vacuum tubes were hot, these early computers required air conditioning. The vacuum tubes were also unreliable by today's standards. Vacuum tubes made the early computers expensive to build, expensive to run, and expensive to maintain. The drawbacks of the vacuum tube were hampering the development of the digital computer.

Nevertheless, the early computers did introduce the important idea of *program storage*. The computers of the late 1940s and early 1950s had used *patch-cord programming*. Using a patch panel, the programmer actually wired in the steps telling the computer what to do with data. Nothing was stored in memory except data.

Later designs provided computers with program storage. This means that the steps telling the computer what to do with data were stored in memory in the form of *digital words*. The only way of knowing that some words were program steps instead of data was to check their location in memory. The idea of program storage was an important, basic addition to the computer's architecture.

The technology of solid-state circuitry also made great strides during the 1950s. The knowledge of semiconductors increased. The use of silicon lowered costs, because silicon is much more plentiful than germanium, which had been the chief material for making semiconductors. Mass-production methods made transistors common and inexpensive.

Naturally, the designers of digital computers jumped at the chance to replace vacuum tubes with transistors and in the late 1950s, they began doing so. But logic circuits, although now made of transistors, were still *discrete*. That is, each logic circuit was built from a number of components such as individual transistors. But these first solid-state computers were already much smaller, much cooler, and much more reliable than vacuum-tube computers.

In the early 1960s, the art of building solid-state computers advanced in two directions. Moving in one direction were the giants like IBM, Burroughs, and Honeywell. They were building huge solid-state computers that still required large, air-conditioned rooms. These computers were very complicated. They could process large amounts of data. These large data processing systems were used for commercial and scientific applications.

These big computers were still very expensive. In order to pay for themselves, they had to be run 24 hours a day, 7 days a week. Two different methods were developed for getting the maximum use out of these expensive machines: the *batch* mode and the *timesharing* mode. In the batch mode, only one large job is run at a time, and one job is run immediately after another. In the timesharing mode, the large computer is used to do many jobs "at once" by working on a part of each job in turn.

Moving in a new direction were some younger, smaller companies. They began building small computers—about the size of a desk. These *minicomputers* were not as powerful as their larger relatives, but they were not as expensive, either. And they still performed many useful functions.

Minicomputers quickly proved useful in the laboratory. Scientists found that "dedicated" computers—computers used for only a single kind of job—had real value. Instead of running many different kinds of jobs on one of the giant computers, scientists ran each kind of job on a separate, dedicated minicomputer.

The idea that a single device with the computer's architecture could be tied up on a single job was a major change. No one could afford to dedicate a computer until the low-cost minicomputer appeared. Often a dedicated minicomputer did a short job and was turned off until that job had to be done again.

Solid-state circuitry continued to develop along with the digital computer. But now the two technologies were moving closer together. Computers use many of the same few logic circuit designs again and again. The need for large numbers of these circuits began to drive the semiconductor industry to develop new products.

In the mid-1960s, *small-* and *medium-scale integration* (SSI and MSI) produced major families of digital logic. The technology of *integrated circuits* (ICs) pushed in two directions. There was a push to develop low-cost manufacturing techniques. At the same time, there was a push to develop circuits that were more complex.

The use of integrated circuits let minicomputers become more and more powerful for their size. The desk-sized minicomputer of the 1960s became as powerful as a room-sized computer of the late 1950s. New $10,000, drawer-sized minicomputers were as powerful as the older $100,000, desk-sized minicomputers. Some computers even began to appear in "bare-board" form. That is, printed-circuit boards with all the logic needed to make a computer processor were for sale. The buyer of such a board had to obtain his or her own power supply and other necessary equipment.

As we all know, integrated-circuit technology has progressed further since the mid-1960s. The late 1960s and early 1970s saw *large-scale integration* (LSI) become common. LSI was making it possible to produce more and more digital circuits in a single integrated circuit.

Most of the early large-scale integrated circuits performed special functions. But a few LSI circuits were produced to perform universal functions. Memory devices are a good example.

The development of the electronic calculator shows the dramatic improvements in large-scale integration. The first electronic calculators required 75 to 100 individual IC packages. Special LSI replaced most of these ICs with five to six LSI circuits. By the mid-1970s, LSI had reduced the calculator to a single circuit.

After the calculator was so reduced, the next natural step was to reduce the architecture of the computer to a single integrated circuit. Designers soon achieved this step, and the resulting circuit was called the *microprocessor*.

The microprocessor made possible the manufacture of powerful calculators and many other products. Like the earlier dedicated minicomputer, the computerlike architecture of the microprocessor could be programmed to carry out a single task. Products

Batch mode

Timesharing mode

Minicomputers

Small- and medium-scale integration (SSI and MSI)

Large-scale integration (LSI)

Electronic calculators

Microprocessor

3

4-bit word

Program control

Central
processing unit
(CPU)

Microprocessing
unit (MPU)

Arithmetic logic
unit (ALU)

like the microwave oven, the telephone dialer, and the automatic temperature-control system became commonplace. With a cheap computer available in the form of an integrated circuit, such products became practical.

Since the early 1970s, the main effort has been to improve the microprocessor's architecture. Every improvement in architecture increases the microprocessor's speed and computing power.

The early microprocessors processed digital data 4 bits at a time. That is, they used a 4-bit word. These microprocessors were slow and did not compare to minicomputers. But new generations of microprocessors came fast. The 4-bit microprocessors grew into 8-bit microprocessors and then into 16-bit microprocessors. Microprocessors' *instruction sets*—the instructions that microprocessors can carry out—increased in size and sophistication. Some microprocessors soon equaled or surpassed the capabilities of modest minicomputers.

Self-Test

Check your understanding by answering these questions.

1. The basic design, that is, the way the data move about inside the microprocessor and how the calculations are done, is called the microprocessor's
   a. Packaging   c. Module
   b. Architecture   d. Power supply

2. A microprocessor's program is stored in memory along with its data. The only way you can tell the difference between program steps and data is by
   a. The word length
   b. The word type
   c. The place you put the program steps
   d. Seeing if the microprocessor will execute them

3. The minicomputer introduced the idea of a separate processor for each task. The microprocessor used to implement a telephone dialer
   a. Is an example of multiple tasks in one processor
   b. Is the same idea
   c. Proves stored programming is not possible
   d. Will be made possible at some future date

4. The integrated circuit is used a lot in computer applications because
   a. Computers use the same logic over and over
   b. All computers must run very fast
   c. Vacuum tubes generate too much heat even though they are faster
   d. (All of the above)

1-2 WHAT IS A MICROPROCESSOR?

The word "microprocessor" tells us something about the device it names. The microprocessor uses the same type of logic that is used in a digital computer's *central processing unit* (CPU). Because of its resemblance to the CPU, the microprocessor is sometimes called a *microprocessing unit* (MPU). Like the CPU, the MPU has digital circuits for data handling and computation under program control. In other words, the microprocessor is a *data processing* unit.

Unlike an ordinary, full-scale CPU, the microprocessor has digital logic made up of one (or at most a few) large-scale integrated circuits. Since LSI circuits are also called *microcircuits*, it is easy to see why the microprocessor has the name it does.

Data processing is clearly one major function of the microprocessor. Data processing includes both computation and data handling.

Computation is performed by circuits that make up what is usually called the *arithmetic logic unit* (ALU). These circuits enable us to use functions that cause data changes. Among these functions are Add, Subtract, AND, OR, Compare, Increment, and Decrement.

The ALU cannot, of course, perform any of these functions without data to operate on. If the ALU is to add two numbers, for example, then each of the numbers must be put in the right place beforehand. The ALU cannot itself move data from place to place either before or after an operation. Instead, the ALU merely performs an operation on whatever data it finds in certain places.

You may find it helpful to think of the ALU as a blindfolded juggler. The juggler can do amazing tricks, but only after being handed objects by someone else. Being blindfolded, the juggler cannot find the objects unaided. Like a blindfolded juggler waiting to be handed objects, the ALU must wait for data to be placed in certain places.

How then does the ALU get the data that it operates on? The MPU has other circuits, outside the ALU, that handle data. These data-handling circuits move data into place so that the ALU can process the data. After the operation, the data-handling circuits move the data elsewhere.

While a juggler cannot change the objects juggled, the ALU can perform operations that actually change data. And the data-handling circuits of the MPU can move the data from place to place as necessary. But what tells the ALU *how* to process the data? What tells the ALU which of the possible operations to perform?

The second major function of the microprocessor is system *control*. The control circuits of the MPU allow the microprocessor to decode and execute the program—a set of instructions for processing the data. The control circuits store program steps (*instructions*) in memory and call (*fetch*) them one at a time. After the instruction is fetched, the microprocessor decodes the instruction. Then the control logic carries out (*executes*) the decoded instruction.

Because the instructions are stored in memory, you can change them when you want to. When you change the microprocessor's instructions, you change what it does to the data. The instructions that you store in memory determine what the microprocessor will do. This is a very important point for you to understand about microprocessors.

To review: The microprocessor has both a control and a processing function. The processing function moves data from place to place and performs operations on the data. The control function determines how the data will be processed. The microprocessor operates in the following steps. First, the microprocessor fetches (gets) an instruction. Then the control logic decodes what the instruction says to do. After decoding, the microprocessor executes (carries out) the instruction. These steps are called the Fetch-and-Execute cycle, or the Fetch/Execute cycle. For each instruction in memory, the microprocessor goes through one Fetch-and-Execute cycle.

Besides fetching and executing instructions, the control logic also performs other major tasks. The control logic controls the microprocessor's relations with everything outside that is connected to the microprocessor. Powerful though the microprocessor is, you should keep in mind that it can do nothing by itself. The microprocessor must have the aid of other circuits. Some memory circuits are required to store the program instructions. Circuits are also needed to move data into and out of the microprocessor; these circuits are called input/output (I/O) circuits. Storage of data requires additional memory. The microprocessor also needs a power supply.

For example, look at even the simplest of hand-held microprocessor-based games. Such games need a keyboard to get data into the microprocessor and a display to get answers out. A battery is necessary to supply power. And, of course, the whole system must be put into a package.

This point is quite important for distinguishing between the microprocessor and the *microcomputer*: The microprocessor is the heart of many products, but the microprocessor is never a complete, working product all by itself.* The microprocessor's control logic can, however, *control* the other necessary parts when they are added.

Self-Test

Check your understanding by answering these questions.

5. A microprocessing unit (MPU) does not include ___?___ circuits.
   a. Logic   c. Memory
   b. Computational   d. (All of the above)

6. The microprocessor's Fetch/Execute cycle is used to get and carry out
   a. Logic work   c. Arithmetic work
   b. Program steps   d. MPUs

7. The ALU is used to do
   a. Addition   c. Instruction decoding
   b. Data moves   d. (All of the above)

8. You can change what a microprocessor will do by
   a. Changing the instructions in memory
   b. Adding more inputs
   c. Adding more outputs
   d. Increasing memory size

Decode

Execute

Fetch

Microcomputer

---

* Some *single-chip microcomputer* ICs do have circuits for input/output, data storage, or program storage, but these circuits are not part of an MPU.

Input/output (I/O)

Random access
memory (RAM)

Alphanumeric
display

Cathode-ray
tube (CRT)

Bus

Clock

Read-only
memory (ROM)

Universal
asynchronous
receiver
transmitter
(UART)

9. The microprocessor generates signals to
   control the ___?___ circuits.
   a. Memory   c. Output
   b. Input   d. (All of the above)

10. A microprocessor is not a stand-alone de-
    vice. That is, it requires at least ___?___
    to operate.
    a. Memory   c. An output
    b. An input   d. (All of the above)

1-3 WHAT IS A MICROCOMPUTER?

Frequently the words "microprocessor" and
"microcomputer" are used to mean the
same thing, but in fact these similar words
have different meanings. As you learned
in the previous section, the microprocessor
is an integrated circuit. It includes circuitry
for only two purposes: data processing and
control.

The microcomputer, on the other hand, is
a complete computing system built around a
microprocessor. A complete computing system has an MPU, and it has memory and
input/output functions. Figure 1-2 shows a
complete microcomputer system. Note that
the system has a mainframe containing an
MPU card, a *random access memory* (RAM)
card, and an input/output (I/O) card. The
mainframe also has a front panel. In the system illustrated, the I/O card is connected to a
video terminal. The video terminal gives an
alphanumeric display (output) on a *cathode-
ray tube* (CRT). That is, it displays both letters
and numbers on a screen that is like a television's picture tube. The terminal also provides for alphanumeric input by a keyboard.
This system also has a power supply and packaging. We say this system is *self-contained*.

Figure 1-3 shows the same system in a block
diagram. Notice how many extra circuits are
needed to make a microprocessor into a microcomputer.

All the cards in the microcomputer are connected by a *bus*. The bus consists of the
many signal lines that let the different cards
"talk" to one another. The word "bus" is
short for *omnibus*, a Latin word meaning "to
all." All the cards are able to communicate
through the bus because each card uses the
same set of signals. Usually any microcomputer card will work if plugged into any slot on
the bus. An electrical schematic of a bus is
shown in Fig. 1-4.

Returning to Fig. 1-3, you can see that the
microprocessor is on the MPU card. The
MPU card also has a *clock generator*, which
generates timing signals for the microprocessor. A *read-only memory* (ROM)
stores a few program instructions. These
instructions are used to input other programs
from magnetic tape or disk. Like all the other
cards, the MPU card has four ICs at the
bottom. These ICs electrically interface the
MPU card circuits to the bus, which usually
requires higher current levels than those
produced by most logic chips.

Besides the ICs that interface with the bus,
the random-access memory (RAM) card has
RAM ICs. This card has all the microcomputer's data- and program-storage space.

On the input/output card, we find a *universal asynchronous receiver-transmitter* (UART)
and a clock IC. The UART converts parallel
data to serial so that the microcomputer can
talk to the video terminal.

A fourth card used in this microcomputer is
for the front panel. Besides the ICs that interface with the bus, the front-panel card has
logic to drive *seven-segment displays*.

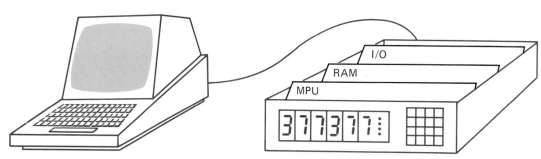

Fig. 1-2 A microcomputer system. Physically the two main
elements of a microcomputer system are the video terminal and
the "mainframe". The mainframe holds the MPU card, the
RAM card, the I/O ports, and the power supply.

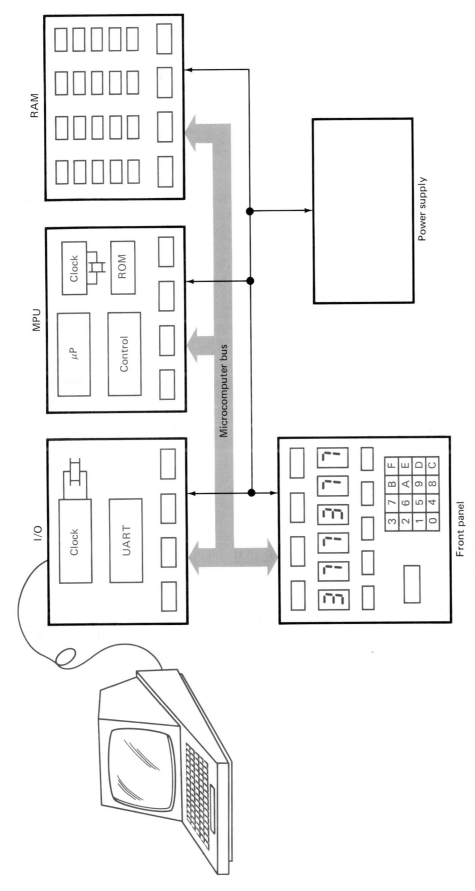

Fig. 1-3   A microcomputer system block diagram.   This block diagram shows the electrical makeup of the mainframe pictured in Fig. 1-2.   The front panel is really a specialized I/O for start-up and diagnostic work.

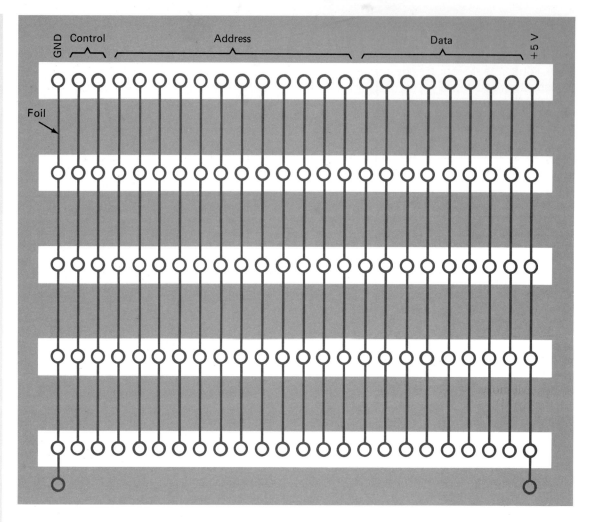

GND Control Address Data +5 V

Foil

(a)

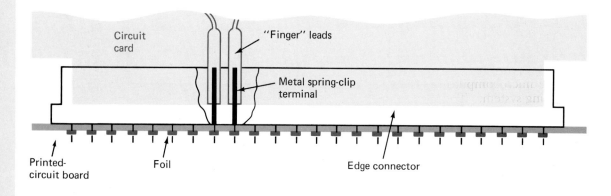

Circuit card "Finger" leads

Metal spring-clip terminal

Printed-circuit board   Foil   Edge connector

(b)

Fig. 1-4 A microcomputer bus. (a) An electrical schematic of a typical microcomputer bus. The edge connector of each card is connected to that of the next card by a series of foils on the bus printed-circuit board. (b) Edge view showing the bus printed-circuit board's edge connector, the printed-circuit board, and the foil, which actually carries the bus signals.

The power supply of this microcomputer system is another separate component. It is connected to all the boards by the bus.

As you can see from this description of the system shown in Fig. 1-3, the microprocessor is a small—but vital—part of a microcomputer. The microcomputer, on the other hand, is a complete system. To repeat: A complete system must have at least an MPU, some memory, and some form of input/output.

Self-Test

Check your understanding by answering these questions.

11. A microcomputer system has at least ___?___ circuits.
    a. Memory (ROM   c. MPU
    or RAM)
    b. Input/output   d. (All of the above)

12. The microcomputer's instructions are stored in the ___?___ circuits.
    a. Memory (ROM   c. MPU
    or RAM)
    b. Input/output   d. (All of the above)

13. The microcomputer's bus is a well-defined set of signal lines that let the different parts of the microcomputer system
    a. Communicate
    b. Get rid of heat
    c. Talk to a serial device
    d. Use power

14. The microprocessor must have timing signals to make the circuits work. These signals originate in the microprocessor's:
    a. ROM   c. Clock
    b. RAM   d. MPU

15. The microcomputer is a complete computing system. The microprocessor is
    a. The IC that generates the bus signals
    b. The IC that controls the system power supply
    c. The IC that contains the microcomputer's MPU
    d. The IC that lets the system talk to serial devices

1-4 WHAT IS THE POWER OF A MICROPROCESSOR?

Almost all microprocessors are made on silicon *chips*. These chips are about $\frac{1}{4}$ inch (in), or 0.64 centimeters (cm), on a side. Since the silicon chip with the microprocessor circuits usually comes inside a 16- to 64-pin IC package, we cannot see the chip. But seeing the chip is unimportant. The appearance of the chip tells us little about the power of the microprocessor "printed" on the chip.

What we mean by the "power" of a microprocessor is its capacity to process data. There are three main measures of the power of a microprocessor: the *length* of the microprocessor's *data word*; the *number* of *memory words* that the microprocessor can address; and the *speed* with which the microprocessor can execute an *instruction*.

Microprocessors are most often compared in terms of the lengths of their data words. Each microprocessor works on a data word of fixed length. Having to handle only one word length makes the design of the processor simpler.

Word lengths of 4 bits, 8 bits, 12 bits, and 16 bits are common today. In the next few years, 32-bit microprocessors will become common too. Data words of three different lengths are illustrated in Fig. 1-5.

The 8-bit data word is so common that it has been given the special name *byte*. Because the byte is so commonly used, 16-bit microprocessors often have instructions that let them process their 16-bit data word in two 8-bit bytes. In Fig. 1-6, you can see that a 16-bit data word is really made up of two 8-bit words. These words are called the *upper* byte, or *hi byte* (bits 8 through 15), and the *lower* byte, or *lo byte* (bits 0 through 7).

Often the byte is used to speak of the size of part of a microcomputer. For example, you might speak of a microprocessor program that has 4000 bytes.

The byte is also used as a sort of common denominator for measuring microprocessor size. The byte is used as a measure rather than the data word because the size of a word varies from one processor to another but a byte is always 8 bits. Given the same number of bytes, the 8-bit processor has half as many words as the 4-bit microprocessor and twice as many words as the 16-bit microprocessor. For example: 4000 bytes on an 8-bit microprocessor equals 4000 words; on a 4-bit microprocessor, 4000 bytes equals 8000 words; on a 16-bit microprocessor, 4000 bytes equals 2000 words.

The 4-bit microprocessor was the first developed. Microprocessors of this word length are still popular in some types of work. Four

Parallel-to-serial conversion

Silicon chips

Data word

Byte

Hi byte

Lo byte

Binary-coded
decimal (BCD)

American
Standard Code
for Information
Interchange
(ASCII)

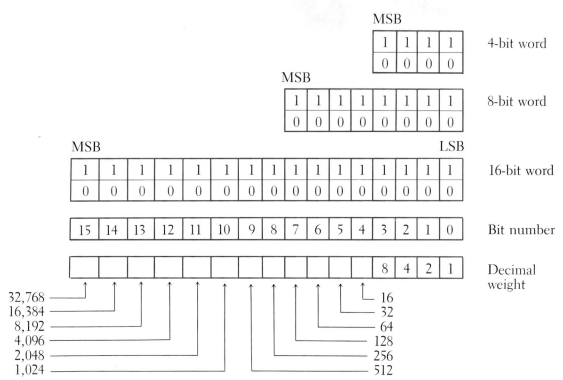

Fig. 1-5 Digital words of 4, 8, and 16 bits. Note the bit positions are usually numbered from right to left starting with bit zero. Bit zero is the least significant bit, and the bit weight increases to the left. Each bit can be a 1 or a 0.

bits is the length of a *binary-coded decimal* (BCD) number. In some applications, including calculators and industrial control systems, the microprocessor deals only with BCD numbers. Consequently, the 4-bit microprocessor is ideal for those applications. Another reason for the continuing use of the 4-bit microprocessor is its extremely low cost.

The 8-bit microprocessor is also both common and inexpensive. The 8-bit word length was the next developed after the 4-bit, because (1) the 8-bit word length is twice 4 bits, (2) the 8-bit word length allows two BCD numbers for each MPU data word, and (3) the 8-bit length can hold the code for a character in the American Standard Code for Information Interchange (ASCII, pronounced "askkey"). ASCII characters are used widely in data processing.

Most of the early 16-bit microprocessors

were standard 16-bit minicomputers in LSI form. Examples are the Digital Equipment Corporation LSI-11, a copy of the PDP-11 minicomputer; the Data General MicroNova, a copy of the Nova minicomputer; and the Texas Instruments 9900, a copy of the 990 minicomputer. More recent 16-bit microprocessors have their own architecture, not taken from a minicomputer.

Each time the microprocessor's word length doubles, the processor becomes more powerful. Greater word lengths have required better and better LSI technology. Superior technology has resulted in other improvements in the 16-bit microprocessors besides their greater word length.

Another common measure of microprocessor power is the number of memory words or memory bytes that the microprocessor can address. Here, too, the length of the data word

Fig. 1-6 A 16-bit digital word showing the hi- and lo-byte breakdown.

Binary address	Memory contents (4 bits long)
1 1 1 1	Data word 15
1 1 1 0	Data word 14
1 1 0 1	Data word 13
1 1 0 0	Data word 12
1 0 1 1	Data word 11
1 0 1 0	Data word 10
1 0 0 1	Data word 9
1 0 0 0	Data word 8
0 1 1 1	Data word 7
0 1 1 0	Data word 6
0 1 0 1	Data word 5
0 1 0 0	Data word 4
0 0 1 1	Data word 3
0 0 1 0	Data word 2
0 0 0 1	Data word 1
0 0 0 0	Data word 0

Fig. 1-7 A 16-word memory addressed by a 4-bit word.

Address

Address range

4K

plays an important role. The length of the data word in memory is the same as the length of the data word used by the microprocessor. A 4-bit microprocessor, for example, stores 4-bit words in memory.

Each word in memory is assigned a location number or *address*. When a word is needed from memory, the computer gets the word by referring to an address. Memory addresses start at 0 and end at some large binary number, the value of which varies from one pro-

cessor to another. The larger the number of memory addresses, the greater the microprocessor's computing power.

Figure 1-7 shows the memory-addressing power of a single 4-bit word. As you can see, the 4 bits can address 16 words in memory. Put differently, the 4-bit word has an *address range* of 16 words.

A single 8-bit word has an address range of 256 memory words. A 16-bit word has an address range of 65,536 memory words.

Of course, most microprocessors can use more than a single word to address memory, and so the memory-address range is not limited by the length of the microprocessor's data word. Memory addresses can be as long as 22 bits and more. Some microprocessors can address millions of memory words.

Figure 1-8 shows the memory-address ranges of some commonly available microprocessors having 4-, 8-, and 16-bit data words. Common address ranges for 4-bit microprocessors are 4096 and 8192 memory words. Eight-bit microprocessors often have an address range of 65,536 memory words. The address ranges of 16-bit microprocessors, as you can see, extend from 32,768 memory words to 4,194,304.

Referring to these large numbers is often necessary when working with microprocessors. Since the numbers are not round figures, they are difficult to remember and awkward to say. A shorthand has developed to simplify describing these memory sizes. The shorthand figures are shown in parentheses in Fig. 1-8. The 4096-word addressing range, for instance, is called a 4K range. The "K," from the prefix "kilo-," meaning "thousand," is a scientific abbreviation for 1000. The ex-

Data-word length	4 bit	8 bit	16 bit
	4,096 (4K)		
	8,192 (8K)		
Memory-address range		65,536 (65K)	
			32,768 (32K)
			65,536 (65K)
			1,048,576 (1M)
			2,097,152 (2M)
			4,194,304 (4M)

Fig. 1-8 Word size and memory-addressing range of some commonly available microprocessors.

**Time to
complete
fetch/execute
cycle**

**Benchmark
program**

pression "4K" represents 4096 rounded off to the nearest thousand. Expressions for the other memory sizes have been shortened in the same way. When the memory sizes get extremely large, the letter "M," from the prefix "mega," meaning "million," is used as shorthand for a million.

Memory sizes of 65 kilobytes are very common for 8-bit microprocessors. The newer 16-bit microprocessors have address ranges extending into megabytes.

In talking about a microcomputer's memory size, you must always take care to explain whether you are talking of bytes or words. Throughout this text we will speak of memory size in bytes. Since a byte is always 8 bits, a 65,536-*word* memory on an 8-bit microcomputer and a 32,768-*word* memory on a 16-bit microcomputer are really the same size. That is, they both have 65,536 *bytes*.

If this comparison is unclear, then compare the memory sizes in bits. Multiply the number of words in each case by the number of bits per word. That is,

65,536 words $\times$ 8 bits per word = 524,288 bits

and

32,758 words $\times$ 16 bits per word
$$= 524,288 \text{ bits}$$

A third common measure of microprocessor power is the speed with which the microprocessor executes an instruction. Speed is determined by the time it takes the microprocessor to complete the Fetch/Execute cycle for one program step.

Some microprocessors are 20 to 100 times faster than others. Slow microprocessors may use a clock that runs at a few hundred kilohertz (kHz). It takes such a microprocessor 10 to 20 microseconds (μs; the Greek letter "mu" stands for one-millionth) to execute one instruction. On the other hand, some microprocessors use clocks that run at 5 to 10 mega-

hertz (MHz). These microprocessors may execute an instruction in only a few tenths of a microsecond.

The microprocessor's speed is related to its maximum clock frequency. Sometimes people compare microprocessors simply in terms of clock frequency. Comparisons are more meaningful, however, when they find out how long a given operation will take on the different processors. Short programs, called *benchmark* programs, are written to make such comparisons easier. Different microprocessors are timed while executing the same benchmark program.

Self-Test

Check your understanding by answering these questions.

16. One of the most common measurements of a microprocessor's power is its
    a. Chip size   c. Number of pins
    b. Word length   d. (All of the above)

17. An 8-bit word is a very common length. It is called a(n)
    a. Byte   c. MPU
    b. CPU   d. Address

18. A 12-bit word length is used on the PDP-8 series of minicomputers and on a few microprocessors. If a PDP-8 can address 32 kilowords of memory, its memory will have ____?____ bits of data.
    a. 32,768   c. 384,000
    b. 262,144   d. 393,216

19. Many 8-bit microprocessors can address 65,536 memory locations. Usually this is shown as 65K. Sometimes the shorthand is 64K. Why do you think the terms 65K and 64K are both used as shorthand for 65,536?

20. Two identical microcomputer systems have different clock rates. System A has a 5-MHz clock and system B has a 1-μs clock. Which system executes an instruction faster? Why?

Summary

1. The microprocessor is a large-scale integrated circuit that uses the architecture of the general-purpose digital computer.

2. The architecture of the digital computer

and the capability of LSI were brought together in the early 1970s. The computer had developed from the post-World War II period, as had solid-state technology.

3. Two important concepts were developed as the computer evolved. First came the concept of program storage. Second came the concept of many independent low-cost processors to do many independent tasks.

4. The MPU (microprocessing unit) has the control and computational functions in microcircuit form.

5. The MPU can do both data-handling and data processing functions. The data processing functions are carried out by the ALU (arithmetic logic unit). The MPU also fetches instructions and executes them (decodes them and carries them out).

6. A microcomputer is a complete computing system based on a microprocessor. It has an MPU and it has memory and input/output functions. It also has power supplies and packaging.

7. The microcomputer's bus allows each part of the microcomputer system to communicate with the other parts by using a common set of signals. Often the signals are a high-powered extension of the microprocessor's internal bus.

8. The microprocessor's data word is a common measurement of the microprocessor's size. Word lengths of 4, 8, and 16 bits are common. The 8-bit word is so common it is called by a special name, "byte."

9. The number of memory locations addressed by the microprocessor is also used to describe the microprocessor. Most 8-bit microprocessors address 65,536 memory locations. Sixteen-bit microprocessors may have addressing ranges in the millions.

10. A shorthand notation is used in specifying the number of bytes. The symbol "K" is used to say "times 1000," and numbers in the kilobyte range that are powers of 2 are rounded to the nearest thousand. The symbol "M" means "times 1 million," and numbers in the megabyte range that are powers of 2 are rounded to the nearest million.

11. The speed of a microprocessor is measured by how long it takes to fetch and execute an instruction. Both the instruction time and the clock frequency are used to describe a microprocessor's speed.

Chapter Review Questions

1-1. Microprocessor architecture is taken from the architecture of a
  a. Calculator LSI chip
  b. Patch-paneled programmed computer
  c. General-purpose digital computer
  d. Vacuum-tube CRT

1-2. The semiconductor technology that finally made the microprocessor possible was a development of
  a. MPUs   c. LEDs
  b. LSI   d. Germanium transistors

1-3. The microprocessor uses the stored-program concept. This means the instructions are stored in the ____?____ along with the data.
  a. Serial I/O   c. Power supply
  b. MPU   d. Memory

1-4. Using the computer's architecture to solve small problems has been made possible only because the microprocessor is so ____?____ compared to the general-purpose digital computer.
  a. Fast   c. Powerful
  b. Extremely low in cost   d. (All of the above)

1-5. What does the abbreviation MPU stand for? This function can be compared to a general-purpose digital computer's ____?____

1-6. The microprocessor's data-handling functions let it
  a. Perform a logic AND function
  b. Move data between microcomputer parts
  c. Make the computation using the data
  d. Operate more quickly than it could if it had only computational functions

13

1-7. To process one of your instructions, the microprocessor must go through a Fetch/Execute cycle. The execute parts are carried out in the
a. ALU
c. I/O
b. Memory
d. ROM

1-8. A microprocessor is at the heart of a microcomputer system. However, the microcomputer must also have ___?___ circuits.
a. Input
c. Output
b. Memory
d. (All of the above)

1-9. You can safely say that the true microprocessor
a. Will always run at almost 1 MHz
b. Will have a minimum of 16 kilobytes of memory
c. Will always be a single chip
d. Will never work by itself

1-10. The purpose of a microcomputer's bus is to
a. Allow the industry to build standard products
b. Allow different parts of the microcomputer system to communicate using a well-defined signal path
c. Provide a standard mechanical connection for the microcomputer system
d. Be sure that signals of 3.58 MHz and higher are properly transmitted

1-11. Often the microcomputer's bus is a set of parallel conductors interconnecting a number of circuit-card connectors. Why do you think it is built this way?

1-12. The 8-bit data word is a very popular length. Two data words are usually used to address a memory location. This means the memory has ___?___ locations.
a. 16K
c. 65K
b. 32K
d. 128K

1-13. A data word ___?___ bits long is used on many microprocessors.
a. 4
c. 16
b. 8
d. (All of the above)

1-14. An 8-bit data word is often called
a. Very Popular
c. An MPU
b. A byte
d. A CPU

1-15. A 16-bit microprocessor must have ___?___ memory locations.
a. 65,536
c. No fixed number of
b. 64K
d. Millions of

1-16. The microprocessor's Fetch/Execute cycle time depends on its
a. Address range
c. Bus size
b. Clock frequency
d. (All of the above)

Answers to Self-Tests

1. b.	7. a.	13. a.	19. Because 64 is 2^6, and therefore 64,000 is thought of as the round number closest to 65,536.	20. System A, because the clock time is 200 nanoseconds (ns) for a 5-MHz clock and 200 ns is 5 times as fast as 1 μs, which is 1000 ns.
2. c.	8. a.	14. c.		
3. b.	9. d.	15. c.		
4. a.	10. d.	16. b.		
5. c.	11. d.	17. a.		
6. b.	12. a.	18. d.		

The Decimal and Binary Number Systems

2

■ The first part of this chapter is a review of the binary and decimal number systems. You are already familiar with the decimal number system. You use it in everyday life. You have done many calculations using the decimal number system as you studied electronic circuits. You should be familiar with the binary number system from your digital circuits studies. Both number systems are very important to the understanding of digital computational circuits and to your understanding of microprocessors. For this reason, we also review the conversion of decimal numbers to binary numbers, as well as the conversion of binary numbers into decimal numbers.

This chapter introduces two commonly used "shorthand" techniques: the octal and the hexadecimal number systems. These are used because they are much simpler ways of representing large binary numbers. We look at both systems because octal notation is used by some microprocessor manufacturers and hexadecimal notation is used by others.

2-1 THE DECIMAL NUMBER SYSTEM

The decimal number system is the most commonly used number system in the world. It uses 10 different characters to show the values of numbers. Because the system uses 10 different characters, it is called the *base 10 system*. The base of a number system tells you how many different characters are used. The mathematical term for the base of a number system is its *radix*.

The 10 characters used in the decimal number system are

0, 1, 2, 3, 4, 5, 6, 7, 8, and 9

As you look at the characters that make up the decimal number system, you see that the character "0" is one of the ten. This is very important to remember. All counting in computer, and therefore microprocessor, systems starts at 0.

What do we do when there are more than 10 objects to be counted? As we all know, we add more numbers to the left of the original column. We can say that the next number to the left tells us how many times we have completely used the column to the right.

For example, what does the number 23 mean? One way to look at this is to say (*a*) we found enough objects to use all the characters (0 through 9) in the right-hand column once (with the left-hand column equal to 0); (*b*) we found enough objects to use all the characters (0 through 9) a second time (with the left-hand column equal to 1); and (*c*) with the left-hand column equal to 2 we had enough objects that we used the first, second, third, and fourth characters in the system. The fourth character is 3.

This way of counting is shown in Fig. 2-1. Note that this shows the decimal number, how we got it, and the number of objects shown by each number. Frequently we drop *insignificant* 0s. These are 0s to the left of the most significant digit. In this figure, an insignificant 0 is shown in the left-hand column beside the first set of numbers 0 through 9.

Normally we say that each column is given a "weight." The weights are powers of 10. The first column is the ones column, the second is the tens column, the third column is

15

00		0	None
01		1	.
02		2	..
03		3	...
04	0	4	....
05		5	.....
06		6	......
07		7	....
08		8	....
09		9	....
10		0	....
11		1	....
12		2	....
13		3	....
14	1	4	....
15		5	....
16		6	....
17		7	....
18		8	....
19		9	....
20		0	....
21	2	1	....
22		2	....
23		3	....

Fig. 2-1   Counting 23 objects. For each of the first nine objects we have a unique character to show the number of objects. We use the characters 0 through 9. After the ninth object we begin to repeat the count characters.

the hundreds column, the fourth column is the thousands column, and so forth. This is shown in Fig. 2-2. We do not usually show the insignificant 0s. They are shown in Fig. 2-2 so that you will know where they are.

Using scientific notation, we can show the first column weight as 10^0, the second as 10^1, the third as 10^2, the fourth as 10^3, and so forth. You can see that the weight of each column is the base of the number system raised to a *power*. The power is the column's position.

As an example, let's look at the number 6321, which is used in Fig. 2-2. Assigning a weight to each column, we represent this as:

$$\begin{array}{cccc} 10^3 & 10^2 & 10^1 & 10^0 \\ 6 & 3 & 2 & 1 \end{array}$$

We can evaluate this as:

$$6 \times 10^3 + 3 \times 10^2 + 2 \times 10^1 + 1 \times 10^0 = 6321$$

As an additional example, let's look at the number 1,260,523.

$$\begin{array}{ccccccc} 10^6 & 10^5 & 10^4 & 10^3 & 10^2 & 10^1 & 10^0 \\ 1 & 2 & 6 & 0 & 5 & 2 & 3 \end{array}$$

We can evaluate this as:

$$1 \times 10^6 + 2 \times 10^5 + 6 \times 10^4 + 0 \times 10^3 + 5 \times 10^2 + 2 \times 10^1 + 3 \times 10^0 = 1,260,523$$

In the decimal number system, we show fractional numbers by putting characters to the right of the decimal point. The decimal

100,000s	10,000s	1000s	100s	10s	1s	$\frac{1}{10}$s	$\frac{1}{100}$s
0	0	6	3	2	1 .	0	0

Fig. 2-2   Assigning a decimal weight to each column of a decimal number. Whether you use them or not, the insignificant 0s are always there.

$$10^3 \quad 10^2 \quad 10^1 \quad 10^0 \qquad 10^{-1} \quad 10^{-2} \quad 10^{-3}$$
$$6 \quad\; 3 \quad\; 2 \quad\; 1 \quad . \quad\; 5 \quad\;\; 6 \quad\;\; 4$$
$$6 \times 10^3 + 3 \times 10^2 + 2 \times 10^1 + 1 \times 10^0 + 5 \times 10^{-1} + 6 \times 10^{-2} + 4 \times 10^{-3} = 6321.564$$

Fig. 2-3 Evaluating a decimal mixed number by using scientific notation. Note that the zero power of any number is equal to 1.

point is used to separate the integer and fractional parts of a number. The more general mathematical term for the decimal point is the *radix point*.

Each column to the right of the decimal point is also given a weight. The column immediately to the right of the decimal point has a weight of $\frac{1}{10}$. The next column to the right has a weight of $\frac{1}{100}$, the next column a weight of $\frac{1}{1000}$, and the next $\frac{1}{10\,000}$, and so forth. As you know from studying scientific notation, these may also be expressed as negative powers of 10. That is, $\frac{1}{10}$ may be expressed as 10^{-1}. (See Fig. 2-3.)

Self-Test

Check your understanding by answering these questions.

1. You will find positive powers of 10 on the ___?___ side of a decimal number's radix point.
   a. Right-hand
   c. Opposite
   b. Left-hand
   d. Wrong

2. To evaluate the value of a column, you ___?___ the column's weight.
   a. Add its number to
   b. Divide its number by
   c. Multiply its number by
   d. Subtract its number from

3. The expression

   $$2 \times 10^4 + 7 \times 10^3 + 3 \times 10^2 + 2 \times 10^1 + 9 \times 10^0$$

   totals ___?___.

4. Negative powers of 10 are used to show ___?___ column weights.
   a. Half
   c. Whole
   b. Integer
   d. Fractional

2-2 THE BINARY NUMBER SYSTEM

In many ways the binary number system is simpler than the decimal number system. The binary number system has only two characters. The binary number system is used in digital electronics because digital circuits have only two states. Most of the time, 0 and 1 are the two characters used.

Sometimes other characters are used. The pairs of binary expressions On and Off, Mark and Space, and High and Low may be used. Binary characters can represent any two-state condition.

When you compare the decimal number system with the binary number system you can see that the binary number uses many more columns. This is because there are only two characters in the binary number system. The decimal number system can represent up to nine units in each column. The binary system can represent up to only one unit in each column.

Like the decimal system, the binary number system assigns a weight to each column. In the decimal number system, each column is assigned a weight that is a power of 10. This is because the decimal number system is the base 10 system. The binary number system is the base 2 system. The assigned weights are powers of 2. The first 13 column weights are shown in Fig. 2-4. As you might expect, the size of the equivalent number is quite small even though there are many columns.

In the following example we evaluate a binary number to find its decimal value.

$$101101_2$$
$$1 \times 2^5 + 0 \times 2^4 + 1 \times 2^3 + 1 \times 2^2 + 0 \times 2^1 + 1 \times 2^0 = 45_{10}$$

4096	2048	1024	512	256	128	64	32	16	8	4	2	1
2^{12}	2^{11}	2^{10}	2^9	2^8	2^7	2^6	2^5	2^4	2^3	2^2	2^1	2^0

Fig. 2-4 The powers of 2 and their decimal equivalents.

$$
\begin{array}{cccccc}
0.5 & 0.25 & 0.125 & 0.0625 & 0.03125 & 0.015625 \\
2^{-1} & 2^{-2} & 2^{-3} & 2^{-4} & 2^{-5} & 2^{-6}
\end{array}
$$

Fig. 2-5 The negative powers of 2 and their decimal equivalents.

Binary point

Bit

Binary digit

Least significant bit (LSB)

Most significant bit (MSB)

Most significant digit (MSD)

Least significant digit (LSD)

The binary number 101101 is the same as the decimal number 45.

Note that when we are using both binary and decimal numbers, the decimal numbers are followed by the subscript 10 and binary numbers are followed by the subscript 2. For example, there is quite a difference between 101_2 and 101_{10}. In the first example we have the binary representation of the decimal number five. In the second example we have the decimal representation of the decimal number one hundred one.

Like the decimal system, the binary number system uses a radix point. It is called the *binary point*. The binary point separates the integer part of the number from the fractional part of the number. It serves the same purpose in binary mixed numbers as the decimal point does in decimal mixed numbers. Each column to the right of the binary point is assigned a fractional weight. Again as in the decimal system, the column weight can be shown as a negative power of the number system's base. In the binary number system the weights are the fractions $\frac{1}{2}$, $\frac{1}{4}$, $\frac{1}{8}$, $\frac{1}{16}$, $\frac{1}{32}$, and so forth These can be expressed as 2^{-1}, 2^{-2}, 2^{-3}, 2^{-4}, 2^{-5}, and so forth. The first six negative powers of 2 and their decimal equivalents are shown in Fig. 2-5.

In the decimal number system each column or place is referred to as a *digit*, or more precisely, a decimal digit. In the binary number system each place is referred to as a *bit*. The term "bit" stands for *bi*nary dig*it*. "Bit" is a very commonly used (and misused) term in digital electronics.

Often when referring to binary numbers you will hear the terms "LSB" (least significant bit) and "MSB" (most significant bit). These are very much like the terms we use when speaking of decimal numbers. In decimal numbers we refer to the most significant digit (MSD) and the least significant digit (LSD). The LSB is the bit with the least weight. The MSB is the bit with the greatest weight. Normally, binary numbers are shown with the MSB as the leftmost bit.

Self-Test

Check your understanding by answering these questions.

5. In the decimal number 2364 the character 2 is the
   a. LSD   c. LSB
   b. MSD   d. MSB

6. Is the number 1210110 a binary number? Why?

7. What does the abbreviation "LSB" stand for?

8. "Bit" is the abbreviation for ____?____.

9. The base of the binary number system is
   a. 10_{10} c. 2_{10}
   b. 1_2 d. 0_{10}

10. Which is the larger number, 1111_2 or 11_{10}? Why?

11. The value 2^{-3} is the same as
    a. $\frac{1}{16}$ c. $\frac{1}{4}$
    b. $\frac{1}{8}$ d. $\frac{1}{2}$

2-3 BINARY-TO-DECIMAL CONVERSION

Often when you are working with microcomputers, you have to change binary numbers to their decimal equivalents. There are many different reasons for doing this. Perhaps the most common reason is the need to display the number for people who cannot read binary numbers. You must use the binary-to-decimal conversion process to make the results meaningful for these people.

The binary-to-decimal conversion process is simple: We add the decimal weights of all bits that are a "1." The following two examples demonstrate this process.

Convert the binary number 1100 1100 to decimal.

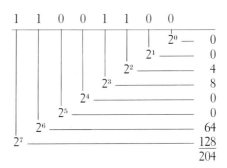

$$11001100_2 = 204_{10}$$

To convert the fractional binary number 101.011 to decimal we do the same:

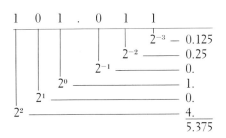

$$101.011_2 = 5.375_{10}$$

Self-Test

Check your understanding by answering these questions.

12. Evaluate the following binary numbers to find their decimal values:
    a. 1011 0110   f. 1000 0001
    b. 0101 0000   g. 0111 1110
    c. 0001 1110   h. 0011 1111
    d. 1000 0000   i. 0.0101
    e. 1111 1111   j. 100.011

2-4 DECIMAL-TO-BINARY CONVERSION

When you are working with a microcomputer, you will often want to make the computer use decimal numbers. To do this you must input decimal numbers, convert them to binary numbers, process the binary numbers with the microprocessor, and then convert the numbers back to decimal. Consequently, we need a way to convert decimal numbers to binary numbers.

In fact, we must have two processes. First, we must have a process that we can do manually while programming the microprocessor. This allows us to put numerical constants into calculating programs and to make other decimal calculations. Second, we must be able to use the microprocessor to convert decimal numbers to binary. Then the user can enter decimal numbers that will be converted to binary by the microprocessor.

Once you learn the first technique, the second technique is a matter of programming.

The process for converting integer decimal numbers into binary numbers is a specific case of the general process for converting a num-

ber in one base to a number in another base. Suppose you wanted to convert the decimal number 10 to a binary number. Converting a decimal integer to a binary integer is done by using the following procedure. Follow the example as you read the procedure.

1. The number to be converted is divided by the base of the number system it is to be converted into. In this case, the decimal number 10 is divided by 2, the base of the binary number system. In dividing by 2, the remainder has to be either 1 or 0. This remainder becomes the least significant bit of the new number.

$$\begin{array}{r} 5 \\ 2\overline{)10} \\ \underline{10} \quad \text{LSB} = 0 \\ 0 \end{array}$$

2. The result from the division in step 1 is also divided by 2. The remainder is either 1 or 0. This becomes the next more significant bit of the resulting number.

$$\begin{array}{r} 2 \\ 2\overline{)5} \\ \underline{4} \quad \text{Next bit} = 1 \\ 1 \end{array}$$

3. Once again, the result of the previous division is divided by 2. The remainder is the next more significant bit.

$$\begin{array}{r} 1 \\ 2\overline{)2} \\ \underline{2} \quad \text{Next bit} = 0 \\ 0 \end{array}$$

4. This process continues until the *result* of the division is 0. The remainder from the last division (either a 1 or a 0) is the most significant bit of the binary number.

$$\begin{array}{r} 0 \\ 2\overline{)1} \\ \underline{0} \quad \text{Next bit (MSB)} = 1 \\ 1 \end{array}$$

The binary integer is 1010.

The following two examples illustrate the procedure:

$$57_{10} = ?_2$$

Division	Remainder	
$\dfrac{28}{2\overline{)57}}$	1	LSB
$\dfrac{14}{2\overline{)28}}$	0	
$\dfrac{7}{2\overline{)14}}$	0	
$\dfrac{3}{2\overline{)7}}$	1	
$\dfrac{1}{2\overline{)3}}$	1	
$\dfrac{0}{2\overline{)1}}$	1	MSB

Therefore $57_{10} = 111001_2$

$$134_{10} = ?_2$$

Division	Remainder	
$\dfrac{67}{2\overline{)134}}$	0	LSB
$\dfrac{33}{2\overline{)67}}$	1	
$\dfrac{16}{2\overline{)33}}$	1	
$\dfrac{8}{2\overline{)16}}$	0	
$\dfrac{4}{2\overline{)8}}$	0	
$\dfrac{2}{2\overline{)4}}$	0	
$\dfrac{1}{2\overline{)2}}$	0	
$\dfrac{0}{2\overline{)1}}$	1	MSB

Therefore $134_{10} = 10000110_2$

The procedure we have learned to convert decimal to binary numbers is for integers. Fractional numbers must be handled separately. But the procedure for fractions is very similar to that for integers.

Once the fractional number and the integer are converted, the results are combined as the right-hand and left-hand numerals around the binary point.

Converting a decimal fraction to a binary fraction is done by using the following procedure, which shows how to convert the deci-

mal number 0.375 to a binary number. Follow the example as you read the procedure.

1. The fraction to be converted is multiplied by the base of the number system it is to be converted into. In this case, the decimal fraction 0.375 is multiplied by 2, the base of the binary number system.

$$2 \times 0.375 = 0.75$$

2. If the result of the multiplication is less than 1, the most significant bit of the new binary number is a 0. If the result is greater than 1, the most significant bit of the new binary number is a 1.

$$0.75 < 1$$

Therefore the MSB is 0.

3. The fractional portion of the previous multiplication is again multiplied by 2. Note: This is only the fractional portion. It does not include the integer portion if the result was greater than 1.

$$2 \times 0.75 = 1.5$$

4. If the result of the multiplication is less than 1, the next most significant bit of the new binary number is a 0. If the result of the multiplication is equal to or greater than 1, the next most significant bit of the new binary number is 1.

$$1.5 > 1$$

Therefore the next most significant bit is 1.

5. This process continues either until the result of the multiplication is exactly 1 or until you have sufficient accuracy.

$$2 \times 0.5 = 1.0$$

The next bit, which will be the LSB, is 1.

The binary fraction is 0.011.

It is important to note that you will not always be able to reach a result of exactly 1 when you multiply repeatedly by 2. Therefore, you stop when you get the accuracy you want—that is, when you have enough bits in your binary fraction for your needs. The integer result of this last step becomes the least significant bit of the binary number.

The following examples illustrate this procedure.

$$0.34375_{10} = ?_2$$

Multiplication	Integer result	
$2 \times 0.34375 = 0.6875$	0	MSB
$2 \times 0.6875 = 1.375$	1	
$2 \times 0.375 = 0.75$	0	
$2 \times 0.75 = 1.5$	1	
$2 \times 0.5 = 1.0$	1	
$2 \times 0 = 0$	0	LSB

Therefore $0.34375_{10} = 0.01011_2$

$$0.3_{10} = ?_2$$

Multiplication	Integer result
$2 \times 0.3 = 0.6$	0
$2 \times 0.6 = 1.2$	1
$2 \times 0.2 = 0.4$	0
$2 \times 0.4 = 0.8$	0
$2 \times 0.8 = 1.6$	1
$2 \times 0.6 = 1.2$	1
$2 \times 0.2 = 0.4$	0
$2 \times 0.4 = 0.8$	0
$2 \times 0.8 = 1.6$	1
$2 \times 0.6 = 1.2$	1
$2 \times 0.2 = 0.4$	0

This conversion will repeat forever. We shall cut it off after eight bits of resolution. Therefore, $0.3_{10} = 0.0100\ 1100$, to eight bits of resolution.

Self-Test

Check your understanding by answering these questions.

13. Converting the integer portion of a number from one radix to another radix is done by using
    a. Addition   c. Multiplication
    b. Subtraction   d. Division

14. Converting the fractional portion of a number from one radix to another radix is done by using
    a. Addition   c. Multiplication
    b. Subtraction   d. Division

15. Convert the following decimal numbers to binary numbers:
    a. 23   *g.* 63
    b. 105   *h.* 29
    c. 32   *i.* 12.125
    d. 15   *j.* 16.375
    e. 206   *k.* 5.015625
    f. 128   *l.* 2.5

2-5 THE OCTAL NUMBER SYSTEM

As its name tells you, the *octal* numbering system refers to the base 8 number system. In the base 8 number system there are eight different characters. In the octal numbering system we use the characters 0, 1, 2, 3, 4, 5, 6, and 7.

Why is the octal numbering system used?

We know that no electronic system uses eight different levels in the way that digital electronics uses two different levels. The octal numbering system is not required by machines. It is a convenience for people. The octal numbering system is used in the world of computers, microcomputers, and microprocessors as a shorthand technique.

Stop and think of some of the common uses for binary numbers. You can see that there is a very real problem because of their length. For example, many microprocessors use an 8-bit word. That is, when they work with a binary number, it has eight bits. An 8-bit number can represent only the decimal values 0 through 255. This 8-bit number has just as many characters as the decimal numbers for any value from 0 to 99,999,999.

Clearly, the binary number that represents a large decimal number like 99,999,999 is very long. In fact, the binary version of 99,999,999 is 27 bits long! Such a long number is very difficult to read. The octal numbering system is used as a shorthand method to reduce the length of binary numbers.

Eight, as we know, is the third power of 2. That is, $8 = 2^3$. Each of the eight octal characters (0 through 7) can be represented by a 3-bit binary number. The 3-bit binary numbers are 000 to 111. They are shown in Fig. 2-6.

To show a binary number in octal form, the bits are grouped by threes. You start at the least significant bit (LSB). Each group of three is converted from the binary number to the equivalent octal number. For example, to convert the binary number 101010111111101 to an octal number, we start at the least significant bit and group by threes.

010   101   011   111   101

Octal number	Binary number	Decimal number
0	0	0
1	1	1
2	10	2
3	11	3
4	100	4
5	101	5
6	110	6
7	111	7
10	1000	8
11	1001	9
12	1010	10
13	1011	11
14	1100	12
15	1101	13
16	1110	14
17	1111	15
20	1 0000	16
62	11 0010	50
100	100 0000	64
156	110 1110	110
200	1000 0000	128

Fig. 2-6 Octal numbers and their binary and decimal equivalents. Insignificant 0s have been omitted to make the table easier to read.

Now we replace each group with the equal octal number

$$2 \quad 5 \quad 3 \quad 7 \quad 5$$

Therefore, 10101011111101_2 is $25{,}375_8$.

To convert 11000111_2 to an octal number, we have

$$\begin{array}{ccc} 011 & 000 & 111 \\ 3 & 0 & 7 \end{array}$$

That is, $11000111_2 = 307_8$. You can see that $25{,}375_8$ and 307_8 are much easier to read than the original binary numbers.

In these two examples, insignificant (leading) 0s were added to make the binary numbers into multiples of three bits. The addition of leading 0s does not change the value of a number.

We can represent fractional binary numbers with fractional octal numbers. Again, we group the bits into threes, but this time we start with the MSB. It is closest to the binary point. In this case we must add insignificant

0s (trailing 0s) to complete a grouping by threes. For example, to convert the binary fraction

$$0.0101101$$

to octal, we group by threes.

$$0. \quad 010 \quad 110 \quad 100$$

Now we replace each group with the equal octal number

$$0. \quad 2 \quad 6 \quad 4$$

That is, 0.0101101_2 is 0.264_8.

Converting 1011.0101_2, we have

$$\begin{array}{ccccc} 001 & 011 & . & 010 & 100 \\ 1 & 3 & . & 2 & 4 \end{array}$$

Therefore, 1011.0101_2 is 13.24_8. Again, the octal shorthand is much easier to read.

Be sure to note that

$$13.24_8 \neq 13.24_{10}*$$

Don't confuse base 8 and base 10 (decimal) numbers. One way to avoid mixing these numbers is to be careful how you say them. For example, when you are reading 13.24_8, say "one three point two four," not "thirteen point twenty-four." Do this whether reading aloud or reading in your head.

As you can see from the examples, the binary number is considerably shortened by conversion to octal. In the case of the 8-bit number, which is frequently used in microprocessors, the range of numbers is from $0000\ 0000_2$ to $1111\ 1111_2$. This reduces to the far simpler 000_8 to 377_8. Since there are only eight bits in the binary number, the octal number never reaches the maximum 777. Making the octal number 777 requires nine bits.

Self-Test

Check your understanding by answering these questions.

16. The octal number system uses the characters
    a. 0 and 1
    b. 1 through 8
    c. 0 through 9
    d. 0 through 7

* $\neq$ is the symbol for "is *not* equal to."

17. By using octal shorthand, the number of characters in a binary byte is reduced to
a. 4   b. 3   c. 2   d. 1

18. Convert the following binary numbers to octal notation:
a. 101   f. 0101 0101
b. 1111 1111   g. 0000.0010
c. 1110 1101   h. 111.111
d. 0000 0000   i. 0110.0110
e. 1000 0000   j. 1000.0001

19. Could the number 137783 be octal? Why? 13777? Why?

2-6 THE HEXADECIMAL NUMBER SYSTEM

Once we have been introduced to the octal numbering system, the hexadecimal numbering system becomes both simple and obvious. The hexadecimal numbering system uses 16 different characters. Conventional computer usage has chosen the 16 characters

0, 1, 2, 3, 4, 5, 6, 7, 8, 9,

A, B, C, D, E, and F

Earlier we saw that the octal number system is used because 8 is the third power of 2. We can see that the hexadecimal system is used because 16 is the fourth power of 2. That is, $16 = 2^4$. This means one hexadecimal character can serve as a shorthand notation for a 4-bit binary number. The relationships between the hexadecimal, binary, and decimal numbers are shown in Fig. 2-7.

Because the word "hexadecimal" is such a mouthful, the term "hex" is often used in speaking of hexadecimal numbers.

The conversion from a binary number to a hexadecimal number is simple. The binary number is collected into groups of four bits. This grouping starts at the least significant bit (the binary point). Each of the groups of four bits is then converted into its equivalent hex number.

The following two examples demonstrate the conversion of binary numbers into hexadecimal numbers. To convert the binary number 1010101111101 to a hexadecimal number, we first group by fours

0010   1010   1111   1101

Note that we can add insignificant 0s as necessary to make groupings that are 4 bits long.

Hexadecimal number	Binary number	Decimal number
0	0	0
1	1	1
2	10	2
3	11	3
4	100	4
5	101	5
6	110	6
7	111	7
8	1000	8
9	1001	9
A	1010	10
B	1011	11
C	1100	12
D	1101	13
E	1110	14
F	1111	15
10	1 0000	16
11	1 0001	17
12	1 0010	18
13	1 0011	19
14	1 0100	20
15	1 0101	21
16	1 0110	22
17	1 0111	23
18	1 1000	24
19	1 1001	25
1A	1 1010	26
1B	1 1011	27
1C	1 1100	28
1D	1 1101	29
1E	1 1110	30
1F	1 1111	31
20	10 0000	32
32	11 0010	50
40	100 0000	64
6E	110 1110	110
80	1000 0000	128

Fig. 2-7 Hexadecimal (hex) numbers and their binary and decimal equivalents.

Now we replace each group with the equal hexadecimal number.

2   A   F   D

Therefore, 1010101111101_2 is $2AFD_{16}$.

Converting 11000111_2 to hex, we have

$$1100 \quad 0111$$
$$C \qquad 7$$

That is, $11000111_2 = C7_{16}$.

Again, you can see that hexadecimal numbers are much easier to read or say than binary numbers. In fact, they are just about as easy to say or read as the octal numbers are. We now know that

$$10101011111101_2 = 25375_8 = 2AFD_{16}$$

and that

$$11000111_2 = 307_8 = C7_{16}$$

Both the octal number and the hexidecimal number are much easier to say and remember than the binary number. You will become quite familiar with both hex and octal.

Always remember that both hex and octal numbers are just ways of showing binary numbers. The microprocessor works on binary bits, not octal or hexadecimal characters!

The hexadecimal numbering system has one distinct advantage over the octal. Microprocessors use 4-, 8-, 16-, or 32-bit words. This means that most microprocessors have a word length that is a multiple of 4 bits.

If you want to put numbers that are multiples of 4 bits in octal form, you must add insignificant 0s to make the number of bits even multiples of 3. You do not need to do this when you are using hexadecimal notation.

For example, an 8-bit number can be broken into two 4-bit numbers. Each 4-bit number can be changed into its equal hex number. This very simple relationship has made hexadecimal notation more popular than octal notation for working with microprocessors.

Octal notation became very popular for use with the Digital Equipment Corporation's PDP-8 family of computers. The PDP-8 computers used a 12-bit word, which is easily represented by four octal numbers.

Converting from binary fractions to hexadecimal fractions follows the same rules you learned for octal fractions. The fractional bits are grouped in fours starting at the fraction's MSB (this is the number to the right of the binary point.) Each grouping of four is converted into its equivalent hex number.

Insignificant (trailing) 0s are added to the binary bits if necessary.

For example, to convert the binary fraction 0.0101101 to hex, we group by fours:

$$0. \quad 0101 \quad 1010$$

Now we replace each group with the equal hexadecimal number:

$$0. \quad 5 \qquad A$$

That is, 0.0101101_2 is $0.5A_{16}$.

Converting 1101.0111_2 to hexadecimal, we have

$$1101 \quad . \quad 0111$$
$$D \quad . \quad 7$$

Therefore, 1011.0111_2 is $D.7_{16}$.

Self-Test

Check your understanding by answering these questions.

20. The hexadecimal system uses the characters ____?____ to represent binary numbers.
    a. 0 through 10   c. 0 through 7
    b. 0 through F   d. 0 and 1

21. Does the number 01C34 probably belong to the decimal, octal, or hexadecimal number systems? Why?

22. Using hex shorthand reduces the length of a binary number by a factor of
    a. 4   b. 3   c. 2   d. 1

23. Convert the following binary numbers to hexadecimal notation:
    a. 101   *f.* 0101 0101
    b. 1111 1111   *g.* 0000 0010
    c. 1110 1101   *h.* 111.111
    d. 0000 0000   *i.* 0110.0110
    e. 1000 0000   *j.* 1000.0001

24. Comment on how the answers to question 23 compare with the answers to question 18 in the self-test on the octal system.

2-7 OCTAL, DECIMAL, AND HEXADECIMAL CONVERSIONS

When you work with microprocessors, you will have to convert decimal numbers to binary numbers and binary numbers to decimal numbers. Often you will want to show these binary numbers in either the octal or the hexadecimal shorthand form. Consequently you will want to make other conversions. For example, you will want to convert octal or hexadecimal numbers back to their binary form. You may also want to convert an octal or hexadecimal number into its decimal equivalent.

When you are converting either octal or hexadecimal numbers to decimal form, you use the same procedure that you used for binary numbers. That is, you assign a weight to each column of the number. Then you multiply these weights by the number in the column and add the results of the multiplications. The following examples show conversions from octal to decimal and hexadecimal to decimal.

$$1172.25_8 = ?_{10}$$

Assign weights:

8^3	8^2	8^1	8^0	.	8^{-1}	8^{-2}	
1	1	7	2	.	2	5	

$$
\begin{aligned}
& 0.015625 \longrightarrow 0.078125 \\
& 0.125 \longrightarrow 0.25 \\
& 1 \longrightarrow 2.0 \\
& 8 \longrightarrow 56.0 \\
& 64 \longrightarrow 64.0 \\
& 512 \longrightarrow 512.0 \\
& \hphantom{512} \quad \overline{634.328125}
\end{aligned}
$$

Therefore $1172.25_8 = 634.328125_{10}$.

$$27A.54_{16} = ?_{10}$$

Assign weights:

16^2	16^1	16^0	.	16^{-1}	16^{-2}	
2	7	A	.	5	4	

$$
\begin{aligned}
& 0.00390625 \longrightarrow 0.015625 \\
& 0.0625 \longrightarrow 0.3125 \\
& 1 \longrightarrow 10.0 \\
& 16 \longrightarrow 112.0 \\
& 256 \longrightarrow 512.0 \\
& \hphantom{256} \quad \overline{634.328125}
\end{aligned}
$$

Therefore $27A.54_{16} = 634.328125_{10}$

The procedure is really quite simple. As we saw with the binary fractions, the numbers can easily get quite long. Often you will wish to round numbers off.

Let's look at converting a number from decimal to octal or hexadecimal. You may use a procedure similar to the one you used to convert decimal numbers into binary numbers.

We learned that that procedure is a general-purpose one. For converting from decimal to octal or hex, instead of dividing (multiplying, in the case of a fraction) the number by 2, we divide (or multiply) the number by 8 or 16. The remainders (or integer products) are used to make up the final number.

In the following examples, you see octal and hexadecimal numbers created from decimal numbers. The process is different for the integer and fractional parts of a decimal number. In both cases, the original decimal number must be split at the radix point into its integer and its fraction. Then separate conversions must be done on both parts. The parts are then put back together in either the octal or the hexadecimal form.

$$634.328125_{10} = ?_8$$

The integer part

Division	Remainder	
$\dfrac{79}{8)\overline{634}}$		
$\dfrac{56}{74}$		
$\dfrac{72}{2}$	2	LSD
$\dfrac{9}{8)\overline{79}}$		
$\dfrac{72}{7}$	7	
$\dfrac{1}{8)\overline{9}}$		
$\dfrac{8}{1}$	1	
$\dfrac{0}{8)\overline{1}}$		
$\dfrac{0}{1}$	1	MSD

Therefore, $634_{10} = 1172_8$

The fractional part

Multiplication		Integer result	
$8 \times 0.328125 = 2.625$		2	MSD
$8 \times 0.625 \quad = 5.0$		5	LSD

Therefore $0.328125_{10} = 0.25_8$, and so 634.328125_{10} is 1172.25_8

$$634.328125_{10} = ?_{16}$$

The integer part

Division	Remainder	
$\begin{array}{r} 39 \\ 16\overline{)634} \\ \underline{48} \\ 154 \\ \underline{144} \\ 10 \end{array}$	$10_{10} = A_{16}$	LSD
$\begin{array}{r} 2 \\ 16\overline{)39} \\ \underline{32} \\ 7 \end{array}$	7	
$\begin{array}{r} 0 \\ 16\overline{)2} \\ \underline{0} \\ 2 \end{array}$	2	MSD

$634_{10} = 27A_{16}$. Note that the remainders must be converted into their hexadecimal form.

The fractional part

Multiplication	Integer result	
$16 \times 0.328125 = 5.25$	5	MSD
$16 \times 0.25 \quad = 4.0$	4	LSD

Therefore, $0.328125_{10} = 0.54_{16}$, and $634.328125_{10} = 27A.54_{16}$.

These two examples show us how to get octal and hexadecimal numbers from decimal numbers. Remember, the reason we do this is to express the number in a shorthand form.

Converting 1172.25_8 and $27A.54_{16}$ to their binary forms, we see that they are the same binary number. That is,

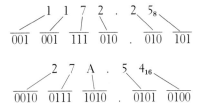

are both

$$1001111010.010101_2$$

which is

$$634.328125_{10}$$

Obviously, there are procedures for converting from octal to hexadecimal, and from hexadecimal to octal. If you ever find such conversion necessary, you can always convert to binary first and then to the desired number system. You will seldom if ever find it necessary to make these conversions.

Self-Test

Check your understanding by answering these questions.

25. Converting decimal numbers into octal or hexadecimal numbers uses the same procedure as converting
    a. Binary numbers into octal
    b. Hexadecimal numbers into binary
    c. Decimal numbers into binary
    d. Binary numbers into hexadecimal

26. For the following decimal numbers, give the binary, octal, and hexadecimal forms:
    a. 126   *f.* 12
    b. 4   *g.* 1
    c. 16   *h.* 127
    d. 63   *i.* 9.25
    e. 101   *j.* 64.015625

27. A real number may have both integer and fractional parts. How would you expect to convert a real decimal number into a real base 4 number? What characters would you use?

Summary

1. The decimal number system uses the characters 0 through 9. We use it every day. Each column of numbers is assigned a weight that is a power of 10. The decimal point separates the integer and fractional parts of a mixed number.

2. The binary number system uses two characters. These are usually 1 and 0. Each character position is called a "bit," for *bi*nary dig*it*. The column weights are powers of 2. The binary point separates the integer and fractional portions of mixed binary numbers.

"LSB" and "MSB" refer to the least and the most significant bit of a binary number.

3. Binary numbers are converted to decimal numbers by adding the column weights for those columns that have a 1.

4. Decimal numbers are converted to binary numbers by a division and multiplication process. Division is used for the integer part of the conversion, and multiplication is used for the fractional part of the process.

5. The octal number system uses the characters 0 through 7. It is used as a shorthand way to represent long binary numbers. For conversion, the binary numbers are grouped by threes and then replaced by the equivalent octal characters.

6. The hexadecimal number system uses the characters 0 through F. It is called the "hex" system for short. Hex is a shorthand way to represent long binary numbers. For conversion, the binary numbers are grouped by fours and then replaced by the equivalent hex characters.

7. Converting from a decimal number to either an octal or a hexadecimal number is done in the same way that a decimal number is converted into a binary number.

Chapter Review Questions

2-1. The *base* of a number system is
   a. The highest number which can be used
   b. The number of characters used in the system
   c. 8 in the decimal system
   d. F in the hexadecimal system

2-2. In the number 426, the character 4 is the
   a. MSD   c. MSB
   b. LSB   d. LSD

2-3. In scientific notation the weight of the thousands column is
   a. 10^0 *b.* 10^1 *c.* 10^2 *d.* 10^3

2-4. The binary number system uses the characters
   a. 0 through 9   c. 0 through F
   b. 0 and 1   d. 0 through 7

2-5. Complete the following:
   $2^0 = 1$ $2^5 =$ $2^9 =$
   $2^1 =$ $2^6 =$ $2^{10} =$
   $2^2 =$ $2^7 =$ $2^{11} =$
   $2^3 =$ $2^8 =$ $2^{12} =$
   $2^4 =$

2-6. An 8-bit binary number can represent ____?____ different decimal numbers.
   a. 8   c. 256
   b. 99,999,999   d. 1024

2-7. A *bit* is a
   a. Binary *increment*   *c.* Least significant number
   b. Binary digit   *d.* Most significant number

2-8. Convert the following binary numbers to decimal numbers:
   a. 1111   *f.* 1101 1101   *k.* 0.0001
   b. 1111 1111   *g.* 0001   *l.* 101.11111
   c. 0100   *h.* 0000 0001   *m.* 1110.1110
   d. 0000 0000   *i.* 0111   *n.* 00.01011
   e. 1101   *j.* 0011 1111

27

2-9. Convert the following decimal numbers to binary numbers:

a.	128	*h.*	29
b.	12	*i.*	255
c.	75	*j.*	1024
d.	256	*k.*	10.5
e.	31	*l.*	16.015625
f.	30	*m.*	12.03
g.	56	*n.*	17.7

2-10. Convert the binary numbers in question 2-8 to a table of equivalent octal, decimal, and hexadecimal numbers.

2-11. Convert the decimal numbers in question 2-9 into a table of equivalent binary, octal, and hexadecimal numbers.

Answers to Self-Tests

1. b.
2. c.
3. 27,329.
4. d.
5. b.
6. No, because the character 2 is not a binary character.
7. Least significant bit.
8. Binary digit.
9. c.
10. 1111_2, because it is equal to 15_{10}.
11. b.
12. *a.* 182   *f.* 129
    b. 80   *g.* 126
    c. 30   *h.* 63
    d. 128   *i.* 0.3125
    e. 255   *j.* 4.375
13. d.
14. c.
15. *a.* 10111
    b. 1101001
    c. 100000
    d. 1111
    e. 1100 1110
    f. 1000 0000
    g. 111111
    h. 11101
    i. 1100.001
    j. 10000.011
    k. 101.000001
    l. 10.1
16. d.
17. b.
18. *a.* 5   *f.* 125
    b. 377   *g.* 00.1
    c. 355   *h.* 7.7
    d. 000   *i.* 06.30
    e. 200   *j.* 10.04

19. The first number could not be octal because the character "8" is not used in the octal system. The second number can be octal or decimal, because the characters used are available in the octal system.

20. b.

21. Hexadecimal, because the character C is not used in the other systems.

22. a.

23. *a.* 5   *f.* 55
    b. FF   *g.* 0.0
    c. ED   *h.* 7.E
    d. 00   *i.* 6.6
    e. 80   *j.* 8.1

24. The hexadecimal and octal 5 are the same. The hexadecimal notation gives fewer characters. Zero in any system is zero.

25. c.

26.

	Binary	Octal	Hexadecimal
a.	01111110	176	7E
b.	100	4	4
c.	10000	20	10
d.	111111	77	3F
e.	1100101	145	65
f.	1100	14	C
g.	1	1	1
h.	01111111	177	7F
i.	1001.01	11.2	9.4
j.	1000000.000001	100.01	40.04

27. Divide the integer part of the decimal number by 4. The remainder becomes the LSD. Keep dividing the results by 4 until the result is 0. The last remainder is the MSD. The fractional part is multiplied by 4. The integer part of the result becomes the MSD of the fraction. The fractional parts are again multiplied by 4 until the desired precision is achieved. The base 4 number system would use the characters 0, 1, 2, and 3.

Inside the Microprocessor

■ **In this chapter, we begin to look at the internal structure of the microprocessor. We will first look at the microprocessor's block diagram in order to learn about the microprocessor's three major functional blocks: the arithmetic logic unit (ALU), the data registers, and the control logic. We will see that the ALU performs all logic and arithmetic operations that change data. We will learn that a register is a fast, internal memory device having enough bits to store one data word.**

We will identify the six registers that almost every microprocessor must have. The others may be thought of as "convenience" registers, and there will be more about them in Chap. 7. We will then look at the microprocessor's control logic.

Finally, we will study the microprocessor's internal bus. We will learn how it carries data from one internal logic function to another. In Chap. 6, we will see that the idea underlying this bus is also used in a microcomputer system.

3-1 THE MICROPROCESSOR BLOCK DIAGRAM

The microprocessor block diagram is designed to help show how a microprocessor works. The block diagram shows a microprocessor's logic functions for data processing and data handling. The diagram also shows how each of these logic functions is connected to all the others. Referring to a block diagram often makes it easier to see how to use a microprocessor to solve problems.

In this text, we will always use the block diagram shown in Fig. 3-1. The 8-bit, register-oriented microprocessor shown is designed to be an example only; it is *not* a commercially available microprocessor. When you work with real, manufactured microprocessors, you will be able to use block diagrams that are provided, along with other data sheets, by the manufacturers. Each block diagram makes it easier to understand the architecture of the particular microprocessor it shows.

Each manufacturer also provides a programming model for each microprocessor. Although a programming model may at first seem much like a block diagram, the two are really quite different. In this chapter, we use

a block diagram. In a later chapter, we will use a programming model. We will learn in that later chapter how to tell the difference between a block diagram and a programming model.

Returning to Fig. 3-1, we find three major logic devices in the microprocessor's block diagram: (1) the ALU, (2) the several registers, and (3) the control logic. Also shown is the microprocessor's system for transmitting data from one of these logic devices to another: the microprocessor's internal data bus.

In Sec. 3-2 we look at the ALU. We will then proceed to the various registers, the control logic, and the internal data bus.

3-2 THE ALU

One of the microprocessor's major logic functions is contained in the arithmetic logic unit (ALU). The ALU contains the microprocessor's data processing logic. Figure 3-2 shows the ALU outlined in black to make it stand out from the other parts of the microprocessor.

Notice that the ALU has two *input ports*, labeled "IN" in the diagram, and one *output port*, labeled "OUT." An input port is the

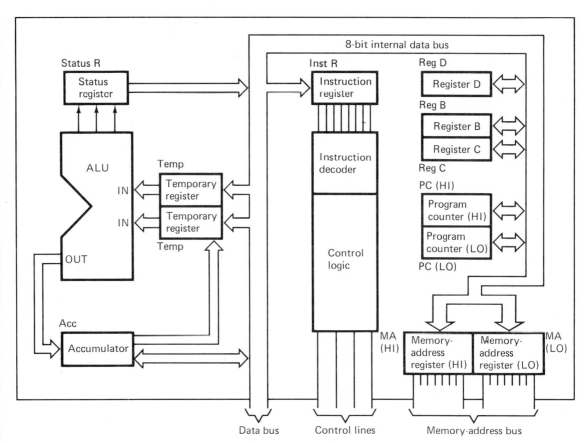

Fig. 3-1 The microprocessor used as a model in this text. This 8-bit register-oriented microprocessor is used throughout this text to illustrate the microprocessor's features. Although this is not a commercially available microprocessor, it does represent many of the functions and features found in commercially available units.

logic circuitry used to get a data word into a logic device. An output port is the logic circuitry used to get a data word out of a logic device. Most logic devices have one or more input ports and a single output port.

Both of the input ports are *buffered* by a temporary register; that is, each port has a register that temporarily stores one data word, holding the word for the ALU. A fuller discussion of the temporary registers takes place in Sec. 3-9 in this chapter.

The ALU's two input ports allow it to take data either from the microprocessor's internal data bus or from a special register called the *accumulator*. The ALU's single output port allows it to send a data word to the accumulator.

The accumulator can store one data word, whether that word has been fetched from memory or has been sent from the ALU's output port. When the ALU adds two data words, for example, one of the two words is

placed in the accumulator. After the addition is performed, the resulting data word is sent to the accumulator and stored there.

The ALU works on either one or two data words, depending on the kind of operation performed. The ALU uses input ports as necessary. Since addition requires two data words, for example, an addition operation uses both ALU input ports.

Complementing a data word, on the other hand, uses only one input port. To complement a data word is to set all the word's bits that are logic "1" to logic "0," and to set all the word's bits that are logic "0" to logical "1." As you can see, the ALU needs to work on only one word to perform a complement operation. That is why the complement operation uses only one input port—the input port connected to the accumulator.

The ALU must be used whenever it is necessary to change or test a data word. The list of ALU functions—the exact ways in which

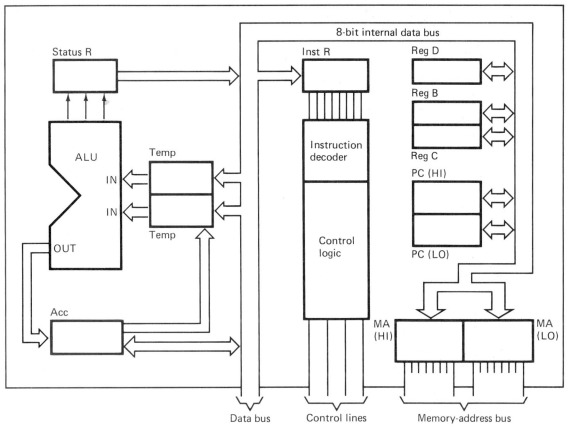

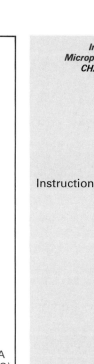

Fig. 3-2 The ALU of the model microprocessor. The micro-processor's arithmetic and logic unit can input data from one or two sources and outputs a single word.

the ALU can change or test data—varies from one microprocessor to another. Some ALUs have many functions. Other ALUs have only a few. ALU functions are part of the microprocessor's architecture.

The ALUs of most microprocessors can perform all the functions listed below:

Add	Complement
Subtract	Shift Right
AND	Shift Left
OR	Increment
EXCLUSIVE OR	Decrement

We will look at these ALU functions in detail later when we study microprocessor instruction sets. The most important point to remember now is that any instruction that changes data *must* use the ALU.

Self-Test

Check your understanding by answering these questions.

1. A microprocessor's block diagram is used to
   a. Describe the detailed gate and flip-flop logic used to construct the microprocessor
   b. Describe how the microprocessor's logic is connected to the memory and I/O devices
   c. Show the logic devices which you can use on your data to solve a problem
   d. (All of the above)

2. Which of the following is not an ALU function?
   a. Add   c. Power-up
   b. Shift Left d. Complement

3. The ALU has two inputs. In the microprocessor used in this text they are connected to the accumulator and the
   a. Program counter
   b. Internal data bus
   c. Control logic
   d. Memory-address register

4. The ALU's main job is to
   a. Perform addition
   b. Act as an output for the accumulator

31

c. Logically or arithmetically modify data words

d. (All of the above)

3-3 THE MICROPROCESSOR'S REGISTERS

Registers are a prominent part of the block diagram of any microprocessor. They are a major logic function. This is true whether a microprocessor has only a few registers or many. Figure 3-3 highlights the registers in the block diagram of our microprocessor. The six basic registers are shown with a black outline. The others, discussed later in this chapter, are shown with a color outline.

The microprocessor's registers can each temporarily store a word of data. You may wish to think of a register as a data latch with enough bits to store one word.

Some microprocessor registers serve a special purpose. That is, they hold data that are used to do a specific kind of job. Other registers serve general purposes. General-purpose registers are available for any use the programmer's imagination can think of. Imaginative use of general-purpose registers often allows one programmer to do a job that another programmer using the same microprocessor cannot do.

Both the number and the use of registers in a microprocessor depends on the microprocessor's architecture. But there are six basic registers that almost all microprocessors have. All the other registers are included to make life easier for the programmer.

The six basic registers are the *accumulator*, the *program counter*, the *status register*, the *instruction register*, the *memory-address register*, and the *temporary data register*. In the next few sections, we will look at each of these basic registers in turn. As you read, pay careful attention to how each of these registers affects the microprocessor's data flow.

Later you may be surprised to find that some of these registers do not appear in cer-

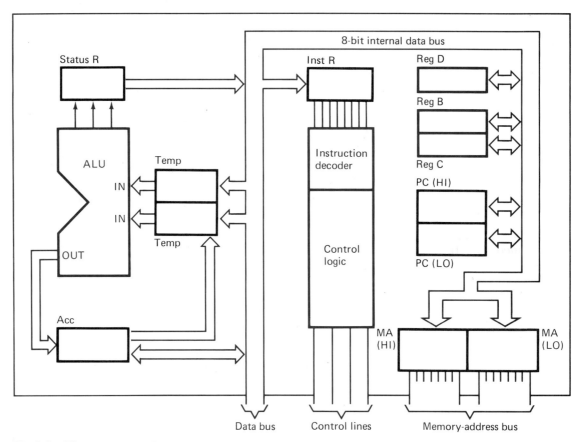

Fig. 3-3 The registers. The microprocessor's major registers are shown outlined in black. The three registers in the colored outline are general-purpose registers found on some microprocessors.

tain microprocessor programming models. The reason for omitting some registers from the programming model is that the programmer cannot do anything to change what happens with them. You must remember, however, that all the registers are present in the microprocessor and are serving a purpose. Otherwise you will not be able to understand how each register affects the microprocessor's data flow. In working with microprocessors, understanding data flow is essential.

3-4 THE ACCUMULATOR

When we looked at the ALU in Sec. 3-2, we had a glimpse of the accumulator's importance. In fact, the accumulator is the microprocessor's major register for data manipulation. Most arithmetic and logic operations on data use both the ALU and the accumulator. Whenever the operation combines two words, whether arithmetically or logically, the accumulator contains one of the words. (The other word may be contained in another register or in a memory location.)

For example, consider how the microprocessor adds two words. Let's call them word A and word B. First, word A is placed in the accumulator. The addition is then executed when word B (the contents of a memory location) is added to word A (in the accumulator). The resulting sum (C) is placed in the accumulator, replacing word A.

The result of an ALU operation is usually placed in the accumulator. It is important to understand that the accumulator's original contents are lost.

Another kind of operation using the accumulator is the *programmed data transfer*. A programmed data transfer moves data from one place in the microcomputer to another. Data movements between an I/O port and a memory location, or between one memory location and another, are examples of programmed data transfers. When a programmed data transfer is executed, the transfer takes place in two stages. First, the data are moved from their source to the accumulator. Then the data are moved from the accumulator to their destination.

We have seen how the microprocessor permits using the ALU to combine the data in the accumulator with other data. The microprocessor also permits working directly on data in the accumulator.

An example is *clearing* the accumulator. This operation sets all the accumulator's bits equal to logic "0." Other accumulator instructions set all the accumulator's bits to logic "1," shift the data to the right or to the left, complement the data in the accumulator, or perform other operations. We will study other accumulator instructions when we look at the microprocessor's instruction set.

No other register is as versatile as the accumulator. We can perform only more limited operations with the other registers. To do real work on a piece of data, we must first move it to the accumulator.

Figure 3-4 shows that the accumulator can receive data from the microprocessor's internal data bus. The accumulator can also send its contents to the internal data bus. Note that the path from the accumulator's output to the ALU is buffered by a temporary register. The need for this temporary register is discussed in Sec. 3-9 in this chapter.

The accumulator works on the same word length as the microprocessor's data word. That is, an 8-bit microprocessor has an 8-bit accumulator.

Some microprocessors, however, have *double-length* accumulators. In such cases, the double-length accumulator may be treated either as one device or as two separate accumulators. Treating the double-length accumulator as one device makes it possible to do a mathematical operation that introduces a carry into the second word. Consider the example of multiplying two 8-bit words. The result is a 16-bit word, which the double-length accumulator can hold.

Some microprocessors have multiple accumulators. A microprocessor, for example, might have one accumulator called accumulator A and another called accumulator B. A microprocessor that has two accumulators needs two different instructions to place the ALU's output in a specific accumulator. One instruction places the data in accumulator A. Another instruction places the data in accumulator B. Similarly, there are two Clear instructions—one to clear accumulator A and one to clear accumulator B.

What is the advantage of a microprocessor's having more than one accumulator? It is in the ability to perform accumulator-to-accumulator operations. Data can be stored temporarily in one accumulator while the other is used to do a different job. When the data in

33

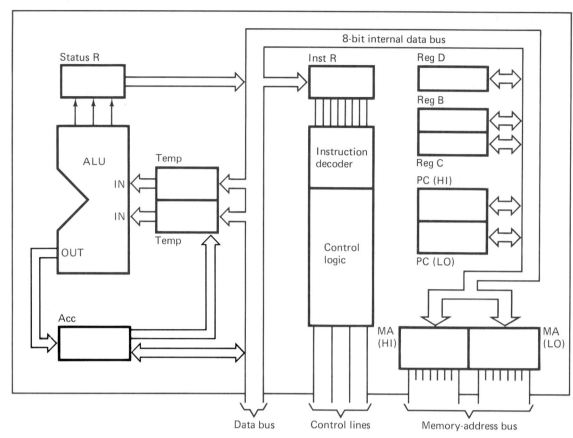

Fig. 3-4 The accumulator, the microprocessor's most important
working register. The accumulator can take data from the ALU
or the bus and can place data on the bus or in the ALU.

the first accumulator are needed again, there
is no need to move the data because they are
already in an accumulator.

By contrast, a microprocessor with one accumulator requires working on the data in the
accumulator and then storing the result in
memory or in another register. In many
cases, the programmer wants to do this any-
way. In other cases, however, having two accumulators can eliminate the need for many
operations.

Self-Test

*Check your understanding by answering these
questions.*

5. Most arithmetic and logic operations in a
microprocessor perform the operation between the contents of a memory location
or a register and the
a. Accumulator
b. Program counter
c. Memory-address register
d. Instruction register

6. The accumulator is connected to the other
logic devices of the microprocessor by the
microprocessor's internal data bus. The
accumulator has
a. 8 bits
b. 16 bits
c. Both input and output ports
d. All logic "0s"

7. When we say that we have cleared or reset
the accumulator, we really mean that we
have
a. Set the accumulator's contents to all
logic "0s"
b. Shorted out the accumulator's outputs
c. Set the accumulator contents to all
logic "1s"
d. Stopped using the accumulator

8. You are using a new 16-bit microprocessor. It has a double-length accumulator.
You expect this accumulator to be able to
store the results of ALU operations.
These results can be up to ___?___ bytes
long.
a. 1   c. 3
b. 2   d. 4

9. A programmed data transfer between input port 200_8 and memory location 7234_8 uses the ___?___ to temporarily hold the data.
   a. Program counter
   b. ALU
   c. Memory location 7233_8
   d. Accumulator

3-5 THE PROGRAM COUNTER

The program counter is one of the most important registers in the microprocessor. As you know, a program is a series of instructions stored in the microcomputer's memory. These instructions tell the microcomputer exactly how to solve a problem. Each instruction is simple and each instruction is exact. But all the instructions must occur in the right order if the program is to work correctly. The program counter's job is to keep track of what instruction is being used and what the next instruction will be.

Often the program counter is much longer than the microprocessor's data word. For example, in most 8-bit microprocessors that address 65K of memory, the program counter is 16 bits long. There is good reason for having such a long program counter. In a general-purpose microcomputer, any one of the 65,536 different memory locations can contain program steps. That is, the program can start anywhere and stop anywhere in the memory-address range of location 0 through location 65,535. The program counter must be 16 bits long in order to be able to point to any one of these different memory locations.

Always remember that wherever the program instructions are located, they must be in order.

In Fig. 3-5, the program counter is outlined in black. Notice that the program counter is connected to the microprocessor's internal data bus. In theory, the program counter could receive program address data from any other logic function that is connected to the internal data bus. In practice, however, the

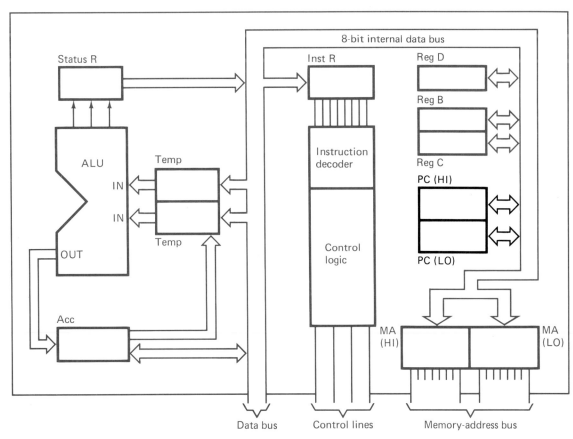

Fig. 3-5 The program counter. Both the hi byte and the lo byte of the program counter are bidirectionally connected to the microprocessor's internal data bus. However, all operations on the program counter work with it as a full 16-bit register.

Subroutine

program counter generally gets its data from the microcomputer's memory.

When the microprocessor starts up, a reset command loads the program counter with data from memory locations determined by the microprocessor's manufacturer. Before running a program, you must put the starting address for the program in the location that the manufacturer has specified. When you start to run the program, the program counter begins at the specified address.

The program counter cannot perform the variety of operations that the accumulator can. The program counter has fewer special instructions than the accumulator has.

Before it can start executing a program, the program counter has to be loaded with a number. This number is the address of the memory location containing the first program instruction.

Note the memory-address register and the memory-address bus, shown below the program counter in Fig. 3-5. The address of the memory location containing the first program instruction is sent from the program counter to the memory-address register. The contents of the memory-address register and the contents of the program counter are now the same. Section 3-6 gives more information on the memory-address register. For now, all you need to know is that the memory-address register, like the program counter, can hold a 16-bit binary number.

The memory address of the first instruction is sent on the memory-address bus toward the memory circuits. The memory then reads the contents of the address specified. These contents should, of course, be an instruction. The memory sends the instruction back to a special register in the MPU—the instruction register, described more fully in Sec. 3-7.

For now, the important point to note is this: Once the microprocessor fetches an instruction from memory, the microprocessor automatically increments the program counter. The program counter is incremented just as the microprocessor is starting to execute the instruction fetched immediately before.

The program counter now points to the *next* instruction. The program counter always points to the next instruction throughout the time in which the current instruction is being executed. This is an important concept to remember, because there are times when you may need to use the current value of the program counter. To know what the current

value is, you must know that the program counter is pointing to the next instruction, not to the current one.

The program counter can be loaded with a new value for special program instructions. You may wish to execute part of a program that is *not* in sequence with the main program. For example, there may be a part of the program that must be repeated exactly many times during the execution of the entire program. Rather than writing the repeated part of the program again and again, the programmer may want to write that part only once, but return to it—going out of sequence —many times. The part of the program to be done out of sequence is called a *subroutine*. Once the program counter is set to the starting address of the subroutine, the program counter then increments through the subroutine in order until it finds an instruction that tells it to return to the main program. Subroutines are explained in detail in Chap. 5.

Self Test

Check your understanding by answering these questions.

10. A 16-bit microprocessor has a memory address range of 2^{16} (65,536). You would expect the program counter in this microprocessor to be ___?___ bits long.
    a. 4   c. 16
    b. 8   d. 32

11. The program counter is one of a microprocessor's ___?___ registers.
    a. Special-purpose   c. Memory
    b. General-purpose   d. (All of the above)

12. Except when it is fetching an instruction, the program counter is pointing to the ___?___ program instruction.
    a. Last   c. Current
    b. Next   d. Subroutine

13. Once the program counter is loaded with a starting address it will
    a. Skip around, pointing to different memory locations as it thinks you need them
    b. Go to a lower memory location after it executes each instruction
    c. Increment to the next program instructed once the current instruction is fetched
    d. Go directly to location 65,536

3-6 THE MEMORY-ADDRESS REGISTER

Every time the microprocessor addresses the microcomputer's memory, the memory-address register points to the memory location the processor wants to use. That is, the memory-address register holds a binary number. That number is the address of a memory location. The memory location pointed to is the one identified by the binary number this register holds.

The output of the memory-address register is called the *memory-address bus*. This output is used to select a memory location or, in some cases, to select an input/output port.

During the Fetch cycle, as described in Sec. 3-5, an instruction is taken from memory. The contents of the memory-address register and the contents of the program counter are then the same. That is, the memory-address register points to the instruction word being fetched from memory. Once the instruction is decoded, the program counter increments.

The memory-address register does not in-

crement. During the Execute cycle, the contents of the memory-address register depend on the instruction being executed. If this instruction requires that the microprocessor address memory, then the memory-address register will be used for a second time during this one instruction. The execution of some instructions does not require addressing memory. An example is the Clear Accumulator instruction. If the instruction being executed does not require addressing memory, then the memory-address register is used only during the Fetch cycle.

In most microprocessors, the memory-address register is the same length as the program counter. Like the program counter, the memory-address register must have enough bits to address any location in the microprocessor's memory. For most 8-bit microprocessors, the memory-address register is 16 bits long. A 16-bit memory-address register may be two separate registers, each with an independent connection to the microprocessor's data bus. If so, these two registers are called the hi-byte and the lo-byte memory-address

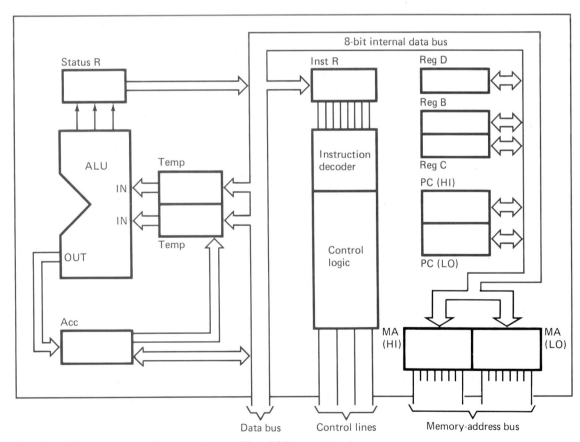

Fig. 3-6 The memory-address register. This 16-bit register is broken into the hi and lo bytes. Both bytes have an independent connection to the microprocessor's data bus.

Introduction to
Microprocessors
CHAPTER 3

Fetch/execute
instruction cycle

Offset
addressing

registers. Figure 3-6 shows two memory-address registers outlined in black and labeled HI and LO.

As Fig. 3-6 shows, the memory-address register is connected to the microprocessor's internal bus. Consequently, the memory-address register can be loaded from several different sources. Most microprocessors have instructions that permit loading the memory-address register from the program counter, from a general-purpose register, or from memory. Some instructions permit setting the memory-address register to a new number by computation: the new number is computed from the program counter's value plus or minus a number that is part of the instruction itself. The term for this kind of memory addressing is *offset addressing*.

Self-Test

Check your understanding by answering these questions.

14. The memory-address register points
    a. To the memory's contents
    b. To the memory location
    c. To a memory register
    d. To an MPU location

15. A certain 16-bit microprocessor can address 4,194,304 memory locations. You would expect this microprocessor to have a memory-address register which is ___?___ bits long.
    a. 8   c. 22
    b. 16   d. 32

16. The memory-address register is connected to the microprocessor's internal data bus. This is so that it can be loaded from
    a. The program counter
    b. The general-purpose register
    c. Memory
    d. (All of the above)

17. The memory address register's outputs make up the microprocessor's
    a. Accumulator
    b. Internal data bus
    c. Memory-address bus
    d. Instruction-decoder input

3-7 THE INSTRUCTION REGISTER

The instruction register holds the instruction that the microprocessor is currently execut-

ing. This is the instruction register's only job, and the instruction register performs it automatically. The instruction register is loaded by starting the microprocessor on a Fetch/Execute cycle—also called an *instruction cycle*.

As we have seen earlier, the instruction cycle consists of a Fetch cycle and an Execute cycle. Except for loading the instruction into the instruction register during the Fetch cycle, the programmer can make no other use of the instruction register. As shown in Fig. 3-7, the instruction register is connected to the microprocessor's internal data bus, but it can only receive data. The instruction register cannot place data on the internal bus.

Nevertheless, the instruction register plays a very important role in the microprocessor. The instruction register is important because its output always drives the part of the control logic known as the instruction decoder.

Remember the sequence of the Fetch/Execute cycle. First an instruction is fetched. Then the program counter points to the next instruction in memory. Whenever an instruction is fetched, a copy of the instruction is taken from the instruction's memory location. The copy is placed on the microprocessor's internal data bus and carried to the instruction register.

Then the instruction is executed. During execution, the instruction decoder reads the contents of the instruction register. The decoder decodes the instruction in order to tell the microprocessor exactly what to do to carry out the instruction. The instruction decoder is discussed in Sec. 3-11, which is about the microprocessor's control logic.

The length of the instruction register varies from one microprocessor to another. In some microprocessors, the instruction word is as long as the data word. In others, the instruction word may be as short as 3 or 4 bits.

Self-Test

Check your understanding by answering these questions.

18. During the execution of an instruction, the instruction register holds the ___?___ instruction.
    a. Previous   c. Next
    b. Current   d. (All of the above)

19. The instruction register's length depends on
    a. The microprocessor's architecutre

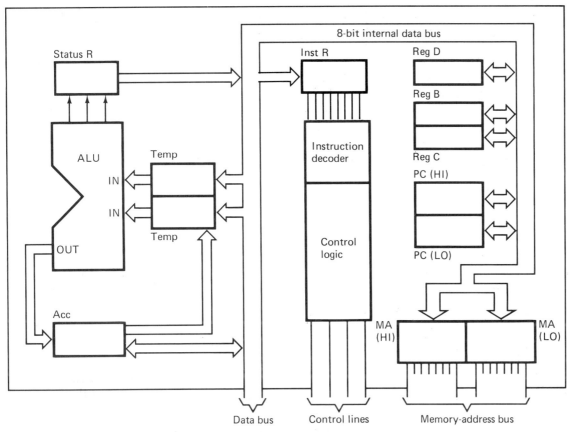

Branch

Fig. 3-7   The instruction register. This register holds the program instruction telling the microprocessor how to operate during its EXECUTE cycle.

b. Whether the microprocessor is an 8-bit or 16-bit design
c. The size of the memory being addressed
d. The microprocessor's speed

20. The instruction register is loaded with the contents of the memory location pointed to by the
a. Accumulator   c. Previous instruction
b. MPU   d. Program counter

3-8 THE STATUS REGISTER

The register that can make the difference between a simple calculator and an authentic computer is the *status register*. The status register is used to store the results of certain tests performed during the execution of a program. ALU operations and certain register operations set the status register's bits.

Storing the results of tests makes possible the writing of programs that *branch*. When the program branches, it starts at a new location. That is, the program counter is loaded with a new starting value. In conditional branching, the branch happens only if the result of a certain test comes out as required. The status register holds the results of such tests. Figure 3-8 shows the status register outlined in black.

The ability to branch is what sets a computer apart from a simple calculator. The status register lets the microprocessor's programmer arrange for the microprocessor to change the order in which the instructions are executed. The microprocessor carries out different programs when different conditions are true. We might even say that the microprocessor makes decisions based on these conditions. No calculator can make decisions.

Status bits have led to a new set of microprocessor instructions. These instructions exist in order to permit the execution of a program to change course on the basis of the condition of a status bit. The usual method of using these special instructions is to write the program so that the program counter is loaded with a new value when a certain status bit is

39

Mathematical
operations

Carry bit

Conditional
instructions

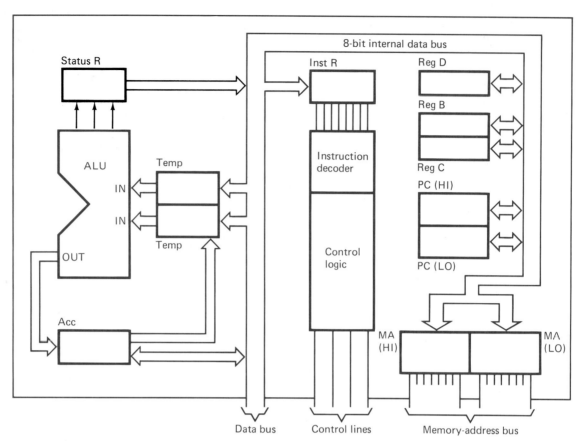

Fig. 3-8   The status register is shown receiving the output of the
ALU. Data operations with many of the different logic devices
set status register bits.

set.   The *conditional* instructions are discussed in detail in Chap. 6.

As already noted in this section, ALU operations set the status register's bits. The status register stores the results of tests for conditions that are generated by ALU operations. Mathematical operations create the most common conditions indicated by the status register. For example, mathematical operations can produce a carry bit, or they can result in a logic "0" (cleared register), or both.

If two 8-bit numbers are added, for example, and their sum is greater than 1111 1111, then a carry bit is generated. The carry is used to set the status register's carry bit.

If we add 1110 1110 and 1111 0000, we get

```
          1110 1110
          1111 0000
        1 1101 1110
       /          |
   carry        8-bit
               result
```

This operation sets the status register's carry bit to logic "1." If we add 0011 1111 and 0100 0001, we get

```
          0011 1111
          0100 0001
        0 1000 0000
       /          |
   carry        8-bit
               result
```

and the carry bit is set to logic "0."

If we add 1101 1110 and 1101 1010 we get

```
          1101 1110
        +  1101 1010
        1 1011 1000
       /      \
   carry    negative
```

This sets the carry bit and the negative bit to logic "1."

If the result of an operation sets all the bits of the accumulator to logic "0," the status register's zero bit is set. In our microprocessor, general-purpose registers can also set the status register's zero bit. For example, we often set the value of a register—let's call it register D—at some specific number and then decrement the register each time we pass through a designated point in the program. The result, each time the designated point is passed, is that register D is decremented and the status register's zero bit is checked. If, after register D is decremented, register D's value is logic "0," the status register's zero bit is set. If decrementing register D does not cause a logic "0" there, then the status register's zero bit is not set. The program that tests for the logic "0" in register D continues until the status register's zero bit is set.

Figure 3-9 shows a short program using the status register to test a decrementing register. First we set the register at 1100. Then we decrement the register. After decrementing the register, we test the status register for a logic "1" in the zero bit. If there is no logic "1" in the zero bit, then we decrement and test again. When a logic "1" is found in the zero bit, the program stops.

Some of the common status register bits are:

1. Carry/borrow. This bit indicates that the last operation caused either a carry or a borrow. The carry bit is set when two binary numbers are added and generate a carry from the eighth bit. A borrow is generated when a larger number is subtracted from a smaller number.
2. Zero. The zero bit is set when the operation causes all of a register's bits to be logic "0." This happens not only when you decrement the register, but also when any operation causes the register's bits all to become logic "0."

1. Load register with 1100_2.
2. Decrement register 1 count.
3. Is status register's zero bit a logic "1"?
4. No. Go back to Step 2.
5. Yes. Stop.

Fig. 3-9 A simple program showing how the status register is used. The instruction in the third line tests the status bit, which was set by the instruction in the second line.

3. Negative. The status register's negative bit is set when a register's most significant bit is logic "1." In 2's complement arithmetic, which we will cover in Chap. 4, a logic "1" in the register's most significant bit means that the number in the register is negative.

Most microprocessors use these three status bits. We use them also on the model microprocessor described in this text.

Many microprocessors, however, also use additional status register bits. The use of other status bits is not standardized. Some nonstandardized status bits in use require a thorough understanding of binary arithmetic, because these status bits are set only when specific arithmetic operations occur.

Other nonstandardized status bits are set for nonregister or non-ALU operations. These status bits are used to indicate that certain microprocessor functions are turned on or are turned off. Such status bits can indicate the hardware status of certain microprocessor options and are examined before the use of those options.

In some microprocessors, you can clear or set all the status bits by using a special microprocessor instruction. In other microprocessors, however, you can only read the status register's value.

To understand how nonstandardized status bits are used in a particular microprocessor, you must study the manufacturer's data sheets.

The status register's length depends on the number of status bits used by a particular microprocessor. In general, those bits not used are permanently set to logic "1."

Figure 3-10 shows the status word as it is used in our microprocessor. The five least significant bits are permanently set to logic

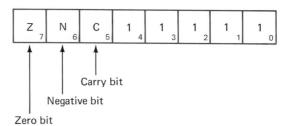

Fig. 3-10 The status word of the model microprocessor. For our model microprocessor there are only three status bits. All other bits are logic "1s."

Decrement

Status bits

Carry/borrow

Zero

Negative

"1." As a result, the word in the status register can be placed on the microprocessor's internal data bus, but the status register cannot receive data from the microprocessor's internal data bus.

In our microprocessor, an instruction that causes a positive number without carry to appear in the accumulator generates 0001 1111 as a status word. An instruction causing a negative number without carry generates 0101 1111.

Self-Test

Check your understanding by answering these questions.

21. Add the following 8-bit binary numbers. After adding these numbers, indicate how the result sets the zero, negative, and carry bits.

Example

```
     1 0 1 0 1 0 1 0
     1 1 1 1 1 1 1 1   Z  N  C
   1 1 0 1 0 1 0 0 1   0  1  1
```

```
a. 0 0 0 0 1 1 1 1
   1 1 1 1 0 0 0 0
```

```
b. 0 0 1 1 1 0 1 1
   1 1 0 0 0 1 0 1
```

```
c. 1 1 1 1 1 1 1 1
   1 1 1 1 1 1 1 1
```

```
d. 0 0 0 0 0 0 0 1
   1 1 1 1 1 1 1 0
```

```
e. 0 1 0 1 0 1 0 0
   1 1 0 0 1 1 0 0
```

```
f. 0 0 0 0 0 0 0 1
   0 1 1 1 1 1 1 1
```

```
g. 0 0 0 0 1 1 1 1
   0 0 0 1 0 0 0 0
```

```
h. 1 1 0 0 0 0 0 0
   1 0 0 0 0 0 0 1
```

22. You want to increment a register three times and set the status register's zero bit on the third increment. What is the 8-bit starting number? What are the three steps?

23. The status register's carry bit can also indicate
    a. A zero   c. A borrow
    b. A negative   d. (All of the above)

3-9 THE ALU's TEMPORARY DATA REGISTERS

Figure 3-11 shows the ALU's temporary data registers outlined in black. We will call the temporary register nearer the bottom of the block diagram the ALU's *accumulator latch*. Each of the temporary data registers has enough bits to store one data word.

We will explain the function of the accumulator latch later in this section. Now we will discuss the ALU's other temporary register, the one nearer the top of Fig. 3-11. Data from the microprocessor's internal data bus are temporarily stored in this register.

The need for the temporary register arises because the ALU has no data storage of its own. The ALU is constructed entirely of combinational logic. Because the ALU has no storage, any data applied to its input immediately appear at its output. The data that appear at the ALU's output, of course, have been modified by some ALU operation determined by the program.

The ALU must take data from the microprocessor's internal data bus, change the data, and then place the changed data in the accumulator. Without the temporary data register, the ALU's tasks would be impossible. Thus, this temporary register is essential to the internal functioning of the microprocessor. The ALU's temporary data registers cannot be used by the programmer.

Unlike the input of the other temporary register, the input of the accumulator latch can come from either the microprocessor's internal data bus or the accumulator's output. If the ALU is combining two words in a logic or arithmetic operation, one of the two words comes from the accumulator. The result of the operation is placed back in the accumulator. The accumulator latch keeps the ALU's input and output from being connected to the same place at the same time.

Like the other temporary register, the accumulator latch is not available for use by the programmer.

Self-Test

Check your understanding by answering these questions.

24. The main purpose of the temporary data register is
    a. To connect the ALU to the microprocessor's internal data bus

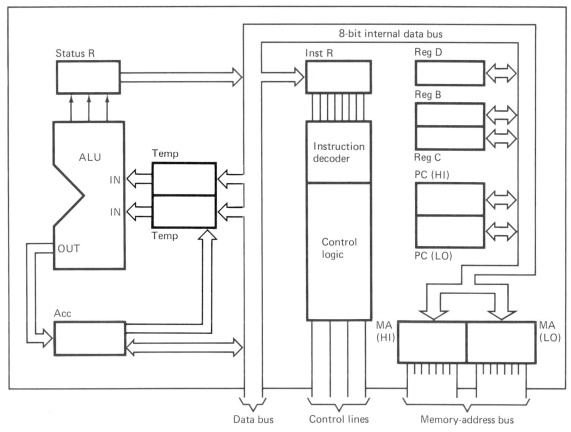

Fig. 3-11 The temporary registers. These registers hold the ALU's input data while the resulting output is placed into the accumulator.

b. To connect the ALU to the accumulator

c. To isolate the ALU's input and output ports in time

d. To provide accumulator storage

25. If you were using a 16-bit microprocessor, you would expect the temporary data register to be ___?___ bits wide.

    a. 32   c. 8
    b. 16   d. 4

26. A word in memory is to be added to the program counter's lower byte. This *offset address* is to be placed in the memory-address register. List the steps you think the microprocessor might take to carry out this instruction. Include the use of any temporary registers.

3-10 THE MICROPROCESSOR'S GENERAL-PURPOSE REGISTERS

In addition to the six basic registers that all microprocessor's have, some microprocessors

have other registers for general programming use. These other registers are called *general-purpose registers*. On some microprocessors, general-purpose registers serve only as simple storage areas. On other microprocessors, however, the general-purpose registers are as powerful as an accumulator. General-purpose registers achieve such power if the ALU can put its data into them.

The model microprocessor used in this text has three general-purpose registers (Fig. 3-12). They are called the B, C, and D registers. Since the ALU of our microprocessor does not put its data into these three registers, they lack the power of an accumulator. Nevertheless, many instructions do use these general-purpose registers.

For many operations, the B, C, and D registers are three identical 8-bit registers. The choice of which one to use for a certain job depends simply on which register is available and most convenient.

Usually operations with the B, C, and D registers affect the status register. Therefore,

43

Register arithmetic

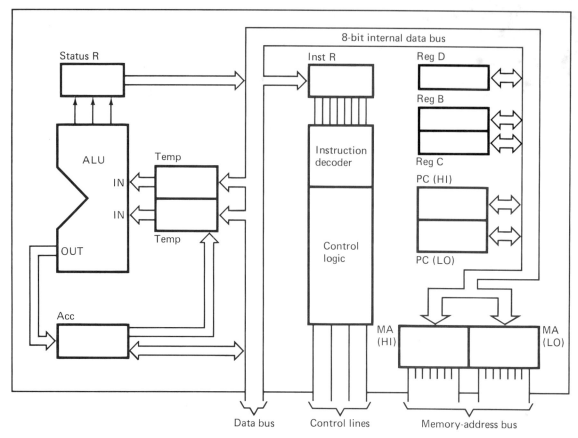

Fig. 3-12 The general-purpose registers. Register D is an 8-bit register. Registers B and C are either individual 8-bit registers or serve as a single 16-bit register.

any of the three can be used as a decrementing counter. What happens if we use the D register, for example, as a decrementing counter? When the D register decrements to 0, the status register's zero bit is set to logic "1."

Together, the B and C registers have a unique function: they can operate as a special-purpose 16-bit register. We then call them the *BC register pair*. When used as the BC register pair, the two registers act as if they were a single, 16-bit register.

Our microprocessor has an addressing mode that places the contents of the BC register pair in the memory-address register. This mode enables us to do register arithmetic on a 16-bit address. For example, we can increment the BC register pair and then use its contents to point to a memory location.

Remember that the B and C registers can also be used independently at any time. While the B and C registers can be used either in combination or independently, the D register is always a single 8-bit register.

Self-Test

Check your understanding by answering these questions.

27. The B, C, and D registers can be used as
    a. A program counter
    b. A memory-address register
    c. General-purpose registers
    d. A DC register pair

28. The BC register pair is used as a memory pointer because
    a. It is near the program counter
    b. It is near the memory-address register
    c. It can be used as two independent 8-bit registers
    d. 16 bits will address all of memory

29. If you need to use a register as a 16-bit decrementing counter, you will probably use the
    a. D register   c. B register
    b. C register   d. BC register pair

3-11 THE MICROPROCESSOR'S CONTROL LOGIC

Another major logic function of the microprocessor is its control logic. The logic in this part of the microprocessor keeps all the other parts working together and in the right time sequence. The control logic takes instructions from the instruction register, figures out what is to be done to the data, and then gives the commands necessary to get the job done.

Usually the microprocessor's control logic is microprogrammed. This means that the architecture of the control logic itself is much like the architecture of a very special-purpose microprocessor. The control logic, then, is like a small microprocessor within the microprocessor. The control logic's chief function is in its instruction decoder. The instruction decoder decodes the instructions stored in the instruction register and issues the control signals necessary to carry out these instructions.

The control logic is shown outlined in black on the block diagram in Fig. 3-13. As you can see, the control logic has control lines to each of the microprocessor's logic functions. These lines include the memory, I/O, and read-write lines. These control lines are usually not shown in a block diagram, because they only complicate the diagram and because the programmer cannot exercise control over the control logic.

One of the control logic's major external inputs is the microprocessor's clock. This clock is the basis of all the timing inside the microprocessor. The control logic converts the clock signal into a multiphase signal.

The diagram in Fig. 3-14 shows how a two-phase clock is derived from a single square wave. (Sometimes a microprocessor will use a four-phase clock.) Looking at this diagram,

Microprogram

Multiphase signal

Square wave

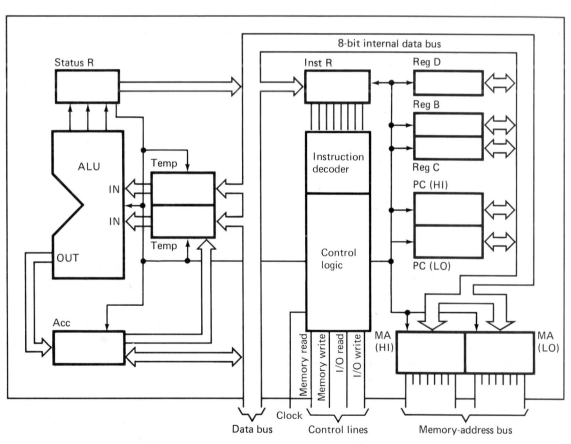

Fig. 3-13 The control logic. The control logic includes the instruction decoder, which gets its signals from the instruction register. The memory and I/O read-write lines send control signals to these external devices telling them what to do and when to do it.

External
oscillator

Internal
oscillator

Crystal-
control

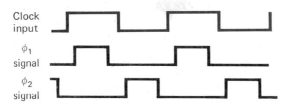

Fig. 3-14 A two-phase clock. The ϕ_1 and ϕ_2 signals are derived from a higher frequency square wave. Sometimes a microprocessor will use a four-phase clock.

you can see that two separate things can happen during a single clock cycle. The first thing can happen in time with the phase 1 (ϕ1) clock signal, and the second thing can happen in time with the phase 2 (ϕ2) clock signal. It is common for the control logic to generate either a phase 1 or a phase 2 clock signal and to output the signal for use by other devices such as memory and I/O.

The microprocessor may take its clock signal from an external oscillator, or the microprocessor may have its own internal oscillator. Frequently, the microprocessor's clock is crystal-controlled.

The control logic does a few other special functions. It controls the microprocessor's power-up sequence. The control logic also processes interrupts. An interrupt is like a request to the control logic from other logic devices such as the memory and I/O. The interrupt requests the use of the microprocessor's internal data bus. The control logic decides when and in what order the other devices can use the internal data bus. In functions of this kind, the control logic serves as a sort of housekeeper for the microprocessor.

3-12 THE MICROPROCESSOR'S INTERNAL DATA BUS

The microprocessor block diagram in Fig. 3-15 outlines the internal data bus in black. Looking at Fig. 3-15, you can clearly see that the ALU and all the other registers are connected by this one 8-bit data bus. All internal microprocessor data transfers take place on this one bus.

The microprocessor's internal data bus is made up of data signals. Although the con-

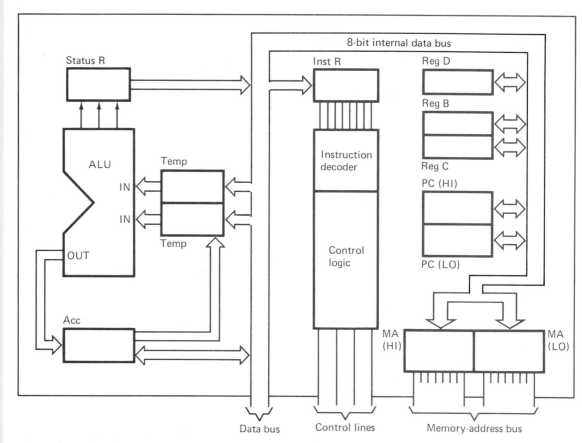

Fig. 3-15 The microprocessor's internal data bus. This becomes the microcomputer's data bus when it leaves the microprocessor.

trol signals coming from the control logic play a vital part in controlling the use of the bus, the control signals are not usually considered part of the bus.

Each of the microprocessor's logic functions is always connected to the internal data bus. Before any function can place data on the bus, however, the function must wait for its signal from the control logic.

Let's look at an example in order to better understand how the microprocessor's internal data bus works. We will look at what happens when the contents of register D are added to the contents of the accumulator. Follow the operations in Figs. 3-16 to 3-19 as you read what happens in each step.

1. The data are placed in the accumulator and in register D, neither of which is connected to any other device at this time. Note that the instruction register contains the instruction "Add." See Fig. 3-16.

2. The accumulator's data are loaded into the accumulator's output latch (a temporary register). Register D's data are placed on the microprocessor's internal data bus. The ALU's other temporary data register is connected to the bus. This temporary register is loaded with a copy of the data in register D. Only register D and the temporary register use the internal data bus at this time. The outputs of the two temporary registers drive the ALU input ports. See Fig. 3-17.

3. The ALU is directed to add the data at its input ports. Its output port is connected to the accumulator. The result of the addition is placed in the accumulator. Note: This addition sets the status register's negative and carry bits:
See Fig. 3-18.

$$\begin{array}{r} 1101\ 1110 \\ +\ \ 1101\ 1010 \\ \hline 1\ 1011\ 1000 \end{array}$$

carry negative

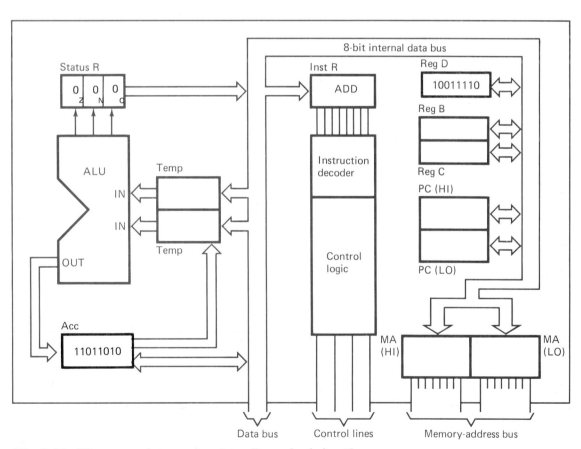

Fig. 3-16 The accumulator and register D are loaded with data. Note that the instruction register contains the instruction ADD. At this time neither register D or the accumulator are connected to any other device.

Bidirectional
communication

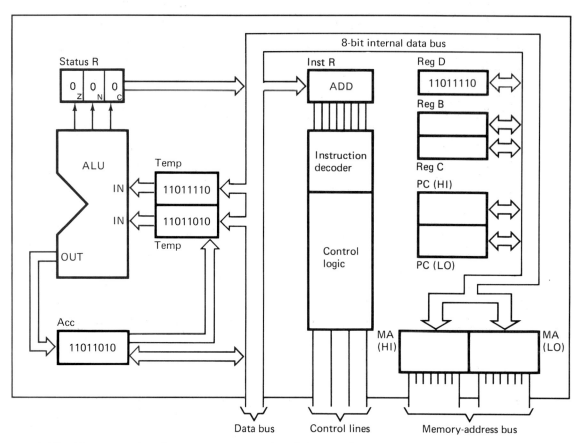

Fig. 3-17   The accumulator's contents are transferred to one of
the ALU's temporary registers. The other temporary register is
loaded with a copy of the data in register D. Only register D and
the temporary register use the internal data bus at this time.

4. The accumulator's input port and the
ALU's output port are both turned off.
The sum resulting from the addition is in
the accumulator. The bus is available for
another operation. See Fig. 3-19.

Almost all the microprocessor's logic devices have bidirectional communication with
the microprocessor's internal data bus. That
is, the devices can either place data on the bus
or receive data from the bus. The data bus itself is entirely bidirectional.

Remember that the data bus moves data
words, not bits. In a 16-bit microprocessor,
for example, all the movements on the internal data bus transfer 2 bytes of data (16 bits).

Self-Test

*Check your understanding by answering these
questions.*

30. The control logic guides the microprocessor through the steps to carry out a pro-

gram. It also does housekeeping functions such as
a. Temporary storage
b. The power-up sequence
c. Adding two numbers
d. Transferring data

31. The microprocessor's bus is bidirectional. This means that
a. All data flow in two directions
b. Data can flow in the direction needed
to complete the transfer
c. Each device has two input ports
d. Each device must have both an input
and an output port

32. All the microprocessor's logic functions
are connected to its internal data bus.
The microprocessor's ___?___ tells them
to talk to the bus, to listen to the bus, or to
do nothing.
a. Accumulator   c. MPU
b. Control logic   d. Instruction register

33. The microprocessor control logic is
driven by a high-frequency square wave
called the microprocessor's clock. The

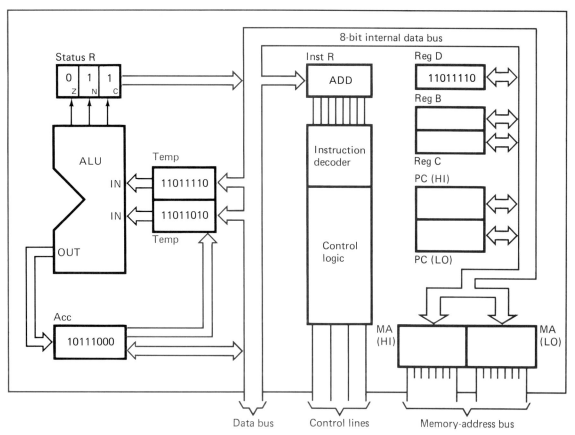

8-bit internal data bus

Status R

0	1	1
Z	N	C

ALU

IN

OUT

Acc

10111000

Temp

11011110

11011010

Temp

Inst R

ADD

Instruction
decoder

Control
logic

Reg D

11011110

Reg B

Reg C

PC (HI)

PC (LO)

MA
(HI)

MA
(LO)

Data bus   Control lines   Memory-address bus

Fig. 3-18 The ALU is told to add. The ALU's output goes to
the accumulator. The status register's negative and carry bits are
set. The accumulator's original contents are lost.

purpose of the microprocessor's clock is to
a. Provide time-of-day information
b. Operate the ALU's data-storage mech-
anism

c. Provide a timing signal to sequence the
control logic
d. Be sure the data in registers are kept
current

Summary

1. A microprocessor has three major logic
functions: the ALU, the registers, and the
control logic.

2. A logic device has a port through which
input or output data pass.

3. The ALU has two input ports and one
output port. One ALU input port comes
from the microprocessor's internal data bus.
The other ALU input port comes from the accumulator. An ALU works on either one or
two data words. The ALU is used to arithmetically or logically change or test data.

4. A register lets you temporarily store a
word of data. Some microprocessor registers
are general-purpose, but a few are very special-purpose.

5. All microprocessors have six basic registers. They are:
a. The accumulator
b. The program counter
c. The status register
d. The instruction register
e. The memory-address register
f. The temporary register
The six registers are needed to make a microprocessor work. However, a programmer
may not have direct access to all of them.

6. The accumulator works with the ALU. It
is the microprocessor's major register for data
manipulation. The accumulator's contents
are usually one-half of an arithmetic or logic
operation. The accumulator is the micropro-

49

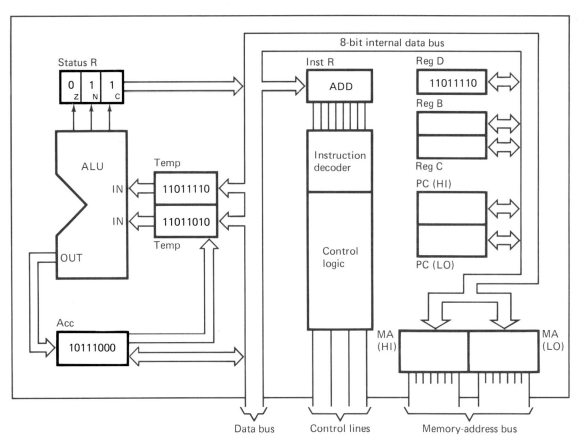

Fig. 3-19   The operation is complete. The new data is in the
accumulator, and the processor waits for the next instruction.

cessor's most versatile register. The accumulator's length is the same as that of the microprocessor's data word. Some sophisticated microprocessors have an accumulator which is twice as long as their data word. Some microprocessors have two accumulators. This feature lets you do accumulator-to-accumulator arithmetic and logic operations.

7. The program counter keeps track of exactly what instruction is to be executed next. The program counter's length must be long enough to address any memory location. Often 8-bit microprocessors have 16-bit program counters.

8. A program can start at any memory location and end at any memory location. However, the program instructions must be in their proper order, no matter where they are located.

9 a. When a microprocessor is first started up it always gets its first instruction from the same memory location.

b. Each program instruction step is then exe-

cuted in sequence unless a special instruction changes the sequence.

c. The program counter points to a memory location. The control logic fetches an instruction from this memory location.

d. Once the instruction is fetched, the microprocessor increments the program counter and starts to execute the instruction.

e. The incremented program counter now points to the *next* program instruction.

f. The memory-address register points to each memory location that the microprocessor wants to use when it wants to use it.

g. The memory-address register drives the microprocessor's memory-address bus.

h. The memory-address register is long enough to address every memory location in the microprocessor's main memory.

i. Typically, an 8-bit microprocessor's memory-address register is 16 bits long. This lets it address 65,536 memory locations from 0 to 65,535.

10. a. The instruction register holds the bi-

nary word that tells the microprocessor what to do to carry out the current instruction.

b. When the instruction is fetched, a copy is taken from its memory location in the program and placed in the instruction register.

c. During execution, the instruction decoder and control logic read the word in the instruction register.

11. The status register records the results of certain register operations.

a. Often the data in the status register control how the rest of the program will execute. They give the program decision-making information.

b. At a minimum, the status register has a zero, a negative, and a carry bit.

c. A logic "1" in the status register's zero bit tells you that the last operation caused a result of all logic "0s."

d. A logic "1" in the status register's negative bit tells you that the last operation caused a logic "1" in the result's most significant bit.

e. A logic "1" in the status register's carry bit tells you that the last operation caused an arithmetic overflow. The result was larger than the register it was put into.

f. Often a status register has additional bits or *flags*. These are peculiar to the particular microprocessor.

g. Some status bits may be used to indicate the status of certain programmable options. The bit tells you whether the option is on or off.

h. Because the microprocessor has a status register, it has conditional instructions that change the course of the program only if the proper bit is set.

12. The temporary registers hold data at the ALU's input while the ALU's combinational logic operates on the data.

13. Many double-width registers are broken into a hi and a lo word. The hi word and lo word are each the same length as a data word.

14. The microprocessor's control logic decodes the instruction and tells the other logic devices what to do and in what order to carry out the instruction. The microprocessor's control logic timing comes from the microprocessor's clock. Usually the clock is a two-phase, nonoverlapping signal.

15. The data path between all the microprocessor's logic devices is called its data bus. The data bus is bidirectional. All the logic devices are always connected to the bus. However, they must wait for a signal from the control logic before they talk to or listen to the bus. Data on the bus move from a source to a destination.

Chapter Review Questions

3-1. List the three major logic functions found in a microprocessor's block diagram.

3-2. The logic functions are connected together by the microprocessor's _____?_____ ?

3-3. Briefly explain what the arithmetic logic unit does. That is, what is its effect on the microprocessor's data?

3-4. List four typical specific functions performed by the ALU.

3-5. The ALU has two input ports. Does it always use both inputs? Why?

3-6. What does a microprocessor's register do?

3-7. The microprocessor's registers are
   a. Connected to the bus
   b. Single-word storage elements
   c. General- or special-purpose
   d. (All of the above)

3-8. The microprocessor's _____?_____ is not one of its six basic registers.
   a. Memory address register   c. Accumulator
   b. Index register   d. Program counter

51

3-9. The accumulator is used for
   a. Pointing to memory locations
   b. Pointing to the next instruction
   c. The storage part of arithmetic or logic operations
   d. Holding the instruction during execution

3-10. The result of an ALU operation is usually placed in the
   a. Program counter   c. Instruction register
   b. Accumulator   d. Temporary register

3-11. You would expect the accumulator in a 12-bit microprocessor to be ____?____ bits long.
   a. 8   b. 12   c. 16   d. 24

3-12. A double-length accumulator for the microprocessor in question 3-11 would be ____?____ bits long.
   a. 8   b. 12   c. 16   d. 24

3-13. Why would you want a microprocessor to have a double-length accumulator?

3-14. Some microprocessors have two accumulators for added flexibility. Give one example of this added flexibility.

3-15. The program counter keeps track of which program instruction is to be executed. It always points to the ____?____ instruction.

3-16. The program counter in a typical 8-bit microprocessor is ____?____ bits long. This means it can address 65,536 different memory locations.
   a. 4   b. 8   c. 16   d. 24

3-17. Why does the program counter need to be able to address any memory location even though a program cannot use all of memory?

3-18. When you power up a microprocessor, the reset command always starts the program counter at
   a. The same location
   b. Memory location 0000
   c. Memory location FFFF
   d. A random memory location

3-19. The memory-address register's output drives the ____?____ bus.

3-20. The data on the memory-address bus are used to select a desired ____?____.

3-21. You would expect a 16-bit microprocessor that can address 1,048,576 memory locations to have a ____?____-bit memory address register.

3-22. The instruction register holds the program's instruction while it is being executed. The instruction register's input is connected to the ____?____ and its output is connected to the ____?____.

3-23. The microprocessor has a two-phase cycle as each instruction is called and carried out. This is called the microprocessor's ____?____ cycle.

3-24. During the ____?____ cycle an instruction is moved from program memory into the instruction register.

3-25. During the ____?____ cycle the instruction is decoded and carried out.

3-26. The instruction register is ____?____ bits long.
   a. 4   b. 8   c. 16   d. No fixed number of

3-27. List the three common status register bits. Briefly explain what setting each of these three bits means.

3-28. The status register is tested by certain program instructions. The results of these decisions are used to make a _____?_____.

3-29. Explain why the microprocessor uses a temporary register. Would you expect the temporary register to be in the same place for different microprocessors? Why?

3-30. The microprocessor's clock provides the control logic with its basic
    a. Register   c. Timing
    b. Reset   d. Instruction

3-31. The job of the microprocessor's control logic is to _____?_____.

3-32. The microprocessor's internal data bus is
    a. Bidirectional
    b. As wide as a data word,
    c. Used to interconnect the logic devices
    d. (All of the above)

3-33. Name one logic device which has bidirectional communications with the internal data bus. Name one that does not.

Answers to Self-Tests

1. c.	8. d.	15. c.
2. c.	9. d.	16. d.
3. b.	10. c.	17. c.
4. c.	11. a.	18. b.
5. a.	12. b.	19. a.
6. c.	13. c.	20. d.
7. a.	14. b.	

21.

	Result	Z	N	C
a.	1111 1111	0	1	0
b.	1 0000 0000	1	0	1
c.	1 1111 1110	0	1	1
d.	1111 1111	0	1	0
e.	1 0010 0000	0	0	1
f.	1000 0000	0	1	0
g.	0001 1111	0	0	0
h.	1 0100 0001	0	0	1

22. The three steps will be:
11111101 start
11111110 1st increment
11111111 2d increment
00000000 3d increment

The zero bit will be set in the third increment. You could use the following:
01111101 start
01111110 1st increment
01111111 2d increment
10000000 3d increment
This time you would check the status register's negative bit.

23. c.   24. c.   25. b.

26. One possible series of steps is:
a. Load offset word into accumulator.
b. Load accumulator into temporary register
c. Load program counter's lower byte into ALU's temporary register.
d. Store result (sum) in accumulator.
e. Load program counter's upper byte into memory-address register's upper byte.
f. Load accumulator into memory-address register's lower byte.

27. c.   31. b.

28. d.   32. b.

29. d.   33. c.

30. b.

Processor Arithmetic

• In this chapter we will learn how a microprocessor does arithmetic with binary numbers. Microprocessors may be programmed to do decimal arithmetic, but they must convert decimal numbers to binary before doing arithmetic operations.

First, we will review decimal addition and subtraction, because binary arithmetic is very much like decimal arithmetic. We will look at how the microprocessor expresses both positive and negative binary numbers. We will learn a system called "2's complement" arithmetic, which makes handling signed binary numbers easy. We will see how 2's complement arithmetic is used in binary addition and subtraction.

We will look at binary multiplication and binary division. We will see that multiplication is really just successive additions and that division is just successive subtractions. We will see how to do general-purpose binary division.

We will look at multiple-precision techniques, which let us work with numbers bigger than the binary equivalent of a single microprocessor word. Finally, we will look at floating-point arithmetic, which is a way to express very large numbers in scientific notation.

4-1 BINARY ADDITION

Binary addition and decimal addition are done in the same general way. In either number system, when we add two numbers we start with the right-hand column. This column represents the least significant number. Any result that is *greater than a single place* causes a carry. We add the carry to the numbers in the next more significant column. Any column may generate a carry.

In the decimal number system, any number greater than 9 generates a carry. In the binary system, any number greater than 1 generates a carry.

Figure 4-1 will help you see both the similarities and the differences between binary and decimal addition. The same addition problem is shown first in the decimal number system and then in the binary number system.

In the decimal version, we add 95 to 99. The addend is 99 and the augend is 95. When we add 9 to 5 in the right-hand column, the result is 4 with 1 to carry. The carry is shown in Fig. 4-1 as an extra 1 at the top of the tens column. In that column, the carried 1 is

Decimal addition	Terms	Binary addition
11	Carry	1111 1110
099	Addend	0110 0011
095	Augend	0101 1111
194	Sum	1100 0010

Fig. 4-1 Decimal and binary addition. When the sum of the addend and the augend cannot be expressed as a single digit a carry is generated. Carries are shown as a 1 in the carry row of the next column.

added to 9 plus 9. The result is 9 with 1 to carry. The carried 1 is added to the 0s in the hundreds column. The result in the hundreds column is 1. The sum of 99 and 95 is 194.

Figure 4-2(a) is a table summarizing the rules for decimal addition. We could have used this table to find the sum of 99 and 95. We can find the result of adding any two *digits* by finding where the row (representing the augend) and the column (representing the addend) intersect. If the row and the column intersect in the shaded area, then the two

+		Addend									
		0	1	2	3	4	5	6	7	8	9
Augend	0	0	1	2	3	4	5	6	7	8	9
	1	1	2	3	4	5	6	7	8	9	0
	2	2	3	4	5	6	7	8	9	0	1
	3	3	4	5	6	7	8	9	0	1	2
	4	4	5	6	7	8	9	0	1	2	3
	5	5	6	7	8	9	0	1	2	3	4
	6	6	7	8	9	0	1	2	3	4	5
	7	7	8	9	0	1	2	3	4	5	6
	8	8	9	0	1	2	3	4	5	6	7
	9	9	0	1	2	3	4	5	6	7	8

(a)

+		Addend	
		0	1
Augend	0	0	1
	1	1	0

(b)

Fig. 4-2 The addition tables. Results in the shaded areas mean there is also a carry. (*a*) Decimal addition. (*b*) Binary addition.

digits generate a carry of 1 into the next more significant column. In the decimal number system, this procedure is so familiar to us that we may forget the rules we are working with. We just do decimal addition automatically.

Since we are unaccustomed to doing binary arithmetic, it may seem awkward at first. But it is really much simpler than decimal arithmetic. Figure 4-2(*b*) summarizes the rules for binary addition. We can find the result of adding any two *bits* by finding where the row (representing the augend) and the column (representing the addend) intersect. If the row and the column intersect in the shaded area, then the two bits generate a carry of 1 into the next more significant column. As you can see, the shaded area in Fig. 4-2(*b*) is only a single square. Figure 4-2(*b*) is so much simpler than Fig. 4-2(*a*) because the binary system has only two characters, 0 and 1.

Now let's return to Fig. 4-1 and add the binary equivalents of 99 and 95, 0110 0011 and 0101 1111. Starting with the least significant bit, we see that both the addend and the augend are 1s. From our binary addition table, we can see that the result is 0 with 1 to carry.

The carry is shown in Fig. 4-1 as an extra 1 at the top of the twos column. In that column, the carried 1 is added to 1 plus 1. We are adding three 1s.

The procedure for adding three 1s is shown in Fig. 4-3. There we see that the addition of three 1s can be broken down into two separate addition problems. Like other binary addition problems, these can be solved by using the rules summarized in our binary addition table. Adding 1 to 1, we get 0 with 1 to carry. That is, we get 0 in the ones place and 1 in the twos place, or 10. Now we add 1 to 10. This gives us 1 in the ones place and no carry to add to the 1 in the twos place. Thus, the binary sum of 1 and 1 and 1 is 11.

Returning to our larger addition problem in Fig. 4-1 the sum in the twos place is 11, or 1 with 1 to carry. The carry is shown as an extra 1 in the fours place. The carried 1 is added to the 0 and the 1 that are already in the fours place. This gives us 0 with 1 to carry to the eights place. The carry is shown as an extra 1 in the eights place. The carried 1 is added to the 0 and the 1 that are already in the eights place. This gives us 0 with 1 to carry to the sixteens place. The carry is shown as an extra 1 in the sixteens place. The carried 1 is added to the 0 and the 1 that are already in the eights place. This gives us 0 with 1 to carry to the sixteens place. The carry is shown as an extra 1 in the sixteens place. The carried 1 is added to the 0 and the 1 that are already in the sixteens place. This gives us 0 with 1 to carry to the thirty-twos place. The carry is shown as an extra 1 in the thirty-twos place. The carried 1 is added to the 1 and the 0 that are already in the thirty-twos place. This gives us 0 with 1 to carry to the sixty-fours place. The carried 1 is added to the two 1s that are already in the sixty-fours place. The result of adding three 1s, as we have seen, is 1 with 1 to carry. The carried 1 is added to the two 0s that are in the one hundred twenty-eights place. This gives us 1 in the one hundred twenty-

From page 54:
Carry

On this page:
Augend

Addend

$$
\begin{array}{c}
1 \\
1 \\
\underline{+1} \\
11
\end{array}
\quad = \quad
\begin{array}{c}
1 \\
\underline{+1} \\
10 \\
\underline{+1} \\
11
\end{array}
$$

Fig. 4-3 Adding three binary 1s. This is done as two separate addition problems. All addition problems can be reduced to adding groups of two digits.

eights place, with nothing to carry. Thus, the binary sum of 0110 0011 and 0101 1111 is 1100 0010.

Once you have added a few binary numbers, you will see that binary addition is easy. The only difficulty is that binary numbers need lots of bits to express large numbers. Consequently there are many columns and many carries in binary addition.

We deliberately chose an 8-bit representation of the binary numbers in the example above. This is because many microprocessors represent binary numbers as 8-bit words. Although neither the addend nor the augend in the example required eight bits, we still showed all eight bits. We did this because we cannot shorten a microprocessor word length just because there are significant leading 0s.

We do try to get rid of insignificant 0s for most decimal addition problems. That is, when we are writing a problem on paper we only show the number of digits necessary to express significant numbers. However, in this problem we did have a carry into the hundreds column. That is why this figure shows the two leading 0s. We must always remember that leading 0s are really there.

Self-Test

Check your understanding by answering these questions.

1. Add the following binary numbers:
   a. 0000 0101
      0001 0001

   b. 1000 1001
      0000 1111

   c. 0111 1111
      0111 1110

   d. 0101 0101
      1010 1010

   e. 101
      011

   f. 1001
      011

   g. 0100 0010 0110 1100
      0101 1110 1001 0110

   h. 0111 1111 1111 1111
      0001 0111 1011 1001

2. Express the following decimal-number addition problems in 8- or 16-bit binary numbers and do the additions.
   a. 101   *c.* 398   *e.* 86
       16   132   25

   b. 225   *d.* 56   *f.* 289
       168   10   493

3. What is the maximum number of bits needed to hold the result of adding two 8-bit numbers?

4. What is the difference between the binary numbers 101, 0101, and 0000 0101? How would this affect any binary sum?

4-2 BINARY SUBTRACTION

The way we do decimal subtraction is the same as the way we do binary subtraction. As with decimal addition and binary addition, we simply have different sets of rules for combining the numbers.

Figure 4-4(a) and (b) shows the subtraction tables for decimal and binary arithmetic. In Fig. 4-4(a) we can see the rules for decimal subtraction. In this figure any subtraction in

—		Subtrahend									
		0	1	2	3	4	5	6	7	8	9
Minuend	0	0	9	8	7	6	5	4	3	2	1
	1	1	0	9	8	7	6	5	4	3	2
	2	2	1	0	9	8	7	6	5	4	3
	3	3	2	1	0	9	8	7	6	5	4
	4	4	3	2	1	0	9	8	7	6	5
	5	5	4	3	2	1	0	9	8	7	6
	6	6	5	4	3	2	1	0	9	8	7
	7	7	6	5	4	3	2	1	0	9	8
	8	8	7	6	5	4	3	2	1	0	9
	9	9	8	7	6	5	4	3	2	1	0

(a)

—		Subtrahend	
		0	1
Minuend	0	0	1
	1	1	0

(b)

Fig. 4-4 The subtraction tables. Results in the shaded areas mean there is a borrow.

Decimal subtraction	Terms	Binary subtraction
1	Borrow	110 0000
109	Minuend	0110 1101
49	Subtrahend	0011 0001
060	Difference	0011 1100

Fig. 4-5 A subtraction problem in decimal and binary arithmetic. The first binary borrow in bit 5 resulted when a 1 was subtracted from 0. The borrow is shown as a 1 in the bit 6 column and borrow row.

which the subtrahend is larger than the minuend is shown in the shaded area. This means that the subtraction causes a borrow. That is, we borrow a 1 from the next more significant column in the minuend.

Looking at Fig. 4-4(b), we can see that the same is true for binary subtraction. That is, when the subtrahend is larger than the minuend, we generate a borrow. In binary subtraction, the only such case is when we subtract 1 from 0. The result is 1, and this operation causes us to borrow a 1.

Figure 4-5(a) shows a decimal subtraction problem. We can see the borrows, the minuend, the subtrahend, and the difference.

In the decimal problem, we start with the far right-hand column. Nine subtracted from 9 gives 0; no borrow is required. In the next column, 4 subtracted from 0 gives 6, but we must borrow 1 from the hundreds column. In the hundreds column we only had 1 to start with. When we borrow 1 from a minuend that is 1, the result is a minuend that is 0. From the minuend of 0 is subtracted a subtrahend of 0 in the hundreds column, giving 0 as a result.

In the binary subtraction in Fig. 4-5(b), we start with the far right-hand column. Here we see that a 1 subtracted from a 1 is 0. No borrow is generated. In the second column, a 0 is subtracted from a 0 and no borrow is generated. In the third column, 0 from 1 is 1, with no borrow. The same is true in the fourth column. In the fifth column, 1 is subtracted from 0. The result is 1, but we must borrow 1 from the sixth column. When we borrow 1 from the minuend in the sixth column, the result is a minuend that is 0. The subtraction therefore is 1 from 0, which leaves 1 and again results in a borrow. In the seventh column we must borrow 1 from the minuend, and therefore the minuend becomes

0. The subtraction is therefore 0 from 0, and the result is 0 with no borrow. Because we are dealing with 8-bit numbers, we must complete the subtraction in the eighth column even though it is all insignificant 0s. Of course, the result is 0.

Once again you will find binary subtraction relatively easy to do. The rules are simple, and it just takes a little practice to become familiar with it.

Self-Test

Check your understanding by answering these questions.

5. Subtract the following binary numbers:
   a. 0101
      0001

   b. 1001
       111

   c. 1111
      1001

   d. 1001
      0001

   e. 1001 0110
      0110 1001

   f. 1111 0001
      0000 0011

   g. 1001 0011 1001 1001
      0101 1101 1111 0000

6. Express the following subtraction problems in either 4-, 8-, or 16-bit binary numbers and do the subtractions.

a.	15	c.	255	e.	29
	− 12		− 24		− 12
b.	8	d.	52	f.	136
	− 2		− 36		− 108

7. What causes a borrow?

8. What is the difference between a borrow and a carry?

4-3 TWO'S COMPLEMENT NUMBERS

When you first look at binary numbers it is very easy to think that the only numbers you can express with them are positive integers. We have already found, however, that a

Subtrahend

Borrow

Minuend

Negative
numbers

Sign and
magnitude
system

2's complement

	Binary	Decimal
Sign bit →	0 0 0 1 1 1 0 0	+28
→	1 0 0 1 1 1 0 0	−28

Fig. 4-6 The sign and magnitude method of representing positive and negative binary numbers. In both cases the 7-bit binary number 0011100 has a *magnitude* of 28. The sign (in the 8th bit) is either 0 (+) or 1 (−).

Binary	Decimal
0 0 0 1 1 1 0 0	+28
1 1 1 0 0 0 1 1	−28

Fig. 4-7 The 1's complement method of representing positive and negative binary numbers. The 1's complement process complements each bit. Both 00000000 and 11111111 are 1's complement 8-bit numbers representing decimal zero.

binary point is used quite commonly. Therefore, we know we can represent binary fractional numbers. Can we express binary negative numbers? How?

A number of different methods have been used to represent negative numbers. Most of these methods do not work well with the binary electronics of the arithmetic and logic unit. These unsuccessful methods did, however, lead to the development of a system that works well.

One of the first systems was called the *sign and magnitude system*. In this system, the most significant bit of the binary number is used as a sign bit. That is, a "0" in the most significant bit means the number is positive. A "1" in the most significant bit means the number is negative. Examples of sign and magnitude method are shown in Fig. 4-6. In both cases the 7-bit binary number 0011100 has a magnitude of 28. The sign bit (the eighth bit) is either "0" (for positive) or "1" (for negative).

Another method that uses "0" in the most significant bit to mean "positive" and "1" to mean "negative" is the 1's complement representation. In the 1's complement method, all bits of a negative number are complemented. That is, all 1s are changed to 0s and all 0s are changed to 1s. This process changes the sign bit as well, thus giving a 1 in the MSB for negative numbers. Although generating the 1's complement is simple, the 1's complement method has a number of disadvantages. It is difficult to work with, and zero can be represented by either all "0s" or all "1s." That is, there are two ways of saying "zero."

Figure 4-7 shows an example of the 1's complement expression of a binary number.

The 2's complement method of representing negative numbers is now very commonly used in microcomputer systems. It solves the problem of the double representation of 0. The 2's complement is made by

taking the 1's complement and adding 1. You can see from Fig. 4-8 that this allows 8-bit binary numbers to represent the decimal numbers from −128 to +127, including 0. In the figure, we can see the two common methods used to represent binary numbers in microprocessors. These are the unsigned binary and the 2's complement systems.

In the left-hand column, we show the 8-bit binary numbers from 0000 0000 to 1111 1111. In the right-hand column we show the decimal equivalents using the unsigned binary system. These go from 0 to 255.

The center column shows the decimal equivalent using the 2's complement system. Here we see the binary numbers from 0000 0000 to 0111 1111 represent the decimal numbers from 0 to +127. Negative numbers are indicated by a "1" in the eighth bit. Therefore the next number in the binary sequence, 1000 0000, represents a negative number. This is −128. The negative numbers continue until 1111 1111 is reached. This represents −1.

Using the 2's complement method, we express 256 different values. There are 127 positive numbers, 0, and 128 negative numbers. As we noted before, taking the 2's complement of a number is quite simple. Just take the 1's complement and add 1. This is shown in Fig. 4-9. You can see that we have generated the 2's complement of 4. The result checks with the table in Fig. 4-8.

There is also a second shorthand method for generating the 2's complement of a binary number. Start at the least significant bit. As long as the least significant bits are "0s," copy them directly. When you reach the first "1," copy it directly. Each bit after that is simply inverted. That is, you take the 1's complement of all bits *following* the first "1" starting from the least significant bit.

Using 2's complement notation, we can ex-

8-bit binary number	Decimal number from 2's complement	Decimal number from unsigned binary
0000 0000	+ 0	0
0000 0001	+ 1	1
0000 0010	+ 2	2
0000 0011	+ 3	3
.	.	.
.	.	.
.	.	.
.	.	.
.	.	.
0111 1100	+124	124
0111 1101	+125	125
0111 1110	+126	126
0111 1111	+127	127
1000 0000	−128	128
1000 0001	−127	129
1000 0010	−126	130
1000 0011	−125	131
.	.	.
.	.	.
.	.	.
.	.	.
1111 1100	− 4	252
1111 1101	− 3	253
1111 1110	− 2	254
1111 1111	− 1	255

Fig. 4-8 Comparison of 8-bit binary numbers and their decimal representations. The binary number does not change. What changes is how you think of the number.

Binary bit pattern

press both positive and negative numbers. Because the logic to do 2's complement arithmetic and the logic for unsigned binary arithmetic are identical, the microprocessor's logic becomes simple. However, we must remember which system we are using. That is, the bit patterns will always be the same, but interpreting the answers depends on our knowing which system we are using. If we add two unsigned numbers, we get a result that is another unsigned number. It is expressed as a binary bit pattern. This bit pattern can be read either as a 2's complement negative number or as an unsigned number.

If an addition or subtraction problem generates a negative number and the input to this computation is intended as 2's complement notation, then the output must be in 2's complement notation. If the result of this computation leaves a logic "1" in the most significant bit, then the result is being expressed as a negative 2's complement number.

If you wish to find the magnitude of a negative 2's complement result, you must store the fact that it is negative and take the 2's complement. That is, you must take the 1's complement of the result, and add 1.

The simplicity of the 2's complement system is shown by a subtraction problem. Subtracting is simply taking the 2's complement of the subtrahend and adding it to the minuend. The difference is expressed in 2's complement form. That is, if the difference is positive, then the most significant bit is "0,"

Binary	Explanation
0000100	4_{10}
1111011	1's complement of 4_{10}
1	Add 1
1111100	2's complement of 4_{10}

Fig. 4-9 Taking the 2's complement. First find the complement of each bit by changing 1s to 0s and 0s to 1s, then add 1.

Binary   Explanation

0001 0111 23_{10}

1110 1000   1's complement of 23_{10}
0000 0001   Add 1
1110 1001   2's complement of 23_{10}

Decimal arithmetic	Binary arithmetic	Explanation for binary arithmetic
58	0011 1010	58_{10}
−23	1110 1001	Add 2's complement of 23_{10}
35	1 0010 0011	Difference (35_{10})

└─ Discard carry for positive results

(a)

Binary   Explanation

0010 0010 34_{10}

1101 1101   1's complement of 34_{10}
0000 0001   Add 1
1101 1110   2's complement of 34_{10}

Decimal arithmetic	Binary arithmetic	Explanation for binary arithmetic
26	0001 1010	26_{10}
−34	1101 1110	Add 2's complement of 34_{10}
−08	1111 1000	Difference (in 2's complement form because MSB is 1)

(b)

To find the absolute value:

Binary   Explanation

1111 1000   Difference in 2's complement

0000 0111   Take 1's complement
0000 0001   Add 1
0000 1000   Result is 8_{10}

(c)

Fig. 4-10   Two binary subtraction problems using 2's complement arithmetic. (a) First, find the 2's complement of 23. Then, add it to 58, thus performing the subtraction. (b) The same process produces a negative result. (c) We find the absolute value of the result from part (b). To do this, we use the 2's complement process.

the magnitude is expressed as a binary number, and the final carry must be discarded. If the difference is negative, the most significant bit is "1" and the number is expressed in 2's complement form. As indicated above, a negative result requires an additional 2's complement operation to show the magnitude in simple binary form.

Two problems that illustrate 2's complement subtraction are shown in Fig. 4-10. In Fig. 4-10(a), we subtract the number 23 from 58. To do the subtraction, 23 is put into 2's complement form. This is done by taking the 1's complement and adding 1. We then add the 2's complement of 23 to the binary 58. We discard the final carry, and the result is a binary number that has a "0" in the most significant bit. Therefore, we can treat the magnitude as that of an unsigned binary number.

In Fig. 4-10(b) we subtract 34 from 26. To perform this subtraction we take the 2's complement of 34. This is done by inverting each bit and adding 1. The 2's complement of 34 is then added to 26. The result is a negative number. This is shown by the "1" in the most significant bit. If we want to express the magnitude as an unsigned binary number, we must take the 2's complement of the difference. This is done by taking the 1's complement of the difference and adding 1. The result is an unsigned binary 8; it is shown in Fig. 4-10(c).

Self-Test

Check your understanding by answering these questions.

9. Today, the most common way to show a negative binary number is to show its ___?___.
   a. 1's complement
   b. 2's complement
   c. Sign and magnitude
   d. Absolute value

10. Complement the following binary numbers
    a. 1011 0110 f. 0000 0001
    b. 0110 1011 g. 1111 1111
    c. 101   h. 0101 0101
    d. 0000 1100 i. 1111 0000 1111 0000
    e. 1   j. 1100 1100 1100 0011

11. Treat each of the binary numbers in question 10 as if it were either an 8- or a 16-bit 2's complement number. Indicate which numbers are positive and which ones are negative.

12. Express the following as 8-bit 2's complement numbers:
    a. 64   g. 32
    b. −56   h. −32
    c. 12   i. 256
    d. 0   j. 16
    e. −128   k. −100
    f. 127   l. −4

13. Why can the same logic be used to add or subtract both 2's complement and unsigned binary numbers? Give an example to show your point.

4-4 BINARY MULTIPLICATION

As with addition and subtraction, decimal multiplication and binary multiplication are very much the same. Each is a quick way to add one number to itself many times. For example, multiplying 7 by 5 is simply a quick way of adding 7 to itself five times.

When we multiply one number by another, we call one number the *multiplicand* and the other the *multiplier*. We use a digit-by-digit method in multiplication. We often generate a carry in decimal multiplication, but we normally solve it in our heads. After the entire multiplicand is multiplied by the least significant digit of the multiplier, the result is called the *first partial product*. The second partial product is generated after the multiplicand is multiplied by the second least significant digit in the multiplier. This process continues until we have generated all the needed partial products.

Because each partial product has been created by a multiplier that is 10 times greater than the previous one, each partial product is shifted to the left by one decimal place. Then all the partial products are added to generate a final product. Of course, the process of adding all the partial products may also generate carries, all of which must be included in the additions.

An example of decimal multiplication is shown in Fig. 4-11. In this problem we multiply 17 by 12. Because there are two digits in the multiplier, we generate two partial products. Adding these partial products together generates a carry in the hundreds column. The product is 204.

```
        17   Multiplicand
    ×   12   Multiplier
        34   1st partial product
        17   2nd partial product
       100   Carry
       204   Total product
```

Fig. 4-11 The parts of a decimal multiplication problem. There will be a partial product for each digit in the multiplier. Normally, we do not show the carry. This is done in our heads, however, it is still there.

Multiplier

Multiplicand

Partial product

Fig. 4-12 The binary multiplication table. Multiplication of two binary digits does not generate a carry.

In Fig. 4-12 we show the binary multiplication table. Of course, we all learned our decimal multiplication table many years ago. It is a large table with 10 places on each side. It gives 100 different products.

The binary multiplication table shown in Fig. 4-12 is quite simple. Again, this is because there are only two binary characters. You can see that the multiplication of two binary digits will never generate a carry.

Let's use this binary multiplication table to multiply 17 by 12, but in binary form. This is shown in Fig. 4-13. The multiplicand and the multiplier are simply 8-bit binary expressions of the numbers 17 and 12.

The first thing you will note in Fig. 4-13 is that there are eight partial products. This is to be expected, because there are eight bits in the multiplier.

Because the rules of binary multiplication are so simple, the multiplication is easy to follow. The first partial product is all 0s. This is because the least significant bit in the multiplier is a 0. If we look at the binary multiplication table in Fig. 4-12 we can see that 0 times anything is 0. The second partial product is just the same: all 0s.

The third partial product is an exact copy of the multiplicand. The only difference is that it is shifted over three binary places, because it is the product of the third-place multiplier and the multiplicand.

The fourth partial product is again a copy of the multiplicand, this time shifted over four places.

The fifth, sixth, seventh, and eighth partial products are all 0s. This is because the fifth, sixth, seventh, and eighth multiplier bits are 0s.

In adding all the partial products we have generated a final (total) product. These additions resulted in no carries. However, since

Binary arithmetic	Terms
00010001	Multiplicand 17_{10}
00001100	Multiplier 12_{10}
00000000	1st partial product
00000000	2nd partial product
00010001	3rd partial product
00010001	4th partial product
00000000	5th partial product
00000000	6th partial product
00000000	7th partial product
00000000	8th partial product
000000000000000	Carry
0000000011001100	Product 204_{10}

(a)

00010001	
00001100	
10001	Multiplicand shifted left 2 times
+10001	Multiplicand shifted left 3 times
11001100	Sum of shifted multiplicands

(b)

Fig. 4-13 Multiplying 17 by 12 with binary multiplication. Both numbers are shown as 8-bit numbers as they might be in an 8-bit microprocessor. A 16-bit product results.

they could have caused a carry, we left room for one.

The result has 16 places, but the eight most significant bits are all 0. Therefore, we may use the eight least significant bits of the final product for the result. We know that binary numbers of 8 bits or less represent decimal numbers smaller than 255.

Because binary multiplication is so simple, a very simple method has been developed. This method is called *shift and add*. The shift and add method works as follows:

1. The first partial product is taken. If the least significant bit of the multiplier is 0, the result is 0. If the LSB of the multiplier is 1, the result is an exact copy of the multiplicand.
2. Each time another bit of the multiplier is worked on, the multiplicand is shifted one bit to the left.
3. Each time there is a 1 in the multiplier bit being worked on, we add the multiplicand *in its shifted position* to the result we already have.
4. The last sum at the end of all the shifts and adds is the product.

Looking at Fig. 4-13(*a*), we can see that this is how this problem was solved. The multiplicand was not shifted for the first partial product. That is because we were working on the least significant bit of the multiplier. Since the least significant bit of the multiplier was 0, the partial product was 0. The multiplicand was shifted one bit to the left for the second multiplier bit. But again no addition took place, because the second bit of the multiplier was also a 0. The multiplicand was shifted one more bit to the left. This time the multiplicand was added to the result, because the third bit in the multiplier was a 1. For the fourth multiplier bit, the multiplicand was shifted one bit to the left for a third time. The multiplicand was again added to the result, because the fourth bit of the multiplier was a 1. No further additions took place, because the fifth, sixth, seventh, and eighth bits of the multiplier were all 0. The shift and add method is shown in simpler form in Fig. 4-13(*b*).

You can easily see how the shift and add method works in binary multiplication. This simple method is made possible because mul-

tiplying a binary number by 0 yields 0 and multiplying a binary number by 1 yields the number itself.

Self-Test

Check your understanding by answering these questions.

14. Multiplication is a process that lets you do repetitive __?__ quickly.

15. The most commonly used procedure for multiplying creates a __?__ for each bit or digit in the multiplier.

16. Multiply the following:

a. 101	*d.* 0101 1101	*g.* 1001
011	0010 1101	1010
b. 0110	*e.* 0001 1011	
0111	1111 1100	
c. 011	*f.* 0111	
011	1000	

17. In a multiplication problem, the magnitude of each partial product is greater than the previous one by a factor the same as the __?__.

18. In binary multiplication, the partial product is __?__ if the multiplier bit is a 1.

19. In binary multiplication, the partial product is __?__ if the multiplier bit is a 0.

20. The binary multiplication procedure is called __?__.

4-5 BINARY DIVISION

Division is the reverse of multiplication. That is, we subtract one number from another until we cannot subtract it anymore. The number of times that we subract the first number tells us how many times it can be divided into the second number.

We can see that this is the reverse of adding one number repeatedly to get a result.

Multiplication by repeated addition and division by repeated subtraction are shown in Fig. 4-14. Here we see that five successive additions of 7 result in the answer 35. In the division column, we can see that 0 will result if we subtract 7 from 35 five times.

The process of division is a little more difficult than that of multiplication. If we look at a decimal long division problem, we see that

Shift and add

Long division

63

Dividend

Divisor

Quotient

Remainder

Process of
inspection

Multiplication		Division	
$7 \times 5 = ?$		$35 \div 7 = ?$	
$+\dfrac{0}{7}$	1	$-\dfrac{35}{7}$	1
$+\dfrac{7}{7}$	2	$\dfrac{28}{}$	
$\dfrac{14}{}$		$-\dfrac{7}{21}$	2
$+\dfrac{7}{}$	3	$-\dfrac{7}{14}$	3
$\dfrac{21}{}$			
$+\dfrac{7}{}$	4	$-\dfrac{7}{7}$	4
$\dfrac{28}{}$			
$+\dfrac{7}{35}$	5	$-\dfrac{7}{0}$	5

Fig. 4-14 Multiplication by repeated addition and division by repeated subtraction.

division requires more understanding of what we are doing.

For example, let's look at the problem shown in Fig. 4-15(*a*). This example is just the reverse of the example we used in Fig. 4-13 when showing binary multiplication. That is, the product (204) is now the dividend, the multiplier (12) now becomes the divisor; and the multiplicand from Fig. 4-13 (17) becomes the quotient.

$$
\begin{array}{r}
17 \\
12\overline{)204} \\
\underline{12} \\
84 \\
\underline{84} \\
0
\end{array}
\qquad
\begin{array}{l}
\text{Quotient} \\
\text{Divisor)Dividend}
\end{array}
$$

(*a*)

$$
\begin{array}{r}
10001 \\
1100\overline{)11001100} \\
\underline{1100} \\
01 \\
\underline{0} \\
011 \\
\underline{0} \\
110 \\
\underline{0} \\
1100 \\
\underline{1100} \\
0
\end{array}
$$

(*b*)

Fig. 4-15 Long division. (*a*) **A numerical example using decimal arithmetic.** (*b*) **A numerical example using binary arithmetic to do the same division as in part** *a*.

Let's look at how we do this division. We begin by using the process of inspection. We inspect the problem and guess that 12 will go into 20 once. We then try this guess. We subtract 12 from 20, and indeed the remainder (8) is less than the divisor. We combine the remainder from the first difference with the next digit of the dividend, and again we guess the result.

Now let us turn to Fig. 4-15(*b*). Here, we face the same problem expressed in binary numbers. The first inspection is easy: 1100 will go into 1100 exactly once. We place the trial 1 in the quotient, perform a multiplication, and then subtract to complete the test. The difference (in this case 0) is less than the divisor, so we can continue. We bring down the next bit in the dividend. This division, too, is obvious. We know that 1100 goes into 1 zero times. This process continues until the division is complete.

You can see that this way of doing division cannot be made into a machine operation as easily as multiplication was. There are too many guesses and tests. However, an ingenious way of doing binary division in microprocessors has been developed. In the following paragraphs, we will see how to do the same job as the binary long division in Fig. 4-15(*b*).

The procedure for binary division is actually quite simple, because each bit of the quotient can be only a "1" or a "0." Once again we will use a shifting process, this time taken from binary long division.

Before we can begin dividing 204 by 12, there is one other step we must do. We must take the 2's complement of 12. This is done so that we can use binary addition, whether to subtract or to add. The 2's complement of 12 is:

0	1 1 0 0	Binary 12
1	0 0 1 1	1's complement of 12
0	0 0 0 1	Add 1
1	0 1 0 0	2's complement of 12

sign magnitude   (that is, -12)
bits   bits

Now that we have the 2's complement of 12, we can start doing the division.

Just as in long division, we will test to see whether the divisor will go into the same number of the dividend's most significant bits. Of course, the microprocessor can't take a guess. Therefore, we start by actually subtracting the divisor from the dividend's most significant bits. If the divisor won't go into that part of the dividend, we can always add the subtracted bits back. We will know if the divisor won't go, because the subtraction will produce a negative number. That is, the sign bit will be a "1."

Trying the first subtraction, we have:

```
0 | 1 1 0 0 1 1 0 0      Dividend
1 | 0 1 0 0 0 0 0 0      Subtract 12
0 | 0 0 0 0 1 1 0 0      First result
"0" here means 1st bit
of quotient is "1"       Quotient = 1XXXX
```

If the divisor will go into the appropriate part of the dividend, then the sign bit will be "0." This means that the result of the division is a positive number. As you can see, our first test has worked. We know that the first bit in the quotient is a "1."

Now let's try the next step. We will again try to subtract the divisor. But we must shift the first result. We shift the first result so that the next operation will generate the second bit in the quotient. Shifting the first result we have:

```
0 | 0 0 0 0 1 1 0 0      First result
0 | 0 0 0 1 1 0 0        Shifted first result
```

We are now ready to do another subtraction. This subtraction gives us:

```
0 | 0 0 0 1 1 0 0        Shifted first result
1 | 0 1 0 0 0 0 0        Subtract 12
1 | 0 1 0 1 1 0 0        Second result
"1" here means 2d bit
of quotient is "0"       Quotient = 10XXX
```

Looking at this subtraction, we can see a "1" in the sign bit, indicating that a negative number has been generated. A negative number means we have tested for "1" in the quotient and the test has *failed*. This means we must do two things. First, we must make this bit in the quotient a "0." In this case, the second bit of the quotient becomes a "0." Second, we must correct for this wrong test. That is, we must add back the divisor, because the negative sign of the result shows that the divi-

sor should not have been subtracted in the first place. Adding back the divisor, we have:

```
1 | 0 1 0 1 1 0 0        Second result
0 | 1 1 0 0 0 0 0        Add back 12
0 | 0 0 0 1 1 0 0        Shifted first result
                          (again)
```

We are now ready to shift again. Shifting, we have:

```
0 | 0 0 1 1 0 0          Shifted first result
                          (again)
0 | 0 0 1 1 0 0          First result shifted
                          twice
```

From this you can see we are back to the first result but have shifted it twice. That is, each time we test, we shift.

Once again, we will try to see if we can make the divisor go into the result. Again, we will subtract a binary 12 from the shifted result. Subtracting, we have:

```
0 | 0 0 1 1 0 0          First result shifted
                          twice
1 | 0 1 0 0 0 0          Subtract 12
1 | 0 1 1 1 0 0          Third result
"1" here mean 3d bit
of quotient is "0"       Quotient = 100XX
```

Looking at the third result, we again see a negative number. Once again, this tells us the shifted result was not equal to or bigger than the divisor. This means that the third bit in the quotient is also a "0." It also means that we must add 12 back to the shifted result. Adding 12 back, we have:

```
1 | 0 1 1 1 0 0          Third result
0 | 1 1 0 0 0 0          Add back 12
0 | 0 0 1 1 0 0          First result shifted
                          twice
```

Now that we have corrected for our mistake, we must shift the result again. This gives us:

```
0 | 0 0 1 1 0 0          First result shifted
                          twice
0 | 0 1 1 0 0            First result shifted
                          three times
```

$$\begin{array}{r} 7 \\ 5\overline{)35} \end{array}$$

(a)

$$\begin{array}{r} 0111 \\ 101\overline{)100011} \\ \underline{000} \\ 1000 \\ \underline{101} \\ 00111 \\ \underline{101} \\ 0101 \\ \underline{101} \\ 000 \end{array}$$

(b)

0 1 0 1	5_{10}	
1 0 1 0	1's complement	
0 0 0 1	Add 1	
1 1 0 1	2's complement	

(c)

Binary arithmetic	Quotient	Process
0 1 0 0 0 1 1		Dividend 35_{10}
1 0 1 1 0 0 0		2's complement of 5_{10}
1 1 1 1 0 1 1	0	1st result
1 1 1 1 0 1 1		1st result
0 1 0 1 0 0 0		Add back 5_{10}
0 1 0 0 0 1 1		Dividend
1 0 0 0 1 1		Dividend shifted 1 time
1 0 1 1 0 0		2's complement of 5_{10}
0 0 1 1 1 1	1	2nd result
0 1 1 1 1		2nd result shifted 1 time
1 0 1 1 0		2's complement of 5_{10}
0 0 1 0 1	1	3rd result
0 1 0 1		3rd result shifted 1 time
1 0 1 1		2's complement of 5_{10}
0 0 0 0	1	4th result

(d)

Fig. 4-16 Dividing 35 by 5. (a) Long division with decimal numbers. (b) Binary long division. (c) Taking the 2's complement of 5. (d) The subtract-and-shift-left method.

Once again, we will try to subtract the divisor. This gives us:

0 | 0 1 1 0 0	First result shifted three times
1 | 0 1 0 0 0	Subtract 12
1 | 1 0 1 0 0	Fourth result

"1" here means 4th bit of quotient is "0"   Quotient = 1000X

The result of this subtraction is also a negative number. This means the fourth bit of the quotient is also a "0." Again, we must correct by adding 12 back to the result.

1 | 1 0 1 0 0	Fourth result
0 | 1 1 0 0 0	Add back 12
0 | 0 1 1 0 0	First result shifted four times

We now have the first result shifted four times.

Again, we shift this result. This gives us the first result shifted five bits. It is:

0 | 0 1 1 0 0	First result shifted four times
0 | 1 1 0 0	First result shifted five times

Again we subtract the divisor from this shifted result. As you can see, we are now going to subtract 12 from 12. That is

0 | 1 1 0 0	First result shifted five times
1 | 0 1 0 0	Subtract 12
0 | 0 0 0 0	Fifth result

"0" here means 5th bit of quotient is "1"   Quotient = 10001

The fifth result is a positive number. Therefore, the fifth bit of the quotient is a "1."

We can stop here because we have our answer. That is, 1100 1100 divided by 1100 is 10001.

You have seen that the process for division is a little more difficult than the process for multiplication. But this kind of division is a process that can be done by simply following the rules one step at a time. As you will see, this is all-important when working with microprocessors. If you can find a set of rules to solve a problem, the microprocessor will execute them faithfully. However, you must be sure that the rules cover all possible situations.

Let's take a look at one more example to be sure we understand the process. The example is shown in Fig. 4-16. In 4-16(a) we see a long division problem, 35 divided by 5. In Fig. 4-16(b) we see the long division done with binary numbers. In Fig. 4-16(c) we generate the 2's complement of the divisor (5). In Fig. 4-16(d) the division is done by using the subtract-and-shift-left method we have just learned.

In the first step the test fails. Therefore, the quotient bit is "0." We must add back the divisor. This gives us the dividend again. The addition is done in the second step. In the third step we shift the result (the dividend). Then we subtract the divisor from the shifted dividend. This time, the result is a positive number. This means the next bit in the quotient is a "1" and the subtraction process was correct. That is, we do not have to add back the divisor. All we need to do is shift the result.

This is done in the fourth step. We also subtract 5 from this shifted result. Once again, this gives us a positive number. This means that the third bit of the quotient is a "1" and we should shift the third result.

In the fifth step we shift the third result and subtract 5. This also leaves us with a positive number, and therefore the quotient's fourth bit is a "1." At this point, we stop the division process because it is complete.

If we carry on the division process, all future quotient bits are "0." Usually we know how many quotient bits we are looking for and where the binary point is. For example, we might divide a 16-bit dividend by an 8-bit divisor until we have an 8-bit quotient. If we know where the dividend and divisor binary points are, then we automatically know where the quotient's binary point is.

Self-Test

Check your understanding by answering these questions.

21. Division is just repeated
    a. Addition   c. Multiplication
    b. Subtraction   d. (All of the above)

22. Explain why division needs a somewhat more complicated set of rules for a processor to follow than multiplication does.

23. Perform the following division problems.

Use the procedure outlined in this section. Check your work with either binary or decimal long division.

a. $101\overline{)11110}$ d. $11\overline{)1001}$

b. $111\overline{)10101}$ e. $1001\overline{)1100011}$

c. $100\overline{)101000}$ f. $1100\overline{)10000100}$

All numbers are positive.

4-6 MULTIPLE-PRECISION ARITHMETIC

Often when working with a microprocessor we will find that the microprocessor's word length does not allow enough precision. This means that we need a way to express larger numbers so that the microprocessor can work with them.

For example, the very popular 8-bit microprocessor lets us use numbers from +127 through 0 to −128.

Obviously, for most work these numbers are nowhere near large enough. Using two 8-bit words to represent a 2's complement number gives a range of −32,768 to +32,767. We are limited to a precision of about 1 part in 60,000. That is, our precision is ±0.0015 percent.

For many applications this *double precision* is good enough. However, there are applications that require even greater precision. Some applications require triple precision. Triple precision uses one sign bit and 23 magnitude bits.

When we are using triple-precision representation in an 8-bit system, the range of numbers is from −8,388,608 to +8,388,607, including 0. This gives much better precision than six digits. That is, the number has a precision greater than 1 part per million.

As usual, we do not get something for nothing. Using multiple-precision notation requires the microprocessor to store more data and to do more work each time a calculation is done.

For example, again suppose you are going to use triple precision on an 8-bit system. You can no longer simply call two numbers from memory, add them in the accumulator, and store them at a location reserved for results. First, you must call the least significant byte of each number. The two bytes are added and the result is stored. Any carries generated must be saved. The middle bytes

Multiple-precision notation

Least significant byte

Most significant byte

Scientific notation

Mantissa

Exponent

of the two numbers are then called. These are added, together with the carries from previous additions, and the result is stored in a space reserved for the middle byte of the result. Finally, the most significant bytes of the two words are called and added, and the carries from the previous addition are added to the sum. The result of this addition is stored in the space reserved for the most significant byte.

As you can see, this addition process takes 3 times as long as a simple 8-bit addition, and of course it uses 3 times as much storage space.

There is also one other hidden problem. If other program steps interrupt the multiple-precision addition, then the status register's contents must be saved. Otherwise the intermediate carries are lost. If they are lost, the addition is no longer valid.

Multiple-precision arithmetic can be done for all four arithmetic operations. That is, we have multiple-precision addition, subtraction, multiplication, and division.

Self-Test

Check your understanding by answering these questions.

24. Explain why multiple precision is used.

25. What is the range of a double-precision 2's complement number in a 16-bit processor?

26. Why does multiple-precision arithmetic mean extra work?

27. You are using an 8-bit microprocessor. What precision is needed to handle each of these numbers?
    a. 1568   d. −129
    b. −10,264,329   e. 12,348
    c. 22,438   f. −1,000,274

4-7 FLOATING-POINT ARITHMETIC

The use of multiple-precision numbers does not solve all our problems. For example, the numbers we have discussed so far are all integers. We have not seen any way to take care of fractions. Nor have we seen a way to represent very large or very small numbers.

These problems are solved by using *float-ing-point arithmetic*. In floating-point arithmetic, the microprocessor keeps track of where the decimal point is. The microprocessor does this by using scientific notation.

We have all used scientific notation in the past. Using scientific notation requires that all numbers be shown as signed decimal fractions lying between 0.1 and 1. Note: The number 10.0 is not used. The number 1 is shown as 0.1×10^1. These signed decimal fractions are multiplied by a signed power of 10. For example, if we wish to present the number 50 in scientific notation we would show it as:

$$0.5 \times 10^2$$

we would show the number −750 as:

$$-0.75 \times 10^3$$

To show a very small number, such as 0.00105, we would write:

$$0.105 \times 10^{-2}$$

When using floating-point notation, the microprocessor stores numbers in the same way. That is, the microprocessor stores both a signed *mantissa* and a signed *exponent*. The mantissa is the number that lies between 0.1 and 1, and the exponent is the *power* of 10.

Let's see how an 8-bit microprocessor stores numbers in floating-point notation. Figure 4-17 shows that four different memory locations are used. The first memory location has the low-order byte of the mantissa. The second memory location has the middle byte of the mantissa. The third memory location has the high seven bits of the mantissa and the sign bit. We can see that the first three bytes of this floating-point package are a triple-precision number. A fourth memory location has a signed 7-bit exponent.

Using this floating-point arithmetic we can represent numbers from $-2^{23} \times N^{127}$ to

Memory location	Contents	
M + 3 (fourth)	+/−	7-bit exponent
M + 2 (third)	+/−	7-bit hi mantissa
M + 1 (second)	8-bit mid mantissa	
M (first)	8-bit low mantissa	

Fig. 4-17 Storing a floating-point number. The number here is in the form
$\pm$XXXXXXXXXXXXXXXXXXXXXXX $\cdot$ $2^{\pm\text{XXXXXXX}}$, where X is an unknown binary digit (bit).

$+(2^{23} - 1) \times N^{127}$, including fractional values as small as $\pm 1 \times N^{-128}$. The value of N is usually 2. However, we can use 10 for some special purposes. Obviously, this is a very wide range of numbers.

Once a microcomputer system has been set up to operate in floating-point notation, all arithmetic operations are usually passed through the *floating-point package*. The floating-point package usually contains a series of subroutines. These subroutines let us place a number in four memory locations using a floating-point format like the one shown in Fig. 4-17. Once we have placed the number in this floating-point "accumulator," we can call subroutines that will perform mathematical operations on the number in the floating-point accumulator and numbers in another set of memory locations.

Most floating-point packages include more than subroutines to do addition, subtraction, multiplication, and division. Many of them include subroutines that do such operations as squares, square roots, sines, cosines, tangents, and logarithms.

Obviously, once a floating-point package has been written, it is used over and over again. Often the floating-point package is treated almost as if it were an extension of the hardware itself. Don't be confused when someone speaks of the "floating-point accumulator." It is not a piece of hardware. As we have just learned, the floating-point accumulator is actually four memory locations that are worked on by a set of subroutines.

The floating-point package works much more slowly than the microprocessor's natural instructions. In fact, a floating-point addition may take 10 to 20 times longer than an addi-tion instruction for a microprocessor's hardware. This is because the floating-point Add subroutine executes 20 or 30 instructions for each operation. Not only does this subroutine always have to work with a triple-precision number, but it also must keep track of the exponent on each calculation.

The floating-point package is almost always used whenever the microprocessor is controlling a system into which people can enter a wide range of numbers. One of the most common applications for the floating-point package is when the microprocessor is executing a higher-level language such as BASIC. All higher-level languages, such as BASIC and FORTRAN, include their own floating-point packages. Usually these floating-point packages are very sophisticated when compared with the ones you might find in a microprocessor control system designed to perform a few limited functions.

Floating-point package

Subroutines

Floating-point accumulator

BASIC

Self-Test

Check your understanding by answering these questions.

28. You would use floating-point arithmetic to represent very ___?___ numbers.

29. Express the following numbers in scientific notation:
    a. 12　　　　　　f. −1000
    b. 222.3　　　　g. −0.000101
    c. −0.334　　　　h. 100
    d. 1,256,000　　i. 22,000,000
    e. 0.0000125　　j. 0.000000021

30. The two numbers used in the floating-point system are called the ___?___ and the ___?___.

Summary

1. Binary and decimal addition are alike; they just use different number systems.

2. When you add two digits and the resultant sum cannot be expressed as a single digit, the result is a carry.

3. There are only four possible results from adding two binary digits. The binary addition rules are:

$$0 + 0 = 0$$
$$0 + 1 = 1$$
$$1 + 0 = 1$$
$$1 + 1 = 0 \text{ plus 1 carry}$$

A carry must be added into the next more significant column. A carry is added according to the rules of addition.

4. Computer arithmetic uses fixed-length binary numbers. Insignificant (leading) 0s are used to fill up the required number of bits.

5. Binary and decimal subtraction processes are alike. Only the number systems are different. If the the subtrahend is larger than the minuend, then subtracting causes a borrow.

6. The rules for binary subtraction are:

$$0 - 0 = 0$$
$$1 - 0 = 1$$
$$0 - 1 = 1 \text{ and } 1 \text{ borrow}$$
$$1 - 1 = 0$$

A borrow must be subtracted from the next column to the left. The borrow is subtracted according to the rules of subtraction.

7. To complement a binary number, change all the "1s" to "0s" and all the "0s" to "1s." This is called a 1's complement.

8. The most common way to express a negative binary number is to show it as a 2's complement number. In 2's complement notation, a "0" in the number's most significant bit means it is a positive number. A "1" in the number's most significant bit means it is a negative number.

9. The 2's complement is made by taking the 1's complement and adding 1. An 8-bit 2's complement binary number can represent decimal numbers from −128 to +127.

10. A short method of generating 2's complement numbers is as follows:
a. Start at the LSB.
b. Copy "0s" directly until you reach the first "1."
c. Copy the first "1" directly.
d. Complement each bit after that.

11. The logic in doing binary arithmetic is the same for both unsigned and 2's complement numbers. To know the value of the answer, we must know which notation we are using. If the result of a 2's complement arithmetic operation is negative, take the 2's complement of the result to get its absolute value.

12. Both binary and decimal multiplications are just quick ways to do a lot of additions. The process of multiplication is repeated for each digit of the multiplier. Each mutiplication results in a partial product. The partial products are added together to form the final product. Each partial product is shifted to the left one digit before adding.

13. The rules for binary multiplication are:

$$0 \times 0 = 0$$
$$1 \times 0 = 0$$
$$0 \times 1 = 0$$
$$1 \times 1 = 1$$

Binary multiplication generates a great many partial products. The partial product is a copy of the multiplicand if the multiplier bit is "1." The partial product is all "0s" if the multiplier bit is "0."

14. The binary multiplication procedure is shift and add. The multiplicand is shifted left and added to the previous result each time there is a "1" in the multiplier. Each "0" in the multiplier causes a shift but no add.

15. Division is really just repeated subtraction. Division is more complicated than multiplication because we guess the partial results and then test our guess. In binary division, we first guess the result is a "1." If the divisor will go into the most significant remaining bits of the dividend, then we keep the "1" in the quotient. If not, then we change the quotient's bit to a "0." We use 2's complement arithmetic for division because we must both add and subtract during the process.

16. Often the microprocessor's word length does not give enough precision. We use multiple words to increase precision. A triple-precision number in an 8-bit microprocessor has 23 magnitude bits and one sign bit. Using multiple precision requires extra data handling and keeping track of any carries or borrows generated by the operations on less significant bytes. Multiple-precision arithmetic is used for all kinds of mathematical operations.

17. Floating-point arithmetic is used to represent very large and very small numbers. It keeps track of the radix point. Floating-point arithmetic uses scientific notation. In floating-point arithmetic, the mantissa lies between 0.1 and 1.

18. The mantissa is multiplied by a power of 10 or 2. The power is called the number's exponent. Most microprocessor software packages have a routine called the floating-point package. The floating-point package has a floating-point accumulator. The floating-point package often has many floating-point instructions for advanced arithmetic operations.

4-1. If you add two digits and the result cannot be expressed as one digit, you have caused a ____?____.
   a. Borrow   c. Carry
   b. Sum   d. Multiplicand

4-2. Fill in the table, showing the results of binary addition:
   a. 0 + 0 = ____?____ + a carry of ____?____.
   b. 0 + 1 = ____?____ + a carry of ____?____.
   c. 1 + 0 = ____?____ + a carry of ____?____.
   d. 1 + 1 = ____?____ + a carry of ____?____.

4-3. Computer arithmetic is done with fixed-length numbers. Unused leading digits are expressed as
   a. Carries   c. Borrows
   b. 1s   d. 0s

4-4. If an addition generates a carry it must be added to ____?____.

4-5. Express the following as 8- or 16-bit binary numbers and find the sums:
   a. 12,525   *c.* 99   *e.* 56,274
         621   107   32,768

   b. 2,048   *d.* 1,296   *f.* 128
          64   151   256

4-6. Fill in the table, showing the results of binary subtraction.
   a. 0 − 0 = ____?____ with a borrow of ____?____.
   b. 1 − 0 = ____?____ with a borrow of ____?____.
   c. 0 − 1 = ____?____ with a borrow of ____?____.
   d. 1 − 1 = ____?____ with a borrow of ____?____.

4-7. A borrow must be subtracted from the ____?____.

4-8. Complete the following binary subtractions. What are the decimal results?
   a. 010111   *c.* 010101   *e.* 0111 1111
         001011   000001   0111 1110

   b. 0110111   *d.* 0001011   *f.* 0000111
          0001011   0000111   0000010

4-9. If you needed to express a binary number in both positve and negative forms, you would probably use ____?____ notation.
   a. Scientific   c. 2's complement
   b. 1's complement   d. Sign and Magnitude

4-10. Two's complement, 1's complement, and sign and magnitude all express a negative number with a(n) ____?____.

4-11. What is the range of a 16-bit 2's complement number?

4-12. What is the range of a 12-bit 2's complement number?

4-13. Show the following numbers in 2's complement form:
   a. +12   *e.* −100   *i.* 0
   b. +16   *f.* +64   *j.* −1
   c. −15   *g.* −70   *k.* −128
   d. +125   *h.* −127   *l.* +127

4-14. Complete the following subtraction problems using 2's complement arithmetic. If the answer is negative, express the number both in 2's complement form and in absolute-value binary form.

a. 0101
   0111

b. 0111 0111
   0011 0101

c. 0110 1011
   0111 1111

d. 0101 1100
   0011 1011

e. 0110 1101 1011 1111
   0111 1101 1100 0101

f. 0111 1111 1000 0000
   0000 1101 0110 1100

4-15. Explain why the shift and add process works so well for binary multiplication.

4-16. Fill in the following binary multiplication table:

a. $0 \times 0 = $ ____?____.
b. $1 \times 0 = $ ____?____.
c. $0 \times 1 = $ ____?____.
d. $1 \times 1 = $ ____?____.

4-17. Perform the following binary multiplications using the shift and add process:

a. 0000 1001
   0000 0101

b. 0100 0110
   0001 0101

c. 0101 0101
   0101 0101

d. 0101 1110
   1000 0101

e. 0111 0111 0110 1110
   0000 1010 0111 0101

f. 1000 0000 0001 0111
   0010 0000 0000 0111

4-18. The result of multiplying the multiplicand by one bit of the multiplier is called a(n) ____?____.

4-19. Divide the following, using the method a microprocessor would use.

a. $01010\overline{)1100100}$

b. $0100\overline{)10000}$

c. $D\overline{)9C}$

d. $0010\overline{)11110}$

4-20. Multiple-precision arithmetic is used to improve

a. Addition
b. Carrying
c. Resolution
d. Precision

4-21. A triple-precision number in an 8-bit microprocessor uses ____?____ magnitude bit(s) and ____?____ sign bit(s).

4-22. Floating-point representation uses multiple-precision and ____?____ notation.

4-23. You would not expect a floating-point package to be able to call the ____?____ function.

a. Addition
b. Sine
c. Log
d. Reset

Answers to Self-Tests

1. a. 0001 0110
   b. 1001 1000
   c. 1111 1101
   d. 1111 1111
   e. 1000
   f. 1100
   g. 1010 0001 0000 0010
   h. 1001 0111 1011 1000

2. *a.* 0110 0101
   <u>0001 0000</u>
   0111 0101

   b.   1110 0001
      <u>1010 1000</u>
   1 1000 1001

   c. 0000 0001 1000 1110
   <u>0000 0000 1000 0100</u>
   0000 0010 0001 0010

   d. 0011 1000
   <u>0000 1010</u>
   0100 0010

   e. 0101 0110
   <u>0001 1001</u>
   0110 1111

   f. 0000 0001 0010 0001
   <u>0000 0001 1110 1101</u>
   0000 0011 0000 1110

3. 9 bits.
4. The only difference is that 0101 and 0000 0101 have insignificant leading 0s. It would not affect any sum.
5. *a.* 0100   *d.* 1000   *g.* 0011 0101 1010 1001
   b. 0010   *e.* 0010 1101
   c. 0110   *f.* 1110 1110
6. *a.* 1111
   <u>1100</u>
   0011

   b. 1000
   <u>0010</u>
   0110

   c. 1111 1111
   <u>0001 1000</u>
   1110 0111

   d. 0011 0100
   <u>0010 0100</u>
   0001 0000

   e. 0001 1101
   <u>0000 1100</u>
   0001 0001

   f. 1000 1000
   <u>0110 1100</u>
   0001 1100

7. A borrow is caused by subtracting a larger digit (bit) from a smaller digit (bit).
8. A borrow comes from subtraction and a carry comes from addition. Both are arithmetic overflows.
9. b.
10. *a.* 0100 1001   *e.* 0   *i.* 0000 1111 0000 1111
    b. 1001 0100   *f.* 1111 1110   *j.* 0011 0011 0011 1100
    c. 010   *g.* 0000 0000
    d. 1111 0011   *h.* 1010 1010
11. *a.* Negative.   *e.* Positive.   *i.* Negative.
    b. Positive.   *f.* Positive.   *j.* Negative.
    c. Positive.   *g.* Negative.
    d. Positive.   *h.* Positive.
12. *a.* 0100 0000   *e.* 1000 0000
    b. 1100 1000   *f.* 0111 1111
    c. 0000 1100   *g.* 0010 0000
    d. 0000 0000   *h.* 1110 0000
    i. 256 cannot be expressed as an 8-bit number. It can be expressed as the 16-bit number 0000 0001 0000 0000.
    j. 0001 0000   *k.* 1001 1100   *l.* 1111 1100
13. The same logic can be used because the binary relationships don't change. All that changes is how you look at the numbers. For example,

1100 can represent either 12 or the 2's complement of 4:

```
  0111      7    or     0111      7
+ 1100    + 12          1100    - 4
 10011     19          10011      3
```

In the second case, we disregard the carry, because we are using 2's complement arithmetic.

14. Additions.
15. Partial product.
16. *a.*
```
  101
  011
  101
  101
  000
01111
```
b.
```
  0110
  0111
  0110
  0110
  0110
  0000
0101010
```
c.
```
  011
  011
  011
  011
  000
01001
```

d.
```
        01011101
        00101101
        01011101
        00000000
        01011101
        01011101
        00000000
        01011101
        00000000
        00000000
0001000001011001
```
e.
```
        00011011
        11111100
        00000000
        00000000
        00011011
        00011011
        00011011
        00011011
        00011011
0001101010010100
```

f.
```
  0111
  1000
  0000
  0000
  0000
  0111
0111000
```
g.
```
  1001
  1010
  0000
  1001
  0000
  1001
1011010
```

17. Number's base.
18. The same as the multiplicand.
19. 0.
20. Shift and add.
21. *b.*
22. Because in division you must guess the correct quotient and then test to see if your guess was right. The processor does not guess.
23. *a.* 110   *d.* 11
    b. 11   *e.* 1011
    c. 1010   *f.* 1011
24. Multiple precision is used when you cannot express a large enough number using one word.
25. $\pm 2^{31} = \pm 2,147,483,648$.
26. Because you must work on it one word at a time. This means you must store many intermediate results and keep track of carries and borrows.
27. *a.* Double.   *d.* Double.
    b. Quadruple. *e.* Double.
    c. Double.   *f.* Triple.
28. Large or small.
29. *a.* 0.12×10^2
    b. 0.2223×10^3
    c. -0.334×10^0
    d. 0.1256×10^7
    e. 0.125×10^{-4}
    f. -0.1×10^4
    g. -0.101×10^{-3}
    h. 0.1×10^3
    i. 0.22×10^8
    j. 0.21×10^{-7}
30. Exponent; mantissa.

An Introduction to Programming

5
5
5
5
5
5
5
5
5
5
5
5
5

■ This chapter introduces the basic concepts of microprocessor programming. You will find that programming a microprocessor is like programming a microcomputer, a minicomputer, or a large computer. In each case, you try to decide the right sequence of operations to make the processor solve a problem.

The product of programming is software. This is simply the name given to the programs, routines, and documentation that a processor uses to solve a problem. Usually, software is just data stored in a processor's memory, or a program written on paper.

After reading the first section of this chapter, you should be able to take a problem stated in words and show how it can be solved by a step-by-step program. You will see that programs can be either mathematical or logical. The next section of this chapter is about flowcharting. When you have finished this section, you will be able to use a flowchart to document a program. Flowcharting provides a graphic model of how the software works.

The third section looks at subroutines. In this section, you will learn how to tell when a subroutine can make a program more compact. In the last part of this chapter, you will review four types of computer languages: machine language, assembly language, high-level interpreters, and high-level compilers. You will see why each of these is used for certain kinds of program development.

5-1 WHAT IS PROGRAMMING?

Often, programming is treated as if it were black magic. Nothing could be farther from the truth. Programming is, very simply, the process of telling the processor exactly how to solve a problem. To do this, the programmer must "speak" to the processor in the processor's language. As you have learned from earlier chapters, the processor faithfully performs each instruction that the programmer gives it. However, *the processor will do nothing that the programmer does not instruct it to do*. The process of programming, therefore, must be very exact. The programmer must tell the processor absolutely everything that it must do and exactly how to do everything step by step.

There is one part of the programming process that you must understand thoroughly. Programming a processor cannot make the processor solve a problem if you, as the programmer, do not know how to solve it. Of

course, this does not mean that you must know in advance the answer to the problem. But you must know how to get the answer.

For example, if you can express a problem as an equation and you can supply numerical input for all the equation's variables, the processor can compute the answer. However, the processor *cannot derive an equation* to solve the problem.

Programming a processor requires you to organize the problem so that the processor can solve the problem. In some cases, organizing the problem may be as simple as converting a problem stated in words into an algebraic expression. In other cases, you start with only an idea about the desired result together with your knowledge of a series of inputs. You must find a set of logic operations on the inputs that will produce the result you want.

Organizing the problem so that a computer can solve it is the major part of programming. This is called *designing* the program.

Once the program is designed, it can be *coded*. That is, the programmer can write down a series of computer instructions that implement the design. Since instructions vary from one processor to the next, the programmer must write for the specific processor intended—the "target" processor.

The next step is debugging the coded program. Debugging is done by loading the code into the target processor and attempting to run the program. Then the programmer must correct any problems that develop. Programmers often break programs into small parts. Each part can then be debugged individually. After each part is debugged, more parts are added until the whole program is debugged.

To code a program is to state it in a computer language. The computer language helps you convert the design into instructions that the processor can follow. Each computer (or microcomputer) language has a set of instructions that you must choose from. The instructions that you write are called *source code*. The computer language translates source code into the binary instructions required by the processor. These binary instructions are called *object code*.

Let us now look at an example of programming. To start with, we use a *story problem*. A story problem is a problem expressed in the English language. The story problem is:

Make a table of data points which will be plotted on an X-Y graph. The relationship of the points is such that the Y axis data are the square of the X axis data. The table of data points should be assembled for integer values of X lying between −3 and 3 inclusively.

Fortunately, we can easily reduce this long problem to a simple equation. The equation is

$$Y = X^2$$

Also, we want to solve the equation for $X = -3, -2, -1, 0, 1, 2,$ and 3.

To solve this problem we simply instruct the computer to perform the following steps:

1. LET X = −3
2. LET Y = X²
3. PRINT X, Y

4. LET X = −2
5. LET Y = X²
6. PRINT X, Y

7. LET X = −1
8. LET Y = X²
9. PRINT X, Y

10. LET X = 0
11. LET Y = X²
12. PRINT X, Y

13. LET X = 1
14. LET Y = X²
15. PRINT X, Y

16. LET X = 2
17. LET Y = X²
18. PRINT X, Y

19. LET X = 3
20. LET Y = X²
21. PRINT X, Y

22. END

As you can see, this is a very simple program. Figure 5-1(*a*) shows the printed data table resulting from this program. Figure 5-1(*b*) shows a hand-made plot of the data. The curve is the familiar parabola.

Reviewing this example, you can see that the story problem was first converted into an equation. Then the problem was converted into a series of instructions for the processor to follow in solving the equation. Executing these instructions resulted in a data table. The data were then hand-plotted.

Let's look at another example. This one does not solve an equation. The problem is:

Clear the microprocessor's first 4,000 memory locations by setting each bit to logic "0."

To solve this problem, we must use the microprocessor's data-handling ability. We will store data words consisting of all "0s" successive memory locations. We will take all-0 words from the microprocessor's accumulator. We will use the following instructions:

1. Set the accumulator's contents all to logic "0."
2. Point the memory-address register to the first memory location.
3. Store the contents of the accumulator in the memory location pointed to by the memory-address register.
4. Point the memory-address register to the next memory location.

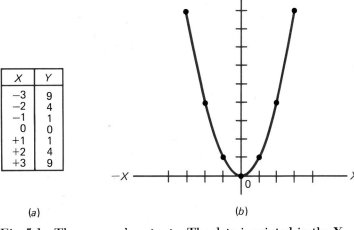

X	Y
−3	9
−2	4
−1	1
0	0
+1	1
+2	4
+3	9

(a)   (b)

Fig. 5-1 The program's output. The data is printed in the **X** and **Y** columns. The plot is made by hand, but could be programmed.

5. Is the memory-address register pointing to location 4001?
6. If yes, halt. If no, return to step 2.

You can see that this program will continue executing until "0s" are placed in all 4,000 memory locations. Once the memory-address register points to location 4001, the program will halt.

In this example, we converted a problem into a series of *logic* instructions. The preceding example used *mathematical* instructions. However, in both examples you can see that the objective is to convert a written description of a problem into a series of instructions that the processor can follow. If we are to implement these programs, we must code them entirely in a computer language.

Self-Test

Check your understanding by answering these questions.

1. Organize the following problem into a series of jobs that might be implemented on a processor.

    You wish to maintain the temperature of the standards laboratory at exactly 68°F (20°C). The temperature is to be maintained regardless of the outside temperature. You have both heating and air conditioning units available. You have one thermostat that tells you when the temperature inside is at or below 68°F. A second thermostat tells you when the temperature is at or above 68°F.

2. Using instructions similar to those in the first example in this section, solve the following problem:

    Plot the data that give the relationship between a number, its square, its cube, its square root, and its cube root. These data are to be plotted for integer values lying between 2 and 5.

3. "Software" refers to a microprocessor's
    a. Read-only memories
    b. Magnetic tapes
    c. Program routines
    d. Paper tapes

4. The basic purpose of programming is to convert a problem into:
    a. A series of instructions in the computer's own language.
    b. An equation that expresses the problem in mathematical terms
    c. A hardware equivalent
    d. A curve that graphs the data versus the result

5. Once the problem has been converted into a series of instructions that can be done by the processor, you then must
    a. Generate software
    b. Code the program into the computer's language
    c. Be sure you have a correct story problem
    d. Run the program

6. Explain why a processor cannot solve a problem if you do not know how to solve the problem.

5-2 FLOWCHARTING

Flowcharting is an important step in the process of documenting a program. That is, it is one way to explain to yourself and to others exactly how a program works. Flowcharting may also be used to help find out how a program will react to different combinations of input data.

Flowcharting has become very popular in documenting computer programs. But flowcharting is not used only in computer programming. Flowcharting is also used to diagram solutions to all kinds of problems. You could even flowchart all the activities you must go through between the time you wake up and the time you leave for school or work.

Flowcharting uses four basic symbols to diagram what a program is to do. These symbols are shown in Fig. 5-2. Each symbol has one or more inputs and one or more outputs. Inputs and outputs are shown as lines with arrowheads. The arrowheads indicate the direction in which the problem's solution is flowing.

The rectangle symbol represents a processing function. That is, the rectangle says that the computer is to do something to the data. A short description of the process that is to be done is written inside the symbol. The rectangle symbol is shown in Fig. 5-2(a).

For example, if your flowchart includes:

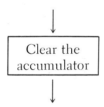

you are saying that, at this point in the program, the accumulator is to be cleared. In this example, the process shown in the rectangle requires one microprocessor instruction.

However, suppose your flowchart included:

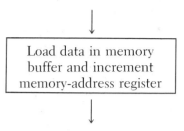

The process described in this processing symbol requires a number of microprocessor instructions.

Both of these examples are correct uses of the processing symbol. The process represented can be as simple or as complicated as you wish.

The diamond, shown in Fig. 5-2(b), is the decision symbol. The decision symbol shows a place in the program at which a choice is made. This choice will determine the direction in which the program will flow from that point. The choice is made based on the result of a test. The description of the test to be done is written inside the diamond. Possible results of the test are written on the lines flowing out of the decision symbol. For example, suppose your flowchart included:

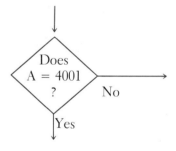

You can see that a test is being made. There can be only one of two results. Either the variable A does equal the number 4001, or it does not.

If it does equal the number 4001, the pro-

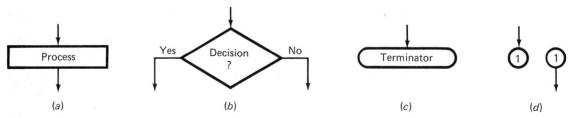

Fig. 5-2 The flowchart's symbols. (*a*) The process rectangle. (*b*) The decision diamond. (*c*) The terminator oval. (*d*) The circle connector.

gram will continue with the instructions following the line labeled Yes. If the number does not equal 4001, that is, if it is either less than 4001 or greater than 4001, the program will follow the instructions on the line labeled No. As you can imagine, this particular test is complex. It uses many microprocessor instructions. But this does not mean that decisions cannot be made using just a few microprocessor instructions or even a single microprocessor instruction.

For example, suppose your flowchart included:

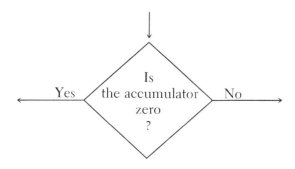

You would recognize that this is a single microprocessor instruction that tests the status register's zero bit. If the status register's zero bit is logic "1," the program will follow instructions on the Yes line. If the status register's zero bit is logic "0," the program's instructions will follow the No line.

The oval symbol is used as a terminator. This symbol is shown in Fig. 5-2(c). In most cases the terminator contains either the word Start or the word Stop. The terminator simply makes it easy to indicate the program's beginning and end.

Figure 5-2(d) shows the connector symbol, the circle. The connector symbol lets you draw large flowcharts that cannot be diagramed on a single page. It also helps make flowcharts clear even when they involve many lines crossing over one another. A number or a letter in the connector circle shows the symbols that are connected together. That is, all circles with the number 1, for example, represent a common point in the program. The connect symbol simply makes the flowchart much easier to read.

Let us now look at an example of a flowchart. We will use the flowchart of the program from Sec. 5-1 that prints the parabola's

data table. This flowchart is shown in Fig. 5-3. We can see that the program simply steps through each of the process blocks between the Start and the End. To make the flowchart a convenient size, we have broken the chart halfway through and used a connector symbol to join the two program halves. Terminator symbols are used to start and end the program.

The program shown in Fig. 5-3 is called a *straight-line*, or *inline*, *program*. No decisions are made between the start and the end. Solving this program is a sequential process. Many simple programs are straight-line programs.

More complicated programs involve program decisions and program loops. A program that includes a decision uses the diamond decision symbol to indicate the program flow. A program with a decision is shown in Fig. 5-4. This program sorts positive and negative integers in the range of -5 to $+5$ into a negative number file and a positive number file. A connector symbol is used to bring the two separate program paths back to the Stop terminator. This program is run once for each integer to be sorted. It is a simple decision program.

Frequently, programs that involve a decision must test and make the decision over and over again. This is called the *iterative* process. An example of this kind of program is our memory-clearing routine in Sec. 5-1 in this chapter. This program uses the iterative process. It is flowcharted in Fig. 5-5.

Looking at this figure, you can follow the program through its operation. After doing this, you will understand the iterative process. The program starts by setting the accumulator to all logic "0s." The program then passes through the connector block to the next processing block. The process done here is to store the accumulator's contents at the memory location pointed to by the memory-address register. In the next processing block, we increment the memory-address register. This makes it point to the *next* memory location.

A decision is made in the next symbol. Does the memory-address register equal 4001? If it does, we may halt the program. If it does not, we loop back to the connector symbol. Following the arrows, we again store the accumulator's contents at the memory location pointed to by the memory-address register. Of course, this time the memory loca-

Oval

Terminator

Straight-line program

Sequential process

Program decisions

Program loops

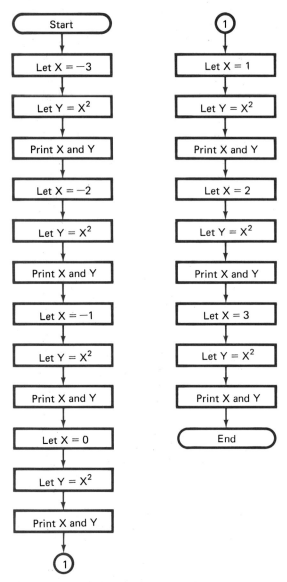

Fig. 5-3 A straight-line program flowchart. Each process block is executed and passes the program operation onto the next process block.

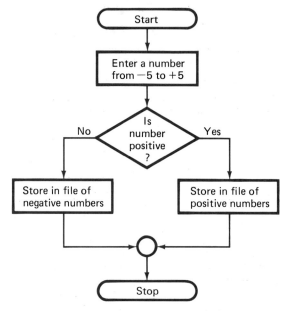

Fig. 5-4 A flowchart of a program that has a decision block. The connector symbol is used to make the chart neat. The Yes and No outputs from the decision symbol can be anywhere so long as it is clear what they are.

tion is the next higher one. Again, we increment and test. The program iterates through the process blocks 4002 times until the test takes the program out of the loop and halts it.

As you can see by looking at Fig. 5-5, this program involves decisions, processes, and connections. Some parts of the program are straight-line. The program also has a decision and a built-in loop. Looking at the flowchart symbols, you can see terminators, process blocks, decision blocks, and connector symbols.

Looking again at Figs. 5-3, 5-4, and 5-5, you

can see that flowcharting is a very simple way to document the programming logic used to solve a problem.

You will find that all programs can be constructed using the sequence, decision, and iterative processes.

Needless to say, flowcharts can become much more complicated than the simple ones shown here. Some flowcharts have symbols that are different from the symbols used here. Some people use special symbols to show certain processes. For example, you will find a special symbol used in some flowcharts to indicate an I/O process. Graphically, the symbol is just a slightly different rectangle. Other graphics are used to add notes to the flowchart. Again, these may vary from programmer to programmer. As long as symbols serve the purpose (to thoroughly document the program), they are quite acceptable.

Self-Test

Check your understanding by answering these questions.

7. Flowchart the word problems given earlier in self-test questions 1 and 2. Do not

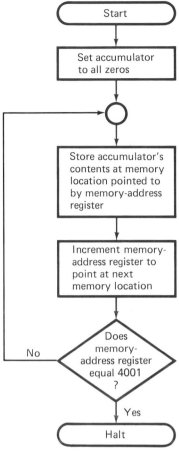

Fig. 5-5 A flowchart of a program that uses the decision symbol in a loop. The program will loop through the two process blocks and the decision block 4002 times and then quit.

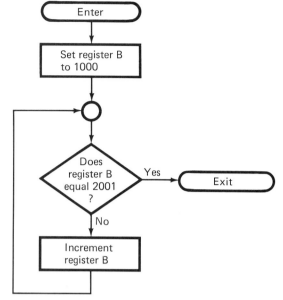

Fig. 5-6. See self-test question 10.

try to flowchart exact computer instructions, but rather flowchart the basic jobs that must be done.

8. Are the flowcharts in your answer to question 7 straight-line programs, or programs with decisions and iterative loops? Explain your answer.

9. Flowchart the following program.
   You are given two positive numbers, A and B. The program inputs A, inputs B, sets flag A if A is the larger number or sets flag B if B is the larger number or if A and B are equal, and then halts.

10. Figure 5-6 is a part of a program. You can tell this because the terminators are marked Enter and Exit, rather than Start and Stop. When the program flow leaves the "Increment Register" pro-

cess symbol, it flows into the connect block. How does the flowchart tell you that the program then flows into the decision symbol instead of flowing into the "Set Register B to 1000" process?

11. The subroutine flowcharted in Fig. 5-6 is often called a *delay* routine. Write a short paragraph to describe what this routine does and why it might be called a "delay routine."

12. Draw the proper flowchart symbols for the following operations:
    a. Is X greater than Y?
    b. Clear register C.
    c. Find the square root of X.
    d. 100 milliseconds (ms)?
    e. Start.
    f. The letter G. (A connection.)
    g. Halt
    h. Input A?
    i. Input A
    j. Exit
    k. $Y = AX^2 + BX + C$.

5-3 SUBROUTINES

A subroutine is a special part of a program. Usually, a subroutine is used more than once during a program's execution. But the programmer writes the subroutine only once. Wherever the subroutine is needed, the programmer uses a short instruction to *call* the subroutine from its one location.

81

Call

Most computer languages have a special instruction to call subroutines. The Call instruction not only calls the subroutine, but also tells the processor to remember exactly where the program was when the subroutine was called. After the call instruction, the program execution moves to the subroutine. The subroutine is executed step by step. The last instruction executed in the subroutine is usually a special "Return" instruction that tells the processor to return to the remembered point in the main program—the point immediately after the call instruction.

The major advantage of subroutines is that they save coding. Subroutines eliminate the need to write the same code again and again. Instead, the programmer writes the code once, in a subroutine, and the program calls the subroutine as often as necessary.

Let's look at an example that shows how a subroutine might be used. Once more, we will use the simple program for generating the data to plot a parabola. As you can see in Fig. 5-7, however, we have added one more formula to this program. The second formula will compute the data needed to plot the parabola $Z = \frac{1}{2}X^2$. In order to have the resulting data table for both parabolas displayed, we must add more print instructions. These instructions are also shown in Fig. 5-7.

Looking at the main program in Fig. 5-7, you can see that the four instructions "Let $Y = X^2$," "Let $Z = \frac{1}{2}X^2$," "Print X and Y," and "Print X and Z" are repeated seven times. These four instructions can be put into a subroutine. Once they are in a subroutine, the subroutine can be called any time we need to use these print instructions.

The program is flowcharted again to Fig. 5-8, but this time we use a subroutine. You can see that using a subroutine shortens the program. The instruction Gosub directs the program to use the subroutine. The subroutine starts at the Enter symbol, sets Y equal to X^2, sets Z equal to one-half of X^2, prints X and Y, prints X and Z, and then returns to the main program. The program returns to the point directly after the Gosub process block. Figure 5-9 shows how the complete program uses the subroutine seven times.

This example shows a very simple approach to a subroutine. This particular problem could be solved another way, but our solution

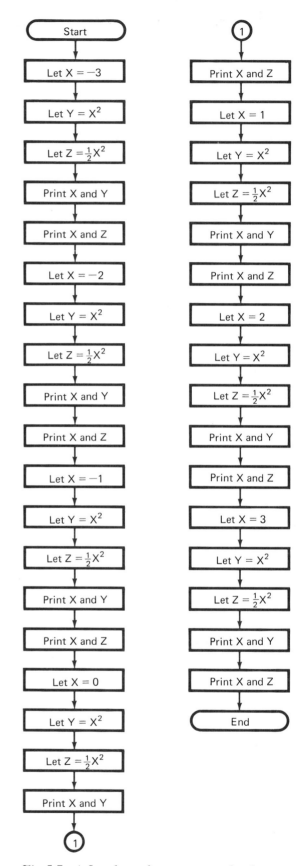

Fig. 5-7 A flowchart of a program to plot the two parabolas $Y = X^2$ and $Z = \frac{1}{2}X^2$.

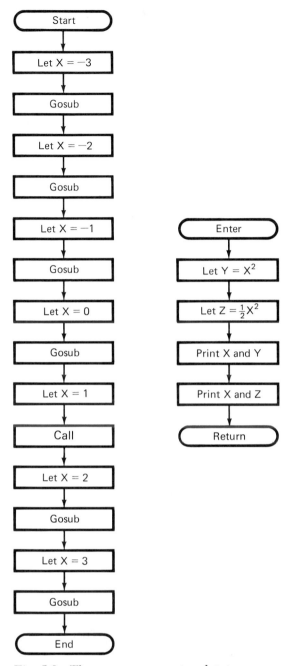

Fig. 5-8 The same program to plot two parabolas, this time using a subroutine for the two print instructions. Each time the program finds a Gosub it executes the subroutine and then returns to the instruction following the Gosub instruction.

does demonstrate the improvement a subroutine can make.

A program can call more than one subroutine. Figure 5-10 shows how a program executes loops through two subroutines. The two subroutines are called subroutine A and subroutine B. Each subroutine is used twice. The program executes in the following order:

Main program	Part 1
Subroutine A	
Main program	Part 2
Subroutine B	
Main program	Part 3
Subroutine A	
Main program	Part 4
Subroutine B	
Main program	Part 5

Although this program starts and stops in the main program, there are no rules requiring this procedure. For example, some programs execute a halt in a subroutine and never return to the main program.

A subroutine can call a subroutine. This is called subroutine *nesting*. Two-level subroutine nesting is shown in Fig. 5-11. The main program calls subroutine A, which in turn calls subroutine B.

In Fig. 5-12 we can see multiple-level subroutines and nesting. The main program is made up of the instructions in parts 1 through 5. Parts 1 to 4 end with a Gosub instruction. The Gosub instructions direct program execution to subroutine A, B, or C. You can see that subroutines A and B contain Gosub instructions too. Subroutine A calls subroutine B and subroutine B calls subroutine C. This is called three-level nesting.

In following the program in Fig. 5-12, you will find that it executes as:

Main program	Part 1
Subroutine A	Part A1
Subroutine B	Part B1
Subroutine C	
Subroutine B	Part B2
Subroutine A	Part A2
Main program	Part 2
Subroutine C	
Main program	Part 3
Subroutine B	Part B1
Subroutine C	
Subroutine B	Part B2
Main program	Part 4
Subroutine C	
Main program	Part 5

This example shows you single-, double-, and triple-level nesting. It also shows how a program can call multiple subroutines.

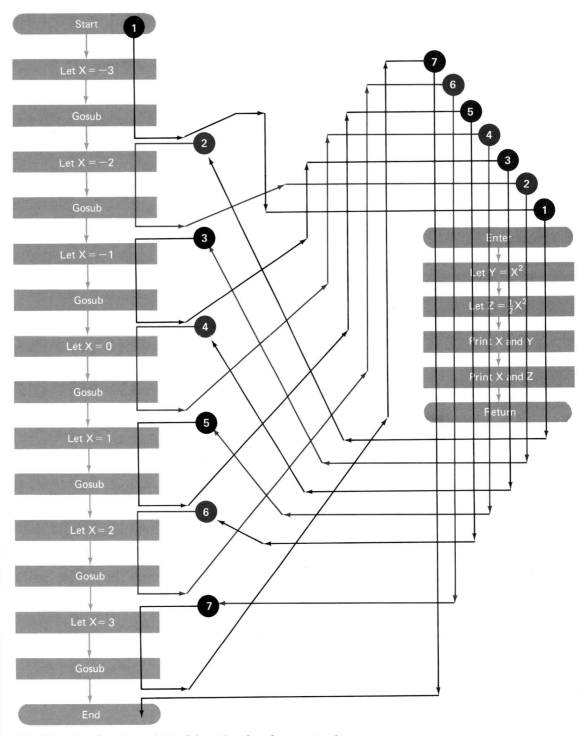

Fig. 5-9 The flowchart of Fig. 5-8, with colored arrows to show
how the program sequences through the subroutine seven times.

The number of subroutine nesting levels
depends on the processor and the programming language. For most modern microprocessors and most modern programming languages, the number of subroutine nesting
levels is very large. As you can see, using a
subroutine does not make the programmer do
a lot of work. That is, the programmer does
not need to remember where the program
must return each time. The microprocessor

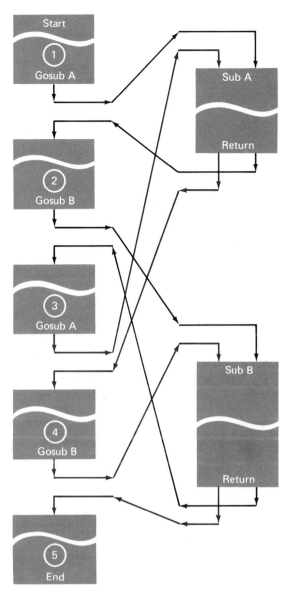

Fig. 5-10 A program with two subroutines. Each subroutine is used twice.

or the programming language keeps track of the place to which the program must return. Later we will see exactly how the microprocessor does this.

Self-Test

Check your understanding by answering these questions.

13. A subroutine is used to
    a. Provide program nesting
    b. Shorten the amount of program code
    c. Provide an Enter and a Return
    d. Allow multiple print statements

14. The purpose of subroutine nesting is to
    a. Keep the routine short
    b. Reduce the number of Gosub instructions
    c. Let the subroutine call commonly used routines
    d. (All of the above)

15. The subroutine often shortens the length of a program. It will shorten the program by
    a. 10 percent
    b. One-seventh
    c. Hardly at all, but it makes the program easier to read
    d. By an amount that depends on how often the subroutine is used

16. (*Optional.*) A program executes in the following sequence:

Main program	Part 1
Subroutine A	Part A1
Subroutine A	Parts A1 and A2
Main program	Part 2

a. Diagram how the program execution flows through the main program and the subroutine.
b. This problem demonstrates that a subroutine may call ___?___.

5-4 PROGRAMMING LANGUAGES

What are programming languages? Programming languages are sets of rules and commands that you, as the programmer, can use to express your program so that the processor can follow and execute it. Like any other language, a programming language has a vocabulary and rules of use. The vocabulary of a programming language is made up of the names of all the language's instructions. The rules tell us how to use these instructions so that the processor will be able to do exactly what we want.

Different programming languages have different conversational levels. A programming language's conversational level is a rough index of how closely its instructions approach English statements. The higher the programming language level, the closer the instructions are to English-language statements.

For example, in *machine language*, the binary number

0100 1111

Vocabulary

Rules of use

Conversational level

Machine language

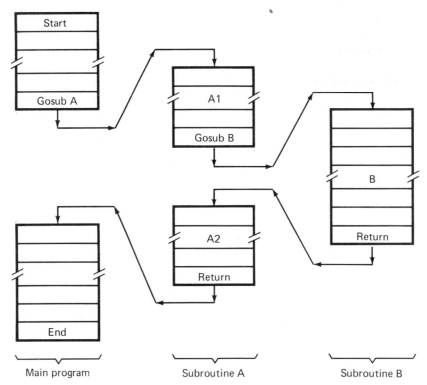

Fig. 5-11 Simple nesting. The main program calls subroutine
A, which in turn calls subroutine B.

may instruct the microprocessor to clear its accumulator. Obviously, there is nothing about this instruction that looks like English. In assembly language, the same operation takes place using the abbreviation

CLA A

This instruction is more like the English word "clear." In the high-level language BASIC, you can set the variable A equal to 0 with the instruction

LET A = 0

As you can see, the BASIC instruction comes very close to reading like an English sentence.

If the conversational programming languages are so much easier to understand, why do we use the lower-level languages? There are two reasons. First, the higher-level languages require many more machine-level instructions to do the same job. For example, the simple BASIC instruction "LET A = 0" may use 100 or more machine-language instructions to execute. The binary word 0100 1111 is a single machine instruction that sets the accumulator to 0. High-level instruc-

tions take more memory space for storage and take much longer to execute. That is, machine-language programs are more efficient than high-level programs.

Second, the use of a high-level language requires a much more sophisticated computer system. Conversational communications require an I/O terminal. And executing a high-level program in a reasonable time requires a powerful processor with a great deal of memory space.

Although there are many levels of programming languages, all these languages must be converted into binary machine instructions before the processor can execute the programming language's instructions. When programming in machine language, you enter binary words directly into program memory. When using a higher-level language, you must take an extra step. You must use a program that changes the higher-level language's statements into machine instructions. Obviously, you must have a more powerful computer system to make this translation.

You can see that the machine-language programming is the basic programming level for all processors. That is, each processor has its own set of machine instructions. Each pro-

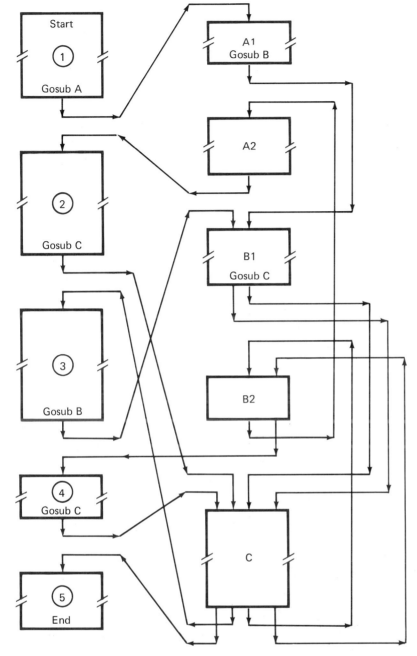

Fig. 5-12 Subroutines with three-level nesting.

cessor can be programmed in its machine instructions. However, the actual machine instructions are often unique to one particular kind of processor. Machine code from one processor will not run on a different kind of processor.

Machine-language programming is used for very short microprocessor programs. If a program is to be more than a few bytes long, machine-language programming becomes difficult. When programming in machine language, you must keep track of the start-ing address and the address of every instruction in the program. You must know the address of every step because you may need to refer to previous instructions. If you find that you have left out an instruction, you must rewrite the entire program.

The most popular way to program a microprocessor is to use assembly-language programming. Assembly-language programming uses an English abbreviation for each binary instruction word. Earlier, we saw an example in which "CLA" was used for the

**Introduction to
Microprocessors
CHAPTER 5**

Source code

Listing

Editor

Source program			Comments
	ORG	000000A	PGM TO START AT 0 OCTAL
START	LXI	B,000100A	POINT BC TO 000100 OCTAL
AGAIN	XRA	A	SET ACC = 0
	STAX	B	PUT ACC (0) INTO MEMORY
	INX	B	NEXT MEMORY LOCATION
	MOV	A,C	PUT C INTO A
	CPI	377Q	IS C AT 377 OCTAL YET?
	JZ	AGAIN	NO. KEEP GOING
	HLT		YES. STOP
	END	START	

(a)

Octal address	Octal machine code	Source program			Comments
000.000			ORG	000000A	PGM TO START AT 0 OCTAL
000.000	001 100 000	START	LXI	B,000100A	POINT BC TO 000100 OCTAL
000.003	257	AGAIN	XRA	A	SET ACC = 0
000.004	002		STAX	B	PUT ACC(0) INTO MEMORY
000.005	003		INX	B	NEXT MEMORY LOCATION
000.006	171		MOV	A,C	PUT C INTO A
000.007	376 377		CPI	377Q	IS C AT 377 OCTAL YET?
000.011	312 003 000		JZ	AGAIN	NO. KEEP GOING
000.014	166		HLT		YES. STOP
000.015	000		END	START	

00011 Statements Assembled
03475 Bytes Free
No Errors Detected

(b)

Fig. 5-13   Using an assembler to generate binary object code.
(a) The source program using the assembler's mnemonics. The
comments are ignored by the assembler. (b) The assembled listing, including the octal memory addresses and the octal machine
code.

Clear instruction. Assembly-language programs are written with symbolic addresses.
That is, the programmer uses names or abbreviations instead of numerical addresses. At
the beginning of the program the programmer
equates the start of the program with a particular numerical address. From then on, the
programmer uses symbolic addresses.

Figure 5-13(a) shows a program in assembly-language source code. Figure 5-13(b)
shows the assembly "listing" for this program. The program clears all memory locations between 000.100 and 000.377 to 0. The
source code was written with only one reference to an actual memory location. This was
the first instruction: ORG 000.000. It tells the

assembler to start the code at memory location 000.000.* After that, the memory locations are referenced by symbolic addresses
such as AGAIN and START.

Figure 5-13(b) shows the actual memory addresses and the machine code. The addresses
and machine code are expressed in octal.
The assembler assigns the memory location
000.003 to the symbolic address AGAIN.

An assembly-language program is written by
using a special computer program called an
editor. The editor lets the programmer easily
construct a series of error-free assembly-lan-

* A dot is used to separate the octal digits representing the upper and lower bytes.

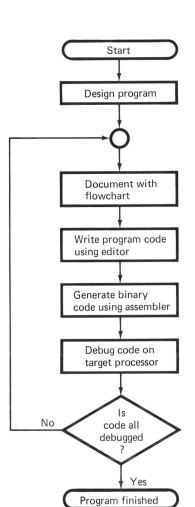

Fig. 5-14 Developing a program. This flowchart is used to show the basic steps used to design and code a program using assembly language. Fully debugged code is fully documented.

Assembler

Linker

Interpreter

Compiler

Parse

that the different programs can "talk" to each other.

Assembly-language programming lets the programmer write long and complicated programs. These programs are as efficient as machine code, because assembly-language programming has only one instruction for every machine instruction.

Starting with Chap. 6, we will write a number of programs using assembly-language abbreviations for the instructions. You will be able to convert some of these programs into machine code so that they will run on a microprocessor system. This is called "hand-assembling" of programs. That is, you are doing by hand what the assembler could do for you.

There are two different ways of translating high-level programs into machine-code instructions. One way is to use a program called an *interpreter*. The other way is to use a program called a *compiler*.

The high-level language BASIC (Beginner's All-purpose Symbolic Instruction Code) is a very good example of a high-level programming language. BASIC usually takes the form of an interpreter. BASIC programming statements are in instructions that are much like ordinary English. The interpreter is a very sophisticated program that makes these complex English statements into simple machine-code instructions.

An interpreter works during the execution of a program. Each line of the high-level program is converted into machine-code instructions just before the execution of the line. The interpreter parses each line. That is, each line is broken down into its basic parts. After the interpreter parses the line, each of the various parts is converted into machine-language instructions by a series of subroutines. As each line is converted into machine-language instructions, it is executed. Once the complete line is executed, the interpreter starts the translation process on the next line of the high-level language.

From this description, you can see that an interpreter takes a very large number of subroutines. These subroutines, the program to parse the instructions, the high-level language's instructions, and the program's data must all be kept in the processor's memory. The interpreter thus requires a microcomputer system with a large memory. Typically, a BASIC interpreter running on an 8-bit

guage addresses, statements, and data. If errors are made, the editor provides an easy way to correct them.

Once the program has been written and edited, it can be assembled. Another program called an *assembler* converts the English abbreviations and symbolic addresses into machine-code instructions at exact addresses. The edit/assembly process is flowcharted in Fig. 5-14. As you can see, you iterate the edit/assembly process until all the code is correct.

Frequently the programmer writes a large program by first preparing a number of short programs. After each program is assembled, the small programs are then linked together. To link the short programs, the programmer uses a program called a *linker*. The linker makes sure that each of the machine-code instructions is given proper memory space and

Object code

FORTRAN

Pascal

Microprocessor development system (MDS)

microcomputer requires from 12 kilobytes to 24 kilobytes of memory.

What is the advantage of using an interpreter? Its main advantage lies in the high-level language. That is, you can easily solve complex mathematical problems without using many, many lines of code. For example, in BASIC you can call subroutines that will do logarithms, sines, square roots, and other mathematical functions in a single statement. To do these in machine language or assembly language would require 1000 to 4000 instructions.

BASIC interpreters are often used on small microcomputer systems of the kind that can replace a minicomputer in a scientific environment. Many medium-sized, general-purpose microcomputer systems offer a BASIC interpreter. So do many personal microcomputers.

There are other languages that use interpreters, but BASIC is by far the most popular language.

As we mentioned earlier, high-level–language programming can also be reduced to machine-language instructions by a compiler. A compiler is very much like an assembler. A compiler works with a high-level language's instructions instead of an assembly language's instructions. The compiler converts the high-level language's instructions into machine-language code. Once the compiler has generated the machine-language code, or object code, the compiler is no longer needed. As a result, a program written in a high-level language and compiled may run in much less memory space than is needed by the same program and an interpreter.

If the object code generated by a compiler is much smaller than the interpreter, why don't we always use a compiler? The answer is that the compiler is much larger than the interpreter. In fact, many compilers are so large that they will not run on microcomputers at all. Some compilers are so large that even a small- to medium-sized minicomputer is too small. These large compilers must run on large scientific computers. The size of a compiler depends on its sophistication, but even a somewhat unsophisticated compiler is a very large program.

We must not, however, underestimate the value of compilers. Compilers are often used to produce object code for microprocessors

that enables these processors to do complex and large-scale mathematical computations. Complex mathematical operations are much more easily expressed in a high-level language than in assembly language. When a mathematical program written in a high-level language is too large to run on a microcomputer, a compiler running on a larger computer may succeed in translating the program into object code that is short enough to run on the microcomputer.

With an interpreter, creating a program of similar complexity to run on the microcomputer would be impossible. The interpreter itself, which must always be present when a program is run, simply takes up too much memory.

Both assemblers and interpreters, on the other hand, have the advantage of built-in editors. Built-in editors are convenient. They allow you to use one program (whether the assembler or the interpreter) to write and then to execute the source code.

Another drawback of assemblers and interpreters, however, is that they must be written to run on a particular microprocessor. Before choosing a microprocessor to do a job requiring high-level programming, it is essential to know what high-level software is available for the microprocessors under consideration.

Two high-level–language compilers are very popular today. One of these is FORTRAN (*FOR*mula *TRAN*slator), which is among the oldest scientific programming languages. FORTRAN is the most standardized scientific language in use today. Although it is complicated and is beginning to show its age, FORTRAN has remained popular.

One of the newer languages that often uses a compiler is Pascal. Pascal is a recently developed scientific language that has become very popular for use with microcomputer systems. This language is named for the French mathematician Blaise Pascal (1623–1662). Pascal is easier to use than FORTRAN and is more compatible with machine-language or assembly-language programming.

Today there is a great deal of code produced by *microprocessor development systems* (MDSs). These are small, general-purpose microcomputer systems designed to help the programmer write and debug code for a *specific* microprocessor. Most microprocessor development systems work with assembly language. However, many of them have an option that lets them generate object code from program statements in either BASIC or Pascal. A microprocessor development system is often necessary for troubleshooting on a complex microcomputer system. We will look at microprocessor development systems in more detail in Chap. 14.

Although microprocessor programming can be done with machine language, assembly language, interpreters, or compilers, the principles of programming remain the same. One proof of this is that flowcharts can be used to document programs written in any of these different kinds of programming languages.

For the rest of this text, we will concentrate on machine-language and assembly-language programming. High-level–language programming is the subject of other courses and does not teach anything about a microprocessor's basic architecture. Both machine-language programming and assembly-language programming require a good knowledge of the microprocessor's architecture before error-free and efficient programming is possible.

Self-Test

Check your understanding by answering these questions.

17. You are going to write a 22-instruction program to set all memory locations to logic "0." Probably you would use
   a. Machine-language programming
   b. Assembly-language programming
   c. A high-level interpreter
   d. A high-level compiler

18. You are going to write a program on a stand-alone microcomputer system. This program will be used to find the roots of a quadratic equation using the formula $(-b \pm \sqrt{b^2 - 4ac})/2a$. To do this you would use
   a. Machine-language programming
   b. Assembly-language programming
   c. A high-level interpreter
   d. A high-level compiler

19. You are writing the software for a microcomputer-based environmental-control system. This is a moderately sophisticated system, and you estimate the software will occupy 14 kilobytes of memory. The software will require a number of routines that are very efficient in program space and execution time. To do this you will probably use
   a. Machine-language programming
   b. Assembly-language programming
   c. A high-level interpreter
   d. A high-level compiler

20. You are servicing a microcomputer-based data-analysis and display system attached to a sophisticated medical instrument. The data processing requires extensive mathematical processing. You suspect that the programs were developed on a large minicomputer system using
   a. Machine-language programming
   b. Assembly-language programming
   c. A high-level interpreter
   d. A high-level compiler

21. In one or two sentences, write a short explanation of each of your answers in questions 17 through 20.

Summary

1. You use a program to tell the processor what to do. You must tell the processor exactly how to go about solving a problem.

2. Designing a program means to organize it so that a processor can solve the problem using the program's steps.

3. Coding the program means to express the design in a series of instructions that the processor understands.

4. Debugging the program means to test the code on the processor and correct the code if it does not work.

5. A programming language is a set of instructions designed for a specific need. A program is coded using some or all of a particular computer language's instructions.

6. "Software" refers to the processor's programs and their documentation.

7. Flowcharts are a very popular way to document software. Flowcharts use four basic symbols. The rectangle indicates a process, the diamond indicates a decision, the circle indicates a connector, and the oval indicates a terminator. The flowchart's arrows indicate

the direction in which the solution is flowing.

8. A straight-line program flows from the beginning to the end with no decisions. More complex programs have decisions and iterative loops. Decisions let the program branch into one of two paths. Iterative loops let the program redo a number of processes until a certain result happens.

9. A subroutine is a part of the program that is used more than once. It is called by a subroutine Call instruction. The subroutine Call instruction remembers where the call happened so that the subroutine Return instruction can go back to where the main program left off. Subroutines save coding time and program memory space, because the same thing need not be recoded. A program can call as many subroutines as needed.

10. A subroutine can call a subroutine. This is called "subroutine nesting." The number of subroutine nesting levels depends on the programming language and the processor.

11. A programming language's level tells us how English-like its instructions are. The higher the programming language's level, the closer it is to plain English.

12. The fundamental language for all processors is machine language. All programs must somehow be made into machine-language programs before they will run.

13. High-level languages are more conversational, but they run more slowly and take more memory space.

14. Assemblers, interpreters, and compilers reduce high-level–language instructions to machine code for a particular processor.

15. Machine-language programming is used for short programs. Machine-language programming makes the programmer do more work than other languages do.

16. Assembly-language programming uses English abbreviations for the processor's binary machine instructions. It also keeps track of memory addresses. Assembly language is just as efficient as machine language. An assembler converts assembly-language source code into machine (object) code for the particular processor.

17. Statements in high-level languages are made into machine code by interpreters or compilers. An interpreter runs on the target processor. It interprets each instruction one line at a time. A compiler runs on a host machine. The compiler generates machine or object code for a particular processor. Many compilers are so large that they will not run on most microcomputers.

Chapter Review Questions

5-1. You want to know how long it takes an object to fall to earth from a given height. Would you expect to use the processor to rearrange the algebraic expression $s = \frac{1}{2}gt^2$, or just to solve the expression for time, given different values of s? Why?

5-2. What work must be done before you code a program?

5-3. To code your program, you will use some or all of the microprocessor's instructions. In other words, a complete set of all these instructions is called a(n) ___?___.

5-4. Most of the time you debug a program on the target microcomputer system. When you are debugging a program, are you looking for design errors or coding errors? Why?

5-5. Designing a program means to convert a statement of the problem into ___?___.

5-6. A flowchart is used to ___?___ a program.
   a. Code
   b. Design
   c. Document
   d. (All of the above)

5-7. The rectangle is used to indicate a
   a. Process
   b. Decision
   c. Connector
   d. Terminator

5-8. The circle is used to indicate a
    a. Process   c. Connector
    b. Decision   d. Terminator

5-9. The oval is used to indicate a
    a. Process   c. Connector
    b. Decision   d. Terminator

5-10. The diamond is used to indicate a
    a. Process   c. Connector
    b. Decision   d. Terminator

5-11. Flowchart the process of designing, coding, debugging, and running a program. Use all four flowchart symbols.

5-12. If your program has nested subroutines, it means that _____?_____.

5-13. Does a subroutine have to be shorter than the main program?

5-14. Does a subroutine have to be called more than once?

5-15. Briefly explain why a subroutine is used.

5-16. Explain the difference between an assembler and a compiler.

5-17. A problem has program solutions in assembly language, FORTRAN, and BASIC. Rank these from 1, the one that will take the most memory space in the target processor, to 3, the one that will use the least memory space in the target processor.

5-18. When you are debugging a program, you find an error in the source code. To correct the source code error, you return to the
    a. Editor   d. Interpreter
    b. Assembler   e. Machine code
    c. Compiler   f. (All of the above)

5-19. You are using a programming language that runs on the target system. It executes each of the high-level statements as it reads them. The programming language is a(n)
    a. Editor   d. Interpreter
    b. Assembler   e. Machine code
    c. Compiler   f. (All of the above)

5-20. All programming languages finally reduce the program to a(n) _____?_____ program.
    a. Editor   d. Interpreter
    b. Assembler   e. Machine code
    c. Compiler   f. (All of the above)

5-21. You are writing a high-level program on an IBM System/370 Model 145 computer. It produces object code for your microcomputer. The IBM System/370 Model 145 is running a(n)
    a. Editor   d. Interpreter
    b. Assembler   e. Machine code
    c. Compiler   f. (All of the above)

5-22. You are using a programming language in which each instruction translates one for one into object code. This programming language is a(n)
    a. Editor   d. Interpreter
    b. Assembler   e. Machine code
    c. Compiler   f. (All of the above)

5-23. A programming language has a vocabulary of _____?_____. It also has _____?_____ that tell us exactly how to use the vocabulary.

Answers to Self-Tests

1. *a.* Is temperature equal to 68°F?
   b. Yes. Turn off heat and air conditioning and go to step *a.*
   c. No. Is temperature greater than 68°F?
   d. Yes. Turn on air conditioning and go to step *a.*
   e. No. Turn on heat and go to step *a.*
2. LET X = 2
   LET Y = X²
   LET Z = X³
   LET U = √X
   LET W = ∛X
   PRINT X, Y, Z, U, and W
   LET X = 3
   LET Y = X²
   LET Z = X³
   LET U = √X
   LET W = ∛X
   PRINT X, Y, Z, U, and W
   LET X = 4
   LET Y = X²
   LET Z = X³
   LET U = √X
   LET W = ∛X
   PRINT X, Y, Z, U, and W
   LET X = 5
   LET Y = X²
   LET Z = X³
   LET U = √X
   LET W = ∛X
   PRINT X, Y, Z, U, and W
3. c.   4. a.   5. b.

6. Because a processor can only follow an exact set of instructions. If you don't know what the procedure is, you can't write the instructions to tell the processor how to solve the problem.
7. See Fig. 5-15(*a*) and (*b*).
8. Figure 5-15(*a*) is a program with decisions and loops. It must decide what the temperature is. Figure 5-15(*b*) is a simple straight-line program. Each instruction is executed in order until it is done.
9. See Fig. 5-16.
10. You know which way the program will flow by the direction in which the arrows point.
11. The program starts by setting register B to 1000. It then keeps checking register B to see whether it has reached 2001. If it has not, register B is incremented one count and checked again. When it is equal to 2001 the program exits.

   The program is called a "delay routine" because it takes the microproces-

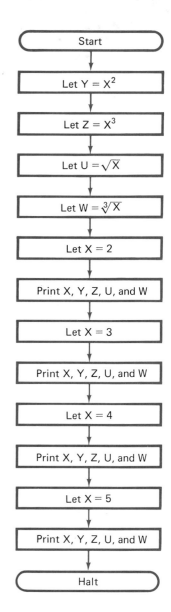

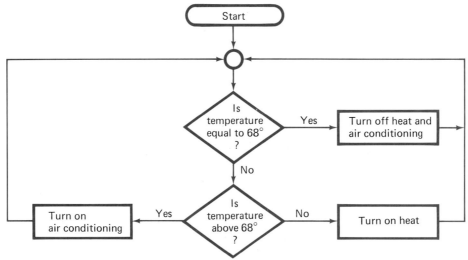

Fig. 5-15   (*a*) A flowchart of the problem in self-test question 1.
(*b*) A flowchart of the problem in self-test question 2.

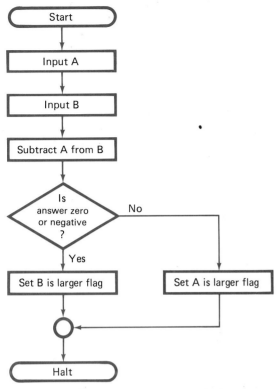

Fig. 5-16   A flowchart of the program in self-test
question 9.

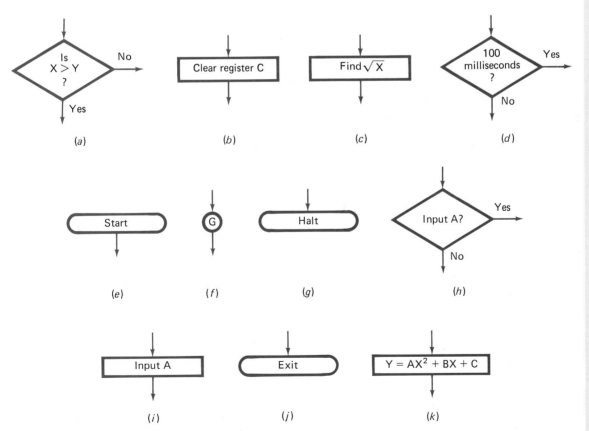

Fig. 5-17   Answers to self-test question 12.

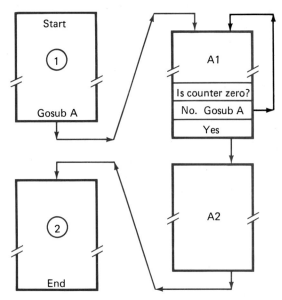

Fig. 5-18 The program execution in self-test question 16.

sor a certain amount of time to execute the instructions going around the loop. In this case it executes them for a delay of $2001 - 1000 = 1001$ times.

12. See Fig. 5-17.
13. b.   14. c.   15. d.
16. *a.* See Fig. 5-18.
    b. Itself.
17. a.   18. c.
19. b.   20. d.
21. (17) Very short programs that work directly with the microprocessor are most easily put in machine language. However, programmers with all the right tools available would most likely write this program in assembly language.

(18) To solve an equation like this will call for a high-level programming language. If it is all to be done on the microprocessor-based system, you probably could not use a compiler. However, there are many interpreters that will work.

(19) If the routines are to be of maximum efficiency, you need to use either machine-language or assembly-language programming. You would never in your right mind tackle a 14-kilobyte machine-language program!

(20) More than likely, the reason for developing the software on another machine was to make use of a very sophisticated compiler or assembler. You would not use assembly language for extensive mathematical programming.

An Introduction to Microprocessor Instructions

■ In this chapter we will answer the question "What is a microprocessor instruction?" You will see how a microprocessor instruction, which is a binary word, is different from other digital words stored in the microprocessor's memory. You will also learn how to break the instruction into its basic parts. You will learn a shorthand way of speaking about a microprocessor instruction and about its various parts.

The first part of a microprocessor instruction tells the microprocessor what to do. The second part tells the microprocessor where to get data. This chapter discusses a number of different basic ways that microprocessors address data and tells why each is used. It also tells when not to use some of the addressing modes.

Finally, this chapter describes a small microcomputer system, which is used to illustrate the microprocessor's instructions as we study them in future chapters and to illustrate how a basic microcomputer is built.

6-1 WHAT IS AN INSTRUCTION SET?

A microprocessor instruction is a binary word. When it is read as an instruction, this binary word tells the microprocessor to do one simple task. No other binary word is used to tell the microprocessor to do this task. Most microprocessor instructions let you move or process data. The data may be in memory, or they may be in one of the microprocessor's registers. A few other microprocessor instructions let you do "housekeeping" functions. These instructions let you control certain microprocessor functions.

When we speak of the microprocessor's *instruction set*, we are talking about all the instructions the microprocessor knows how to use.

The microprocessor's instruction word is the same length as its data word. That is, the instruction word in an 8-bit microprocessor is 8 bits long. The instruction word in a 16-bit microprocessor is 16 bits long. However, an *instruction* may take one, two, or three instruction words. Therefore, an 8-bit microprocessor's instruction may be 8, 16, or 24 bits

long. Later in this chapter, we will see how all these bits are used.

The instruction is sent to the microprocessor's instruction register, decoder, and control logic. These logic functions determine which instruction it is, and they send the signals to the microprocessor's other logic functions. The other functions carry out the instruction.

The instruction is placed in the instruction register during the microprocessor's Fetch cycle. It is during the Execute cycle that the microprocessor's decoding and control logic makes the microprocessor do what the instruction tells it to do.

If we look more closely at a microprocessor instruction, we find that the instruction must do two things. First, the instruction must tell the microprocessor what to do. That is, it must give the microprocessor a command. For example, the instruction must tell the microprocessor to add, clear, move, shift, or do anything else.

Second, the instruction must give the microprocessor some address information. That is, it must tell the microprocessor the location of the data to work on. For example, the instruction may say: Add from memory to

From page 97:
Housekeeping
functions

Instruction
register

Decoder

Control logic

Fetch cycle

Execute cycle

On this page:
Op code
(operation code)

Address

the accumulator, clear the accumulator, move data from register A to register B, shift the accumulator, and so on. You can see that each of these examples not only tells the microprocessor what to do, but also tells the microprocessor which logic function it is to work on.

An instruction can be broken into two parts, called the *op code* (operation code) and the *address*. This is shown in Fig. 6-1. The op code tells the microprocessor what to do, and the address tells the microprocessor where to do it. Often you will find that the first word of a multiple-word instruction is the op code and that either the second word or the second and third words are address words. However, this does not mean that all single-word instructions do not have addresses. We will look more closely at addressing modes later in this chapter.

This text introduces eight major kinds of instructions. However, we will find that most microprocessors have many more than eight different instructions. Typically, today's microprocessors have a minimum of 50 to 75 instructions. Some of the more powerful microprocessor systems have hundreds of instructions.

There are many more instructions than there are op codes. This is because each op code can be combined with a number of different addressing modes.

For example, most microprocessors have a Clear op code. You may ask, Clear what? The answer is, it depends on the microprocessor's instruction set. For some microprocessors, there may be only a single clear instruction: Clear Accumulator. For other microprocessors, there may be a number of clear instructions, such as Clear Accumulator A; Clear Accumulator B; Clear Register A; Clear Register B; Clear Register C; Clear Register D; or Clear Memory Location N. In this example you can see that seven different addresses turn one op code, Clear, into seven different instructions.

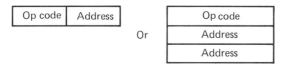

Fig. 6-1 The op code and the address parts of an instruction word. The op code (operation code) tells the microprocessor what to do. The address tells the microprocessor where to do it.

Self-Test

Check your understanding by answering these questions.

1. The microprocessor's op code tells the microprocessor
   a. What to do
   b. Where to do it
   c. What to do and where to do it
   d. (All of the above)

2. A microprocessor instruction may be ___?___ as long as its data word.
   a. Just   c. Three times
   b. Twice   d. (Any of the above)

3. The address portion of the microprocessor's instruction tells you
   a. What action to take using the op code
   b. Where to take the action using the directions given by the op code
   c. Where to find the instruction
   d. How long the instruction will be

4. The number of times a microprocessor's instruction set uses a particular op code depends on
   a. The op code's length
   b. How many different address modes the op code uses
   c. The amount of microcomputer memory
   d. (All of the above)

6-2 THE MNEMONICS

A microprocessor instruction is a binary number. Even 1-byte binary numbers are difficult to remember. It would be very difficult to remember instructions consisting of 2 and 3 bytes of binary numbers. You have learned how octal and hexadecimal numbering systems are used as a shorthand method to express large binary numbers. We could use the octal or hexadecimal shorthand when writing instruction codes. But there would still be a problem—the numbers do not give us any indication of the instructions that they stand for. Instructions in octal or hexadecimal would be difficult to learn and to use.

To solve this problem, we have mnemonics (pronounced ni MON-iks). A mnemonic is an abbreviation that reminds us of what it stands for. In most instruction-code mnemonics, the op code is abbreviated to three letters. For example, the mnemonic for "Clear" is usually CLA. If the microprocessor has two accumulators, for example, the two Clear Accumulator instructions might be CLA A and CLA B. The op code is CLA in both. The address is either accumulator A or accumulator B.

Obviously, when numerical data or a memory location goes with the op code, a number is still used. For example, the mnemonic JMP (meaning "Jump") needs an address to jump to. A jump instruction might read

$$JMP\ 177756_8$$

Here, the address is expressed as a six-digit octal number, meaning memory location 1111111111101110_2. The mnemonic JMP is much more meaningful than an actual op code such as 303_8 (11000011_2). This mix of mnemonics and numbers is used to make the instructions easy to remember.

We will use mnemonics when writing programs. You will find that mnemonics are not only handy when you are thinking about microprocessor instructions, but that they are also built into an assembler. Remember, an assembler is a program that converts mnemonics into binary instructions.

This text develops a mnemonic for each instruction that we study. Of course, somewhere there must be a table that matches mnemonics with the actual binary numbers that are the op codes and the addresses. Usually the op codes and addresses are shown in octal or hexadecimal. The manufacturer's literature for most microprocessors includes a card with an instruction-set summary. Such cards include both the mnemonic and the op code. The exact op code is not needed until you are ready to program a particular microprocessor.

Self-Test

Check your understanding by answering these questions.

5. As we have learned, both 303_8 and JMP mean "jump" for a certain microprocessor. Which of these two is the op code and which is the mnemonic? Why?

6. Many mnemonics are almost self-explanatory. What would you guess the following mnemonics to mean?

CLA	MOV	INC	AND
NOP	HLT	ADD	DEC

7. Some mnemonics are 4 letters long instead of 3. Should this change the length of the instruction that the mnemonics represent? Why?

8. One of an assembler's jobs is to convert assembly-language source code into binary object or machine code for the target microprocessor. To do this, you would expect the assembler to have a table where it can look up the microprocessor's ___?___ for each mnemonic.

9. A microprocessor has a unique binary word for each of its instructions. Would you expect a microprocessor to have a unique mnemonic for each of its instructions? Why?

6-3 THE MICROPROCESSOR'S ADDRESSING MODES

We stated in Sec. 6-1 that a microprocessor instruction must have an op code and an address. A few instructions, however, do not need an address. For example, no address is necessary for the instruction telling the microprocessor to halt.

Instructions that do not require addresses are exceptions. Think of the 8-bit microprocessor with a 65K memory. The programmer must be able to gain access to the contents of any one of the 65,536 addresses. Therefore, the memory-address instruction for such a microprocessor must have a 16-bit address field in addition to the op code.

How can a 16-bit address field and an op code fit into one 8-bit instruction? The answer, of course, is that they cannot.

For most microprocessors, the instruction length is variable. The instruction can be 1, 2, or 3 *instruction words* long as needed to do the job. This does not mean that the instruction word has a variable number of bits. An 8-bit microprocessor cannot have 7-, 12-, or 14-bit instructions. Instructions must come in one, two, or three words (bytes). An 8-bit microprocessor, therefore, can have 8-, 16-, or 24-bit instructions.

The length of the address is what makes one instruction longer than another. Although exact instructions vary from one microprocessor to another, most microprocessors share certain basic ways of addressing data. These basic ways of addressing data are called *addressing modes*. In the next few sections, we

Addressing mode

will look at the addressing modes used by our 8-bit model microprocessor.

6-4 INHERENT ADDRESSING

There are some single-byte instructions. In an 8-bit microprocessor, a single-byte instruction can have only 256 different combinations of bits. This is enough combinations for all the different instructions that our microprocessor can use. But our microprocessor has 65,536 different memory locations. Obviously, 8 bits cannot include both an op code and a memory address capable of addressing all of the 65,536 memory locations. Nor can an 8-bit instruction contain both an op code and a full byte of data. A full byte of data would use all 8 bits just for data.

How can 1-byte instructions address any data then? The answer is that 1-byte instructions do not address main memory. Instead, 1-byte instructions work on data that are already available in a particular register, register pair, or memory location pointed to by a register pair. An example of a 1-byte instruction is the instruction Move Register A to Register B. In this instruction, a single byte contains the op code Move and identifies the source of the data (register A) and the destination of the data (register B). This is shown in Fig. 6-2. The source of the data and the destination of the data are built into the instruction. That is why the addressing mode is called *inherent* or *implied* addressing.

Single-byte instructions are executed faster than any other instructions. As you know, the microprocessor must complete both the Fetch and the Execute cycles to complete the execution of an instruction. A single-byte instruction is executed in two microprocessor cycles. The Fetch takes one cycle and the Execute takes another cycle. As you read on, pay close attention to how many cycles are needed to carry out instructions that use other addressing modes. You will see that instruc-

tions using the inherent addressing mode are the fastest instructions to execute.

6-5 IMMEDIATE ADDRESSING

Immediate addressing is easy to understand. Instructions that use immediate addressing use the first byte for the op code. Immediately following the op code are the data. There may be either 1 or 2 bytes of data. These data are not taken from memory. Instead, the data are supplied by you, the programmer. Immediate addressing, therefore, requires no memory address. Immediate addressing requires only an op code immediately followed by the data to be operated on.

When is immediate addressing useful? A good example is a program that requires loading the accumulator with the same 8-bit number each time the program is run. In the instruction's first byte you put the op code that tells the microprocessor to load its accumulator with the contents of the byte that immediately follows the op code. In that second byte you put the data that you want to be put into the accumulator.

The instruction described is called the Load Register Immediate instruction. Figure 6-3 shows how the Load Register Immediate instruction appears when it is in memory. Figure 6-3 shows the op code in the instruction's first byte and the data in the instruction's second byte. Of course, both the op code and the data will contain binary information rather than the names used in Fig. 6-3.

The immediate addressing mode uses two microprocessor cycles. During the first cycle, the instruction is fetched. When the instruction is executed, the second byte (the data) is processed according to what the first byte (the op code) tells the microprocessor's logic to do.

In immediate addressing, the data must immediately follow the instruction in memory. A microprocessor often needs to use information stored at other memory locations. Immediate addressing will not work in such cases. This leads us to the next form of addressing.

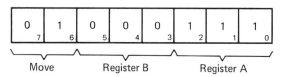

Fig. 6-2 The instruction Move A, B uses inherent addressing. The op code is the simple word 01. The addresses are A = 111 and B = 000.

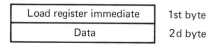

Fig. 6-3 The Load Register Immediate instruction, where the data are in a byte following the op code byte.

6-6 DIRECT ADDRESSING

Instructions that use direct addressing may have either 2 or 3 bytes. The first byte of these instructions is the op code. The second and, if present, third bytes are a memory address. The memory address points to the memory location that contains the data to be worked on. The second and third bytes can address a full 65,536 memory locations.

Direct addressing is in many ways the easiest addressing mode to understand. In inherent addressing, the address is "built in" and the programmer does not have to address a

memory location to get data. In immediate addressing, the data are the byte immediately following the op code. Again, the programmer does not have to address a memory location to get data. In direct addressing, however, the programmer is for the first time actually giving the address of the data needed.

An example of an instruction using direct addressing is shown in Fig. 6-4. The Store Accumulator Direct instruction stores the accumulator contents in memory location 000E. (Memory addresses are given as hexadecimal numbers, but data are given in binary form.)

Figure 6-5 shows what happens when this instruction is executed. As you can see in Fig. 6-5(a), before execution the accumulator contains the binary word 1010 1010. Memory location 000E contains the binary word 0000 0000. Memory location 0003 contains the Store Accumulator Direct instruction. Memory locations 0004 and 0005 are the locations for the address part of the instruction. That is, the data contained in memory loca-

Store accumulator direct	1st byte
00_{16}	2nd byte
$0E_{16}$	3rd byte

Fig. 6-4 An instruction using direct addressing. The Store Accumulator Direct instruction stores the accumulator's contents in memory location $000E_{16}$. Using this instruction, the 2nd and 3rd bytes can address a full 65K memory locations.

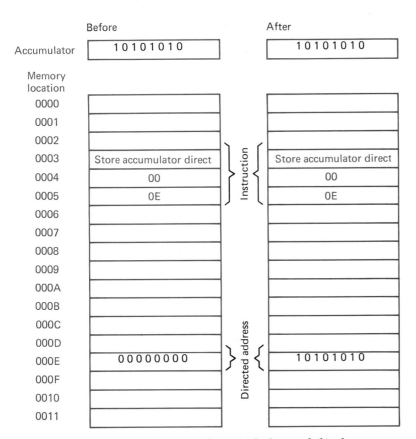

Fig. 6-5 The memory and accumulator (a) before and (b) after executing the Store Accumulator Direct instruction.

tions 0004 and 0005 "direct" the microprocessor to memory location 000E.

As shown in Fig. 6-5(*b*), after the instruction at memory location 0003 is executed, the accumulator's contents can also be found in memory location 000E.

Let's look at another example. Figure 6-6 is a flowchart of a program, and Fig. 6-7 shows what happens in memory and the accumulator as each instruction is executed. Before this program started, the accumulator was loaded with the results of a previous operation. This program starts at memory location 0000 by clearing the accumulator. Then the program loads the accumulator with the contents of memory location 000E. Then the program halts. Figure 6-7 shows that the contents of memory location 000E are the binary number 0101 0101. Look at the contents of the accumulator before and after the second instruction. You can see that after the load instruction is executed, 0101 0101 is the value in the accumulator.

We could have set the accumulator to 0101 0101 using the immediate addressing mode. But using the immediate mode would have tied the data to the memory location immediately following the instruction. What if later there is a need to use other instructions to work on the same data? The data will be difficult to get at. Using direct addressing, on the other hand, would make it easier for other instructions to use the same data. Direct addressing also allows the microprocessor to be directed to any memory location. In this example, any number of instructions can address the data that are stored in memory location 000E.

For example, we can expand the program as shown in Fig. 6-8. In this figure we again start at memory location 0000, but we have added one more program instruction. After the accumulator is loaded with the contents of memory location 000E, register B is loaded with the contents of location 000E. Figure 6-9 shows how the two registers (the accumulator and register B) are loaded. This time both the accumulator and register B start with random data from previous operations. In this example, you can see that two separate direct instructions are using the same data. That is, they both address memory location 000E. Note that clearing the accumulator does not affect register B, and loading the accumulator with 0101 0101 also does not affect register B. Only the Load Register B instruction puts a copy of the same data in both the accumulator and register B. When the program halts, both registers contain 0101 0101.

When you use direct addressing, you use extra microprocessor cycles. First, the microprocessor must fetch the instruction's op code. When the instruction is decoded, the microprocessor knows that it must fetch two additional bytes of information. These bytes of data make up the address of the memory location where the data are stored. Each additional fetch takes one more microprocessor cycle.

Once the op code and the two address bytes are fetched, the microprocessor still must execute the instruction. This takes a fourth cycle.

From this you can see that executing an instruction that uses direct addressing takes twice as long as executing an instruction that uses immediate addressing. Of course, direct addressing is necessary when you need to be able to place data at any location in memory. When you write programs, however, you should use as few direct addressing instructions as possible, because they take longer to execute.

Some microprocessors use a direct addressing mode that takes three microprocessor cycles. This mode uses only 2 bytes for each instruction. The first instruction word is the op code. The second instruction word is the address. This is shown in Fig. 6-10.

However, a single data word is not long enough to address the entire contents of a 65-kiloword memory. In an 8-bit microprocessor, for example, the 8-bit word used in the

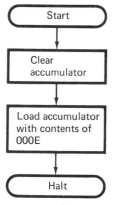

Fig. 6-6   A simple straight-line program to clear the accumulator and then load it with the contents of memory location 000E.

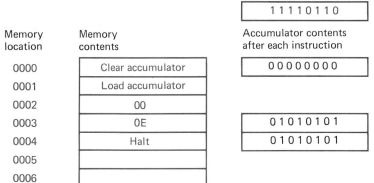

Memory location	Memory contents
0000	Clear accumulator
0001	Load accumulator
0002	00
0003	0E
0004	Halt
0005	
0006	
0007	
0008	
0009	
000A	
000B	
000C	
000D	
000E	0 1 0 1 0 1 0 1

Accumulator contents

| 1 1 1 1 0 1 1 0 |

Accumulator contents after each instruction

| 0 0 0 0 0 0 0 0 |

| 0 1 0 1 0 1 0 1 |
| 0 1 0 1 0 1 0 1 |

Memory page 0

Fig. 6-7 Executing the program flowcharted in Fig. 6-6. The program starts at memory location 0000. Before the program started, a previous operation left the accumulator set to 1111 0110. The Clear instruction makes the accumulator 0000 0000. After the Load instruction executes, we find 0101 0101 in the accumulator and in memory location 000E.

second byte of the instruction can address only 256 memory locations. Therefore, a special op code tells you that the instruction is a direct-address instruction using a single address byte. Usually, these addresses start at

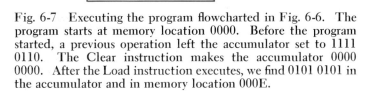

Fig. 6-8 Expanding the program from Fig. 6-6 to include a step to load register B. Both the accumulator and register B are loaded with the *contents* of memory location 000E.

the "bottom" of memory. That is, they start at address location 0. Sometimes this single-byte range is called memory page 0.

For example, an 8-bit microprocessor using a single byte of address information might address the first 256 memory locations. These are memory locations 0 to 255 ($0000\ 0000$ to $1111\ 1111$ or 00_{16} to FF_{16}). On the other hand, the 2-byte address word addresses the first 65,536 memory locations. These are memory locations 0 to 65,535 ($0000\ 0000\ 0000\ 0000$ to $1111\ 1111\ 1111\ 1111$ or 0000_{16} to $FFFF_{16}$).

Figure 6-11 shows these two different addressing ranges. What is the advantage of direct addressing limited to one-word addresses? The answer is that it saves one microprocessor cycle. It saves time. This can be a valuable addressing mode for 8-bit microprocessors if there are a few bytes of data that must be addressed frequently. These few bytes can be stored handily in the first 256 bytes of memory.

When you use a 16-bit microprocessor that has 65K of memory, direct addressing limited to one-word addresses is the only form of direct addressing needed. This is because a

103

Extended direct
addressing

Memory location	Memory contents
0000	Clear accumulator
0001	Load accumulator
0002	00
0003	0E
0004	Load register B
0005	00
0006	0E
0007	Halt
0008	
0009	
000A	
000B	
000C	
000D	
000E	0 1 0 1 0 1 0 1

Accumulator contents
1 1 1 1 0 1 1 0

Register B contents
1 1 1 0 1 1 0 1

Accumulator contents after each instruction
0 0 0 0 0 0 0 0

Register B contents after each instruction
1 1 1 0 1 1 0 1

0 1 0 1 0 1 0 1

1 1 1 0 1 1 0 1

0 1 0 1 0 1 0 1
0 1 0 1 0 1 0 1

0 1 0 1 0 1 0 1
0 1 0 1 0 1 0 1

Fig. 6-9 Executing the program flowcharted in Fig. 6-8. Again, the program starts at memory location 0000. In this case both the accumulator and register B contain random data from previous operations. Clearing the accumulator sets it to 0 but does *not* affect register B. Loading the accumulator puts 01010101 in the accumulator but again *does not change register B*. Only the **Load Register B** instruction puts a copy of the same data in both the accumulator and register B.

16-bit word can address every location in a 65K memory. You may find 16-bit microprocessors that have only instructions one and two words long.

How do you tell the two addressing modes apart if the microprocessor has both two-word and three-word direct addressing instructions? The manufacturer usually gives each form of direct addressing a different name. The op code for each form of addressing is also different. For example, some manufacturers call 2-byte direct addressing "direct addressing" or "page 0 addressing." However,

Op code	1st byte
Address	2nd byte

Fig. 6-10 A direct-address instruction that uses only two words. In this example, the words are bytes. Consequently the direct address range is only 256 memory locations. However, if the words were 16-bits long, this direct address instruction would have a range of 0 to 65,535 memory locations.

these manufacturers refer to the 3-byte direct addressing as "extended direct addressing."

6-7 REGISTER INDIRECT ADDRESSING

Most microprocessors offer another memory addressing mode that uses a single instruction word. This addressing mode is called *indirect addressing*. It is also called *register indirect addressing*. In the register indirect addressing mode, the instruction contains the op code and also indicates which register points to the memory location that contains the data needed. That is, the instruction does not contain the data needed, as in immediate addressing; the instruction does not contain the address of the data needed, as in direct addressing; but the instruction indicates *which register contains the address of the data needed*. In an 8-bit processor, the register indirect addressing mode indicates which register pair points to the correct memory address.

Indirect addressing is very convenient for

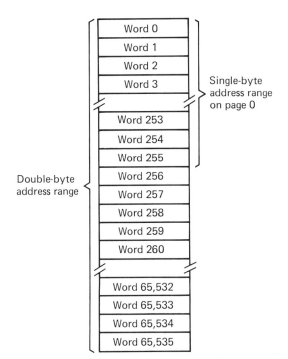

Fig. 6-11 A memory map showing the range of single- and double-byte direct addressing. The double-byte address range is 0 to 65,535, and the single-byte range is 0 to 255. Often the single-byte range is called a *memory page*.

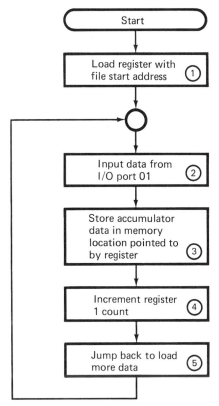

File format

Sequential memory locations

Fig. 6-12 A program to load data into sequential memory locations using register indirect addressing. The register used as a memory pointer is loaded in the first instruction. This makes the register point to the first file memory location. In all instructions after that, the register is incremented to point to other sequential memory locations.

moving data to and from frequently used memory locations. This is especially true when the data are in list or file format. That is, it is very helpful when you want to store or read data in sequential memory locations.

A program that files data in sequential locations (that is, one location after the next) is shown in Fig. 6-12. This program uses register indirect addressing. It inputs data from an I/O port to the accumulator. The data are then stored in sequential memory locations. This example may use instructions that you do not yet fully understand. These instructions are explained in greater detail in Chap. 10. What you need to see here is how the indirect memory addressing mode is used.

The program is shown in flowchart form. In the flowchart, each numbered box shows the programming logic for one instruction. Follow the flowchart as you read the numbered steps.

1. The first step in the program is to establish a point where the data file will start. Therefore, to start the program you give the register these data. You use the Load Register Immediate instruction. The reg-

ister now contains the starting address of the data file.

2. We are now ready to load the accumulator. This second instruction inputs data from the I/O port and places them in the accumulator. The Input instruction brings data from I/O port 01.

3. This instruction uses a Store instruction with an indirect address. It stores the accumulator's data in the memory location pointed to by the register. Note: You do not store the data in the register. Rather, you store data in the memory location *pointed to* by the register. Once the data are stored, you will want to get another byte of data and store it in the next memory location.

4. To make the register pair point to the next sequential memory location, you increment the register by one count.

5. Once the register is incremented, it now points to the new memory location. You

105

Introduction to Microprocessors
CHAPTER 6

Jump
instruction

Hypothetical
microcomputer
system

RAM

Read-write
memory

may now repeat the Input and Store instructions. A jump instruction returns you to the Input instruction. You jump back to a point that is *after* the loading of the register that points to memory. You do this because you do not want to reload the register. If you did reload the register you would destroy the incremented memory pointer and keep loading data in the same memory location.

Self-Test

Check your understanding by answering these questions.

10. The kind of memory addressing that takes the least time is
    a. Direct addressing
    b. Extended addressing
    c. Immediate addressing
    d. Inherent addressing

11. When you use immediate addressing, you expect the second byte to be
    a. A memory address between 0_{10} and 255_{10}
    b. 8 bits of data
    c. Easily referred to by many instructions
    d. (All of the above)

12. A 16-bit microprocessor uses a 22-bit address field. That is, it can address 4,194,304 memory locations. A direct-address instruction can address any memory location in a single instruction. The first instruction word is the op code. How many *bytes* are used to make up its longest instruction? Why?

13. Indirect register addressing is so named because the register addressed by the instruction
    a. Is where the data would be stored
    b. Tests the data indirectly
    c. Points to the memory location
    d. Is only used for memory locations 0_{10} to 255_{10}

14. Rank the three memory-addressing modes by speed.

15. Explain why you think direct addressing or register indirect addressing is the simplest form of memory addressing.

6-8 AN ELEMENTARY MICROCOMPUTER

During the rest of this text, we are going to study how to make the microprocessor do what we want. That is, we are going to look at the way the microprocessor solves problems. However, we have already learned that the microprocessor cannot do anything by itself. To be useful, the microprocessor must be part of a microcomputer system.

Microcomputer systems vary from big to small. Obviously, the example of a hand-held microprocessor-based game is an example of a small microcomputer system. On the other hand, a full microcomputer system might have the maximum amount of memory, a CRT terminal for data I/O, a printer for hard copy, and floppy disks for mass storage. Such a system might easily be packaged in a large video terminal about the size of a 15-in [38.1 cm] portable TV with a typewriter keyboard. This system would be a powerful, small, general-purpose computer built around a microprocessor. We find many such computers in the hobby and industrial computer fields.

As you can see, the size of a microcomputer system can vary greatly. No matter what the size, the microprocessor must be joined with the other components of microcomputer system in order to function.

It is hard to study a microprocessor without the other components. Consequently, we will develop a microcomputer system in block diagram form. We will use this hypothetical microcomputer system to demonstrate how the microprocessor works. A block diagram of this system is shown in Fig. 6-13. You can see that the top half of the diagram is made up of the microprocessor we studied in Chap. 3. The added, lower half of the block diagram shows the microcomputer's memory and the I/O ports.

Figure 6-13 also shows a detailed block diagram of the memory used in our microcomputer system. This memory has only sixteen 8-bit words. Our microprocessor can address 65,536 words. Sixteen words, of course, is a much smaller memory than that used by most microcomputer systems. But this microcomputer is designed only to show how a microprocessor works. In later chapters our microcomputer will have a larger memory.

The microcomputer's memory is random-access memory (RAM). This means we can access any word (byte) of memory as easily as we can access any other byte. We do not have to go through any sequence of memory locations to get to any particular byte. Our microcomputer's memory is also *read-write* memory. We can, upon command, either

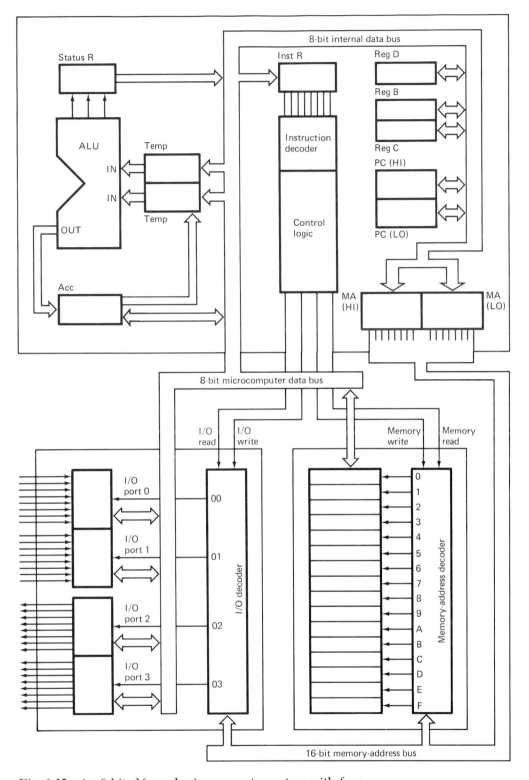

Fig. 6-13   An 8-bit, 16-word microcomputer system with four I/O ports. The microprocessor's internal data bus becomes the microcomputer's data bus to transfer data to and from memory and I/O. The microprocessor's 16-bit memory-address bus is connected to the address decoders in both the memory and I/O sections. Note that the memory uses memory address lines A0 to A3, and the I/O uses memory lines A0 and A1. Both I/O and memory use all 8 data bus bits D0 and D7.

read data from the memory word or write data into the memory word. Writing data into the memory word is also called *storing*.

The microcomputer's memory system is connected to the microprocessor by three different kinds of connections:

1. The memory-address lines
2. The data lines
3. The control lines

Most devices connected to a microprocessor have all these connections.

The data on the memory-address lines are used to identify the memory locations or devices with which the microprocessor wants to communicate. These memory-address lines only carry data out of the microprocessor. They are unidirectional.

At any given time, the data lines carry a single word of data into or out of the microprocessor. They are bidirectional lines. The data lines carry data words from the microprocessor's internal data bus to and from memory or I/O.

The control lines let the microprocessor control or operate external devices. These lines tell external devices when to put data onto the data bus and when to take data from the data bus. The control lines also make sure that data transfers take place in the proper order. For example, the control lines make sure that the memory is not told to read data from the bus until the address lines have a stable address at their output.

Each one of the memory words has a number. This number is the address or location of the memory word. When we wish to read from or write into a certain memory word, we address that word's location. The address is a binary word. That binary word appears on the microprocessor's address bus. The binary word is then decoded by the memory's address decoder. When the memory address bus has a valid memory address, the microprocessor's control logic puts out a Memory Read or Memory Write pulse on its control lines. These pulses tell the memory system either to place data on the bus or to write data from the bus into the selected memory location.

Whenever data are written into a memory location, the location's old contents are erased. But reading data does not erase the contents. You may read data from a memory

location as many times as you want. Such reading is called a nondestructive Read operation.

The input/output section of the microcomputer is made up of I/O ports 00, 01, 02, and 03. These four ports are equally split between input ports and output ports. That is, there are two of each.

Ports 00 and 01 are inputs. These ports each have eight input lines. When port 00 or port 01 is addressed, the data on these input lines are placed on the microcomputer's data bus. The microprocessor then places these data in the accumulator.

Ports 02 and 03 are output ports. These ports each have eight output lines. The status of each output line is held by a data latch. When port 02 or port 03 is addressed, the 8 bits of data on the microcomputer's data bus are stored in the addressed output port's data latch. These data are then held for use by the outside world. The data are held until the port is addressed again or until power is shut off.

I/O ports 00 to 03 are called parallel I/O ports. That is, the data are connected to the outside world through eight parallel lines. A parallel I/O port is the basic I/O design.

A serial I/O port uses a *shift register* to convert parallel data to serial data or to convert serial data to parallel data. Serial I/O is used whenever data must be sent over long distances. After the distance reaches a certain point, it is easier to install parallel-to-serial converter circuits than it is to run eight parallel lines. Our microcomputer will not have a serial I/O port until Chap. 12.

The I/O address decoder is just like the memory-address decoder. Since there are only four I/O ports, however, only two address lines are needed. The I/O address decoder decodes all addresses sent out from the microprocessor. However, the I/O ports respond to their addresses only when an I/O Read or an I/O Write pulse happens at the same time the address is decoded.

The microcomputer's bus is made up of a few basic signals. There are eight data lines, all bidirectional. That is, they carry data both into and out of the microprocessor. They are an extension of the microprocessor's internal data bus. The microprocessor's 16-bit memory-address bus is connected to the address decoders in both the memory and I/O sections. The 16 memory-address lines are used to address memory and I/O devices. Four additional lines have the memory and I/O read-write signals. The bus also contains power and ground. There are also a few other timing and control signals. These are discussed in a later chapter.

Self-Test

Check your understanding by answering these questions.

16. A microcomputer uses a 16-bit memory-address bus. This gives the microcomputer the ability to address
    a. 65,536 memory words
    b. 16 eight-bit memory words
    c. 65,536 eight-bit memory words
    d. 32,768 single-byte memory words

17. A microcomputer's bus is made up of the ___?___ lines.
    a. Data
    b. Memory-address
    c. Control and power
    d. (All of the above)

18. A microcomputer has four I/O ports. The four ports each have eight data lines. These ports are
    a. Parallel input/output ports
    b. Used to output addresses
    c. Serial input ports
    d. Serial output ports

19. The purpose of the 8-bit bidirectional data bus is *not* to
    a. Connect memory and I/O devices to the microprocessor's internal data bus
    b. Address I/O devices
    c. Move data from the microprocessor to the memory
    d. Move input data to the microprocessor's internal data bus

20. A microprocessor's control lines
    a. Issue Memory Read pulses
    b. Issue Memory Write pulses
    c. Issue I/O read-write pulses
    d. (All of the above)

21. A microprocessor's address bus is
    a. 8 bits wide
    b. 16 bits wide
    c. Bidirectional
    d. Unidirectional

Summary

1. An instruction is a binary word that tells the processor to do one task. Most instructions let you move or process data.
2. A microprocessor's instruction set is all the instructions that the microprocessor can carry out.
3. An instruction may be made up of one, two, or three instruction words.
4. The instruction has two parts: the op code and the address.
5. The microprocessor has many addressing modes for each op code. This makes many different instructions possible.
6. A mnemonic is a three-or four-letter abbreviation that stands for the binary op code. The mnemonic's operand is also an abbreviation unless the binary number is meaningful like a specific memory location or data.
7. You write code for an assembler using mnemonics.
8. The instruction's op code is contained in the first word. A second word or second and third words are added if a memory location or a data word is part of the instruction.

9. The instruction's speed is measured by the number of microprocessor cycles it takes. The simplest instructions take two cycles.
10. Inherent addressing means that the first instruction word has both the op code and the address. Usually this means that the address is a register.
11. An instruction with immediate addressing has the data to be worked on as the instruction's second word.
12. An instruction using direct addressing points *directly* to a memory location.
13. A direct instruction must be two or three words long. The second word or the second and third words are the address of a memory location.
14. The length of the address part of the instruction depends on how much memory a microprocessor can address and on the length of a data word.
15. Direct addressing in most 8-bit microprocessors takes two address words (bytes) to address 65,536 words. Some microprocessors have a shortened form of direct addressing.

The shortened form addresses only a small amount of memory. The extended form of direct addressing addresses all memory locations.

16. Register indirect addressing points to a register that points to the memory location. It is a single-word instruction.

Chapter Review Questions

6-1. A microprocessor instruction is a(n) ____?____ word that has a unique meaning to the processor's control logic.
    a. Decimal   c. Binary
    b. Hexadecimal   d. Octal

6-2. A microprocessor's instruction word tells the microprocessor
    a. That the data are in memory
    b. That the data are in a register
    c. That there are 8-bits of data
    d. What to do

6-3. In an 8-bit microprocessor, an instruction can be ____?____ bits long.
    a. 8   c. 24
    b. 16   d. (All of the above)

6-4. What is meant by a microprocessor's "instruction set"?

6-5. What are the two parts of an instruction? What does each part do?

6-6. A mnemonic is an English abbreviation that is used in place of the microprocessor's ____?____ .

6-7. Why do we use mnemonics?

6-8. There may be a number of different forms of the same instruction. Each one uses the same op code but has a different
    a. Length   c. Data word
    b. Addressing mode   d. Speed

6-9. The object of the op code is the op code's operand. Some operands are given as binary (hex or octal) numbers and some are English abbreviations. Why?

6-10. The instruction's op code is its ____?____ word. The other word(s) is (are) memory locations or data.
    a. First   c. Third
    b. Second   d. (All of the above)

6-11. An instruction using inherent addressing will be ____?____ bytes long in an 8-bit microprocessor.
    a. 1   c. 3   e. 5   g. 7
    b. 2   d. 4   f. 6   h. 8

6-12. You find a microprocessor instruction that has data in its second byte. This instruction uses ____?____ addressing.
    a. Direct   c. Inherent
    b. Immediate   d. Register indirect

6-13. An 8-bit microprocessor's second and third instruction bytes point to a memory location. This instruction uses ____?____ addressing.
    a. Direct   c. Inherent
    b. Immediate   d. Register indirect

6-14. The instructions in the _____?_____ addressing mode use the greatest number of microprocessor cycles.
    a. Direct   c. Inherent
    b. Immediate   d. Register indirect

6-15. The _____?_____ addressing mode lets you address any memory location with a single-word instruction.
    a. Direct   c. Inherent
    b. Immediate   d. Register indirect

6-16. Try to guess what the following instructions are and what addressing mode they use:
    a. CLA A   *e*. AND B
    b. STA 34 DE   *f*. LDA 2E
    c. ADD 56   *g*. HLT
    d. INC B   *h*. JMP 105A

6-17. The microprocessor's internal data bus is connected to the microcomputer's
    a. Memory-address bus
    b. Data bus
    c. Memory-address decoder
    d. I/O address decoder

6-18. The microprocessor's control lines do not issue
    a. Memory Read pulses
    b. Memory Write pulses
    c. Memory-address pulses
    d. I/O read-write pulses

Answers to Self-Tests

1. a. 2. d. 3. b. 4. b.
5. 303_8 is the op code, and JMP is the mnemonic. The mnemonic is the English abbreviation used to represent instruction. The op code is the digital word expressed in octal in this example.
6. CLA = Clear
   NOP = No Operation
   MOV = Move
   HLT = Halt
   INC = Increment
   ADD = Add
   AND = Logic AND
   DEC = Decrement
7. No. The mnemonic is just an abbreviation and has nothing to do with the actual binary number's length.
8. Op code.
9. Yes. Somehow you must be able to tell all instructions apart.
10. d.   11. b.

12. Four bytes, because it needs more than 16 bits and adding the third word adds another 16 bits (2 bytes).
13. c.
14. Fastest   Inherent
    Next   Immediate
    Slowest   Direct
15. Register indirect needs to have the register pair preset, but direct takes three bytes.
16. a.   17. d.   18. a.
19. b.   20. d.   21. d.

The Data-Transfer Instructions

■ This chapter gives you a more detailed look at the microprocessor's data-transfer instructions. These instructions are the ones used to move data from one location in the microprocessor to another. These instructions are very important because in using a microprocessor you continually move data back and forth between different locations.

The instructions in this chapter have been developed for our model microprocessor. However, our microprocessor's instructions are very much like those used by almost every commercially available microprocessor. Therefore, you can learn a great deal from them. You will learn some of the elements common to many microprocessor instruction sets. You will also learn to analyze the information usually given about a particular microprocessor's instruction set. Then you will be able to learn the instruction set of a new microprocessor quickly and thoroughly. This knowledge is essential for programming, for designing hardware, and for servicing the microprocessor.

After you have studied the microprocessor's instruction set, you will look at a very detailed example of a program. You will see how the microprocessor uses its instructions to solve a problem.

7-1 HINTS ON STUDYING THE INSTRUCTION-SET SECTIONS

In the following sections, each new instruction is introduced in paragraph form. The paragraph and the accompanying data give you all the basic information that you need to know about the instruction.

In most cases, you will find the microprocessor instructions self-explanatory. When they are not self-explanatory, however, the description in the paragraph explains them clearly.

After you review each instruction you should know all eight items on the following checklist.

1. The instruction's name
2. The type of addressing that the instruction uses
3. The instruction's mnemonic
4. How the instruction will be found in memory
5. How to show the instruction's operation using symbols from Boolean algebra
6. How to explain what the instruction does
7. How long the instruction is
8. How executing the instruction affects the microprocessor's status register

All the paragraphs about instructions are presented in the same format. You will find that most manufacturers show information about their microprocessors in a format similar to the one used here.

Figure 7-1 shows a sample paragraph introducing one of the instructions of our textbook microprocessor. The dark numbers in Fig. 7-1 show where each of the eight items on our checklist can be found. Note that each box shown above the paragraph stands for one byte in the instruction.

As you read each of these paragraphs and study the accompanying information, be sure that you find each of the eight items on the checklist. Later you can use the same checklist as you review a commercial microprocessor's instruction set. If the manufacturer's literature on the microprocessor does not contain all eight items about each instruction,

STORE ACCUMULATOR, DIRECT

3

STA A, Address

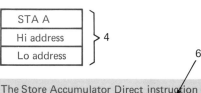

The Store Accumulator Direct instruction copies the data in the accumulator into memory. The memory location is pointed to by the second and third bytes of the instruction. For example, the instruction STA A, 001F copies the contents of the accumulator into the memory location 001F. When the instruction is executed you will find the same data in both the accumulator and memory location 001F. This is a 3-byte instruction which takes five microprocessor cycles. This instruction does not change any status register bits.

Fig. 7-1 Reading the instruction data. This figure is typical of how a microprocessor manufacturer presents data on a microprocessor's instructions.
1. Instruction name
2. Addressing
3. Mnemonic
4. Memory map
5. Boolean description
6. A written description
7. Instruction's length
8. Status register impact

then the manufacturer has not provided all the necessary information.

When studying instructions, you should be aware that manufacturers do not all use the same name for the same instruction. Be sure that you understand exactly what each instruction does in the particular microprocessor that you are working with. Our eight-point checklist will help you gain the necessary understanding of each instruction.

7-2 THE DATA-TRANSFER INSTRUCTIONS

In this section we look at the data-transfer instructions, also called the "data-handling" instructions. These instructions are used to move data to and from the microcomputer's different data-storage areas. The storage areas include both memory locations and reg-

isters. Depending on what parts of the microcomputer are involved in the data transfer, these instructions are referred to as Load instructions, Move instructions, or Store instructions.

The data-transfer instructions probably should be called "copy" instructions, because they really just move a *copy* of the data. For example, one instruction transfers data from the accumulator to a memory location. After the execution of this instruction, the same data will be found in both the memory location and the accumulator. Rarely is a data-transfer instruction designed to destroy the source data.

Like any other instruction, a data-transfer instruction can be broken into two parts: its op code and its address. All data-transfer instructions must specify both a source and a destination for the data.

The op code of a data-transfer instruction specifies both the data source and the form of addressing. The addressing can take one of three forms: immediate, direct, or indirect. The destination is specified by the address.

An 8-bit microprocessor can have 1-, 2-, and 3-byte data-transfer instructions. In the following paragraphs, we will look at data-transfer instructions of each length.

LOAD REGISTER IMMEDIATE   Data → r
LDA r, Data

LDA r
Data

The Load Register Immediate instruction loads register r with the data contained in the instruction's second byte. For example, LDA A loads the data into the accumulator. LDA B loads the data into register B. The Load Register Immediate instruction is a 2-byte instruction that takes 3 microprocessor cycles. If executing this instruction yields a zero result or a "1" in the MSB, then the appropriate bit in the status register is set.*

LOAD REGISTER DIRECT   M → r
LDD r, Address

LDD r
Hi address
Lo address

* Remember that our microprocessor's negative bit is set if a "1" appears in the most significant bit of the result.

Load register
direct

Load
accumulator
indirect

Load register
pair immediate

Move register to
register

Store
accumulator
direct

Store
accumulator
indirect

The Load Register Direct instruction copies data from the addressed memory location to the register r. The second and third bytes of the instruction point to the memory location from which the data are copied. For example, LDD C, 0F1C copies the data in memory location 0F1C into register C. This is a 3-byte instruction that takes four microprocessor cycles. If executing this instruction yields a zero result or a "1" in the MSB, then the appropriate bit in the status register is set.

LOAD ACCUMULATOR INDIRECT   M → A
LDI A

LDI A

The Load Accumulator Indirect instruction copies data from the memory location to the accumulator. The BC register pair points to the memory location from which the data are copied. Note: The BC register pair must contain the correct address before this instruction can be used. This is a single-byte instruction that uses two microprocessor cycles. If executing this instruction yields a zero result or a "1" in the MSB, the appropriate bit in the status register is set.

LOAD REGISTER PAIR IMMEDIATE
LRP B,Data
M → C
(M + 1) → B

LRP B
Hi byte of data
Lo byte of data

The Load Register Pair Immediate instruction loads the 16-bit BC register pair with the data contained in the instruction's second and third bytes. This is a 3-byte instruction that takes three microprocessor cycles. Note: This instruction saves three microprocessor cycles over using an LDA B followed by an LDA C. Executing this instruction does not change any status register bits.

MOVE REGISTER TO REGISTER   r2 → r1
MOV r1,r2

MOV r1,r2

The Move Register to Register instruction loads register r1 with a copy of the data in register r2. For example, the MOV B,A loads a copy of the data in the accumulator (register A) into register B. This is a single-byte in-

struction that takes two microprocessor cycles. If executing this instruction yields a "1" in the MSB or a zero result, then the appropriate bit in the status register is set.

STORE ACCUMULATOR DIRECT   A → M
STA A,Address

STA A
Hi address
Lo address

The Store Accumulator Direct instruction copies data from the accumulator into memory. The second and third bytes of the instruction point to the memory location that receives the copied data. For example, the instruction STA A,001F copies the contents of the accumulator into memory location 001F. After the instruction is executed, the same data will be in both the accumulator and memory location 001F. This is a 3-byte instruction that takes five microprocessor cycles. This instruction does not change any status register bits.

STORE ACCUMULATOR INDIRECT
STI A
A → M

STI A

The Store Accumulator Indirect instruction copies data from the accumulator into memory. The BC register pair points to the memory location that receives the copied data. Note: The BC register pair must contain the correct address before this instruction can be used. This is a single-byte instruction that uses two microprocessor cycles. This instruction does not change any status register bits.

Self-Test

Check your understanding by answering these questions.

1. The Move instruction is used to
   a. Transfer the instruction's second data byte into the indicated register
   b. Transfer the accumulator's contents into memory
   c. Transfer the contents of one register to another register
   d. Transfer indirectly addressed data into a register

2. Explain the difference between the LDA A and the LDD A instruction. Which one takes the greatest execution time?

3. Show how the LDA B and the LDA C instructions can be used to take the place of the LRP B instruction. What is the disadvantage of using the two-instruction method?

4. Explain the difference between the STA A and the LDD A instructions. Why don't they both do the same job?

5. You have data in the B register. You need to store these data in memory location 01FF. What two instructions would you use? Give a brief description using a flowchart showing what each instruction does.

6. The BC register pair is being used as a 16-bit counter. Approximately once every 0.1 second(s), the counter program "wakes up." When the program wakes up it brings the data into the BC register pair, adds the appropriate number of counts, and stores the 16-bit number back in memory. The 16-bit number is kept in memory locations 00F0 (hi byte) and 00F1 (lo byte). What data-transfer instructions are needed to do this job? Complete the flowchart shown in Fig. 7-2. What memory locations do the instructions occupy?

7-3 A PROGRAM EXAMPLE

In this section, we watch a microprocessor as it solves a problem step by step. We will use the program described earlier that brings data

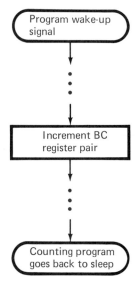

Fig. 7-2 The flowchart for self-test question 6.

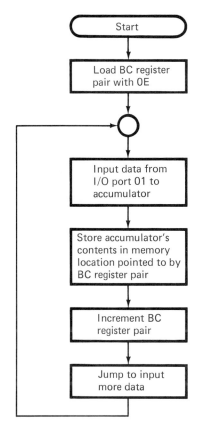

Fig. 7-3 A data-storage program. This program uses the BC register pair for register indirect addressing.

Data file

in from I/O port 01 and places the data in sequential memory locations. In other words, the program creates a data file. We first looked at this program in Fig. 6-12.

The program is flowcharted again in Fig. 7-3. This time the flowchart process blocks use data-transfer instructions. Data are input at port 01. The Input instruction transfers the data from port 01 to the accumulator. From the accumulator, the data are moved into sequential memory locations. The data file starts at memory location 000E.

Looking at the flowchart you can see that this is really only part of a program. There is no terminator. We have not provided a way to end the program. We will see later how the program can be ended.

This program uses three instructions that you have not yet studied. These are the Input, Increment, and jump instructions. We will review each instruction in detail later. To understand this example, you need to know only a little about these new instructions.

The Input instruction can be treated as a 2-

115

byte Load Accumulator Direct data-transfer instruction.

The Increment instruction adds one count to the register each time it is executed.

The jump instruction loads the program counter with a new value that is contained in the instruction's second and third bytes.

As we step through this program, we will take "stop-action snapshots" of the microcomputer system. We will take one snapshot as each microprocessor cycle is completed. That is, we will look at the state of the microcomputer system after each Fetch cycle and after each Execute cycle. You will be able to see how data flow from the I/O port to the register, and then to the memory location.

As you follow this example, be sure to note the changes in the black-outlined parts of the figures showing the microcomputer system. Compare each figure to the previous figure. It is important that you follow each change throughout the program's execution.

In this example, all memory and register contents are shown in hexadecimal notation. Subscripts are not shown. You should keep in mind that the actual contents of these locations are eight bits at either a logic "1" or logic "0." That is, you should not forget that you are working with binary hardware. The hexadecimal numbers are simply a convenient way to represent the status of the hardware.

In some diagrams, you can see blank memory locations and registers. That is, no data are shown. Blanks indicate that the data in the register or memory location are random and, therefore, are of no interest for our present purposes. Of course, no register or memory location is ever truly without data. Both register and memory locations always contain some number between all logic "0s" (00) and all logic "1s" (FF).

Figure 7-4 (page 118) shows the microcomputer system just before we are ready to execute the program. As you can see, the program is stored in memory locations 0000 through 0009. The program starts at memory location 0000. We have set the program counter to all "0s." Setting the program counter before the program execution is called "initializing" the program counter. Program execution will start with the instruction loaded at memory location 0000.

Figure 7-4 shows blanks for the contents of other memory locations and registers. As explained above, blanks indicate that the con-

tents do not matter at the time shown by the figure.

Figure 7-5 (page 119) shows the first Fetch cycle. The instruction Load Register Pair Immediate takes one Fetch and two Execute cycles—a total of three microprocessor cycles. Looking at Fig. 7-5, you can see this instruction is 3 bytes long. The 3-byte instruction is stored in memory locations 0000, 0001, and 0002.

In Figure 7-5 we begin executing the first instruction's Fetch cycle. The program counter's contents are loaded into the memory-address register. This places the binary value for memory location 0000 on the memory-address bus. Once the memory-address lines are valid (that is, once the voltages have settled), the control logic puts out a Memory Read command. The address information on the memory-address bus is decoded and the decoder selects memory word 0000.

When the memory receives the Read command, the contents of memory word 0000 (Load Register Pair Immediate) are placed on the microcomputer's data bus.

Because this is the Fetch cycle, the instruction is transferred to the microprocessor's instruction register. The instruction register is connected to the microprocessor's internal data bus during the Fetch cycle.*

The first instruction's Fetch cycle is complete. The contents of the program's first instruction have been transferred to the microprocessor's instruction register. The microprocessor can now begin executing this instruction.

Figure 7-6 (page 120) shows what happens during the first half of the Load Register Pair Immediate's execution cycle. That is, it shows the results of executing the second microprocessor cycle in this three-cycle instruction. When the Load Register Pair Immediate instruction is decoded, the control logic immediately notes that this is a 3-byte instruction. As you can see, the program counter is incremented three counts. It is now pointing to the *next* instruction. This instruction just happens to be in memory location 0003.

The memory-address register points to location 0001. This is because the control logic knows that memory location 0001 contains

* Remember, the Fetch cycle loads the instruction register. All other cycles are Execute cycles, even though they may be getting data from memory. They are Execute cycles because the instruction is being executed.

the instruction's second byte. Memory location 0001 has the data that we want to put in the BC register pair's hi byte.

Memory address 0001 is placed on the memory-address bus. The address is decoded by the memory-address decoder circuits. The decoder activates memory location 0001. Then the contents (00) of memory location 0001 are placed on the data bus. The data (00) are loaded into the hi byte of the general-purpose BC register pair. Execution of the first half of the Execute cycle is now complete.

The second half of the first instruction's Execute cycle is shown in Fig. 7-7 (page 121). Note: The program counter is still pointing to memory location 0003, the address of the *next* instruction. You are not ready to change the program counter yet.

The control logic now points the memory-address register to memory location 0002. This location contains the third byte of the Load Register Pair Immediate instruction. The memory-address register places the address on the memory-address bus, and then the memory-address decoder decodes the address. The control logic generates a Memory Read pulse and the contents of memory location 0002 are placed on the data bus. The data (0E) from this location are transferred to the lower byte of the BC register pair.

The instruction Load Register Pair Immediate is now complete. The BC register pair is loaded with the data 000E. The control logic knows that is has finished executing a complete instruction cycle. Now the control logic starts a new Fetch cycle.

In Figs. 7-8, 7-9, and 7-10 (pages 122 to 124) we observe the microcomputer system as it completes the three-cycle, 2-byte Input instruction. The Input instruction causes data to be transferred from input port 01 to the accumulator. Our microprocessor is not powerful enough to move data directly from an input port to a memory location.

Figure 7-8 shows this instruction's Fetch cycle. The program counter's contents are loaded into the memory-address register. The memory-address register places the address (memory location 0003) on the memory-address bus. The memory-address decoder decodes the memory address. The control logic generates a Memory Read pulse telling the memory to place the contents of memory location 0003 on the data bus. Then the

Input instruction is transferred into the microprocessor's instruction register. That completes the Fetch cycle.

Figure 7-9 shows the first half of the Execute cycle. The Input instruction is decoded. Because the instruction is 2 bytes long, the control logic immediately increments the program counter so that it points to memory location 0005. This, of course, is the address of the *next* instruction.

Because this is a 2-byte instruction, the control logic makes the memory-address register point to the next memory location, which is location 0004. The memory-address register places this address on the memory-address bus. The memory-address decoder decodes the memory address. A Memory Read pulse tells the memory to place the contents of memory location 0004 on the microcomputer's data bus. The data (01) are stored in the memory-address register's lo byte on $\phi 2$ of the microprocessor's clock. Note that the memory-address register holds two different numbers during this cycle: first the memory address, and then the data 01.

In Fig. 7-10 we execute the third cycle of the program's second instruction. This is the last half of the Execute portion of this instruction. The memory-address lines are XX01. The X's indicate that the contents of the hi byte do not matter. The address 01 is on the lo byte's eight lines. This time, the control logic issues an I/O Read pulse. Therefore, the I/O logic, not the memory logic, is used. The I/O decoder receives an I/O Read pulse. This pulse tells the data-input circuits to place the data currently at input port 01 on the microcomputer's data bus. The data from port 01 are transferred to the microprocessor's accumulator.

This completes the execution of the second instruction. The contents of input port 01 (the first data word) are now stored in the accumulator.

In Figs. 7-11 and 7-12 (pages 125, 126), the microcomputer system executes the 2-cycle, 1-byte Store Indirect instruction. This instruction stores the contents of accumulator (the first data word) in the memory location pointed to by the BC register pair.

Figure 7-11 shows this instruction's Fetch cycle. The program counter's contents are transferred to the memory-address register. The memory-address register places the address 0005 on the memory-address bus. The

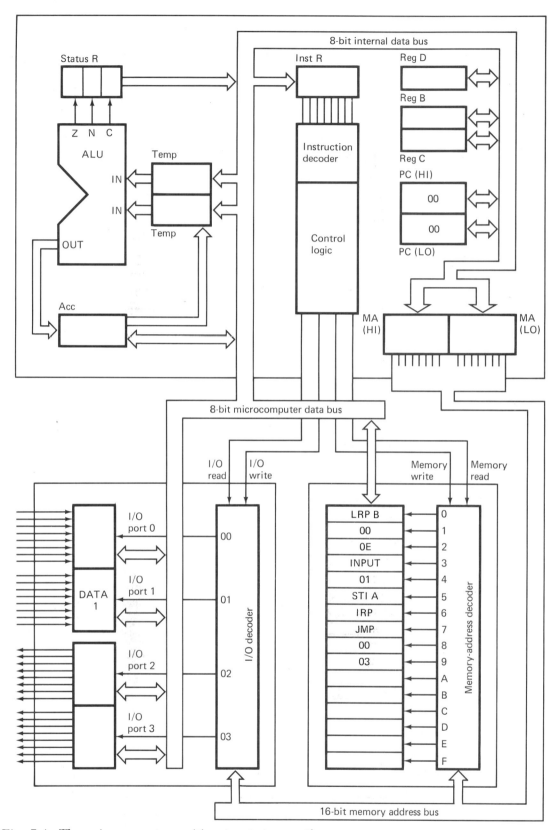

Fig. 7-4 The microcomputer waiting to start executing a program. Memory locations 0000 through 000F are marked as 0 through F at the memory-address decoder's outputs.

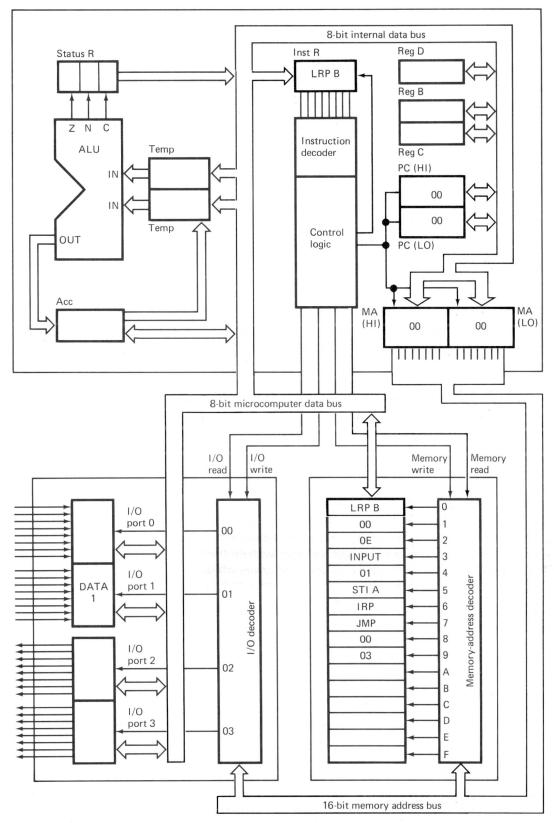

Fig. 7-5 The first Fetch cycle. The LRP B instruction is loaded into the microprocessor's instruction register.

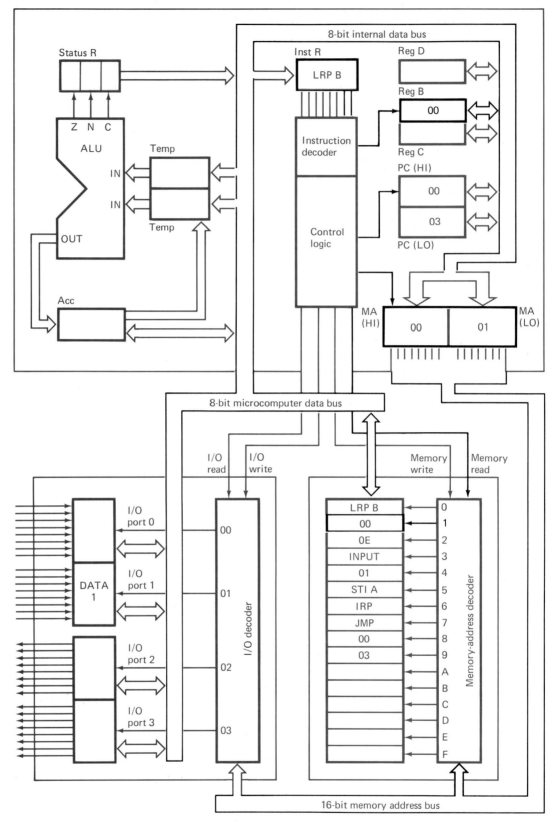

Fig. 7-6 The first half of the Execute cycle. The data from memory location 0001 is loaded into register B. This is the first half of a Load Register Pair instruction.

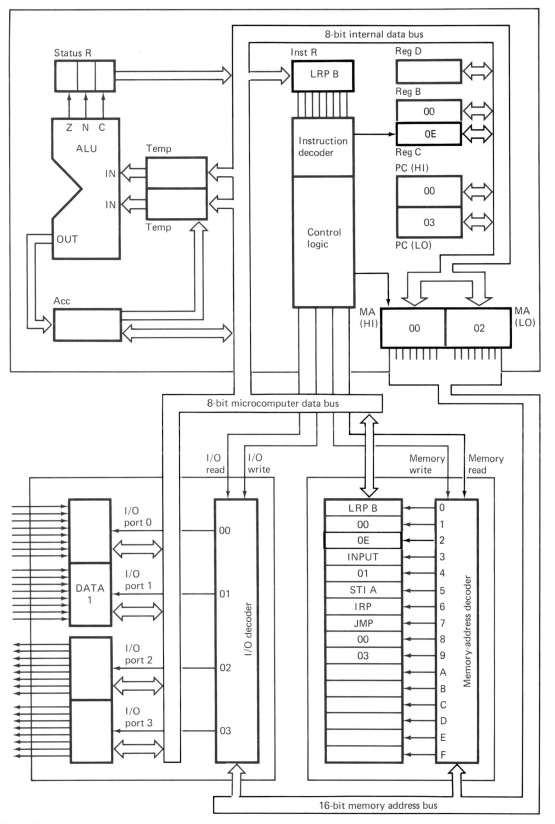

Fig. 7-7   The second half of the Execute cycle.   The data from
memory location 0002 is loaded into register C completing the
Load Register Pair instruction.

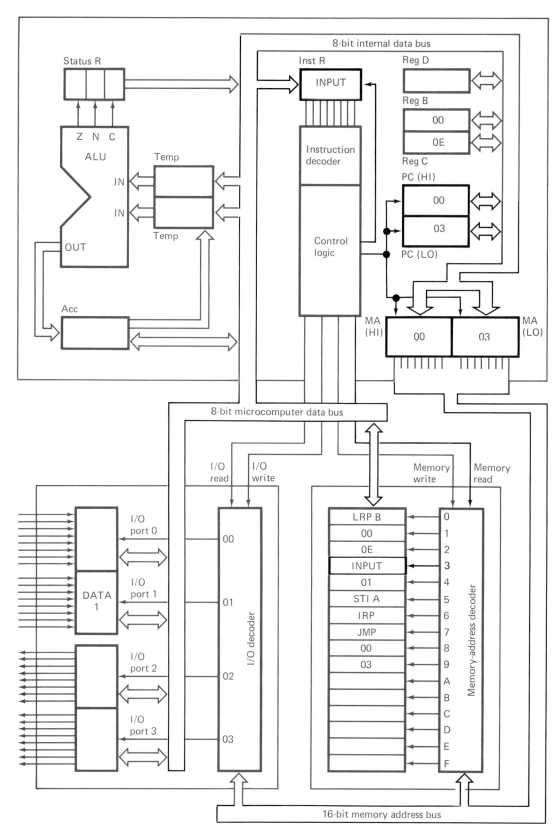

Fig. 7-8   Fetching the Input instruction.   The beginning of the
second instruction.

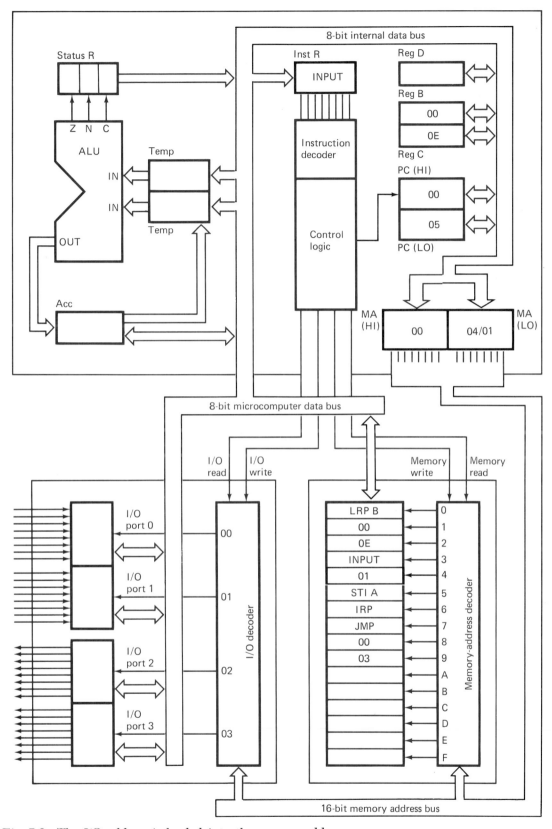

Fig. 7-9 The I/O address is loaded into the memory-address
register's lo byte.

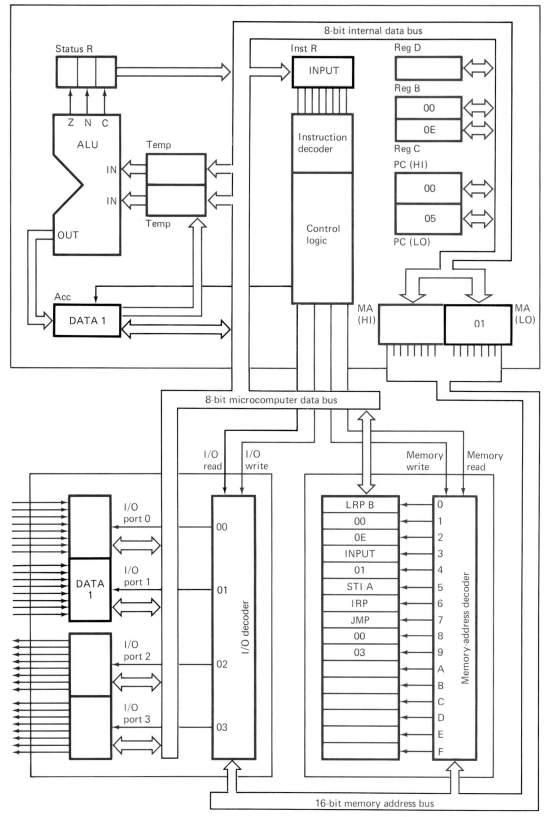

Fig. 7-10 The first I/O data transfer. The 8-bit data word
(DATA 1) is transferred from the 8-input lines on I/O port 01
to the accumulator.

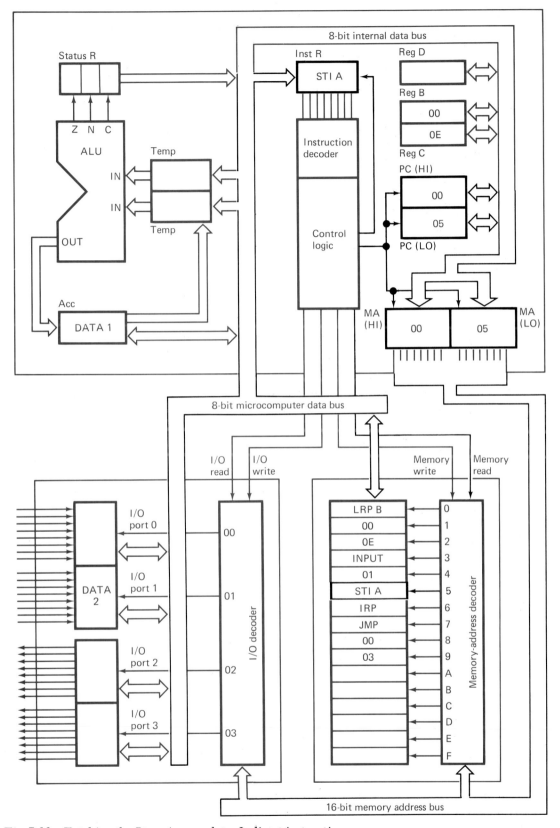

Fig. 7-11 Fetching the Store Accumulator Indirect instruction.

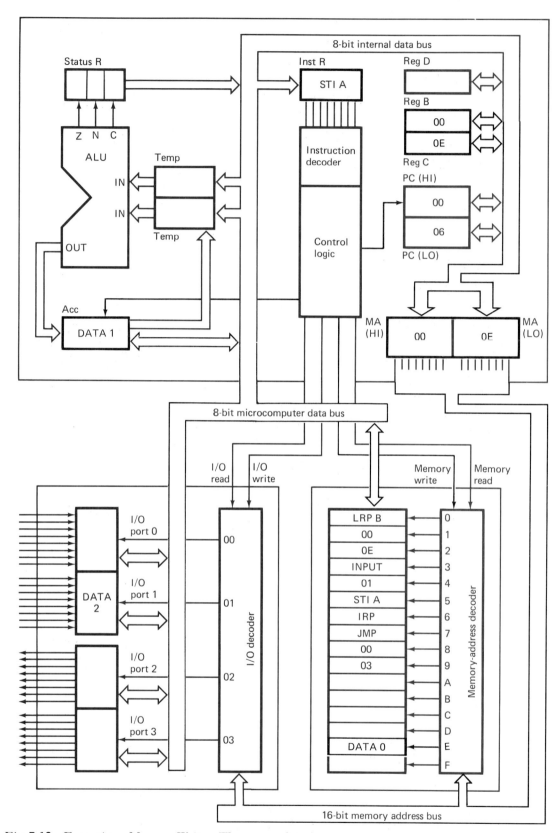

Fig. 7-12 Executing a Memory Write. The accumulator's contents (DATA 1) are written into memory location 000E. The memory address comes from the BC register pair.

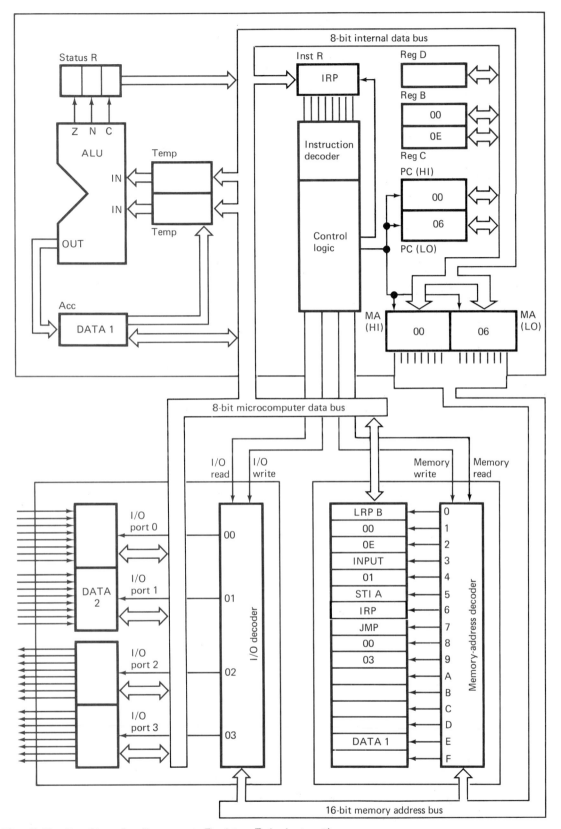

Fig. 7-13 Loading the Increment Register Pair instruction.
The previous data (DATA 1) are still in the accumulator and
will be until it is overwritten or cleared.

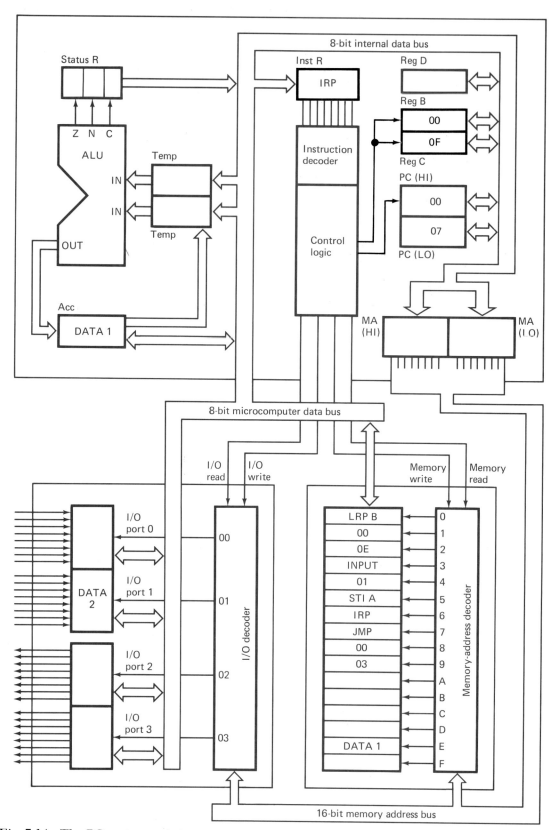

Fig. 7-14 The BC register pair is incremented from 000E to
000F. The program counter is also incremented to point to the
JMP instruction.

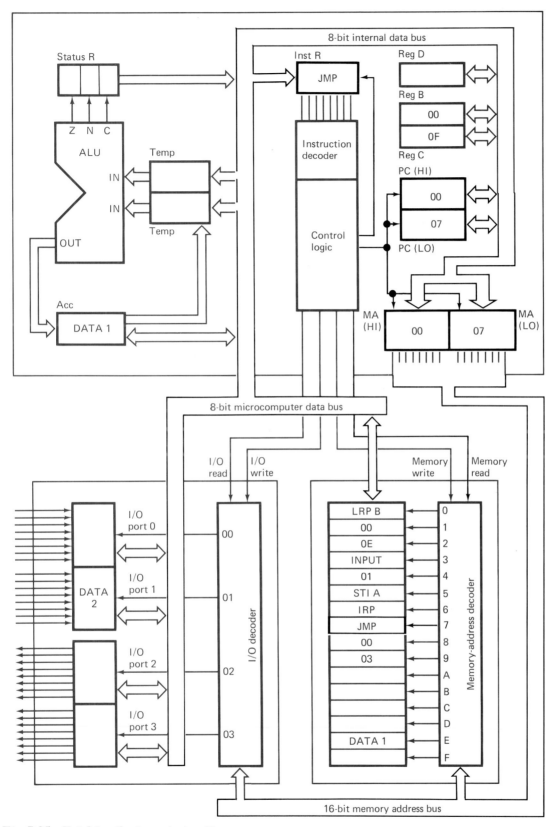

Fig. 7-15   Fetching the jump instruction.

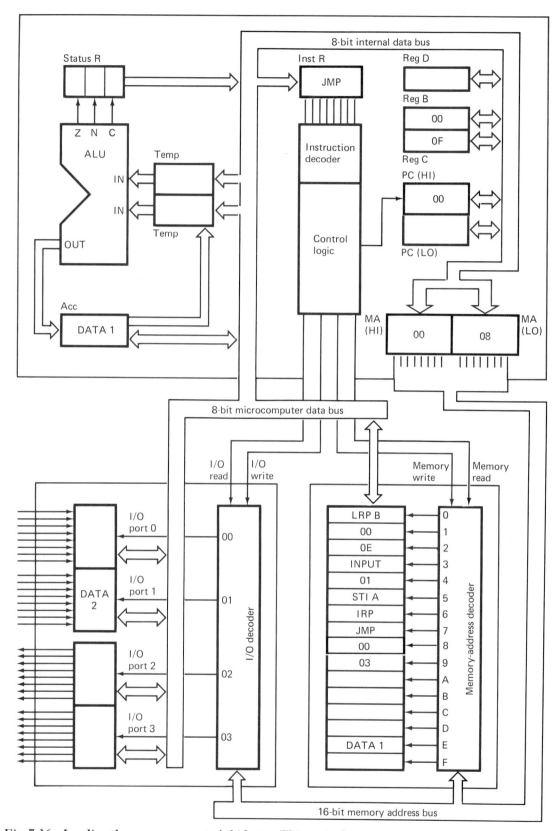

Fig. 7-16 Loading the program counter's hi byte. This part of
the instruction starts the actual modification of the program
counter's contents.

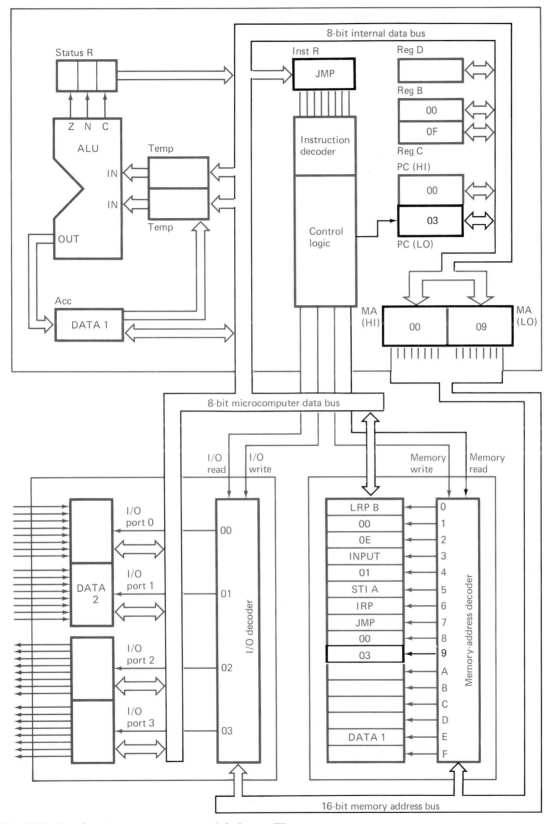

Fig. 7-17 Loading the program counter's lo byte. The program counter now points to memory location 0003_{16}. The microprocessor will take the next instruction from this memory location instead of taking the next higher instruction after JMP.

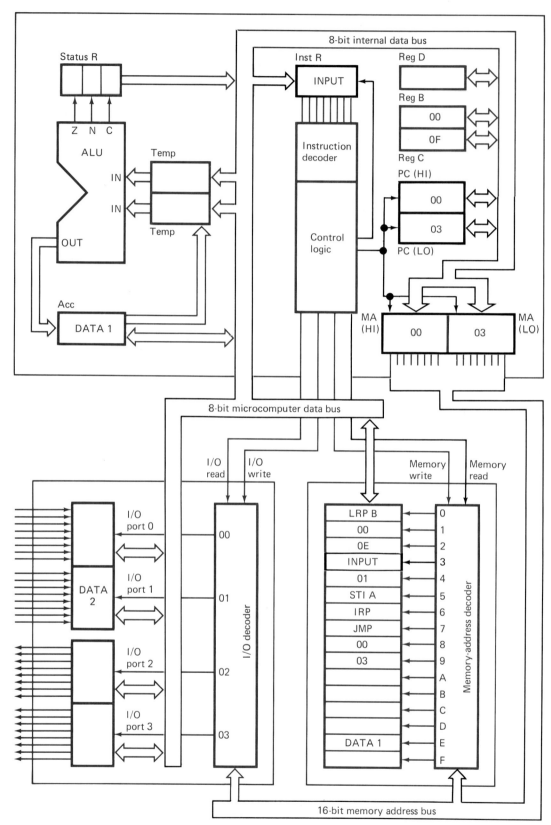

Fig. 7-18 Fetching the Input instruction for the second time.
We have jumped back to get more data.

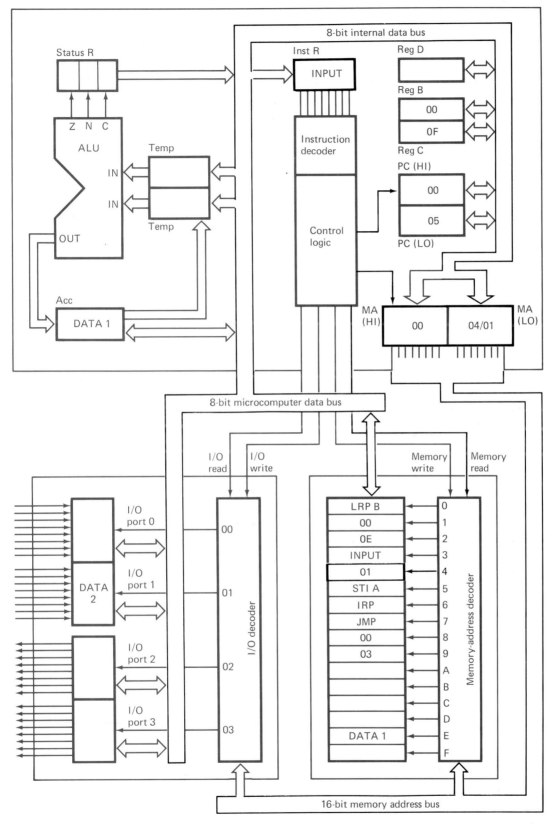

Fig. 7-19 The I/O address is loaded into the memory-address register's lo byte.

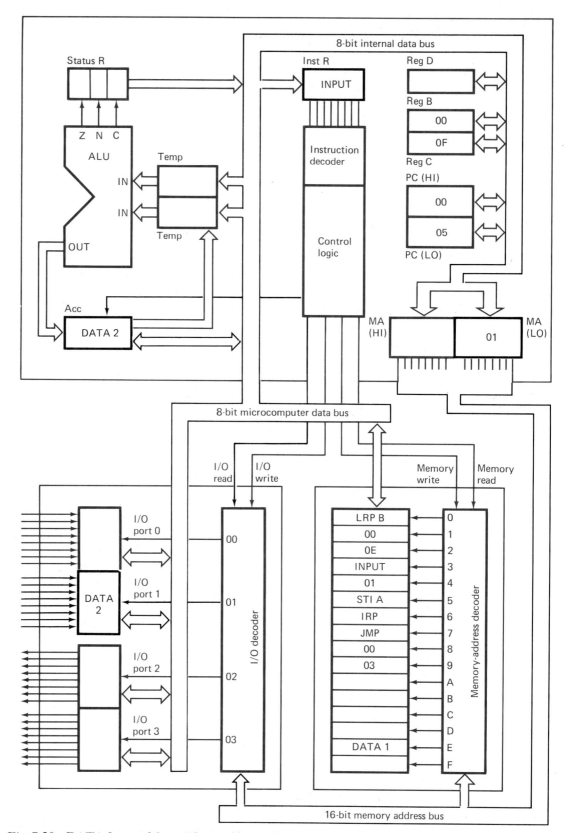

Fig. 7-20   DATA 2 moved from I/O port 01 into the accumulator.   Note that DATA 2 overwrites DATA 1 in the accumulator.

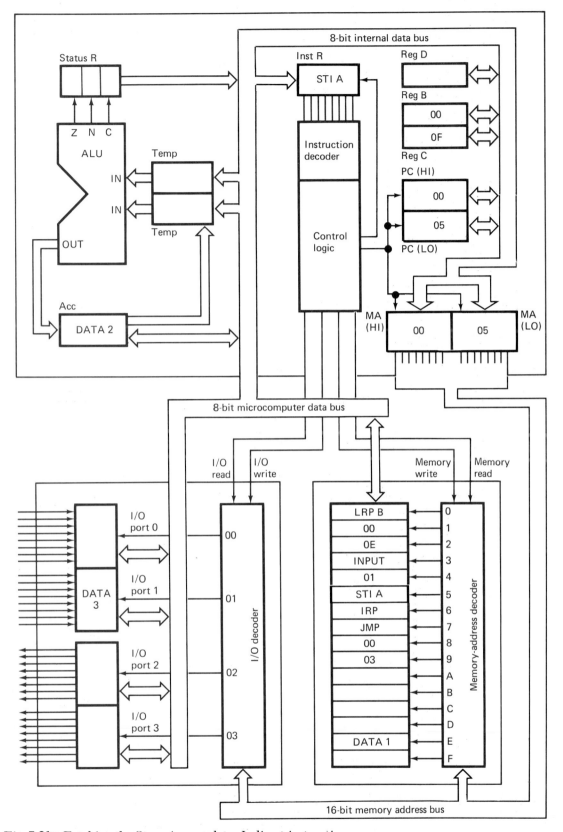

Fig. 7-21   Fetching the Store Accumulator Indirect instruction
for the second time.

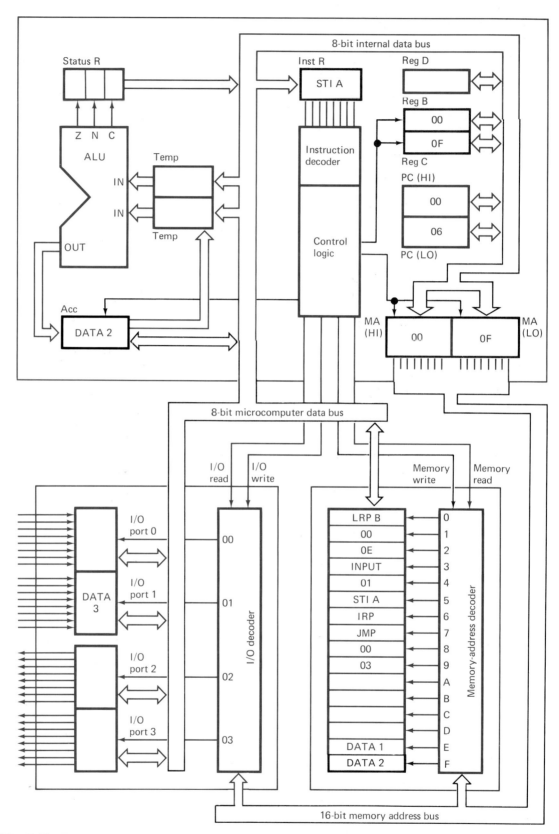

Fig. 7-22 The Execute cycle of the second Store Accumulator Indirect instruction. DATA 2 is stored at memory location 000F using the Store Accumulator Register Indirect instruction. Note that the memory address register was loaded with the BC register pair's contents. The incremented value points to the new memory location.

memory-address decoder receives and decodes this address. The control circuits send a Memory Read pulse. The memory system places the contents of memory location 0005 on the data bus. The contents of memory location 0005 (Store Indirect) are transferred to the microprocessor's instruction register.

Figure 7-12 shows the microcomputer's state after this instruction is executed. In decoding the Store instruction, the control logic finds that this is a single-byte instruction. The control logic increments the program counter by one location. The program counter now points to the next instruction.

The contents of the BC register pair (000E) are transferred to the memory-address register. Using this information as a memory address, the memory-address register places 000E on the memory-address bus. At the same time, the accumulator's contents are placed on the microprocessor's data bus. Address 000E is decoded by the memory-address decoder. When the Memory Write pulse is received from the control logic, the information on the data bus is written into memory location 000E. Memory location 000E now contains a copy of the accumulator's data. These data are the first data word read from input port 01. The Store instruction is complete. The first data word is now stored in the data file.

In Figs. 7-13 and 7-14 (pages 127 and 128), we see the Fetch and Execute cycles for the Increment BC Register Pair instruction. This instruction makes the BC register pair point to the next higher memory location. After the instruction is executed for the first time, the contents of the BC register pair will change from 000E to 000F. This is how you build a sequential data file.

Figure 7-13 shows this instruction's Fetch cycle. The program counter's contents are loaded into the memory-address register. The memory-address register places address 0006 on the memory-address bus. The memory-address decoder receives this address and the Memory Read pulse. The contents of memory location 0006 are placed on the microcomputer's data bus. The instruction Increment Register Pair is transferred into the instruction register.

In Fig. 7-14 we see this instruction's Execute cycle. Because this is a single-byte instruction, the program counter increments only one count. The program counter now points to the next instruction.

The instruction tells the microprocessor's control logic to increment the BC register pair. As you can see, the contents of the BC register pair are incremented one count.

In this case, a single instruction increments a 16-bit register. The carry from the most significant bit of the low-order byte to the least significant bit of the high-order byte is performed automatically if it is required. Such handling of the carry is possible because this instruction treats a register pair as a single 16-bit register.

During the Execute cycle, the memory-address register's contents do not matter, because there is no memory reference during the Execute cycle.

In Figs. 7-15, 7-16, and 7-17 (pages 129 to 131), we show the Fetch and Execute parts of the 3-cycle, 3-byte jump instruction. This is the last instruction in our program. The jump instruction returns program control to the Input instruction. That is, after the jump instruction executes, we are ready to loop back and input more data.

In Fig. 7-15 we show the jump instruction's Fetch cycle. The memory-address register is loaded with the program counter's contents. The memory address 0007 is placed on the memory-address bus. The memory-address decoder decodes this address. When the Memory Read pulse comes, the memory places the contents of location 0007 on the microcomputer's data bus. The contents of memory location 0007 (a jump instruction) are transferred to the instruction register.

The first half of the instruction's Execute cycle is shown in Fig. 7-16. In this part of the instruction cycle, the program counter's hi byte is loaded with the data contained in the jump instruction's second byte. Remember, the jump instruction changes the program counter's contents. The program counter will not point to the next higher instruction in the program. When the jump instruction is complete, the program counter will point to the location addressed by the jump instruction. Of course, this location contains the instruction that you wish to *execute* next—but not the next instruction in the normal, ascending sequence.

Because this is the second byte of a 3-byte instruction, the memory-address register points to memory location 0008. The memory address 0008 is placed on the memory-address bus. The memory-address decoder decodes this address. A Memory Read pulse tells the memory to place the contents (00) of memory location 0008 on the data bus. The data (00) are transferred to the program counter's hi byte. The program counter's hi byte now contains 00.

Figure 7-17 shows the second half of the Execute cycle. Because this is a 3-byte instruction, the memory-address register points to location 0009, the jump instruction's third byte. The memory-address register places the address 0009 on the memory-address bus. This is decoded by the memory-address decoder. When the Memory Read pulse is received, the contents (03) of memory location 0009 are placed on the data bus. The contents are transferred to the program counter's lo byte. The program counter's lo byte now contains the data 03. The instruction is complete. The program counter will be used at the beginning of the next instruction cycle. The program counter now points to memory location 0003.

We have now done one complete cycle of the program. If we let the program run, it will continue indefinitely. We look at a few more steps before commanding the program to halt.

In Fig. 7-18 (page 132) we see the Fetch cycle of the 3-cycle, 2-byte Input instruction. During the Fetch portion of this instruction, the memory-address register is loaded with the program counter's contents. The memory-address register again places the address 0003 on the memory-address bus. The memory-address decoder decodes this address. When the memory system receives a Memory Read pulse, the contents (Input) of memory location 0003 are placed on the microcomputer's data bus. Because this is a Fetch cycle, the contents are transferred to the instruction register.

During this instruction's second cycle (Fig. 7-19, page 133), we begin the first half of the Execute cycle. The memory-address register points to the instruction's second byte. Because this is a 2-byte instruction, the program counter is incremented twice to point to the next instruction. The memory-address register points to memory location 0004. A Memory Read pulse tells the memory to place the contents of memory location 0004 on the data bus. These data are stored in the memory-address register's lo byte on the $\phi 2$ clock cycle.

The Input instruction's third cycle com-

pletes the last half of the Execute cycle. This is shown in Fig. 7-20 (page 134). The memory-address register places the address 01 on the memory-address bus.

This time, however, there is no Memory Read pulse or Memory Write pulse. Instead, there is an I/O Read pulse. When the I/O Read pulse is received, the data contained in the input data register 01 are placed on the microcomputer's data bus. Then these data are transferred to the accumulator.

The instruction is now complete. The new data (the second data word) are now in the accumulator. We have completed the second reading from I/O port 01.

In Fig. 7-21 (page 135) the accumulator's data are transferred to the second location of the data file in memory. The transfer is done by using the single-byte, 2-cycle Store Indirect instruction.

During this instruction's Fetch cycle, the program counter's contents are transferred to the memory-address register. Address 0005 is decoded from the memory-address bus. When the Memory Read pulse is received, the contents of memory location 0005 are placed on the data bus. The Store instruction is transferred to the instruction register.

During the Store instruction's Execute cycle (Fig. 7-22), page 136), the program counter's contents are incremented by 1. The program counter now points to the next instruction.

The contents (000F) of the BC register pair are transferred to the memory-address register. Using 000F as a memory address, the memory-address register places 000F on the memory-address bus.

The accumulator's contents (the second data word) are placed on the microcomputer's data bus. When the Memory Write pulse is received, the contents of the data bus are written into memory location 000F.

The second data word from input port 01 is now stored in memory. This data word is in our data file's second memory location.

The next instruction is Increment BC Register Pair. We do this again so that the register pair will point to the third location in our data file. That is memory location 0010.

This process continues until we halt the microcomputer. The sequential data file can be as long as we wish, so long as we do not run out of memory. As noted above, in this particular program we do not have a built-in halt.

Self-Test

Check your understanding by answering these questions.

7. In the example the program counter's sequence is:

0000
0003
0005
0006
0007
0003
0005
0006
0007

Why isn't the sequence

0000
0001
0002
0003
etc.

8. During the microprocessor's Fetch cycle, data in the addressed memory location are transferred by the data bus to ___?___ . Why?

9. The Store instruction uses more Memory Read cycles than Memory Write cycles to write data into a memory location. Why?

10. Flowchart a program that writes a data file from memory location 0100 to memory location 01FF. The program should store the data 00 in location 0100, 01 in location 0101, 02 in location 0102, and so on. Indicate the data-transfer instructions that you would use to write this program.

11. During the Input instruction of the text example program, what keeps the microcomputer from reading 0E from memory location 0001?

12. If you let the text example program run, what would finally stop it?

Summary

1. The data-transfer instructions tell the microprocessor to move data from one place to another.
2. Data are moved between memory locations and registers.
3. Data-transfer instructions are usually designed to copy the source data in the destination location. The source data are not destroyed. Each data-transfer instruction can affect the status register differently.
4. The Load Register instructions are used to put data into a particular register. The Load Register Pair instructions put data into a double-width register. The data are stored in two successive memory locations.
5. The Move instructions move data from one register to another.
6. The Store instructions store data in a given memory location.

Chapter Review Questions

7-1. What do the data-transfer instructions do? What locations are affected?

7-2. Why do we say a data-transfer instruction should be called a "data-copy" instruction?

7-3. Identify the instructions that you would use to do the following jobs:
a. Transfer data to the accumulator from a specific memory location pointed to by the instruction's second and third bytes.
b. Place a copy of the contents of the accumulator into a memory location pointed to by the BC register pair.
c. Fill the B register with the data in the instruction's second byte.
d. Transfer the data in register C to register B.
e. Copy the contents of the accumulator into memory location FFAE.
f. Put the contents of the accumulator into register D.

7-4. Tell what the following instructions do.
    a. LDA B,04   *g.* MOV D,B
    b. MOV A,C   *h.* STI A
    c. STA E6B4   *i.* LDD D,00A1
    d. LRP B,501C   *j.* STA 0000
    e. LDI A   *k.* LDA A,FF
    f. LDA C,00   *l.* LRP B,FFFF

7-5. Write a short program that moves data from memory location 001F to memory location 007E. The program should also leave a copy of the data in register C.

Answers to Self-Tests

1. c.
2. The LDA A instruction loads the accumulator with the data in the second byte. The LDD A instruction loads the accumulator with the data in the memory location pointed to by the instruction's second and third bytes. The LDD A takes one more MPU cycle.
3. LRP B,Data is the same as LDA B,Data followed by LDA C,Data. The second method uses more memory.
4. The STA A instruction stores the accumulator in memory. The LDD A instruction stores memory data in the accumulator. These are exactly opposite jobs.
5. MOV A,B and STA A,01FF. Data are moved into the accumulator, from which a Store instruction puts them in memory. See Fig. 7-23.
6. See Fig. 7-24.
7. Because the program counter moves to the next instruction in sequence, not just to the next byte.
8. The instruction register. This is done so that the instruction decoder and control logic can execute the instruction.
9. The Store instruction

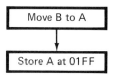

Fig. 7-23 The flowchart of self-test question 5.

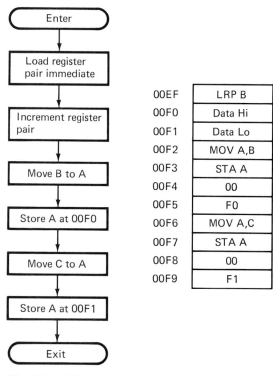

Fig. 7-24 The completed flowchart and memory map of self-test question 6.

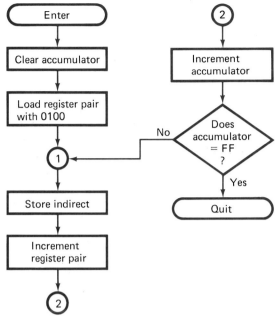

Fig. 7-25 The flowchart of self-test question 10.

uses Memory Read instructions to Fetch the instruction and to get the two address bytes. One Write cycle is used to put the data into memory.

10. See Fig. 7-25.

11. The memory is not accessed by the I/O Read pulse.

12. It would keep going until it had stored data at memory location FFFF. The counter would then increment to 0000 and the program would begin to write data over the program. As soon as data were written into memory location 0003, the microprocessor would crash.

The Arithmetic Instructions

- In this chapter you will learn about some of the most valuable microprocessor instructions. These instructions let you combine two binary numbers using the rules of arithmetic. You will know how to use all the arithmetic instructions needed to perform binary arithmetic. You will find that the microprocessor really does all arithmetic operations by using the Add instruction in many different ways.

First, we will study the simple Add instruction. We will learn how it works with its different memory-addressing modes. We will then learn how to use the Add with Carry instruction, and we will see how this instruction is used in multiple-precision arithmetic. Second, we will look at a special microprocessor instruction called the Subtract instruction. You will learn that this instruction does nothing that cannot be done by using the Add instruction and the Complement instruction. We will see why the Subtract instruction is faster. We will also use the Subtract with Carry instruction to do multiple-precision subtraction.

Last, we will look at the Decimal Adjust instruction. We will learn how this instruction can be used to help us do high-speed BCD (*B*inary-*C*oded *D*ecimal) additions.

8-1 THE ADD INSTRUCTION

As powerful as we may think microprocessors are, most of them can really only execute one arithmetic instruction. That instruction is Add. What makes the microprocessor's arithmetic capabilities so powerful is that it can do an Add in many different ways. It can also do an Add very fast.

For example, the microprocessor can add one binary number to the *complement* of another binary number. This process carries out a subtraction. The microprocessor can add many times over. Repeated addition is multiplication. Repeated subtraction is division. In an earlier chapter we saw how to do binary arithmetic. In this section, we will see how the microprocessor carries out the Add instruction.

We will now look at the four different Add instructions. You can see that the only difference between these Add instructions is the source of the data.

ADD FROM REGISTER
ADD r
A + r → A

ADD r

The Add from Register instruction adds the contents of register r to the contents of the accumulator (register A). The result (the sum) is placed in the accumulator. The original contents of the accumulator are lost. This is a single-byte instruction that uses two microprocessor cycles. If executing this instruction yields an MSB of "1" or a zero result or a carry, then each appropriate bit in the status register is set.

ADD FROM MEMORY DIRECT
ADD M, Address
A + M → A

ADD M
Hi address
Lo address

The Add from Memory Direct instruction adds the contents of memory (at the location given by the address) to the contents of the accumulator (register A). The second and third bytes of the instruction point to the memory location containing the augend. The result (the sum) is placed in the accumulator. The original contents of the accumulator are lost. This is a 3-byte instruction that uses four microprocessor cycles. If executing this instruction yields an MSB of "1" or a zero result or a carry, then each appropriate bit in the status register is set.

ADD FROM MEMORY INDIRECT
ADI M
A + M → A

ADI M

The Add from Memory Indirect instruction adds the contents of memory to the contents of the accumulator (register A). The memory location containing the augend is pointed to by the BC register pair. Note: The BC register pair must be loaded before this instruction can be used. The result (the sum) is placed in the accumulator. The original contents of the accumulator are lost. This is a single-byte instruction that uses three microprocessor cycles. If executing this instruction yields a "1" in the MSB or a zero result or a carry, then each appropriate bit in the status register is set.

ADD IMMEDIATE DATA
ADD I,Data
A + Data → A

ADD I	1st byte
Data	2d byte

The Add Immediate Data instruction adds the contents of the instruction's second byte to the contents of the accumulator. The result (the sum) is placed in the accumulator. The original contents of the accumulator are lost. This is a 2-byte instruction that takes three microprocessor cycles. If executing this instruction yields a "1" in the MSB or a zero result or a carry, then the appropriate status bit is set.

We can now look at an example of how the Add instruction can be used. The program is flowcharted in Fig. 8-1. Figures 8-2, 8-3, 8-4, 8-5, and 8-6 (pages 144 to 148) show the microprocessor executing a simple program. In this program we also use the Load Immediate data-transfer instruction. It is used to place the decimal number 12 in the accumulator. The program uses the Add Immediate instruction to add the number 41 to the number 12. The result (53) is left in the accumulator. After the addition is complete, we halt the processor.

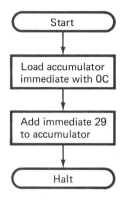

Fig. 8-1 Adding two numbers with a simple Add instruction. The Load instruction puts the addend in the accumulator. The augend is added using the Add instruction.

Remember: Although the illustrations show hexadecimal numbers, the microprocessor is really using binary numbers. That is, the addition being done is

Binary	Decimal	Hexadecimal
0000 1100	12	0C
0010 1001	41	29
0011 0101	53	35

From this you can see that the illustrations will use the hexadecimal numbers 0C, 29, and 35.

Figure 8-2 shows the microcomputer after the Fetch is executed. This is a 3-cycle, 2-byte instruction. To start, the program counter is set to 0000. This makes it point to the program's first instruction.

During the instruction's Fetch cycle, the memory-address register is loaded with the program counter's contents. The memory-address decoder decodes the data on the memory-address bus. When the Memory Read pulse is received, the LDA instruction from memory location 0000 is loaded onto the microcomputer's data bus and from there into the microprocessor's instruction register.

During the Execute cycle (Fig. 8-3), the program counter is incremented twice. It now points to 0002. This is the location of the next instruction: the Add instruction. The memory-address register points to the first instruction's second byte. This contains the data 0C. The memory-address decoder decodes the address. When the Memory Read pulse is received, the data (0C) are placed on the microcomputer's data bus. Executing the LDA instruction loads the data (0C) into the accumulator. You can see that executing

From page 142:
Add from register

Add from memory direct

On this page:
Add from memory indirect

Add immediate data

143

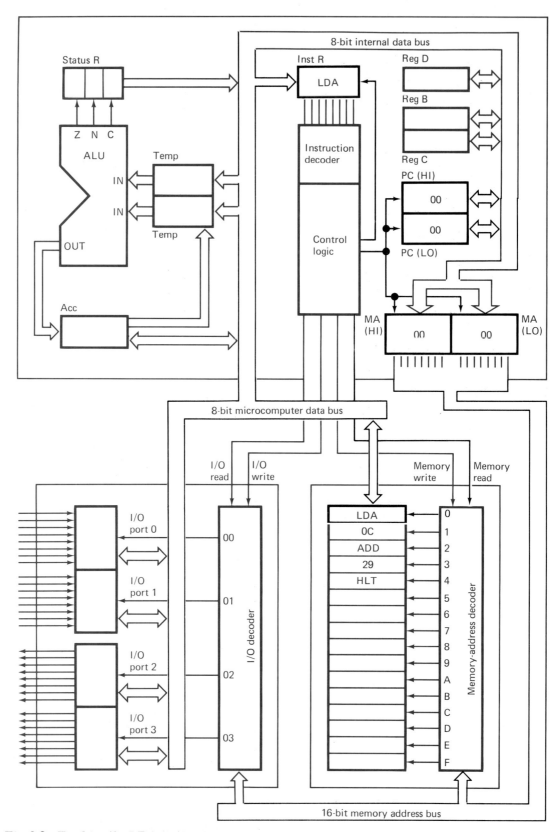

Fig. 8-2   Fetching the LDA instruction.

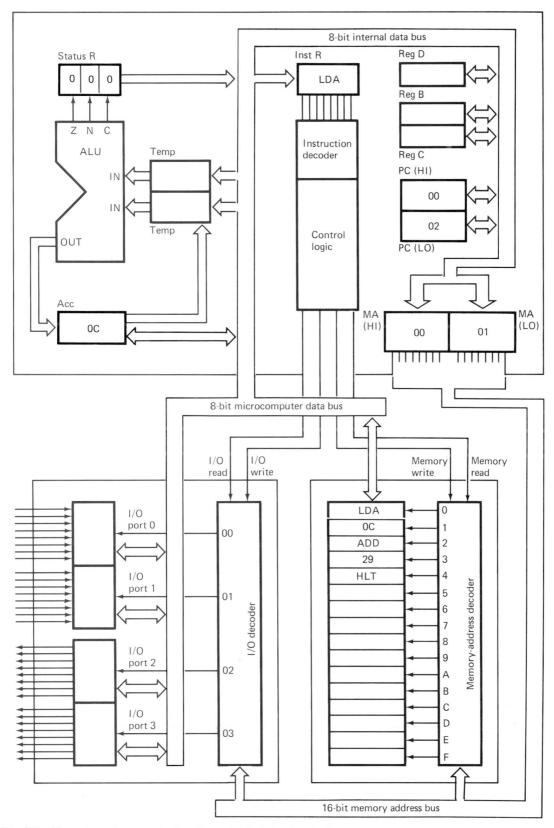

Fig. 8-3   Executing the LDA instruction.   Note: The data in the LDA's second byte is loaded in the accumulator, and the status register is set.

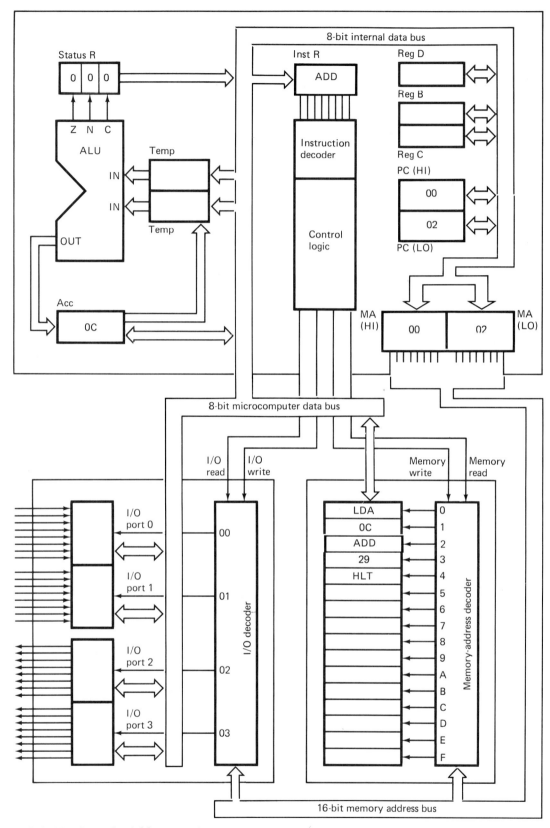

Fig. 8-4 Fetching the Add instruction.

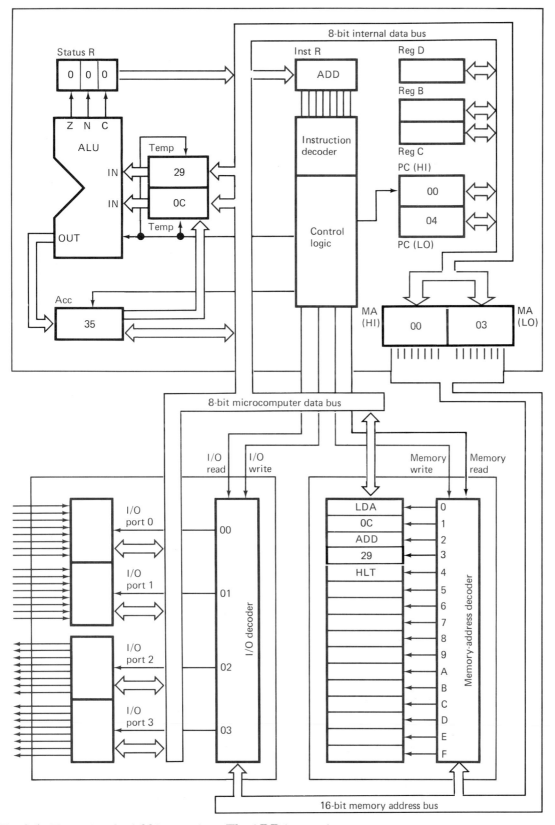

Fig. 8-5   Executing the Add instruction. The ADD instruction causes the accumulator to place its contents in the accumulator's temporary register. The ALU then adds the contents of the accumulator's temporary register to the Add Immediate's data, which is in the ALU's temporary register.

147

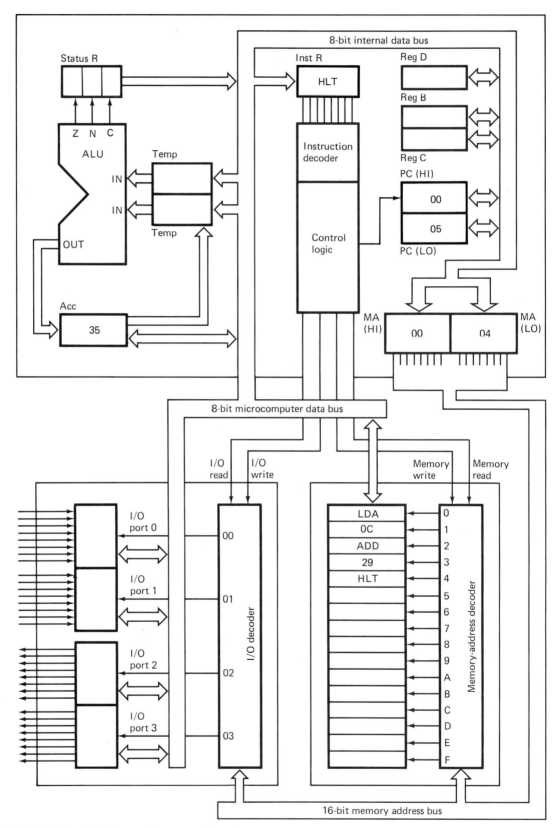

Fig. 8-6 The Halt instruction stops the microcomputer.

this instruction sets all the status register's bits to "0." That is, the data are not 0, the MSB is not a "1," and the operation does not cause a carry.

In Fig. 8-4 we see the Fetch part of the Add instruction. During the Fetch cycle, the program counter is loaded into the memory-address register. The memory-address decoder decodes the address. When the Memory Read pulse is received, the Add instruction is placed on the data bus. This instruction is loaded into the microprocessor's instruction register.

During the Execute part of this instruction (Fig. 8-5), the program counter is incremented twice. It now points to the Halt instruction at location 0004. The accumulator's contents are moved to the accumulator's temporary register. At the same time, the memory-address decoder points to the data in the instruction's second byte. The memory-address decoder selects location 0003. When the Memory Read pulse is received, the data (29) are placed on the microcomputer's data bus. The data bus loads the ALU's temporary register.

The ALU then adds the contents of the ALU's temporary register and the contents of the accumulator's temporary register. The result (35) is placed in the accumulator.

Once again the status register's zero, negative, and carry bits are set as required. In this case they are set to all "0s."

In Fig. 8-6 we see the results of executing the Add instruction. During the Fetch phase the program counter's contents were loaded into the memory-address register. The memory-address decoder decoded the address from the memory-address bus. When the Memory Read pulse was received, the Halt instruction was placed on the microcomputer's data bus. Then this instruction was placed in the instruction register.

During the Execute phase of the Halt instruction, the program counter is incremented to point to location 0005, the next instruction. However, the instruction and control logic decodes the Halt instruction and stops the microprocessor's operation.

The program is now complete. The accumulator contains the data (35). This is the result of adding 0C and 29.

This may seem like a lot of work to add two numbers. Certainly adding in this way would be tedious for a human being. But the micro-

processor can do it so fast! Assume each microprocessor cycle takes 1 microsecond (μs). How fast can the microprocessor do this addition from start to finish?

Instruction	Cycles (1 μs/cycle)
LDA r	3
ADD I	3
	6

The total program takes six cycles, or 6 μs at 1 μs per cycle. The microprocessor can execute 166,667 of these programs in one second! With a 200-nanosecond (ns) cycle time we can do 833,333 complete programs per second!

Self-Test

Check your understanding by answering these questions.

1. Often after an Add instruction is executed, the result is stored in memory. Flowchart such a program and explain how the Store instruction is executed. How does the Store instruction affect program execution time if the microprocessor cycle is 1 μs?

2. Suppose you wish to use the example program over and over. You want to add whatever might be at memory locations 0008 and 0009. You want to put the result in memory location 000A. What instructions would you use? How would this program be different from the one in the example?

3. Change the example program so that it uses the Add from Register instruction. Explain how this program is different from the example program and from the program in self-test question 2.

8-2 ADDING WITH CARRY

In addition to the four Add instructions that we have just studied, there are four other Add instructions. These are much like the first four instructions. The difference is that the addition in these new instructions includes the contents of the status register's carry bit. That is, the contents of the memory location are added to the contents of the accumulator, and then the contents of the status register's carry bit are added to that sum.

Binary	Data source	Decimal
1	Carry	1
0001 1001	Addend	25
0000 1110	Augend	14
0010 1000	Sum	40

Fig. 8-7 An Add with Carry. The LSB is the sum of 0 from the augend, 1 from the addend, and 1 from the status register's carry bit.

Add from register with carry

Add from memory direct with carry

Add from memory indirect with carry

Add immediate data with carry

Multiple precision arithmetic

Double precision

Triple precision

Low-order byte

High-order byte

An example is shown in Fig. 8-7. Here we add the decimal numbers 25 and 14. If we just add these two numbers, then the result is 39. However, as you can see from Fig. 8-7, there is a third number added. This number is a 1. It is the result of a carry from an earlier arithmetic operation. Therefore, we see that 1 + 25 + 14 is equal to 40. The Add with Carry instruction is the only way that the microprocessor can add more than two numbers using a single Add instruction. In other cases when you want to add three numbers, you must use one Add instruction to add the first two numbers, and then use another Add instruction to add the third number to the sum of the first two numbers.

The Add with Carry instructions let you add two numbers and also include the carry bit generated from a previous operation. Of course, each of these Add with Carry instructions also sets the status register's zero, negative, and carry bits as required. Consequently we lose the original contents of both the accumulator and the status register, as we did with the other Add instructions.

The Add with Carry instructions are:

ADD FROM REGISTER WITH CARRY
ACD r
A + r + C → A

ACD r

1 byte
2 cycles

ADD FROM MEMORY DIRECT WITH CARRY
ACD M,Address
A + M + C → A

ACM M
Hi address
Lo address

3 bytes
4 cycles

ADD FROM MEMORY INDIRECT WITH CARRY
ACI M
M + A + C → A

ACI M

1 byte
2 cycles

ADD IMMEDIATE DATA WITH CARRY
ACD I,Data
Data + A + C → A

ACD I
Data

2 bytes
3 cycles

We will now look at a program that demonstrates Add with Carry. We will not only find out how the Add with Carry instructions work; we will also learn how the microprocessor does multiple-precision arithmetic. Earlier we learned that multiple-precision arithmetic is used when part of a calculation or the final result of a calculation does not fit into one data word.

For example, in an 8-bit microprocessor, one word can represent only the numbers between 0 and 255. In order to represent values greater than 255, we must use more than one microprocessor word. Multiple-precision arithmetic means using more than one word to represent a single number.

If we use an 8-bit microprocessor, then double precision—the use of two words to represent a single number—can represent the numbers 0 to 65,535. Using triple precision, we are able to represent the numbers 0 to 16,777,215. Single-, double-, and triple-precision 8-bit words are shown in Fig. 8-8.

Double-precision addition, for example, is done by first adding the low-order bytes. This is done by using the simple Add instruction. It does not use a carry input. Of course, this addition may *generate* a carry bit. The numbers' high-order bytes are then added by using an Add with Carry instruction. The Add with Carry instruction used in case the lower order Add should generate a carry. If the lower order add does generate a carry, the carry will be included; if no carry is generated, the carry input will be zero.

If the number is triple-precision, a second Add with Carry is needed. This third instruction adds the most significant or high-order bytes of the two numbers.

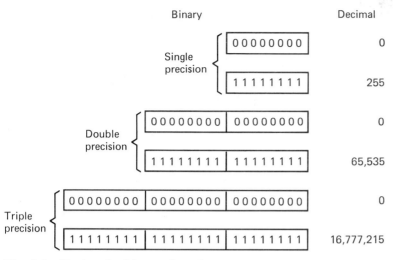

Fig. 8-8 Single-, double-, and triple-precision numbers in an
8-bit system. The resolution is 1 part in 255, 1 part in 65,635,
and 1 part in 16,777,215, respectively.

Any carry generated by the last multiple-precision arithmetic operation must either be stored as a significant bit of the result or be lost. In most cases, we do not expect the last operation to generate a carry. That is, we use a precision large enough to hold the greatest expected result as well as its sign bit.

Let's look at an example where double precision is needed. In Fig. 8-9 we see the addition of two large numbers. Because the result is less than 65,535, we may perform this addition using double-precision arithmetic.

The binary numbers are expressed in *unsigned* binary form. We can tell this by looking at the result, which has a "1" in the MSB. Be sure to note that the result represents 63,580, not −30,812.

You can see in the example that the augend, the addend, and the sum are broken into high- and low-order bytes. Simple binary addition is used to add the augend's and the addend's lo bytes. We use the Add instruction for this addition, which generates the sum's lo byte. A *carry* bit is also generated.

When this operation is performed, the status register's carry bit is set. We must use the Add with Carry instruction to add the augend's and the addend's hi bytes. When we use this instruction, the logic "1" in the status register's carry bit is an input to the calculation. As you can see from Fig. 8-9, the first four bits of the result's hi byte are changed because of this carry bit.

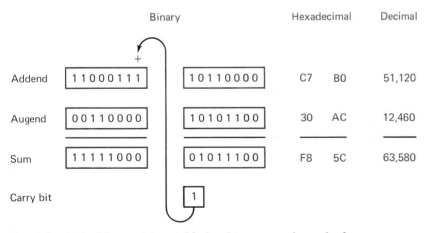

Fig. 8-9 A double-precision Add that has a carry from the lo
byte to the hi byte. This addition uses two 16-bit, unsigned binary numbers.

151

Memory map

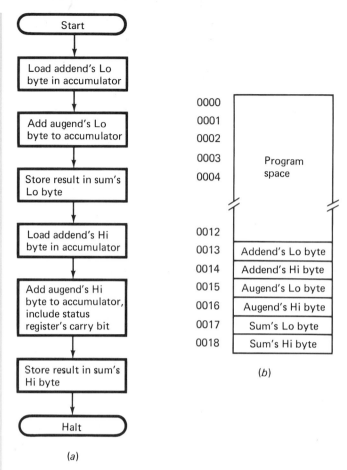

(a)

(b)

Fig. 8-10 A flowchart and a memory map for the double-precision addition program. The memory map shows that we have reserved 6 bytes of memory space to hold the addition problem's numbers in double-precision form.

The program is flowcharted in Fig. 8-10(a). You can see that the lo bytes are added first. The hi bytes are added second. The addition of the hi bytes includes the carry.

Figure 8-10(b) is a memory map. It shows how the microprocessor's memory is used for this program. In this case, the program is stored in memory locations 0000 through 0012. Memory locations 0013 and 0014 contain the addend's lo and hi bytes, respectively. The augend's lo and hi bytes are stored in memory locations 0015 and 0016. The sum's lo and hi bytes are stored in memory locations 0017 and 0018.

Figure 8-11 shows the complete program used to carry out this addition. Figure 8-11 has three columns. The left-hand column shows the hexadecimal memory address. The center column shows the memory contents at that address. The memory contents are shown as mnemonics for instructions and as hexadecimal numbers for addresses. The

program starts at memory location 0000. Data storage is found in the last six memory locations, with the data shown in hexadecimal form. You can compare Fig. 8-11 with the addition shown in Fig. 8-9. The right-hand column of Fig. 8-11 contains comments to help you follow the program. You will often find handwritten programs shown in a similar form.

Looking at this program, you can see that the Add Direct instruction has been used often. The Add Direct instruction is used because the memory locations for the double-precision augend, addend, and sum are not part of the instruction that adds them. In fact, this program will add any numbers that are put into the augend and addend locations. The Store instruction is used to determine the sum's location. Note: If the program ever resulted in a carry when the hi bytes were added, the carry would be lost. In other words, this program can add only un-

Memory address	Memory contents	Comments
0000	LDD A	Load accumulator direct
0001	00	} Addend's address (Lo byte)
0002	13	
0003	ADD A	Add to accumulator
0004	00	} Augend's address (Lo byte)
0005	15	
0006	STA A	Store direct
0007	00	} Sum's address (Lo byte)
0008	17	
0009	LDD A	Load accumulator direct
000A	00	} Addend's address (Hi byte)
000B	14	
000C	ACD A	Add with carry direct
000D	00	} Augend's address (Hi byte)
000E	16	
000F	STA A	Store direct
0010	00	} Sum's address (Hi byte)
0011	18	
0012	HLT	Halt
0013	B0	Lo byte } Addend (51,120)
0014	C7	Hi byte
0015	AC	Lo byte } Augend (12,460)
0016	30	Hi byte
0017	5C	Lo byte } Sum (63,580)
0018	F8	Hi byte

Fig. 8-11   A program listing to perform a double-precision addition. Direct addressing is used so that the memory locations reserved for data can be addressed.

signed binary numbers whose sum is less than 65,535 or signed binary numbers whose sum lies between $-32,768$ and $+32,767$.

Using the microcomputer system diagram, let's follow this program as it executes. In each diagram, we will see the results of executing a complete instruction. We will no longer show a separate diagram for each microprocessor cycle.

Figure 8-12 (page 154) shows what the first instruction does. This instruction tells the microcomputer to load the contents of memory location 0013 into the accumulator.

During the Fetch cycle, the program counter's contents are transferred into the memory-address register. The memory-address decoder decodes the memory address. When the Memory Read pulse comes, the contents of memory location 0000 are placed on the microcomputer's data bus. Because this is the Fetch cycle, the contents of memory location 0000 are placed in the instruction register. The instruction logic decodes a Load Accumulator Direct instruction.

During the execution phase of this instruction, the contents of memory locations 0001 and 0002 are loaded into the memory-address register. The memory-address register points to location 0013. The contents of memory location 0013 are loaded into the accumulator. We have now placed the lo byte of the addend in the accumulator.

In Fig. 8-13 (page 155), we see the result of the second instruction. This Add Direct instruction adds the contents of the memory location to the contents of the accumulator.

During the Fetch cycle, the program counter's contents are loaded into the memory-

153

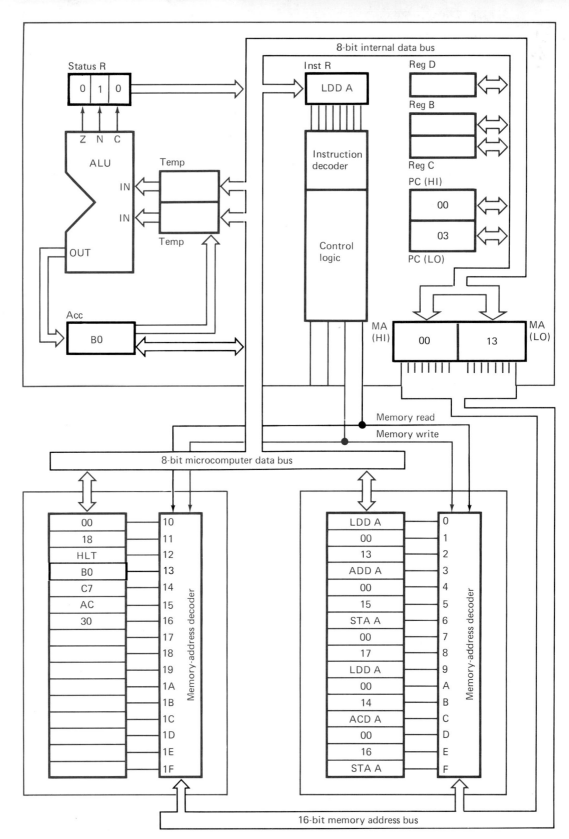

Fig. 8-12   A look at the microcomputer system after the LDA
A,0013 instruction is executed.   The LDA A,0013 instruction
transferred the data from memory location 0013 to the accumulator.   In doing this, the status register's negative bit was set.

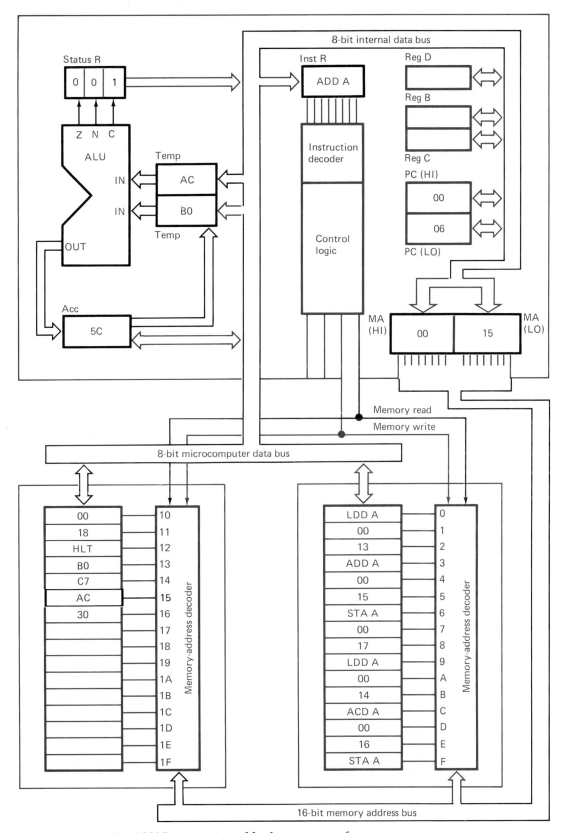

Fig. 8-13 The ACD M,0015 instruction adds the contents of
memory location 0015 to the accumulator. This operation has
an arithmetic carry that sets the status register's carry bit. However, the result is not negative, so the status register's negative bit
is cleared.

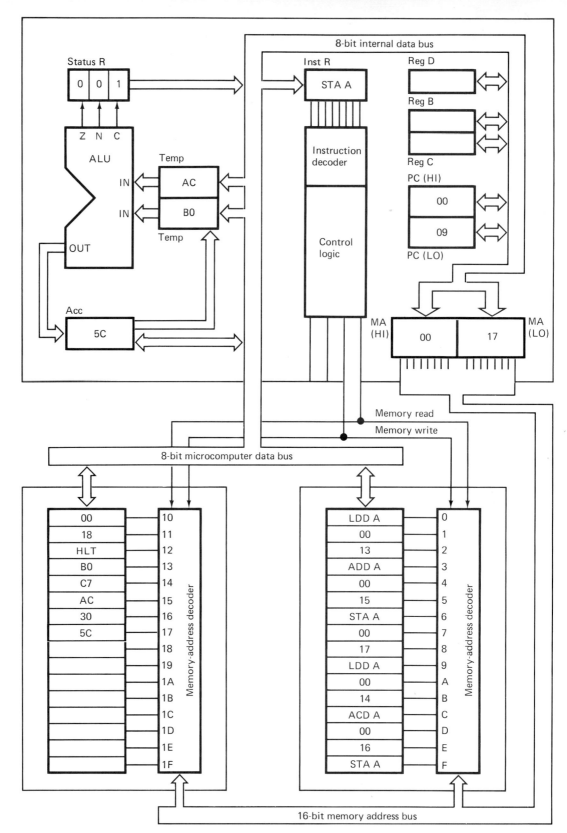

Fig. 8-14   Storing the accumulator's contents in memory. The
Store Direct instruction uses a Memory Write pulse to put the
data into memory location 0017.

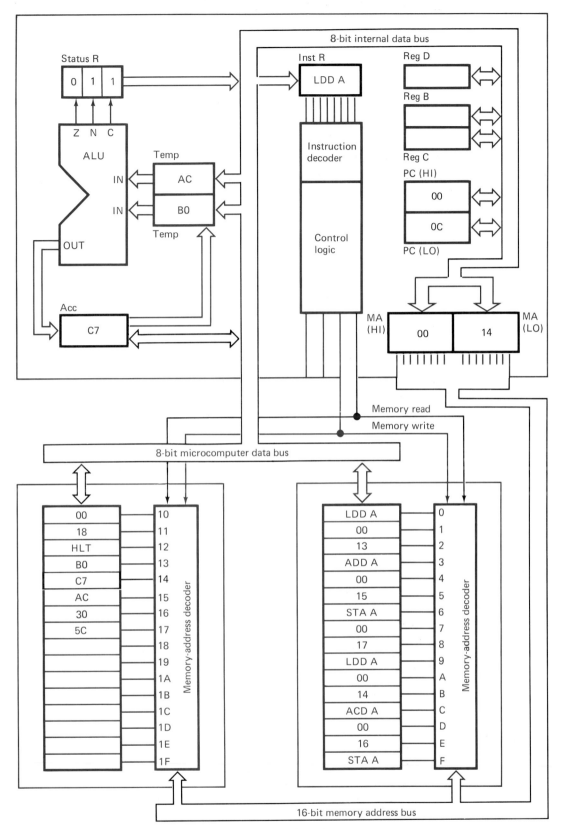

Fig. 8-15   Loading the accumulator with the augend's hi byte.
Although the status register's zero and negative bits are affected
by the Load Accumulator Direct instruction, the carry bit remains unchanged.   The carry bit still has the carry from the previous Add.

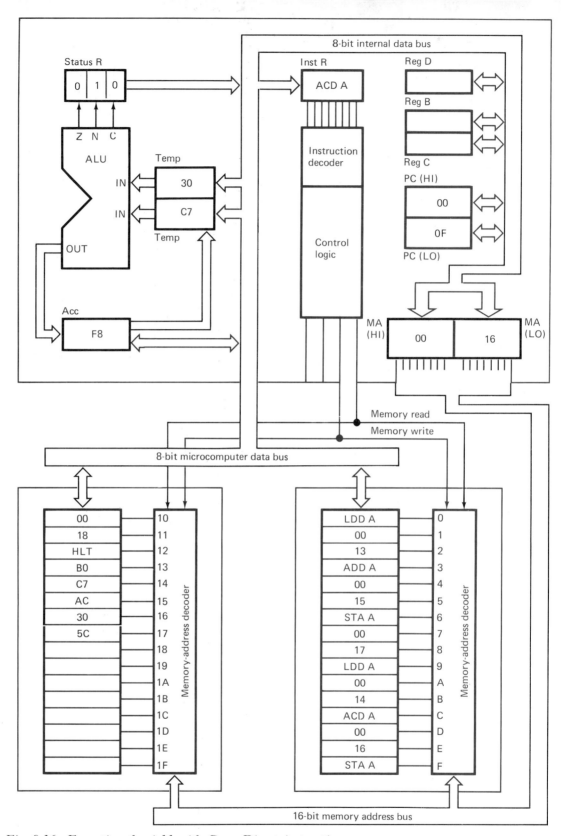

Fig. 8-16 Executing the Add with Carry Direct instruction.
The contents of memory location 0016 are added to the accumulator's contents, which have been moved to the accumulator's
temporary data latch. The status register's carry bit is also
included. In this example, the carry bit was a one, as shown
in Fig. 8-15. The addition causes a new status word that reflects
the logic 1 in the accumulator's MSB.

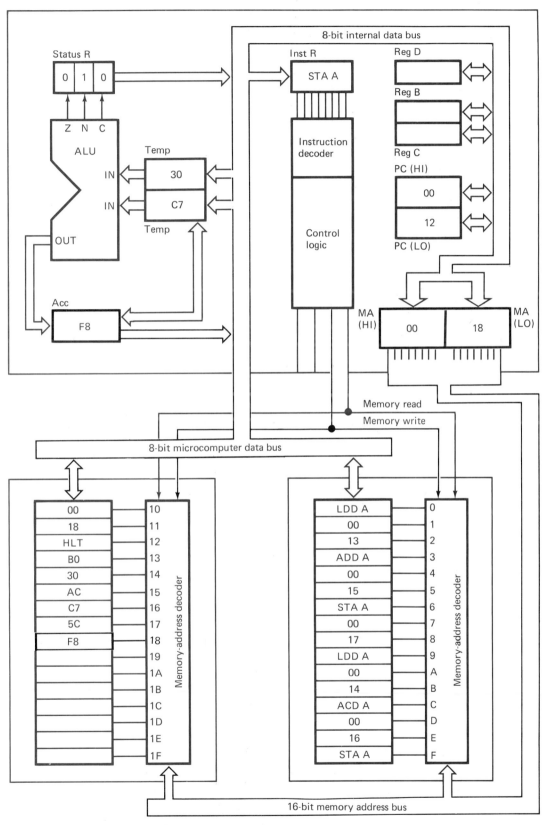

Fig. 8-17   Storing the sum's hi byte at memory location 0018.
The double-precision addition is now complete.

address register. The Memory Read pulse causes the Add Direct instruction to be loaded into the instruction register.

During the Execute phase of the second instruction, three separate actions occur. First, the program counter is incremented to point to the next instruction. This is location 0006. Second, the microprocessor's control logic moves the instruction's next 2 bytes into the memory-address register. This makes the memory-address register point to location 0015. Third, the accumulator's contents are transferred to the accumulator's temporary register.

The contents of memory location 0015 are placed in the ALU's temporary register. The ALU generates the sum of the numbers at its two inputs and places the sum in the accumulator. You can see that the status register's carry bit is set. This shows that the addition of the two numbers caused a carry.

In Fig. 8-14 (page 156), the Store Direct instruction inputs the accumulator's contents in memory location 0017. Memory location 0017 now contains the sum's lo byte. Executing this instruction causes three Memory Reads and one Memory Write.

During the Fetch portion of this cycle, the instruction is placed in the instruction register. To execute this instruction, the hi and lo bytes of the memory location are read from memory and placed in the memory-address register. The memory-address register now points to location 0017. The accumulator's contents are placed on the microcomputer's data bus. The microprocessor's control logic issues a Memory Write pulse. This pulse commands the memory to store the data on the data bus in memory location 0017.

In Fig. 8-15 (page 157), the accumulator is again loaded by using a Load Accumulator Direct instruction. The operation of this cycle is identical to the previous one shown in Fig. 8-12. However, memory location 0014 is now the source of the data. Location 0014 contains the addend's hi byte.

In Fig. 8-16 (page 158), an Add Direct with Carry instruction is executed. This instruction adds the augend's hi byte, the carry bit, and the accumulator's contents. The result is placed in the accumulator. During the Fetch portion of this instruction, the contents of the program counter are placed in the memory-address register. Location 000C is decoded by the memory-address decoder.

When a Memory Read pulse is received, the contents of memory location 000C are placed on the microcomputer's data bus. The Add Direct with Carry instruction is placed in the microprocessor's instruction register.

During the Execute cycle, the program counter is incremented to point to location 000F. The memory-address register is loaded with the contents of the instruction's second and third bytes. The memory-address register now points to location 0016. The accumulator's contents are placed in the accumulator's temporary register. Finally, the contents of memory location 0016, the carry bit, and the contents of the temporary register are all added together. The resulting sum is placed in the accumulator.

Note: On the completion of this instruction, the carry bit is reset to "0" because the Add with Carry instruction does not generate a carry. The status register's negative bit, however, is set. This is because the result has placed a "1" in the accumulator's most significant bit. The accumulator now contains the sum's hi byte.

In Fig. 8-17 (page 159), the accumulator's contents are stored at location 0018. This instruction is identical to the instruction that we carried out in Fig. 8-14. However, this time the hi byte is stored in memory location 0018.

We have now completed the addition of two double-precision numbers resulting in a double-precision sum. Looking at Fig. 8-17 we can see that the result is stored in memory locations 0017 and 0018. From this example, you can see that a triple-precision calculation might be handled by simply carrying out one more addition with carry.

Self-Test

Check your understanding by answering these questions.

4. The purpose of the Add with Carry instruction is to
   a. Generate a carry bit if needed
   b. Set the carry bit
   c. Include a carry from a previous operation
   d. Store the carry bit

5. What would happen if the program in Fig. 8-9 were changed so that the Add instruction in memory location 0003 became the Add with Carry and the instruction in

memory location 000C became the Add instruction?

6. Explain how you would change the program in Fig. 8-9 into a triple-precision addition program.

7. How does changing the instruction from Add to Add with Carry affect execution time? What is the effect on the memory space needed to store the instructions?

8. In one way, the Add with Carry instruction uses only the status register's carry bit. In another way, the Add with Carry instruction involves the status register's zero, carry, and negative bits. Explain.

9. Explain why a multiple-precision Add uses both the Add and the Add with Carry instructions.

8-3 THE SUBTRACT INSTRUCTIONS

From your knowledge of computer arithmetic, you know that the only irreplaceable arithmetic instruction is the Add instruction. For example, a microprocessor can do subtraction by complementing a number, adding 1, and then adding the result to another number. However, it is quicker and easier to let the microprocessor do subtraction directly than to write a program to do the job. You will find that many microprocessors have instructions that are not essential but do make the programmer's task easier. The Subtract instruction is one of these "convenience" instructions.

In the following paragraphs, we look at the eight Subtract instructions that our microprocessor uses. You will find these instructions much like the Add instructions. For example, like the result of the Add instructions, the result of the Subtract instructions (the difference) is placed in the accumulator. The original minuend is lost. Like the Add instructions, the Subtract instructions set any of the status register's three bits if the results warrant.

The Subtract instructions all use 2's complement arithmetic. Subtraction is done by complementing each bit of the minuend, adding 1, and then adding the result to the subtrahend. A logic "1" in the most significant bit indicates a negative number. Likewise, a logic "0" in the most significant bit indicates a positive number. Remember that 2's comple-

ment 8-bit numbers have a range of $+127$ to -128, including 0.

The Subtract instructions subtract the data that the instruction points to from the data in the accumulator. In other words, the accumulator is always the minuend. The address in the Subtract instruction tells the microprocessor where to find the subtrahend.

The Subtract instructions follow.

SUBTRACT FROM REGISTER
SUB r
$A - r \rightarrow A$

SUB r

The Subtract from Register instruction subtracts the contents of register r *from* the contents of the accumulator (register A). The result (the difference) is placed in the accumulator. The original contents of the accumulator are lost. This is a single-byte instruction that uses two microprocessor cycles. If executing this instruction yields a negative or zero result or a carry, then each appropriate bit in the status register is set.

SUBTRACT FROM MEMORY DIRECT
SUB M,Address
$A - M \rightarrow A$

SUB M	1st byte
Hi address	2d byte
Lo address	3d byte

The Subtract from Memory Direct instruction subtracts the contents of a memory location from the contents of the accumulator (register A). The second and third bytes of the instruction point to the memory location containing the subtrahend. The result (difference) is placed in the accumulator. The original contents of the accumulator are lost. This is a 3-byte instruction that uses 4 microprocessor cycles. If executing this instruction yields a negative or zero result or a carry, then each appropriate bit in the status register is set.

SUBTRACT FROM MEMORY INDIRECT
SUI M
$A - M \rightarrow A$

SUI M

The Subtract from Memory Indirect instruction subtracts the contents of a memory location *from* the contents of the accumulator

Subtract from
register

Subtract from
memory direct

Subtract from
memory indirect

(register A). The BC register pair points to the memory location containing the subtrahend. Note: The BC register pair must contain the correct address before this instruction can be used. The result (the difference) is placed in the accumulator. The original contents of the accumulator are lost. This is a single-byte instruction that uses three microprocessor cycles. If executing this instruction yields a negative or zero result or a carry, then each appropriate bit in the status register is set.

SUBTRACT IMMEDIATE DATA
SUB I,Data
$A - Data \rightarrow A$

SUB I
Data

The Subtract Immediate Data instruction subtracts the contents of the instruction's second byte from the contents of the accumulator. The result (difference) is placed in the accumulator. The original contents of the accumulator are lost. This is a 2-byte instruction that takes 3 microprocessor cycles. If executing this instruction yields a negative or zero result or a carry, then each appropriate bit in the status register is set.

Just as there are four Add instructions without carry and four Add with Carry instructions, there are also four subtract instructions without borrow and four Subtract with Carry instructions. A borrow happens when the subtrahend is *larger* than the minuend. When this is the case, the carry (borrow) bit is set. Even though these instructions actually borrow, they are called the "Subtract with Carry" instructions. The reason for the name is that the borrow operation sets the status register's carry bit.

Using the Subtract with Carry instruction, the microprocessor can do subtractions with multiple precision. The Subtract with Carry instructions are like the Subtract instructions without borrow, except that the Subtract with Carry instructions include the current contents of the status register's carry bit in the calculation. As with the other Subtract instructions, the results are placed in the accumulator. The negative, zero, and carry bits are set if the calculation yields a negative or zero result or a borrow.

Here are the Subtract with Carry instructions.

SUBTRACT FROM REGISTER WITH CARRY
SCB r
$A - r - C \rightarrow A$

SCB r	

1 byte
2 cycles

SUBTRACT FROM MEMORY DIRECT WITH CARRY
SCB M,Address
$A - M - C \rightarrow A$

SCB M	1st byte
Hi address	2d byte
Lo address	3d byte

3 bytes
4 cycles

SUBTRACT FROM MEMORY INDIRECT WITH CARRY
SCI M
$A - M - C \rightarrow A$

SCI M	

1 byte
2 cycles

SUBTRACT IMMEDIATE DATA WITH CARRY
SCB I,Data
$A - Data - C \rightarrow A$

SCB I	1st byte
Data	2nd byte

2 bytes
3 cycles

A double-precision subtraction problem illustrates the use of both the Subtract and the Subtract with Carry instructions. The example is shown in Fig. 8-18, where the decimal number 12,460 is subtracted from the decimal number 30,812. The subtraction is shown in decimal, hexadecimal, and binary form. In fact, the figure breaks the subtraction into the hi byte and the lo byte. Looking at the lo byte, we see that a borrow is needed to complete the subtraction. That is, for the lo bytes shown, the minuend is smaller than the subtrahend. Consequently, the status register's carry bit is set.

When the hi-byte subtraction is performed, a Subtract with Carry instruction is used. We can see that this subtraction includes the minuend, the subtrahend, and the borrow bit. Both the subtrahend and the contents of the

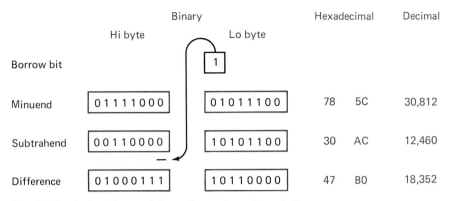

	Binary		Hexadecimal	Decimal
	Hi byte	Lo byte		
Borrow bit		1		
Minuend	0 1 1 1 1 0 0 0	0 1 0 1 1 1 0 0	78 5C	30,812
Subtrahend	0 0 1 1 0 0 0 0	1 0 1 0 1 1 0 0	30 AC	12,460
Difference	0 1 0 0 0 1 1 1	1 0 1 1 0 0 0 0	47 B0	18,352

Fig. 8-18 A double-precision subtraction whose lo-byte operation generates a borrow. The borrow bit is subtracted from the hi-byte operation.

status register's carry bit are subtracted from the minuend.

The program is flowcharted in Fig. 8-19(*a*). Figure 8-19(*b*) shows the program's memory map. Memory locations 0013 and 0014 hold the lo and hi bytes of the minuend. Memory locations 0015 and 0016 hold the lo and hi bytes of the subtrahend. Memory locations 0017 and 0018 are for the lo and hi bytes of the difference.

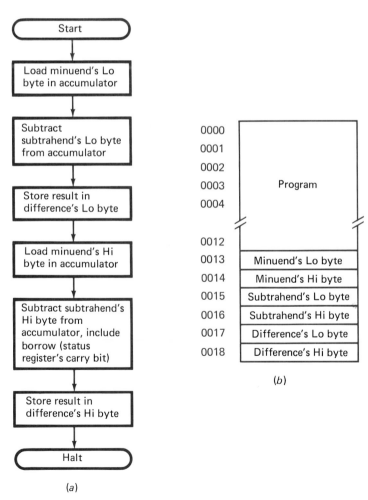

(*a*)

0000	
0001	
0002	
0003	Program
0004	
0012	
0013	Minuend's Lo byte
0014	Minuend's Hi byte
0015	Subtrahend's Lo byte
0016	Subtrahend's Hi byte
0017	Difference's Lo byte
0018	Difference's Hi byte

(*b*)

Fig. 8-19 (*a*) A flowchart and (*b*) a memory map for the double-precision subtraction program. Compare this flowchart with the one used for double-precision addition in Fig. 8-10.

163

Memory address	Memory contents	Comments
0000	LDD A	Load accumulator direct
0001	00	} Minuend's address (Lo byte)
0002	13	
0003	SUB M	Subtract from memory direct
0004	00	} Subtrahend's address (Lo byte)
0005	15	
0006	STA A	Store accumulator direct
0007	00	} Difference's address (Lo byte)
0008	17	
0009	LDD A	Load accumulator direct
000A	00	} Minuend's address (Hi byte)
000B	14	
000C	SCB M	Subtract with borrow
000D	00	} Subtrahend's address (Hi byte)
000E	16	
000F	STA A	Store accumulator direct
0010	00	} Difference's address (Hi byte)
0011	18	
0012	HLT	Halt
0013	5C	Lo byte } Minuend (30,812)
0014	78	Hi byte
0015	AC	Lo byte } Subtrahend (12,460)
0016	30	Hi byte
0017	B0	Lo byte } Difference (18,352)
0018	47	Hi byte

Fig. 8-20 A program listing for the double-precision subtraction problem. Note: this program uses both the SUB M and the SCB M instructions.

Figure 8-20 shows a program listing much like the one used for the double-precision Add addition. The program is altered to do a double-precision subtraction. In the following paragraphs, we briefly step through this program.

In the first program instruction, we use an LDD A instruction to load the accumulator with the contents of memory location 0013. The minuend's lo byte is stored there.

In the program's second instruction, we subtract the contents of memory location 0015 from the contents of the accumulator. The lo byte of the subtrahend is at memory location 0015. Since this subtraction causes a borrow, the status register's carry bit is set to logic "1."

The SUB M instruction is used. When this subtraction takes place, we do not want to use any borrows (carries) from a previous operation. Since this is the first subtraction in this double-precision operation, any carry bit from a previous operation is irrelevant. If we now used the SCB M instruction, we would have to use additional instructions to make sure that the status register's carry bit was set to "0" prior to our performing this subtraction. Using a Subtract instruction without carry saves us this extra effort.

The result of the lo-byte subtraction is now in the accumulator. The third instruction stores the accumulator's contents in the memory location where we have decided to store the difference. An STA A instruction stores the accumulator's contents at memory location 0017.

The fourth instruction is another LDD A instruction. This instruction loads the minuend's hi byte into the accumulator.

Using the fifth instruction, we subtract the subtrahend's hi byte from the minuend's hi byte. The subtrahend's hi byte is stored in memory location 0016. We use an SCB M instruction to subtract the contents of memory location 0016 from the contents of the accumulator. The SCB M instruction also subtracts the contents of the status register's carry bit from the result. For this particular instruction, the status register's carry bit is set to logic "1," because the previous subtraction (the lo byte of the double-precision subtraction) needed a borrow from the hi byte. The result in the accumulator is the difference's hi byte.

In the sixth instruction, we again use the STA A instruction to store the difference's hi byte in memory location 0018. The difference of the complete subtraction is now stored at memory locations 0017 and 0018.

This example of double-precision arithmetic shows one of the reasons why microprocessors have so many different yet similar instructions. The difference between a Subtract with Carry instruction and a Subtract instruction allowed us to avoid an extra instruction (to clear the status register's carry bit). If we had used the CLA A (Clear Accumulator) instruction at the beginning, then the program would have taken two additional microprocessor cycles. We were able to avoid the extra instruction because our microprocessor has the flexibility of two different kinds of Subtract instructions. In this case, a Subtract instruction (without carry) was the more efficient.

Self-Test

Check your understanding by answering these questions.

10. Rewrite the program flowchart in Fig. 8-19 to do a triple-precision subtraction.

11. What Subtract condition causes the status register's carry bit to be set to logic "1"? Give an example.

12. What Subtract condition causes the status register's zero bit to be set to logic "1"? Give an example.

13. What Subtract condition causes the status register's negative bit to be set to logic "1"? Give an example.

14. Once a Subtract operation sets the status register's negative bit, what must you do to display the number in unsigned binary format?

8-4 THE DECIMAL ADJUST INSTRUCTION

The Decimal Adjust instruction gives the microprocessor some ability to work with BCD (binary-coded decimal) numbers. Of course, software could add this ability to a microprocessor. But as we have seen earlier, special built-in convenience instructions can save many program steps.

Why should we want the microprocessor to handle BCD numbers easily? The answer to this question lies in the use of the microprocessor. Many microprocessors are used in simple, noncomputer systems. These systems quite often use BCD-oriented inputs and outputs.

For example, microprocessors are now used in electronic counters. The microprocessor's input is BCD data from the high-speed decade counters. The high-speed decade counters are used to count the instrument's input signal. The microprocessor does calculations on the BCD data such as time-to-frequency conversions, averaging, auto-ranging, etc. The microprocessor's output, which drives the electronic counter's displays, is also BCD data. A block diagram of an electronic counter system is shown in Fig. 8-21. The figure shows that the single-chip microcomputer both inputs and outputs BCD data.

In this example, you can see a practical reason for a microprocessor that can handle BCD data. When BCD capability is necessary, we want to save the microprocessor the additional task of converting BCD data to binary data. You also want to avoid having to convert binary results back to BCD, which is needed to drive displays. There are many other applications in which it is easier to use BCD data at the input and output than to do BCD-to-binary and binary-to-BCD conversions. For example, point of sale (POS) terminals (used in department stores, fast food restaurants, etc.), quite often have BCD keyboards and displays. Microwave ovens and

CLA A (clear accumulator)

BCD (binary-coded decimal)

Decade counters

Point of sale (POS) terminals

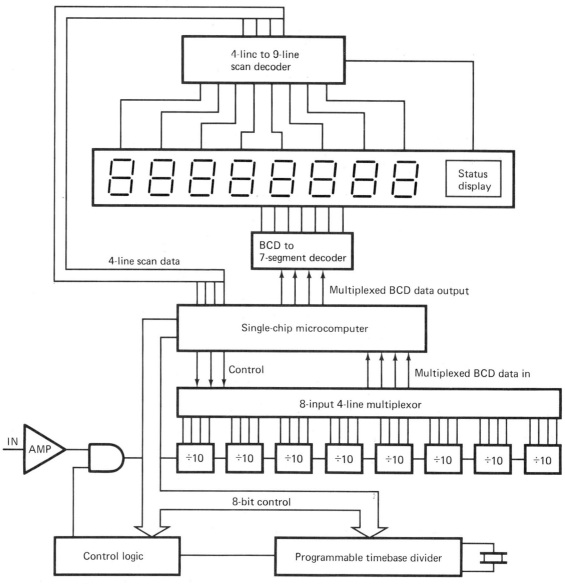

Fig. 8-21 A microcomputer-based time and frequency meter.
The microcomputer controls the instrument, selecting decimal
points, status displays, and time-base frequencies. It also provides computations on the data, such as l/X and averages.

self-contained electronic games are house-
hold products that use BCD data.

The Decimal Adjust instruction enables the
microprocessor to handle BCD numbers con-
veniently. Before looking at the Decimal Adjust instruction, however, let's see what it does.

Using binary numbers to encode decimal
data requires representing the ten digits 0
through 9. Encoding the digit 9_{10} as 1001_2 obviously takes 4 bits. Four bits must be set
aside for all BCD numbers. All the 4-bit binary numbers *above* 1001_2, however, are *not*
legal BCD numbers. Consequently, when
two BCD digits are added, unless the sum is

9_{10} or less the sum will not be in proper BCD
format. The Decimal Adjust instruction corrects a BCD calculation in which the result is
greater than 1001_2.

The Decimal Adjust instruction takes the
form:

DECIMAL ADJUST ACCUMULATOR
DAD A
A $\rightarrow$ 2-byte BCD

DAD A

1 byte
2 cycles

The Decimal Adjust instruction is executed just after two BCD numbers have been added. The sum must still be in the accumulator. This instruction adjusts the results to make certain that they are in correct BCD format.

The Decimal Adjust instruction sets the zero and negative bits of the status register if the results warrant. The status register's carry bit is set if the value of the most significant BCD number is *greater than* 9 (1001_2).

The following example shows how the Decimal Adjust instruction is used. Figure 8-22(*a*) shows the addition of two 4-digit decimal numbers. As stated earlier, one common way to express numbers for use in electronic products is in BCD. Figure 8-22(*b*) shows the BCD representation of this addition problem. In this case, simply adding the BCD numbers yields a result that is neither BCD nor binary. You will remember that any 4-bit number *greater* than 1001_2 is not a legal BCD number.

The correction to BCD is also shown in Fig. 8-22(*b*). In each case where this addition results in a BCD number greater than 1001_2, the number 0110_2 is added to the result. We start with the BCD pair representing the least significant digits. Any carry generated by the BCD correction must be included in the next digit's BCD correction. You can see that we are able to correct the BCD sums. Each column now has a correct BCD answer.

A program to do this 4-digit BCD addition problem is flowcharted in Fig. 8-23. This program is very much like our double-precision addition program. The major difference is that the BCD Decimal Adjust instruction is executed after each addition.

The program listing is shown in Fig. 8-24. The program is just a few instructions longer than the program that showed double-precision binary addition. This program lets us add two BCD numbers as long as the result lies between 0 and 9999. We can see why pure binary addition is more efficient when it can be used. Ordinary double-precision addition lets us have results between 0 and 65,535 with fewer instructions. When BCD operations are necessary, we pay a price.

In the first instruction, the lo byte of the addend is loaded into the accumulator. Note that this lo byte contains *two* BCD numbers. They are the addend's two least significant digits, the BCD numbers 8 and 9. When two BCD numbers are put into a single byte, we say we are using "packed" BCD.

In the program's second instruction we add the augend's lo byte to the addend's lo byte. The augend's lo byte contains the packed BCD numbers 7 and 6. Referring to Fig. 8-22, we can see that the accumulator contains 1111 1111 after this addition. These, of course, are not BCD numbers.

The program's third instruction is the Decimal Adjust instruction. This instruction changes the accumulator's contents from 1111 1111 to 0110 0101. The status register's carry bit is also set because this decimal adjustment causes a carry.

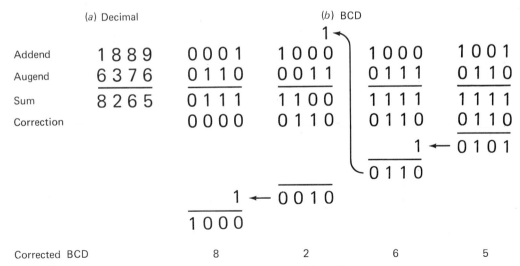

Fig. 8-22 Addition of BCD numbers in a binary adder. Because the result can exceed 1001_2 (9_{10}), we must be able to adjust to legal BCD numbers. This is done by adding 0110 to the result, or by using the microprocessor's **DAD** instruction.

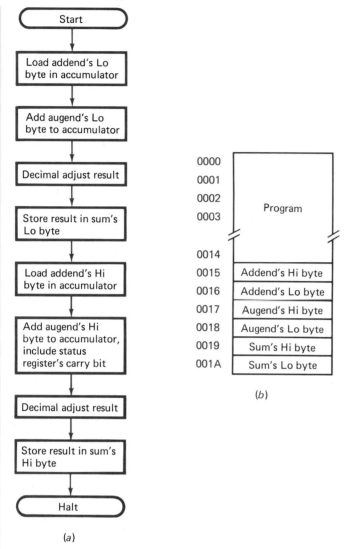

```
                      ┌──────────────┐
                      │    Start     │
                      └──────┬───────┘
                             │
                      ┌──────▼───────┐
                      │ Load addend's Lo
                      │ byte in accumulator
                      └──────┬───────┘
                             │
                      ┌──────▼───────┐
                      │ Add augend's Lo
                      │ byte to accumulator
                      └──────┬───────┘
                             │
                      ┌──────▼───────┐
                      │ Decimal adjust result
                      └──────┬───────┘
                             │
                      ┌──────▼───────┐
                      │ Store result in sum's
                      │ Lo byte
                      └──────┬───────┘
                             │
                      ┌──────▼───────┐
                      │ Load addend's Hi
                      │ byte in accumulator
                      └──────┬───────┘
                             │
                      ┌──────▼───────┐
                      │ Add augend's Hi
                      │ byte to accumulator,
                      │ include status
                      │ register's carry bit
                      └──────┬───────┘
                             │
                      ┌──────▼───────┐
                      │ Decimal adjust result
                      └──────┬───────┘
                             │
                      ┌──────▼───────┐
                      │ Store result in sum's
                      │ Hi byte
                      └──────┬───────┘
                             │
                      ┌──────▼───────┐
                      │    Halt      │
                      └──────────────┘
```

(a)

0000	
0001	
0002	Program
0003	
0014	
0015	Addend's Hi byte
0016	Addend's Lo byte
0017	Augend's Hi byte
0018	Augend's Lo byte
0019	Sum's Hi byte
001A	Sum's Lo byte

(b)

Fig. 8-23 A flowchart and a memory map for a 4-digit BCD addition program. After each addition, the decimal adjust instruction corrects for the binary addition of BCD data.

The fourth instruction stores the adjusted BCD numbers 6 and 5 in memory location 001A. These are the sum's two least significant digits.

The fifth instruction loads the addend's two most significant digits from their memory location into the accumulator.

The sixth instruction adds the augend's two most significant digits to the addend's two most significant digits. Looking at the program, you can see that this is done by using an Add with Carry instruction. The Add with Carry is used because we must include any carry from the first Decimal Adjust instruction. This carry is stored in the status register's carry bit.

Again looking at Fig. 8-22, we see that the accumulator must now contain the binary numbers 0111 1100. These are not BCD numbers. Again we use the Decimal Adjust instruction. The result of using the Decimal Adjust instruction is the numbers 1000 and 0010. These are the BCD numbers 8 and 2.

You should note that the Decimal Adjust instruction is used throughout this program. If the two numbers resulting from the addition are already correct BCD numbers, no adjustment is made. That is, the Decimal Adjust instruction looks to see if the BCD numbers are over 1001_2 before it makes the adjustment.

The Store instruction is used again to put

Memory address	Memory contents	Comments
0000	LDD A	Load accumulator direct
0001	00	} Addend's address (Lo byte)
0002	16	
0003	ADD M	Add from memory direct
0004	00	} Augend's address (Lo byte)
0005	18	
0006	DAD	Decimal adjust
0007	STA A	Store accumulator direct
0008	00	} Sum's address (Lo byte)
0009	1A	
000A	LDD A	Load accumulator direct
000B	00	} Addend's address (Hi byte)
000C	15	
000D	ACD M	Add with carry
000E	00	} Augend's address (Hi byte)
000F	17	
0010	DAD	Decimal adjust
0011	STA A	Store accumulator direct
0012	00	} Sum's address (Hi byte)
0013	19	
0014	HLT	Halt
0015	0 0 0 1 1 0 0 0	Hi byte } Addend (1,889)
0016	1 0 0 0 1 0 0 1	Lo byte
0017	0 1 1 0 0 0 1 1	Hi byte } Augend (6,376)
0018	0 1 1 1 0 1 1 0	Lo byte
0019	1 0 0 0 0 0 1 0	Hi byte } Sum (8,265)
001A	0 1 1 0 0 1 0 1	Lo byte

Fig. 8-24 A program listing for adding two 8-bit packed BCD numbers. Memory locations 0015 through 001A contain the data in packed BCD form.

these two BCD numbers in memory location 0019. This is the sum's hi byte. We now can see that the memory locations 0019 and 001A contain the BCD sum 8265.

The purpose of the Decimal Adjust instruction is to correct the results of adding two BCD numbers with a binary adder. The Decimal Adjust instruction cannot correct for the subtraction of two BCD numbers using binary subtraction. The Decimal Adjust instruction corrects the results of addition only.

There is software that allows arithmetic processing of any operation in BCD. There is also software to convert BCD to binary and binary to BCD. Obviously, this software results

in programs that are much longer than a single instruction.

Self-Test

Check your understanding by answering these questions.

15. We do not need both a Decimal Adjust and a Decimal Adjust with Carry instruction. Why?

16. The Decimal Adjust instruction is useful only when you want to add two BCD numbers. If you also need to subtract BCD numbers, would you still use the Decimal Adjust instruction? Why?

Counting

Increment
register

Decrement
register

Increment
register pair

Decrement
register pair

17. The Decimal Adjust instruction must inspect the results in the microprocessor's accumulator and correct differently for each of four different conditions that may happen. Two of these conditions are: (1) The least significant BCD digit is greater than 1001_2, but the most significant digit is less than 1001_2. You add 0110_2 to correct. (2) Both the BCD digits exceed 1001_2. You must add $0110\ 0110_2$ to correct. What are the other two conditions?

18. You want to add BCD numbers with sums from 0 to 999,999. Flowchart a program to do this. Draw a memory map showing the space reserved for the augend, the addend, and the sum.

19. A binary number of how many bits would be needed to do the job outlined in self-test question 18? If you were using an 8-bit microprocessor, would there be any difference between the number of bytes reserved for a binary unsigned augend and the number of bytes for a BCD augend?

20. When more than one BCD number is put into a microprocessor's data word, we say we are using "packed" BCD. For example, an 8-bit microprocessor packs two BCD digits into one word. How do the ranges of a double-precision binary word and a double-precision packed BCD word compare in a 16-bit microprocessor?

8-5 THE INCREMENT AND DECREMENT INSTRUCTIONS

Increment and Decrement are really just special arithmetic instructions. The Increment instruction adds a binary "1" to a register's current contents. The Decrement instruction subtracts a binary "1" from the register's current contents. The Increment and Decrement instructions are used in applications that involve counting. That is, they are used when a register is keeping track of how many times a certain operation is done.

Although our microprocessor has Increment and Decrement instructions only for registers, many microprocessors have instructions to increment and decrement memory locations.

The Increment and Decrement instructions are single-byte, two-cycle instructions. Note: Neither the Increment Register instruction nor the Decrement Register instruction affects the status register's carry bit.

INCREMENT REGISTER
INC r
$r + 1 \rightarrow r$

| INC r |

The Increment Register instruction adds a binary "1" to the contents of the indicated register. If executing this instruction yields a "1" in the MSB or a zero result, then the appropriate bit in the status register is set.

DECREMENT REGISTER
DEC r
$r - 1 \rightarrow r$

| DEC r |

The Decrement Register instruction subtracts a binary "1" from the register's contents. In all other respects this instruction is identical to the Increment Register instruction. If executing this instruction yields a "1" in the MSB or a zero result, then the appropriate bit in the status register is set.

INCREMENT REGISTER PAIR
IRP
$BC + 1 \rightarrow BC$

| IRP |

DECREMENT REGISTER PAIR
DRP
$BC - 1 \rightarrow BC$

| DRP |

The Increment Register Pair and Decrement Register Pair instructions operate on the BC register pair. The only difference between these instructions and the previous Increment and Decrement Register instructions is that these instructions operate on the BC register pair as if it were a single 16-bit register.

This means that incrementing the BC register pair from 00FF to 0100 or decrementing it from 0100 to 00FF can be done automatically. We do not have to issue a separate instruction to make sure that there is a carry between the B and C registers. However, if you use the simple Increment Register or Decrement Register instruction, there will be no carry from the B to the C register. Depending on the instruction chosen, these registers can be used either as two 8-bit registers or as a single 16-bit register. Incrementing or decrementing a register pair affects only the zero bit in the status register. The zero bit is set when all 16 bits of the BC register pair are logic "0" following an Increment or Decrement Register Pair instruction.

The Decrement instruction is often used to tell when a certain part of the program has been done a given number of times. As with any other programming problem, there are a number of ways to do this job. We can use the Increment instruction. That is, each time the program passes through a certain point, we can increment a register. We can then test the register's contents using a Compare instruction. If the Compare instruction sets the status register's zero bit, then we can jump to any specified part of the program.

The Decrement instruction lets us do the same job with fewer instructions. First, we preset the register to a binary number. We set this number equal to the number of counts that we wish to check for. Second, each time the program passes through a certain point, we decrement the register. Third, after we have decremented the register, a Jump If Zero instruction checks to see if decrementing the register has caused the status register's zero bit to be set. If so, the program jumps to the specified location. If decrementing has not set the status register's zero bit, then the program continues. This technique saves one instruction.

When using the Decrement instruction to act as a counter, you must be very careful about where you place the Decrement instruction in the program. For example, the number of operations counted if we decrement before the instruction is different from the number if we decrement after.

Let's suppose that you want to count the number of times that a Store Indirect instruction is used. Figure 8-25(a) and (b) show two different ways to do this. The program in Fig. 8-25(a) starts with a Load B Immediate instruction. Register B is loaded with the number 03. We choose this number because we wish to execute three Store Indirect instructions.

As the figure shows, some other, unspecified program instructions are then executed. These instructions lead up to the Store Indirect instruction. Following the Store Indirect instruction, register B is decremented. The program jumps to an instruction ending the program if decrementing register B causes register B's contents to be all logic "0."

As you can see by looking at the program outlined in Fig. 8-25(a), we complete three Store instructions. After the third Store, the Decrement instruction results in all logic "0s" in the B register. This causes the Jump If Zero to execute, and the program ends.

In Fig. 8-25(b), the program is organized a little differently. It starts in the same way. That is, register B is loaded with the number 03. After some other, unspecified program instructions are executed, we decrement the B register. A Jump If Zero is then executed, followed by the first Store Indirect instruction.

After the second Store Indirect instruction is executed, some additional program instructions are executed. Just before the third Store Indirect instruction is to be executed, the third Decrement B is executed. This causes the contents of register B to become all logic "0." The next instruction is the Jump If Zero. The microprocessor immediately jumps to the instructions ending the program. The third Store Indirect instruction is never executed. This is because the Decrement and the Jump If Zero instructions are executed before rather than after the Store Indirect instruction.

This example shows two things. First, it shows how the Decrement instruction may be used as a counter. The counter keeps track of how many times we have done things. It lets us end the program after a desired number of counts have been completed. Second, it shows us that programming logic must be well thought out. The exact position of the Decrement instruction in the program can change the number of instructions that are executed.

Of course, there are two ways to fix this problem. First, we can use program A. Second, we can change the data contained in program B's first instruction. That is, we can initially set register B to 04 when we really want three counts. We compensate for the one count that we know will be lost.

We have used the Increment Register Pair instruction in a number of previous examples. As we have noted, the Decrement Register Pair is identical to the Increment Register Pair except that we subtract a binary "1" from the register instead of adding a binary "1" to the register. Of course, one of the many common uses of a 16-bit register is to point to memory locations.

171

Sequence		Instruction		Register B	Stores
1		LDA	B,03	03	
.	PGM	.		.	
.		.		.	
17		STI	A	03	1
18		DEC	B	02	
19		JZ	99	02	
.	PGM	.		.	
.		.		.	
39		STI	A	02	2
40		DEC	B	01	
41		JZ	99	01	
.		.		.	
.		.		.	
.		.		.	
70		STI	A	02	3
71		DEC	B	00	
72		JZ	99		
99		HLT			

(a)

Sequence		Instruction		Register B	Stores
1		LDA	B,03	03	
.	PGM	.		.	
.		.		.	
17		DEC	B	02	
18		JZ	99	02	
19		STI	A	02	1
.	PGM	.		.	
.		.		.	
39		DEC	B	01	
40		JZ	99	01	
41		STI	A	01	2
.	PGM	.		.	
.		.		.	
70		DEC	B	00	
71		JZ			
72		STI	A		
99		HLT			

(b)

Fig. 8-25 Two ways to code the logic for a down-counter. (a)
The Store instruction is executed three times before the program
is halted. (b) The Store instruction is executed twice before the
program is halted.

Usually we want to increment through successive memory locations. Sometimes, however, we wish to decrement through successive memory locations. In that case, we use the Decrement Register Pair instruction.

The Decrement Register Pair instruction can also be used as a simple counter.

For example, suppose you wish to store data in a memory buffer 24,576 bytes long. You need to know how many bytes of available buffer space are left at anytime. The simplest way to keep track of this is to use the BC register pair as a counter. A program might operate like the one in Fig. 8-25. The only difference between these two programs is the number loaded into the BC register pair at the beginning of the program. As each byte of data is added to the memory buffer, the program decrements the number in the BC register pair. If data are later taken out of the buffer, perhaps to be placed on magnetic tape, the program increments the BC register pair by the number of bytes taken out of the buffer. Whenever you need to know how many bytes of data are left in the buffer, you simply call the BC register pair.

Self-Test

Check your understanding by answering these questions.

21. Show what happens to the register contents and to the status register's contents as each of the following registers is incremented:

		Z	N	C
a.	1001 0111			
b.	1111 1111			
c.	0000 0000			
d.	0000 1111			
e.	1111 0000			

		Z	N	C
f.	1111 1111 1111 1111			
g.	0000 0000 0000 0000			
h.	0000 0000 1111 1111			
i.	1111 1111 0000 0000			

22. Show what happens to the register contents and to the status register's contents as each of the registers in question 21 is decremented.

23. Sometimes an incrementing or decrementing counter is used as a clock. That is, a small subroutine is written that indicates when a certain time interval has passed. How do you think this is done? On what property of the microprocessor does this clock depend for its accuracy?

24. How would a decrementing register be used as part of multiplication? Flowchart a simple program to multiply two 8-bit numbers using a decrementing register. What are the disadvantages of this kind of multiplication?

Summary

1. The microprocessor's only indispensable arithmetic instruction is the Add instruction. All other instructions are based on the Add instruction. The Add instructions affect all the status register's bits. There are also add instructions that include the status register's current contents.

2. The Add with Carry instructions are used to include any carry caused by a previous operation. Often the Add with Carry instruction is used to help add two multiple-precision numbers.

3. A multiple-precision number is a number that is expressed in more than one word because one word is not large enough. Adding two double-precision numbers uses a simple Add for the lo byte and an Add with Carry for the hi byte.

4. A Subtract instruction simply adds the subtrahend's 2's complement to the minuend. The Subtract instruction is a convenience in programming. When you use the Subtract instruction, the addressed data are subtracted from the data in the accumulator.

5. A borrow is generated when the subtrahend is larger than the minuend. Subtracting two numbers may cause a borrow, and the borrow sets the status register's carry bit to logic "1."

6. A Subtract with Carry instruction subtracts the subtrahend and the carry from the minuend. A Subtract followed by a Subtract with Carry is used to do double-precision subtraction.

7. Often microprocessors need to handle BCD data. BCD data are used by many simple devices.

8. The Decimal Adjust instruction corrects

173

for the binary addition of two BCD numbers. The Decimal Adjust instruction corrects for packed BCD. A Decimal Adjust instruction usually cannot correct for subtracting two BCD numbers in a binary arithmetic unit.

9. "Packed BCD" refers to putting two or four BCD numbers in a single 8- or 16-bit word.

10. BCD arithmetic has a lower range than binary arithmetic for the same word length.

11. The Increment instructions add a binary "1" to a register's contents.

12. The Decrement instructions subtract a binary "1" from the register's contents.

13. The Increment Register Pair and Decrement Register Pair instructions work on the register pair as if it were a single 16-bit register instead of two 8-bit registers. The Increment and Decrement instructions are used to make counters that check off events or cause delays.

14. When a register or a memory location is used as a counter, the exact construction of the program logic can change the final count.

Chapter Review Questions

8-1. The Add instruction is the microprocessor's basic ___?___ instruction.
    a. Logic   c. Carry
    b. Arithmetic   d. Transfer

8-2. In the ADD r instruction, the mnemonic ADD is the op code and the r is the
    a. Arithmetic result   c. Address
    b. Accumulator   d. Carry bit

8-3. In the text microprocessor, the Add from Memory Direct instruction is a ___?___-byte instruction.
    a. 1   b. 2   c. 3   d. 4

8-4. The Add instructions add the indicated data to the accumulator. The accumulator's original contents are
    a. The addend   c. Stored
    b. The sum   d. Lost

8-5. The Add instruction will not set the status register's ___?___ bit.
    a. Zero   c. Negative
    b. Carry   d. (None of the above)

8-6. The Add with Carry instruction
    a. Includes the status register's carry bit
    b. Sets the status register's carry bit on every operation
    c. Includes the status register's borrow bit
    d. (None of the above)

8-7. You are using an 8-bit microprocessor. You need a decimal result in the range from $-1,000,000$ to $+1,000,000$. For this you choose signed arithmetic and ___?___ precision.
    a. Single   c. Triple
    b. Double   d. Quadruple

8-8. The Add Immediate instruction is 2 bytes long. The Add Immediate with Carry instruction is ___?___ bytes long.
    a. 1   b. 2   c. 3   d. 4

8-9. When you are doing a multiple-precision addition, the carry from a previous operation is
    a. Stored in the sum's hi byte
    b. Lost if not stored in memory
    c. Stored in the addend's hi byte
    d. Stored in the status register's carry bit

8-10. A memory map is used to
    a. Flowchart a program
    b. Diagram how a program uses memory
    c. Diagram the program counter sequence
    d. (All of the above)

8-11. The Subtract instruction really just adds
    a. The subtrahend's 2's complement
    b. The subtrahend's complement
    c. With borrow
    d. (None of the above)

8-12. The Subtract instruction subtracts
    a. The addressed data from the borrow
    b. The addressed data from the accumulator
    c. The accumulator from the addressed data
    d. The addressed data from the status register's carry (borrow) bit

8-13. The Subtract instructions set the status register's ____?____ bit if the result warrants.
    a. Zero   c. Negative
    b. Carry   d. (All of the above)

8-14. The Subtract with Carry instruction subtracts the data and
    a. Subtracts the borrow bit also
    b. Always sets the carry bit
    c. Adds the borrow bit
    d. (None of the above)

8-15. The Decimal Adjust instruction lets you
    a. Work with decimal numbers
    b. Correct BCD arithmetic operations
    c. Correct the binary addition of BCD numbers
    d. Perform BCD division

8-16. BCD data are used
    a. On all microwave oven controllers
    b. On all POS terminals
    c. On many simple products
    d. To drive all seven-segment displays

8-17. Packed BCD lets you put ____?____ BCD number(s) in each byte.
    a. 1   b. 2   c. 3   d. (None of the above)

8-18. To perform BCD subtraction you must
    a. Use a BCD software routine
    b. Use the 2's complement routine
    c. Include the status register's borrow (carry) bit.
    d. First convert the BCD to decimal

8-19. The Increment instruction ____?____ the register.
    a. Adds a carry to   c. Adds a binary "1" to
    b. Subtracts a binary   d. Clears
    "1" from

8-20. Both the Increment and Decrement instructions can be used to make a:
    a. Software up-counter
    b. Software down-counter
    c. Software timer
    d. (All of the above)

8-21. Flowchart a multiple-precision addition.

8-22. Why would you expect a multiple-precision multiplication to use an Add with Carry?

8-23. Explain the difference between how the Add Immediate and the Add Immediate with Carry instructions affect the status register's carry bit.

8-24. Explain what causes a borrow.

8-25. What does a memory map tell you?

8-26. *a.* The BC register pair contains FFFF. It is incremented. What happens?
b. Again, the BC register pair contains FFFF. The C register is incremented. What happens?

Answers to Self-Tests

1. See Fig. 8-26. The Store instruction adds 5 μs.
2. The first instruction LDA A is changed to LDD A,0008. It loads the accumulator with the data you have in memory location 0008. The second instruction ADI is changed to ADD M,0009. It adds the contents of memory location 0009 to the accumulator. The third instruction becomes STA A,000A. It is different because it uses all direct addressing.
3. LDA B,29
   LDA A,0C
   ADD B
   HLT
   The main difference between the example and

self-test question 2 is the use of LDA B,29 to put 29_{16} into register B.
4. c.
5. The first Add instruction might include a carry from a previous operation. The second Add instruction would not include the carry at all.
6. First, you would add one more byte to the memory locations of the addend, the augend, and the sum. Second, you would add another routine made up of LDA A, ACD M, and STA A to add the third bytes.
7. It does not change the execution time. It does not change the memory space needed.
8. It adds data that already *include* the carry bit as a source. Its execution may *set* any of the status register's bits.
9. The Add at the beginning avoids false carry bits. Follow-on Adds include any previously generated carries.
10. See Fig. 8-27.
11. The carry bit is set to logic "1" when the subtraction requires a borrow. This is caused when the subtrahend is larger than the minuend. For example,

$$\begin{array}{r} \text{borrow} \begin{cases} {}^{\nearrow}1\ 0011 & 3 \\ 0101 & -\ 5 \\ \hline {}^{\searrow}1\ 1110 & -2 \end{cases} \end{array}$$

12. The zero bit is set to logic "1" when the result causes all "0s." For example,

$$\begin{array}{r r} 1101 & 13 \\ \underline{1101} & \underline{-13} \\ 0000 & 0 \end{array}$$

13. The negative bit is set when the MSB is of the result logic "1." For example,

$$\begin{array}{r r} 0000\ 1111 & 15 \\ \underline{0001\ 0000} & \underline{-\ 16} \\ 1\ \ 1111\ 1111 & -1 \end{array}$$
$\quad\ \ \uparrow\qquad\ \uparrow$
borrow negative result

14. Complement and add 1. You also must store the negative information somewhere so that you can turn on the display's minus sign.
15. Because the Decimal Adjust instruction includes any carries.
16. You *might* continue to use the Decimal Adjust instruction for addition, but you would have to use a software routine to subtract.
17. (3) The least significant BCD digit is less than 1001_2, but the most significant digit is greater than 1001_2. You add $0110\ 0000_2$ to correct. (4) The least significant BCD digit is less than 1001_2, and the most significant digit is less than 1001_2. You do not have to correct.
18. See Fig. 8-28.

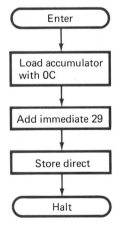

Fig. 8-26 The program of self-test question 1.

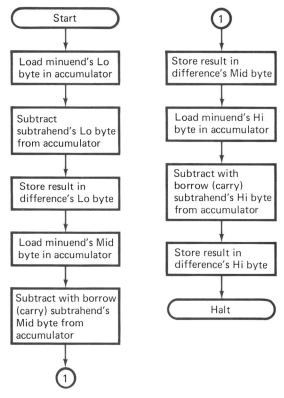

Fig. 8-27 A flowchart to illustrate self-test question 10.

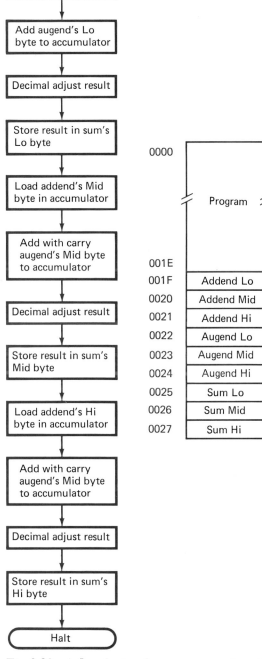

Fig. 8-28 A flowchart and a memory map for self-test question 18.

19. You would need a 20-bit number, which can represent decimal numbers from 0 to 1,048,576. There would be no difference, because either way you would need 4 bytes.

20. A double-precision 16-bit binary word has a range of ±2,147,483,648, or 0 to 4,294,967,296. The double-precision packed BCD word has a range of 0 to 99,999,999.

21.

	Register	Z	N	C
a.	1001 1000	0	1	0
b.	0000 0000	1	0	0
c.	0000 0001	0	0	0
d.	0001 0000	0	0	0
e.	1111 0001	0	1	0
f.	0000 0000 0000 0000	1	0	0
g.	0000 0000 0000 0001	0	0	0
h.	0000 0001 0000 0000	0	0	0
i.	1111 1111 0000 0001	0	1	0

22.

	Register	Z	N	C
a.	1001 0110	0	1	0
b.	1111 1110	0	1	0
c.	1111 1111	0	1	0
d.	0000 1110	0	0	0
e.	1110 1111	0	1	0
f.	1111 1111 1111 1110	0	1	0
g.	1111 1111 1111 1111	0	1	0
h.	0000 0000 1111 1110	0	0	0
i.	1111 1110 1111 1111	0	1	0

23. The counter is incremented when a time pulse comes. It depends on the microprocessor's clock oscillator for its accuracy.

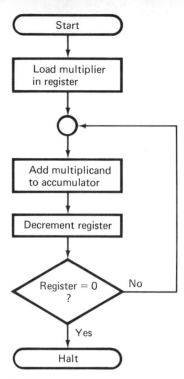

Fig. 8-29   A flowchart to illustrate self-test question 24.

24. The decrementing register would be used to count off successive additions of the multiplicand. See Fig. 8-29 for a flowchart of such a program. The main disadvantage is that it takes a lot of time. For example, to multiply 12 by 200 takes 200 additions.

The Logic Instructions

■ In this chapter, we will learn about several powerful instructions. Like the arithmetic instructions, these new instructions let us work on the data in the microprocessor's accumulator. However, as the chapter title tells you, these instructions do not perform arithmetic operations, but rather logic operations.

In the first part of this chapter, you will look at four instructions. Using these instructions, you will be able to perform the basic logic operations. These logic instructions are the AND, OR, EXCLUSIVE OR, and Complement (NOT) instructions. This chapter also introduces you to the Compare instruction. This powerful instruction is the basis for making tests. You will find that you must make tests in order to solve problems that involve decisions.

The last part of this chapter introduces the Rotate instructions and the Shift instructions. You will see what these two kinds of instructions do and how they differ. You will learn how to use the Rotate and the Shift instructions together to do a multiple-precision shift.

9-1 THE AND, OR, EXCLUSIVE OR, AND COMPLEMENT (NOT) INSTRUCTIONS

When you first think of a microcomputer system, you think of using the microprocessor to do "number crunching"—solving high-powered arithmetic problems. However, many of the microprocessor's applications are for logic operations rather than arithmetic. A microprocessor can replace many logic circuits.

For example, let's look at the single-chip microcomputer system block-diagrammed in Fig. 9-1. This microcomputer system performs a remote-display function. Since this is the only job that this microcomputer system is built to do, we say that this system is "dedicated".

The microprocessor in Fig. 9-1 reads data sent to it over a serial line. In serial transmission, the data arrive at the microprocessor one bit at a time. The microprocessor converts these data to parallel data to be displayed on the four 7-segment displays. The microprocessor also performs the display-scanning function. That is, it lights up display 1, then display 2, then display 3, and finally display 4.

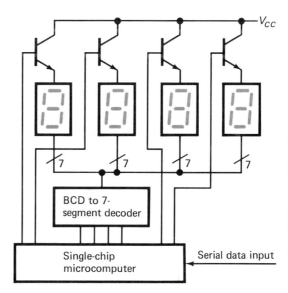

Fig. 9-1 A single-chip microcomputer replacing many logic circuits.

The microprocessor does the display scanning so fast that we cannot see the displays going on and off.

This same job can be done with a large number of small- and medium-scale integrated TTL circuits. However, the remote display is less expensive to build with the sin-

179

AND		
INPUT		OUTPUT
Accumulator bit	Memory or register bit	Accumulator result bit
0	0	0
0	1	0
1	0	0
1	1	1

OR		
INPUT		OUTPUT
Accumulator bit	Memory or register bit	Accumulator result bit
0	0	0
0	1	1
1	0	1
1	1	1

XOR		
INPUT		OUTPUT
Accumulator bit	Memory or register bit	Accumulator result bit
0	0	0
0	1	1
1	0	1
1	1	0

NOT	
INPUT	OUTPUT
Accumulator bit	Accumulator result bit
0	1
1	0

Fig. 9-2 The AND, OR, EXCLUSIVE OR, and NOT truth tables as used by a microprocessor's logic instructions.

gle-chip microcomputer. In this example, the microcomputer system simply replaces discrete logic. The microprocessor does no number crunching.

We must be able to state the results of logic operations in a logical format. In many cases this requires performing logic operations on the data that we are working with. For exam-ple, we may want to AND the data, OR the data, use the EXCLUSIVE OR function, or use the NOT function.

All these operations are available in our microprocessor. Of course, each logic function has a number of addressing modes. We will look at these various logic functions in this section.

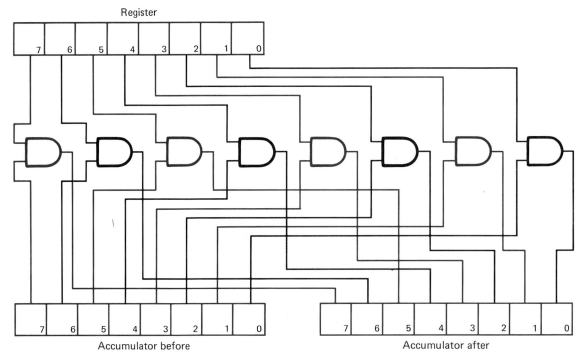

Fig. 9-3 The gate equivalent of the logic AND instruction. Each bit is ANDed separately, and the result is placed in the accumulator.

The following paragraphs look at all of these instructions. We will then look at some examples showing their operation.

Figure 9-2 shows the truth tables used for the AND, OR, EXCLUSIVE OR, and NOT functions. Note: When reading the expressions for the logic instructions, be sure that you do not confuse the logic OR operation (+) with a mathematical Add operation (+).

Each logic operation is a bit-by-bit operation. You can think of it as a simple two-input gate. One input is connected to one of the accumulator's bits. The other input is connected to the same bit position in the memory word or register word. An 8-bit microprocessor has eight of these two-input gates, one for each bit in the microprocessor's word. The drawing in Fig. 9-3 is provided to give you a mental picture of what is happening during the AND operation. In actual practice, the microprocessor uses the ALU to perform the logic operations. Note: Be sure to remember that we always label the bits 0 to 7 from right to left.

As we just noted, a logic instruction operates between the accumulator and some other register word or memory word. Once the logic operation is complete, the result is placed in the accumulator. If the result is zero or if the MSB is a "1," the appropriate status bit is set. The AND, OR, and EXCLUSIVE OR logic instructions do not affect the carry bit. This means that the original contents of the accumulator and the status register are lost.

The following four instructions summarize the logic AND instructions:

AND REGISTER WITH ACCUMULATOR
AND r
$A \cdot r \rightarrow A$

AND r

1 byte
2 cycles

AND MEMORY DIRECT WITH ACCUMULATOR
AND M,Address
$A \cdot M \rightarrow A$

AND M
Hi address
Lo address

3 bytes
4 cycles

AND MEMORY INDIRECT WITH ACCUMULATOR
ANI M
$A \cdot M \rightarrow A$

ANI M

1 byte
3 cycles

AND IMMEDIATE WITH ACCUMULATOR
AND I,Data
$A \cdot Data \rightarrow A$

AND I
Data

2 bytes
3 cycles

The following four instructions summarize the logic OR instructions:

OR REGISTER WITH ACCUMULATOR
OR r
$A + r \rightarrow A$

OR r

1 byte
2 cycles

OR MEMORY DIRECT WITH ACCUMULATOR
OR M,Address
$A + M \rightarrow A$

OR M
Hi address
Lo address

3 bytes
4 cycles

OR MEMORY INDIRECT WITH ACCUMULATOR
ORI M
$A + M \rightarrow A$

ORI M

1 byte
3 cycles

OR IMMEDIATE DATA WITH ACCUMULATOR
OR I,Data
$A + Data \rightarrow A$

OR I
Data

2 bytes
3 cycles

AND register with accumulator

AND memory direct with accumulator

AND memory indirect with accumulator

AND immediate with accumulator

OR register with accumulator

OR memory direct with accumulator

OR memory indirect with accumulator

OR immediate data with accumulator

Exclusive OR register with accumulator

Exclusive OR memory direct with accumulator

Exclusive OR memory indirect with accumulator

Exclusive OR immediate data with accumulator

Bit mask

The following four instructions summarize the logic EXCLUSIVE OR instructions:

EXCLUSIVE OR REGISTER WITH ACCUMULATOR

XOR r

$A \oplus r \to A$

XOR r

1 byte
2 cycles

EXCLUSIVE OR MEMORY DIRECT WITH ACCUMULATOR

XOR M,Address

$A \oplus M \to A$

XOR M
Hi address
Lo address

3 bytes
4 cycles

EXCLUSIVE OR MEMORY INDIRECT WITH ACCUMULATOR

XOI M

$A \oplus M \to A$

XOI M

EXCLUSIVE OR IMMEDIATE DATA WITH ACCUMULATOR

XOR I,Data

$A \oplus Data \to A$

XOR I
Data

2 bytes
3 cycles

When you use a logic instruction, you must be sure to remember that the logic operation is carried out on a bit-for-bit basis. For example, the instruction AND B is executed in Fig. 9-4.

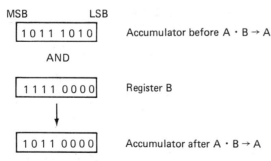

Fig. 9-4 The logic AND function. The accumulator is ANDed with register B.

You can see that the most significant bit of the result in this example is a logic "1." This is because the accumulator's most significant bit *and* register B's most significant bit were both logic "1." However, the next most significant bit (bit 6) of the result is logic "0." This is because we did *not* have a logic "1" in the accumulator's bit 6 *and* a logic "1" in register B's bit 6.

The example in Fig. 9-4 also shows one common application of the AND instruction. This application is called a *bit mask*. For example, suppose you wish to test for all logic "0s" in the accumulator's most significant bits. You want to be sure that the accumulator's four least significant bits are *not* part of the test. However, because of the data source in this case, you know that these four least significant bits may be any value between 0000 and 1111. You must get rid of these four bits before making the test.

To see if all eight bits of the accumulator are logic "0s," you check the status register's zero bit. You will remember that the status register's zero bit is set to logic "1" if and only if every bit in the accumulator is logic "0."

Before testing the status register's contents to see if the zero bit is logic "1," you must first AND the accumulator's contents with the bit pattern in register B. The bit pattern in register B in Fig. 9-4 will eliminate the four least significant bits from the test.

You can see that this AND operation does not change the bit pattern in the accumulator's four most significant bits. However, the AND operation sets the bit pattern in the accumulator's four least significant bits to all logic "0s," because register B's four least significant bits are all logic "0." We call this "masking" the accumulator's lower four bits.

The mask can be any pattern desired. For example, the mask could be every other bit, the center four bits, or the three least significant bits. Since the AND instruction has different addressing modes, we can store the mask in memory and address it directly, store the mask in memory and address it indirectly, store the mask in another register, or store the mask as the data in the byte following the AND Immediate instruction. Storing the mask as the immediate-data byte is probably the most common way to process a mask instruction.

Figure 9-5 shows a logic OR operation. This, too, is a bit-by-bit operation. The result in the accumulator is logic "1" any time there

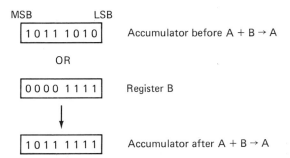

MSB   LSB

Fig. 9-5   The logic OR function. A (the accumulator) is ORed with register B.

is a logic "1" in the accumulator's bit *or* in the matching bit in the memory location or register location.

Looking at Fig. 9-5, you can see that the OR instruction can also be used as a bit mask. In this example, the bits are copied where the mask has logic "0." They are blocked where the mask has logic "1." This mask leaves logic "1" in the bits that are masked out. Depending on the results needed, you can use either an OR mask or an AND mask.

An example of an EXCLUSIVE OR operation is shown in Fig. 9-6. There is a logic "0" in the accumulator for each bit where the accumulator's original contents and the immediate data word's contents match; that is, where both corresponding bits are logic "1" or logic "0."

In this example, a match is found on bits 1, 2, 6, and 7. A match is *not* found on bits 0, 3, 4, and 5.

This example shows the basis for one common use of the EXCLUSIVE OR operation. The EXCLUSIVE OR is valuable for performing tests. Each bit in the tested data is converted to logic "0" *if* it matches the same bit in the mask. After the EXCLUSIVE OR is done, each bit can be tested. The test is done by shifting the tested bit into the accu-

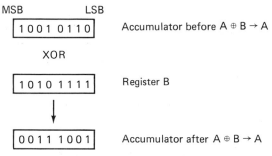

MSB   LSB

Fig. 9-6   The logic EXCLUSIVE OR function. A (the accumulator) is EXCLUSIVE ORed with register B.

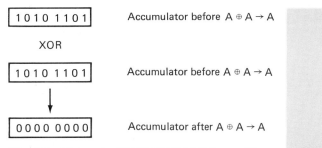

Fig. 9-7   Using the EXCLUSIVE OR as a Clear instruction.

mulator's most significant bit. The status register's negative bit is then tested. If the negative bit is logic "0," the accumulator's most significant bit is logic "0." Therefore, the data matched the mask at that bit position.

This simple test is used to bring in a number of independent bits through a single parallel I/O port and then to test each bit individually. Bits that fail the test (that is, don't match the mask) are immediately identified because they are logic "1s."

Another use of the EXCLUSIVE OR instruction is to clear a data word. Some microprocessors do not offer a Clear instruction. The EXCLUSIVE OR may be used as a Clear instruction. This is done by EXCLUSIVE ORing the word you wish to clear with the word itself. Looking at Fig. 9-7, you can see how this works. Any bit that is EXCLUSIVE ORed with itself always produces logic "0." Therefore, the entire word becomes logic "0" if it is EXCLUSIVE ORed with itself.

The Complement Accumulator instruction complements the accumulator on a bit-by-bit basis. That is, each bit that is logic "1" becomes a logic "0," and each bit that is logic "0" becomes logic "1." The Complement Accumulator instruction performs the logic NOT operation. You can see that this instruction also performs a *1's complement* on a data word. Figure 9-8 shows the accumulator be-

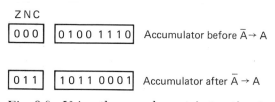

Z N C

Fig. 9-8   Using the complement instruction to perform a logic NOT. This instruction complements, negates, or inverts each accumulator bit on a bit-by-bit basis. Both the negative and the carry bits are set.

fore and after the Complement Accumulator instruction is executed.

It is often necessary to perform a 2's complement. This can be done by executing a 1's complement instruction and then incrementing the accumulator. Incrementing the accumulator adds 1 to the complemented number. This produces the 2's complement.

COMPLEMENT ACCUMULATOR
CMA
$\overline{A} \rightarrow A$

CMA

Executing the CMA (Complement Accumulator) instruction sets the status register's zero bit or negative bit if the result is zero or the MSB is a "1." The carry bit is always set. The Complement Accumulator instruction is a single-byte, 2-cycle instruction.

The following example shows one use of the Complement instruction. We know that arithmetic instructions in the microprocessor can be done in one of two forms. You must use either unsigned binary numbers or signed binary numbers in 2's complement form. If you use the 2's complement form, subtraction becomes very easy. However, negative numbers will be expressed in 2's complement form. They must be converted into unsigned binary numbers before people can read them. After converting a negative 2's complement number into an unsigned binary number, you must somehow show that the number is negative. Many displays include a minus sign (−) for this purpose. Converting a 2's complement negative number into an unsigned binary number is done by taking the 1's complement of the negative number and adding 1. This is shown in Fig. 9-9.

In Fig. 9-9(*a*) we see a simple subtraction problem. The result is negative. That is, the subtrahend is larger than the minuend. We can see that the answer is negative because its most significant bit is logic "1." The answer is in 2's complement form.

In Fig. 9-9(*b*), we see the method used to convert the answer into an unsigned binary number. The answer is complemented. That is, all logic "1s" are changed to logic "0s," and all logic "0s" are changed to logic "1s." To do this in a microprocessor, we use the Complement Accumulator instruction. To get the answer in unsigned binary form, we simply Increment the accumulator by using the Increment Accumulator instruction. After complementing and incrementing, the result shows that the answer's absolute value is 10_{10}. An earlier test of the most significant bit, however, told us that the answer is negative. The binary answer can be displayed as decimal 10. However, the negative indicator must also be turned on to show that the answer is really decimal −10.

The Complement Accumulator instruction can also follow an AND instruction, for example, to make a NAND instruction. Likewise, the Complement instruction will make the OR a NOR and the EXCLUSIVE OR an EXCLUSIVE NOR.

Self-Test

Check your understanding by answering these questions.

1. Find the correct results for the following operations:

   a. 0011 1000   *b.* 1111 0000
        AND   OR
      1010 1010   1010 1010

	Decimal	Binary			
Minuend	60	0 0 1 1 1 1 0 0	Answer	1 1 1 1 0 1 1 0
Subtrahend	70	0 1 0 0 0 1 1 0	Complement	0 0 0 0 1 0 0 1
Difference	−10	1 1 1 1 0 1 1 0	Difference	0 0 0 0 1 0 1 0
		(*a*)		(*b*)	

Fig. 9-9 Using the Complement and Increment instructions to perform a 2's complement operation. Many microprocessors have a single instruction that combines these two instructions into a single 2's complement instruction.

c. 0001 0000
   XOR
  1111 0110

g. 1111 1111
   OR
  1010 1010

d. 0111 0000
   OR
  1010 0000

h. 0000 0000
   OR
  1010 1010

e. 1111 1111
   AND
  1010 1010

i. 1111 1111
   XOR
  1010 1010

f. 0000 0000
   AND
  1111 1111

j. 0000 0000
   XOR
  1010 1010

2. Complement the following data words:
   a. 0011 1000   f. 0000 0000
   b. 1111 0000   g. 1010 1010
   c. 0001 0000   h. 0101 0101
   d. 0111 0000   i. 0000 1111
   e. 1111 1111

3. The EXCLUSIVE OR operation can be used to test for two identical binary words That is, you can do an EXCLUSIVE OR operation and then test the status register's zero bit. The test will tell you if the accumulator's bits are all logic "0." What is the disadvantage of using the EXCLUSIVE OR operation to do this? Note: The disadvantage is great enough that most microprocessors are equipped with an instruction that avoids the disadvantage.

4. The EXCLUSIVE OR performed on one word with itself may be used to set the accumulator to all logic "0s." What logic instruction operating with what data sets the accumulator to all logic "1s"?

5. You are trying to pack BCD data in an 8-bit microprocessor. You have brought the first BCD data word (1001) in and shifted it into the accumulator's four most significant bits. The accumulator now contains:

$$\boxed{1001\ 0000}$$

The second BCD data word is in register B:

$$\boxed{0000\ 1000}$$

What logic operation would you use to make a packed BCD word from these two words? What would the packed BCD word look like when your operation is complete?

6. The data originally in the accumulator were

$$\boxed{1111\ 1000}$$

What operations were used to prepare and move the data now stored in register B as shown in self-test question 5?

7. An AND instruction is followed by a Complement instruction. What is the *logical* relationship of the resulting data to the original data?

8. Flowchart a program to perform a single-byte subtraction and to display the absolute value of the result along with a sign.

9-2 THE COMPARE INSTRUCTION

Often we wish to compare two binary numbers. Most often, we check to see if the two numbers are equal. Sometimes we may want to know which number is larger or smaller.

The EXCLUSIVE OR instruction can check for equality. For example, we can use the EXCLUSIVE OR Immediate instruction. With this instruction, we are testing to see if the data in the accumulator are equal to the data in the instruction byte. To test for equality, move the word that you wish to test into the accumulator. Then execute the EXCLUSIVE OR Immediate instruction. If the two words are equal, the accumulator's contents become all "0s." You can easily see if this happens by testing the status register's zero bit.

This way of comparing two words has a major disadvantage. The accumulator's original contents are lost. If you need to use those data again, you must store them before using the EXCLUSIVE OR to test for equality. Storing the data requires extra instructions.

A similar test can be run by using the Subtract instruction. The reference data are subtracted from the data in the accumulator. If the two data words are equal, the status register's zero bit is set. If the data in the accumulator (A) are less than the reference data R_D, that is, if

$$A < R_D$$

then the carry bit is set because a borrow takes place. If the data in the accumulator are greater than the referenced data, that is, if

$$A > R_D$$

no status register bits are set.

185

Introduction to
Microprocessors
CHAPTER 9

Compare
register with
accumulator

Compare
memory direct
with
accumulator

Compare
memory indirect
with
accumulator

Compare
immediate data
with
accumulator

ASCII keyboard

Parity bit

Control C

The Subtract instruction lets you test for "less than" and "greater than" as well as for equality. This makes the Subtract instruction an even more valuable test. However, this Subtract way of comparing has the same disadvantage as the EXCLUSIVE OR way. That is, the accumulator's original contents are lost.

The Compare instruction overcomes the disadvantage. The Compare instruction works almost the same way as the Subtract instruction. However, the Compare instruction *does not* put the results in the accumulator. The status register's zero, negative, and carry bits can be set, even though the results are not placed in the accumulator. The original data in the accumulator remain unchanged.

The Compare instruction has the usual addressing modes. That is, it can compare any register with the accumulator, it can compare directly addressed memory with the accumulator, it can compare indirectly addressed memory with the accumulator, or it can compare immediate data with the accumulator. These four instructions are shown below.

COMPARE REGISTER WITH
ACCUMULATOR
CMP r
A—r

| CMP r |

1 byte
2 cycles

COMPARE MEMORY DIRECT WITH
ACCUMULATOR
CMP M,Address
A—M

| CMP |
| Hi address |
| Lo address |

3 bytes
4 cycles

COMPARE MEMORY INDIRECT WITH
ACCUMULATOR
CMI M
A—M

| CMI M |

1 byte
2 cycles

COMPARE IMMEDIATE DATA WITH
ACCUMULATOR
CMP I,Data
A—Data

| CMP I |
| Data |

2 bytes
3 cycles

Again, be sure to note that the Compare instructions *do not* place the result in the accumulator. The only result that a Compare instruction may have is that the status register's zero, carry, and negative bits can be set.

The Compare instructions make it possible for the program to make a decision. If the test shows that two words are equal, for example, the program can branch one way. If the words are not equal, the program can proceed another way. The read-file program flowcharted in Fig. 9-10(a) uses the Compare instruction.

This program inputs data words from I/O port 01. Since the words are from an ASCII keyboard, they are 8-bit words. These words have 7 bits of data plus a *parity* bit.* Each word represents a different alphanumeric character or symbol. When the program is in its normal mode, each ASCII character is stored in a sequential memory location. The memory map in Fig. 9-10(b) shows how memory is used.

This program watches for the special ASCII character Control C. The Control C character signals the end of the transmission. We use the compare instruction in this program to detect a Control C. When a Control C character is detected, the program will halt. The exact program listing is given in Fig. 9-11.

Let us now follow the program through, instruction by instruction. The BC register pair points to the next available data-file space. For that reason, this program's first instruction loads a 16-bit address into the BC register pair. The address points to the data file's first memory location. In this example, the data file starts at memory location 0010.

The second instruction inputs data from I/O port 01. The Input instruction transfers the I/O port's contents to the accumulator.

While the data are in the accumulator, we can use the Compare instruction to see if this

* A parity bit is used in data transmission to detect any errors in the data received.

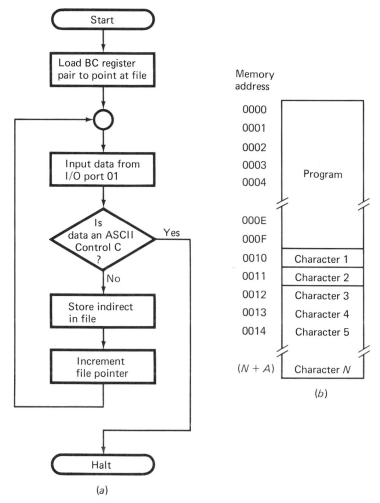

Start

Load BC register
pair to point at file

Input data from
I/O port 01

Is
data an ASCII
Control C
?

Yes

No

Store indirect
in file

Increment
file pointer

Halt

(a)

Memory
address

0000
0001
0002
0003
0004

Program

000E
000F
0010   Character 1
0011   Character 2
0012   Character 3
0013   Character 4
0014   Character 5

(N + A)   Character N

(b)

Fig. 9-10   (a) A program to put ASCII characters in sequential
memory locations and test for the Control C character.   (b) The
program's memory map showing the memory space reserved for
the data storage.

word is the unique binary word that represents the character Control C. We can do
this *without* destroying the contents of the accumulator. We do not want to modify the accumulator's contents, because we will store
the contents in the data file if we do not detect
a Control C.

A Control C is represented by the 8-bit binary word 0000 0011. This is 03 in hexadecimal. Therefore, the Compare Immediate instruction's second byte is loaded with 03. If
the I/O data in the accumulator are 03, then
the Compare instruction sets the status register's zero bit to logic "1." If the data in the
accumulator are not 03, then the Compare instruction does not set the status register's zero
bit.

The fourth instruction (Jump If Zero) is
directed by the status register's zero bit. We

will look at this instruction in more detail in
Chap. 10. The Jump If Zero instruction sets
the program counter to the value 000F *if* the
status register's zero bit is set to logic "1." If
the jump does happen (because the Compare
instruction has found a Control C in the accumulator), the program counter jumps to location 000F. The instruction executed at 000F
is a Halt. This stops the program.

If the ASCII character in the accumulator
is not a Control C, the status register's zero bit
is not set. Therefore, no jump takes place.
The next consecutive instruction (at location
000A) is the next one executed. This is a
Store Indirect instruction. It stores the accumulator's contents in the memory location
pointed to by the BC register pair. When this
program is executed, the BC register pair
points to memory location 0010. This is be-

187

Memory address	Memory contents	Comments
0000	LRP B	Load BC register pair immediate
0001	00	} File start address for BC
0002	10	
0003	IN	} Read I/O port 01
0004	01	
0005	CMP I	Compare immediate
0006	03	Hexadecimal for Control C
0007	JZ	Jump if zero (Compare worked)
0008	00	} Halt location
0009	0F	
000A	STI A	Store accumulator indirect
000B	IRP	Increment BC register pair
000C	JMP	Jump back to start (input)
000D	00	} Address of input
000E	03	
000F	HLT	Halt
0010		} Start of data file
0011		
0012		
0013		
0014		
0015		
0016		
0017		
0018		} Data file
0019		
001A		
001B		
001C		
001D		
001E		
001F		

Fig. 9-11 A program listing for the program flowcharted in Fig. 9-10.

cause we originally set (*initialized*) the BC register pair at 0010 using the Load Register Pair instruction.

After the Store Indirect instruction, we increment the BC register pair. The BC register pair now points to the data file's next memory location. That is, that location is now ready to receive the second input data word.

The next instruction is an unconditional jump. It tells the program counter to return to location 0003. When the program counter returns to location 0003, the next instruction

executed is the Input 02 instruction. This restarts the entire process of filing data.

As you can see, this program continues to execute until a Control C is received. Once the Control C is received, the program halts. Usually this program is used as part of another program, that is, as a subroutine. The subroutine is called whenever there is a need to input an ASCII character into the data file. There may also be another subroutine to limit the size of the data file.

When the Compare instruction detects a

Control C in the accumulator, the program may be set to call another subroutine rather than simply to halt the program. Whatever is done next, the basic form of the input sequence remains the same.

Self-Test

Check your understanding by answering these questions.

9. A Control D in ASCII is a hexadecimal 04. (*a*) How would you modify the program listing in Fig. 9-11 to halt on a Control D instead of a Control C? How would (*b*) the flowchart and (*c*) the memory map in Fig. 9-10 change? (*d*) How would you modify the program to halt on both a Control C and a Control D?

10. Explain the major difference between the Compare instruction and the EXCLUSIVE OR instruction or the Subtract instruction.

11. Often a microprocessor is used to monitor analog data. The microprocessor is to raise a flag (give a warning) if the data exceed a certain value. The analog data are converted into digital words between 0000 0000 and 0100 0000 by an analog-to-digital converter. Suppose that you want to cause a flag if the digital value for the analog data exceeds 0010 0000. How can you use the Compare instruction to do this? Explain by using a flowchart.

12. Flowchart the part of a program that uses the Compare instruction and the status register's bit-test instruction to send the program on three different paths. The paths are "less than," "equal to," and "greater than."

9-3 THE ROTATE INSTRUCTIONS AND THE SHIFT INSTRUCTIONS

The next four instructions we will look at are the Rotate and the Shift instructions. Some microprocessor literature calls all these instructions Rotate instructions, some literature calls them all Shift instructions, and some literature uses a mixture of these terms. Therefore, you must study the manufacturer's data sheet and make sure that you understand exactly what happens with each Rotate instruction or Shift instruction.

Frequently, the literature on these instructions includes diagrams like the ones we shall use. These diagrams are very helpful in understanding how each instruction works. If the manufacturer's literature on an instruction does not include such a diagram, you can easily draw one.

The Rotate and the Shift instructions are single-byte, 2-cycle instructions. If executing any of these instructions yields a "1" in the MSB or a zero result, then the appropriate bit in the status register is set. The carry bit is part of the operation and is affected directly as data are moved into and out of it.

ROTATE ACCUMULATOR LEFT
RAL

| RAL | | C | ← | MSB | LSB | ← |

The Rotate Accumulator Left instruction moves all the data in the accumulator *and the carry bit* 1 bit to the left. That is, the contents of each bit are moved into the *next more significant* bit. The contents of the accumulator's most significant bit are moved into the status register's carry bit. The contents of the status register's carry bit are moved into the accumulator's least significant bit.

It is important for you to understand that the status register's carry bit is included in this instruction. The accumulator's most significant bit does not move directly into the accumulator's least significant bit. The most significant bit must first pass through the status register's carry bit.

ROTATE ACCUMULATOR RIGHT
RAR

| RAR | | C | → | MSB | LSB | |

The Rotate Accumulator Right instruction simply moves the data in the other direction. That is, the contents of the accumulator's least significant bit are moved into the status register's carry bit. The contents of the status register's carry bit are moved into the accumulator's most significant bit. Each bit in the accumulator is moved into a less significant bit. Again, note that the accumulator's contents are rotated through the status register's carry bit.

When we use either the Rotate Accumulator Left or the Rotate Accumulator Right instruction, no data are lost. That is, all data are moved around in a closed loop. If you rotate 9 times in an 8-bit microprocessor, for ex-

Shift
accumulator left

Shift
accumulator
right

Replicate

Bit bucket

ample, the result is no change in the contents of the accumulator or the contents of the status register's carry bit.

SHIFT ACCUMULATOR LEFT
SAL

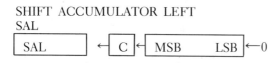

The Shift Accumulator Left instruction is also called an Arithmetic Shift Left. This instruction is the one commonly used in multiplication problems. Refer to the diagram for the Shift Accumulator Left instruction. You can see that the accumulator's most significant bit is moved into the status register's carry bit. A logic "0" is moved into the accumulator's least significant bit. Each bit of the accumulator is moved into the next more significant bit, and whatever is in the status register's carry bit is lost.

SHIFT ACCUMULATOR RIGHT
SAR

The Shift Accumulator Right instruction is like the Rotate Accumulator Right instruction. The accumulator's least significant bit is moved into the status register's carry bit. Each of the other accumulator bits is shifted into the next less significant bit.

A unique feature of the Arithmetic Shift Right is that the accumulator's most significant bit is replicated. That is, instead of filling the most significant bit with a logic "0," this instruction fills that bit with an exact copy of the bit that was in it before the shift. If the most significant bit is a logic "1" before the shift, it will be a logic "1" after the shift. If it is logic "0" before the shift, it will be logic "0" after the shift. This replication of the most significant bit is necessary to complete some 2's complement arithmetic operations.

There are two points you should keep in mind when you are thinking about rotating and shifting. First, shifting or rotating is the same as multiplying or dividing by 2. This is shown in Figs. 9-12 and 9-13.

In Fig. 9-12 you can see what a Shift Left does. One Shift Left doubles the decimal value from 60 to 120. A second Shift Left doubles it again to 240. That is, each Shift Left multiplies by 2.

In Fig. 9-13, you can see what a Shift Right does. One Shift Right halves the number.

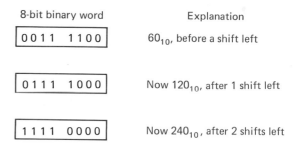

8-bit binary word	Explanation
0011 1100	60_{10}, before a shift left
0111 1000	Now 120_{10}, after 1 shift left
1111 0000	Now 240_{10}, after 2 shifts left

Fig. 9-12   Shifting left to multiply by 2.

The original 60 becomes 30. Two Shift Right operations halve the number again. The result is now 15. You can see that each Shift Right divides by 2.

The second point you should note is that data *shifted* out of the end of a register are lost. This does not happen with a Rotate, because that is a closed-loop operation. Often it is said that the data shifted out of the end are shifted into the "bit bucket." That is, the data are lost forever.

The following example demonstrates the use of the Shift and the Rotate instructions. Actually, this use of the Shift and the Rotate instructions is a necessary part of doing a multiplication. As you know, binary multiplication is done by the Shift and Add technique. But what happens when the binary number exceeds the range of 0 to 255? As we have found in addition and subtraction, multiple-precision arithmetic must be used. As in addition and subtraction, the objective of double-precision multiplication is to make two 8-bit registers look like one 16-bit register. Therefore, before we can do multiple-precision multiplication, we must be able to do multiple-precision shifting.

An example of triple-precision shifting is shown in Fig. 9-14. In Fig. 9-14(*a*) we see three data bytes. These three data bytes contain the binary multiplicand. As you know from previous studies of binary arithmetic, the multiplicand must be shifted to the left to

8-bit binary word	Explanation
0011 1100	60_{10}, before a shift right
0001 1110	Now 30_{10}, after 1 shift right
0000 1111	Now 15_{10}, after 2 shifts right

Fig. 9-13   Shifting right to divide by 2.

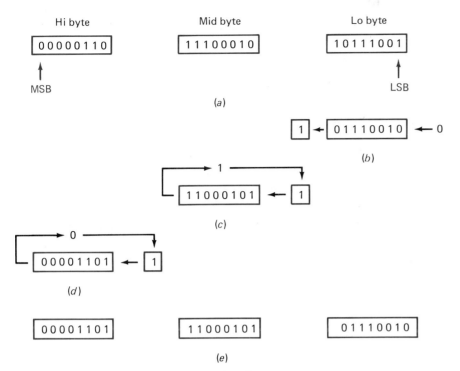

Fig. 9-14 A triple-precision 1-bit Shift Left.

make partial products. The shifting must be done on a byte-by-byte basis. The least significant byte is shifted by using an Arithmetic Shift Left. This places the most significant bit in the status register's carry bit, and the least significant bit is replaced with a binary "0." This is shown in Fig. 9-14(b).

We cannot use the Arithmetic Shift Left instruction to shift the second byte. This is because the contents of the status register's carry bit, which come from the first byte's MSB, must be shifted into the second byte's LSB. Therefore, we use the Rotate Accumulator Left instruction. This is shown in Fig. 9-14(c). The Rotate Accumulator Left instruction places the contents of the status register's carry bit in the accumulator's LSB. The accumulator's MSB is then placed in the status register's carry bit.

The third and most significant byte is also shifted by using the Rotate Accumulator Left instruction. This is shown in Fig. 9-14(d). The contents of the status register's carry bit (which come from the middle byte's Rotate instruction) are now shifted into the most significant byte's LSB. The MSB shifts a logic "0" into the status register's carry bit.

You can now see that using one Arithmetic Shift Left and two Rotate Accumulator Left operations lets you make a single-bit Shift Left

in triple-precision arithmetic. The result of the triple-precision Shift Left is shown in Fig. 9-14(e).

Looking at how this is done, you can see that this whole operation shifts only one bit at a time. That is, the least significant byte must be shifted first. Then the next most significant byte is shifted. Then the most significant byte is shifted. If additional shifting is needed, you must start again with the least significant byte and work your way to the most significant byte.

This shift in triple-precision arithmetic must be done one bit at a time because the status register's carry bit is only a single-bit register. If you shift more than one bit at a time, some bits of information will be lost.

Self-Test

Check your understanding by answering these questions.

In the questions 13 through 16, show in diagram form what happens to the data after:
a. One Shift Left operation
b. Two Shift Left operations
c. One Shift Right operation
d. Two Shift Right operations
e. One Rotate Left operation

191

f. Two Rotate Left operations
g. One Rotate Right operation
h. Two Rotate Right operations

	C		Accumulator							
13.	0	1	1	0	1	0	1	0	0	
14.	0	0	0	1	0	1	1	1	1	
15.	1	0	1	1	1	1	1	1	1	
16.	0	1	1	1	1	1	1	1	0	

17. You have a microcomputer system monitoring a building's environmental system. You can input one 8-bit data word that gives the on or off status for the different system parts. A logic "1" means the part is on, and a logic "0" means the part is off. The status word bits are assigned as follows:

7	6	5	4	3	2	1	0
A/C no. 1	Hot water no. 3	A/C no. 2	A/C no. 3	Hot water no. 2	Hot water no. 4	A/C no. 4	A/C no. 5

Flowchart a subroutine that will quickly scan the status word once that word is in the accumulator. This quick scan is to see if *any* air conditioning (A/C) unit is *off*. Indicate the instruction that you will use and the value of any special data words that you will need.

Summary

1. The microprocessor's logic instructions let you work on data using Boolean algebra operations. The four basic Boolean operations are the AND, OR, EXCLUSIVE OR, and NOT operations.

2. The logic instructions operate between data in the referenced location and data in the accumulator.

3. The result of a logic instruction is placed in the accumulator. The logic instructions operate on the data on a bit-by-bit basis.

4. The AND Immediate is often used as a mask. If you put a logic "1" in the mask bit, it lets the data in that bit position be copied to the result's bit. If you put a logic "0" in the mask bit, it causes a logic "0" in that bit position of the result.

5. The logic OR can be used as a mask. Logic "1s" in the mask cause logic "1s" in the result. Logic "0s" in the mask let the data be copied to the result.

6. The EXCLUSIVE OR sets all bit positions that contain a match to logic "0." The EXCLUSIVE OR can be used to test for a bit-for-bit match to the mask. The EXCLUSIVE OR of a word with itself clears the accumulator.

7. The Complement instruction performs the logic NOT operation. Complementing the accumulator results in the 1's complement. Incrementing a 1's complement results in a 2's complement.

8. The Compare instruction checks for "greater than," "equal to," or "less than." The Compare instruction leaves no result in the accumulator. This instruction only sets the correct status register bits.

9. A data file is made up of a series of sequential memory locations.

10. Incrementing the BC register pair is a good way to point to successive memory locations.

11. The Rotate instructions use a closed loop. This means that the accumulator's MSB is connected to its LSB through the status register's carry bit. The Rotate Left instruction moves data into more significant bits. The Rotate Right instruction moves data into less significant bits.

12. The Shift instructions do not use a closed loop. Data shifted out of the carry bit are lost. The Shift Left instruction shifts a logic "0" into the LSB and shifts the MSB into the carry bit. The Shift Right instruction shifts a copy of the MSB into the MSB and shifts the LSB into the carry bit.

13. The Shift instructions are also called Arithmetic Shift instructions. A Shift Left or Rotate Left multiplies the data by 2. A Shift Right or Rotate Right divides the data by 2.

14. Both Shift and Rotate instructions are used to do a multiple-precision shift. The Shift is used on the least significant byte. The Rotate is used on other bytes to include the carry bit.

Chapter Review Questions

9-1. Boolean operations are implemented by the ____?____ instructions.
   a. Arithmetic
   b. Data-transfer
   c. Conditional
   d. Logic

9-2. Which of the following instructions does not operate between the addressed device and the accumulator?
   a. AND
   b. OR
   c. EXCLUSIVE OR
   d. NOT

9-3. The logic operations operate on
   a. The accumulator
   b. The referenced register
   c. A bit-by-bit basis
   d. A byte

9-4. The logic operations do not affect the status register's ____?____ bit.
   a. Zero
   b. Negative
   c. Carry
   d. (They do not affect any bits.)

9-5. The result of a logic AND, OR, EXCLUSIVE OR, or NOT operation is placed in the
   a. Status register
   b. Addressed memory location
   c. Accumulator
   d. (There is no result.)

9-6. Briefly explain what a bit mask does.

9-7. Explain the difference between using the AND bit mask and using the OR bit mask.

9-8. What results are placed in the accumulator when an EXCLUSIVE OR Immediate $C7_{16}$ executes while the accumulator contains 38_{16}?

9-9. What is the result of executing an EXCLUSIVE OR of a word with itself?

9-10. Flowchart the steps needed to convert memory location 02DE to its 2's complement.

9-11. Complement the following data words. Show the contents of the status register for each operation.
   a. 0010 1100
   b. 1111 1111
   c. 1000 0000
   d. 0000 0001
   e. 0000 0000
   f. 1100 1100
   g. 1010 1010
   h. 0101 0101

193

9-12. What is the difference between a 1's complement and a 2's complement? What instruction do you use to convert from one to the other?

9-13. An EXCLUSIVE OR operation is followed by a Complement operation. Each bit position where there is a ____?____ will be set to logic "1."

9-14. The Compare instruction is the same as a(n) ____?____ instruction but with no results left in the accumulator.
a. Add
b. Subtract
c. AND
d. EXCLUSIVE OR

9-15. The Compare instruction is used to ____?____ data.
a. Test
b. Store
c. Move
d. Clear

9-16. The Compare Immediate instruction is used to
a. Check for a Control C
b. Check for a Control D
c. Check to see if the accumulator's contents match the instruction's second byte
d. (All of the above)

9-17. Explain what the CMP M,A3D1 instruction does.

9-18. What instructions would you use to see if the D register contains FA_{16}?

9-19. Briefly explain the main difference between the Rotate and the Shift instructions.

9-20. Briefly explain the main difference between the Left and Right Shift and the Left and Right Rotate instructions.

9-21. How is the carry bit affected in a Rotate instruction?

9-22. How is the carry bit affected in a Shift instruction?

9-23. Which Shift or Rotate instruction replicates the accumulator's MSB? What does this mean?

9-24. What happens to data shifted out of the carry bit during an Arithmetic Shift operation?

Answers to Self-Tests

1. a. 0010 1000
   b. 1111 1010
   c. 1110 0110
   d. 1111 0000
   e. 1010 1010
   f. 0000 0000
   g. 1111 1111
   h. 1010 1010
   i. 0101 0101
   j. 1010 1010

2. a. 1100 0111
   b. 0000 1111
   c. 1110 1111
   d. 1000 1111
   e. 0000 0000
   f. 1111 1111
   g. 0101 0101
   h. 1010 1010
   i. 1111 0000

3. The data being tested are in the accumulator. They will be lost.

4. The OR I,Data where the data are FF (1111 1111).

5. OR B packs the two words and makes the accumulator contain 1001 1000.

6. First, the accumulator was ANDed with the mask 0000 1111:

1111 1000	Data (D)
0000 1111	Mask (M)
0000 1000	D AND M

   Second, the masked data were moved into register B with a MOV B,A.

7. The logic is NAND.

8. See Fig. 9-15.

9. a. Change the CMP I,03 to a CMP I,04.
   b. The new flowchart decision block is shown in Fig. 9-16.
   c. There is no change in the memory map.
   d. Add a second CMP I instruction following the first. This would be followed by a second JZ instruction.

10. The EXCLUSIVE OR and

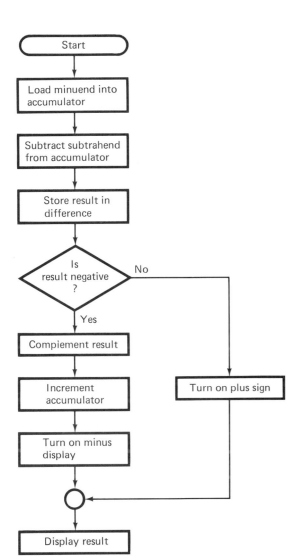

Fig. 9-15   The flowchart of self-test question 8.

Subtract instructions leave a result in the accumulator. The Compare instruction has no result except setting the status register's bits if necessary.

11. See Fig. 9-17.

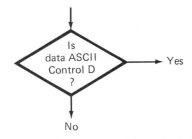

Fig. 9-16   The flowchart decision block for self-test question 9(b).

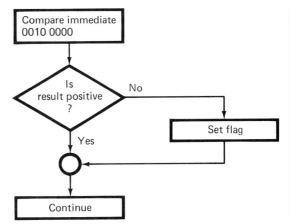

Fig. 9-17   A flowchart for self-test question 11.

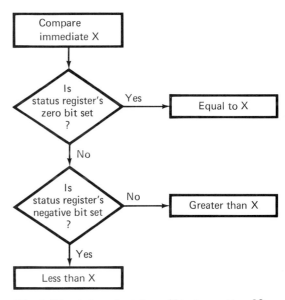

Fig. 9-18   A flowchart for self-test question 12.

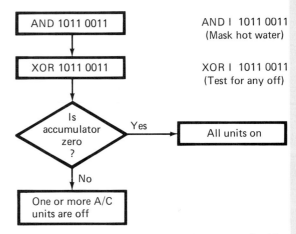

Fig. 9-19   A flowchart of the subroutine of self-test question 17.

12. See Fig. 9-18.

13.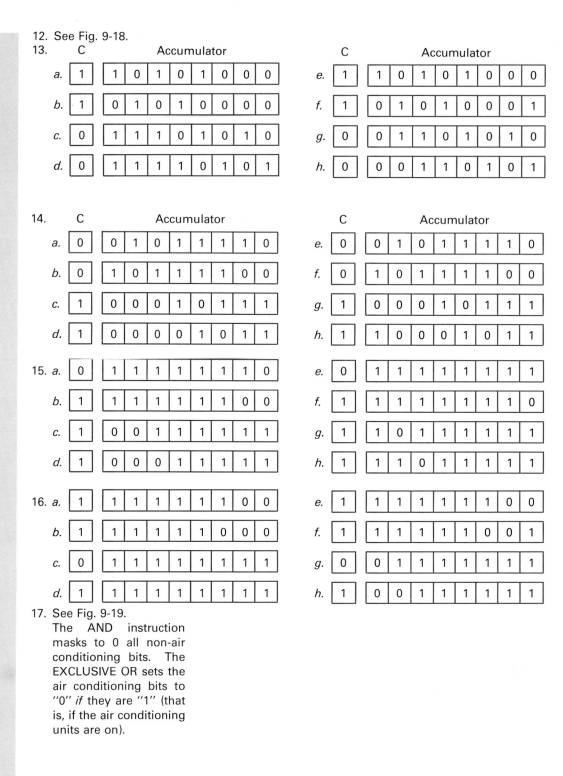

	C	Accumulator		C	Accumulator
a.	1	1 0 1 0 1 0 0 0	e.	1	1 0 1 0 1 0 0 0
b.	1	0 1 0 1 0 0 0 0	f.	1	0 1 0 1 0 0 0 1
c.	0	1 1 0 1 0 1 0	g.	0	0 1 1 0 1 0 1 0
d.	0	1 1 1 0 1 0 1	h.	0	0 0 1 1 0 1 0 1

14.

	C	Accumulator		C	Accumulator
a.	0	0 1 0 1 1 1 1 0	e.	0	0 1 0 1 1 1 1 0
b.	0	1 0 1 1 1 1 0 0	f.	0	1 0 1 1 1 1 0 0
c.	1	0 0 0 1 0 1 1 1	g.	1	0 0 0 1 0 1 1 1
d.	1	0 0 0 0 1 0 1 1	h.	1	1 0 0 0 1 0 1 1

15.

	C	Accumulator		C	Accumulator
a.	0	1 1 1 1 1 1 0	e.	0	1 1 1 1 1 1 1
b.	1	1 1 1 1 1 0 0	f.	1	1 1 1 1 1 1 0
c.	1	0 0 1 1 1 1 1	g.	1	1 0 1 1 1 1 1
d.	1	0 0 0 1 1 1 1	h.	1	1 1 0 1 1 1 1

16.

	C	Accumulator		C	Accumulator
a.	1	1 1 1 1 1 0 0	e.	1	1 1 1 1 1 0 0
b.	1	1 1 1 1 0 0 0	f.	1	1 1 1 1 0 0 1
c.	0	1 1 1 1 1 1 1	g.	0	0 1 1 1 1 1 1
d.	1	1 1 1 1 1 1 1	h.	1	0 0 1 1 1 1 1

17. See Fig. 9-19.
The AND instruction masks to 0 all non-air conditioning bits. The EXCLUSIVE OR sets the air conditioning bits to "0" *if* they are "1" (that is, if the air conditioning units are on).

The Jump Instructions and the Subroutine Instructions

■ The jump instructions and the subroutine instructions both let you change the program's direction. There are two ways to change a program's direction. One way you can change it is *unconditionally*. That means that you can change the program's direction any time an instruction is executed. The other way is *conditionally*. That means that the program changes direction if and only if the result of a certain test is as you specify.

What makes a microprocessor so powerful is its ability to make decisions. The jump instructions and the subroutine instructions are a part of the decision-making process. The Compare instruction and the arithmetic and logic instructions set the status register's zero, negative, or carry bit, and sometimes they set more than one of these bits. The jump instructions and the subroutine instructions test the status register's bits and decide how the program will continue.

The jump instructions, which are also called the *branch* instructions, let you make program loops and program branches. The subroutine instructions make programs much shorter because they let you reuse common subprograms. The microprocessor's *stack* and *stack pointer* make it possible to return to the main program after a subroutine is executed.

10-1 THE JUMP, OR BRANCH, INSTRUCTIONS

The jump, or branch, instructions make the microprocessor powerful. They make decision making possible. In some earlier programming examples, we have seen limited use of jump instructions. You have seen that jump instructions determine, based on the result of a test, which program path will be followed. The tests used with jump instructions are tests of the status register's zero, negative, and carry bits.

In our microprocessor, we call these instructions the "jump" series. In some microprocessors, similar instructions are called "branch" instructions. In most cases, there is little or no difference between jump and branch instructions. With any instruction set, however, you should study the manufacturer's published information very carefully. This information will tell you exactly what is meant by the particular manufacturer's definition of "jump" or "branch."

The differences between one jump instruction and another are in what each instruction tests and in what addressing mode it uses. If you look at a number of different microprocessor families, you will find that there are many different jump instructions.

The following paragraphs describe the jump instructions used by our microprocessor. Each instruction is a 3-byte, 5-cycle instruction. All of this microprocessor's jump instructions use direct addressing. You will find that most microprocessors have only a Jump Direct form.

In the Jump Direct form, the 2 bytes following the jump instruction point to a memory location. These 2 bytes are a memory address. The memory location specified contains the next instruction to be executed.

The memory location can be either just a few instructions away or very far away. Note: When a jump instruction is executed, it leaves behind no reference about the point of departure from the current program. If you want to return to the original program, *you* must somehow store that reference. Another kind of instruction stores the return reference automatically. Instructions of that kind are used when a return to the original program is desired.

When the jump instruction is executed, the

program counter's contents are changed. The contents of the second and third bytes of the jump instruction are transferred into the program counter during the instruction's Execute cycle. When the microprocessor executes the next Fetch cycle, it takes the instruction from the memory location pointed to by the jump instruction's second and third bytes.

This causes a transfer to another point in the program. The program then continues executing the new series of instructions, one after the other. The execution of the new series of instructions continues until another jump instruction is executed.

The following paragraphs introduce seven very common jump instructions.

JUMP UNCONDITIONAL
JMP, Address
Hi add. → PC$_H$
Lo add. → PC$_L$

JMP	1st byte
Hi address	2d byte
Lo address	3d byte

The Jump Unconditional instruction's name tells you how it works. When this instruction is executed, *no* test takes place. The microprocessor's program counter is automatically loaded with the contents of the instruction's second and third bytes. Program execution transfers to this new starting point when the next instruction starts its Fetch/Execute cycle.

JUMP IF ZERO
JZ, Address
If Z = 1, then
Hi add. → PC$_H$
Lo add. → PC$_L$

JZ	1st byte
Hi address	2d byte
Lo address	3d byte

JUMP IF NOT ZERO
JNZ, Address
If Z = 0, then
Hi add. → PC$_H$
Lo add. → PC$_L$

JNZ	1st byte
Hi address	2d byte
Lo address	3d byte

The Jump If Zero and the Jump If Not Zero instructions test the status register's zero bit. The Jump If Zero instruction causes a change in the program counter's contents *if* the status register's zero bit *is* logic "1." That is, the jump takes place if the accumulator is all logic "0s." You will remember that the status register's zero bit is set to logic "1" only when *all* the accumulator bits are logic "0."

The Jump If Not Zero instruction causes a change in the program counter's contents if the status register's zero bit is set to logic "0." In this case, the jump takes place if the accumulator *is not* all logic "0s." Remember that the status register's zero bit is set to logic "0" when *any* of the accumulator's bits is logic "1."

Some programmers speak of the Jump If Zero instruction as the Jump If Equal (JE) instruction. This instruction has earned this second name because it is frequently used following a Compare instruction. If the two words being compared are equal, then the status register's zero bit is set to logic "1." In that case, the program jump will occur. You can see why the JZ instruction can be thought of as Jump If Equal. Likewise, the JNZ instruction can be thought of as Jump If Not Equal instruction (JNE).

JUMP IF CARRY
JC, Address
If C = 1, then
Hi add. → PC$_H$
Lo add. → PC$_L$

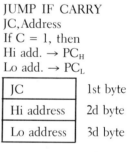

JC	1st byte
Hi address	2d byte
Lo address	3d byte

JUMP IF NOT CARRY
JNC, Address
If C = 0, then
Hi add. → PC$_H$
Lo add. → PC$_L$

JNC	1st byte
Hi address	2d byte
Lo address	3d byte

The Jump If Carry instruction and the Jump If Not Carry instruction test the status register's carry bit. When the Jump If Carry instruction executes, it loads the program counter with the instruction's second and third bytes *if* the status register's carry bit is set to logic "1."

When the Jump If Not Carry instruction executes, it loads the program counter with the instruction's second and third bytes *if* the status register's carry bit is set to logic "0." Frequently these instructions are used after an arithmetic instruction.

JUMP IF NEGATIVE
JN,Address
If N = 1, then
Hi add. → PC$_H$
Lo add. → PC$_L$

JN	1st byte
Hi address	2d byte
Lo address	3d byte

JUMP IF NOT NEGATIVE
JNN,Address
If N = 0, then
Hi add. → PC$_H$
Lo add. → PC$_L$

JNN	1st byte
Hi address	2d byte
Lo address	3d byte

The Jump If Negative instruction tests the status register's negative bit. If the status register's negative bit is set to logic "1," then the Jump If Negative instruction is executed. Program control is transferred to the new address.

The Jump If Not Negative instruction also tests the status register's negative bit. This instruction executes if the status register's negative bit is set to logic "0." This instruction may also be called the Jump If Positive instruction. You can see that if the status register's negative bit is logic "0," then the accumulator's contents must be positive.

Self-Test

Check your understanding by answering these questions.

1. Flowchart the steps that you would use to make a "greater than" or "equal to" decision. What instructions would you use?

2. You are using the microprocessor's B register as a decrementing counter. How do you preset the counter? How do you test for the end of 10 counts? Show a flowchart and the instructions that you would use.

3. The JNN 006A instruction is found at memory location 012A. This instruction transfers program control to the instruction at memory location (a) __?__ if the instruction at memory location 0129 has cleared the microprocessor's (b) __?__. Explain.

4. In question 3, program control is transferred to the instruction at memory location (a) __?__ if the instruction at memory location 0129 has *set* the (b) __?__ MSB. Explain.

5. You would expect that a JE instruction might follow a(n) (a) __?__ instruction. The instruction can also be expressed as (b) __?__.

6. The instruction at memory location 00AC is an Add from Memory Indirect. It adds the number 01 to the number FF already in the accumulator. This instruction is followed by a JC, 00B9 instruction. Executing the instruction at memory location 00AD will cause __?__. Flowchart the program.

10-2 A PROGRAM EXAMPLE

In the following example, we will see several uses of jump instructions. We will see jump instructions used to sort data, to redirect the program, and to test down-counters. This program also shows other programming techniques, such as using a register as a memory pointer, using a temporary-storage register, and making multiple use of a single instruction.

This program's memory map is shown in Fig. 10-1. The program is flowcharted in Fig. 10-2.

Let's first take a look at exactly what the program does. Note: This program is shown here as a complete program starting at memory location 0000 and ending at memory location 0025 with a Halt. Most likely you would find the program actually used as a subprogram. The subprogram would be called when the particular function was needed by a more complex program.

The flowchart shows how one might solve this particular problem by using our microprocessor. However, before we created this flowchart we had to define an *algorithm* for solving this problem. An algorithm is a set of rules or processes to solve a problem in a given number of steps. A flowchart is a way of documenting an algorithm. Figure 10-2 docu-

Jump if negative

Jump if not negative

Subprogram

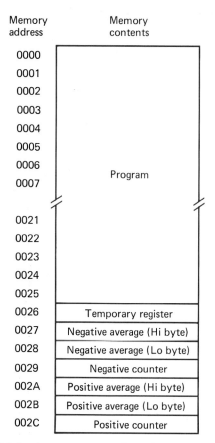

Memory address	Memory contents
0000	
0001	
0002	
0003	
0004	
0005	
0006	
0007	Program
0021	
0022	
0023	
0024	
0025	
0026	Temporary register
0027	Negative average (Hi byte)
0028	Negative average (Lo byte)
0029	Negative counter
002A	Positive average (Hi byte)
002B	Positive average (Lo byte)
002C	Positive counter

Fig. 10-1   A memory map for a data-sorting routine. This program reserves data space in memory locations 0026 to 002C. Program space is in memory locations 0000 to 0025.

ments our algorithm for this particular problem.

Basically the program sorts 2's complement data into positive data, negative data, and data with a value of 0. If the data have a value of 0, the data are not used. The positive and negative data are added to their respective sums in memory. Later, the sums are used to find the average of the positive and the negative data points.

To aid in the averaging process, the program keeps two counters. One counter keeps a record of all positive data measurements. The other counter keeps a record of all negative data measurements.

A third down-counter (register D) is preset to hexadecimal FF. It is decremented each time a valid (positive or negative) measurement is made. When register D reaches zero, 256 measurements have been made. This stops the process.

Let us assume that the data come from a bipolar 8-bit analog-to-digital converter (ADC). The ADC's output is a 2's complement number, and the MSB is the sign bit. The remain-

ing 7 bits are a binary number telling the analog signal's voltage level. For this ADC,

$$0111\ 1111 = +1.27 \text{ volts (V)}$$
$$0000\ 0000 = 0.00 \text{ V}$$
$$1000\ 0000 = -1.28 \text{ V}$$

When the In instruction is executed, one ADC 8-bit output word is transferred to the microprocessor's accumulator.

The memory map in Fig. 10-1 shows how we allocate the microcomputer's memory for this program.

Memory location 0026 is used as a temporary register. We must put the input data here while the microprocessor performs another operation. As in this example, a temporary register is often used so that intermediate programming steps do not cause a loss of data.

Memory location 002C is used to store the positive counter. The data stored in this memory location show the number of positive data measurements made. We start the program with the contents of this memory location set to 0. Each time a positive data word is measured, the contents of memory location 002C are incremented.

Memory location 002B is used to store the low byte of the positive data sum. Each time a positive data word is found, the contents of memory location 002B are added to the data word. The result (that is, the new sum) is then stored back in memory location 002B. Of course, the new value overwrites the old sum. The old sum is lost.

There can be as many as 256 positive measurements. Each measurement might have 7 significant bits. Therefore, we must make room for more than 8 bits in the sum. Memory location 002A is used to capture the overflow. After each measurement is made (and the low byte is stored), the high byte in memory location 002A is added to any carry generated by the low-byte addition.

These three data bytes and the overflow make up all the data about positive measurements. The data in memory locations 0029, 0028, and 0027 store the same information for negative data.

Looking at the memory map, you can see that the entire 38-byte program uses memory locations 0000 through 0025.

The flowchart in Fig. 10-2 explains how the program works. A detailed program listing is

200

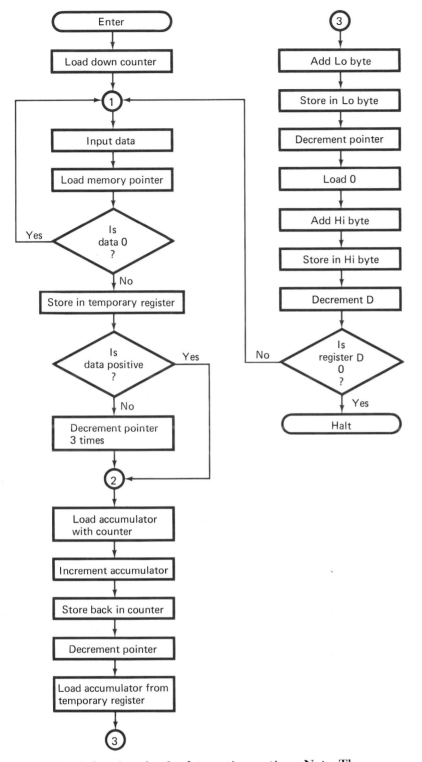

Fig. 10-2 A flowchart for the data-sorting routine. Note: The connect points are used for multiple paths and for clarity. Each decision symbol represents a jump.

given in Fig. 10-3. You should refer to both as we go through this program. The program listing is well "documented." In fact, you can probably follow the listing by itself. However,

most programmers do not document their programs quite this thoroughly. You should use this opportunity to learn to "read between the lines." You will often have to read be-

Memory address	Memory contents	Comments
0000	LDA D	Main counter (register D) set to 256_{10}
0001	FF	256_{10}
0002	IN	Input
0003	01	Port 01
0004	JZ	Back to input if data is 0
0005	00	
0006	02	
0007	LRP B	Pointer (BC pair) to top of file
0008	00	
0009	2C	
000A	STA A	Copy data into temporary register
000B	00	
000C	26	
000D	JNN	Positive? Skip over decrements
000E	00	
000F	13	
0010	DRP B	Negative? Decrement 3 times
0011	DRP B	
0012	DRP B	
0013	LDI A	Counter into accumulator
0014	INC A	Add 1
0015	STI A	Put incremented counter back
0016	DRP B	Pointer to Lo byte
0017	LDD A	Get data from temporary register
0018	00	
0019	26	
001A	ADI M	Add Lo byte of average
001B	STI A	Put new average Lo byte back
001C	DRP B	Pointer to Hi byte
001D	LDA A	Load 0 (data Hi byte)
001E	00	
001F	ACI M	Add Hi byte of average with carry
0020	STI A	Put new average Hi byte back
0021	DEC D	Decrement main counter
0022	JNZ	Not 0? Back to IN
0023	00	
0024	02	
0025	HLT	Zero. Quit
0026	00	Temporary register
0027	00	Negative average Hi byte
0028	00	Negative average Lo byte
0029	00	Negative counter
002A	00	Positive average Hi byte
002B	00	Positive average Lo byte
002C	00	Positive counter

Fig. 10-3 A program listing for the data-sorting routine. Note that the initial values in the data storage area (memory locations 0027 to 002C) are set to zero. The comments after the jump instruction are in the form of a question telling us what happens if the condition is true. If the condition is not true, the comment following the jump instruction's address tells us what will happen.

tween the lines as you read other program listings.

The program's sorting routine is quite common. We use two Jump Conditional instructions. The first instruction tests for data with a value of 0. If the data are not 0, then they must be either positive or negative. Therefore, we pass the data on to the next test. The next test checks for positive data. Obviously, if the data are not positive then they must be negative. Here you see how two Jump Conditional instructions sort data into one of three types.

At the beginning of the program, a Load Immediate instruction initializes the D register to FF. The D register is used as the main down-counter. The D register is decremented after each valid measurement. When the D register reaches 0, the program stops. Note: If we needed to, we could also include, at this point, a series of instructions to initialize memory locations 0026 to 002C with "0s."

The IN instruction simply transfers the data word from I/O port 01 to the accumulator.

We must now initialize the BC register pair. This is done each time we execute the In instruction. The BC register pair points to the memory locations containing the positive and negative sums and counters. We start by presetting the BC register pair to point to the positive counter. This counter is at memory location 002C. A series of three Decrement Register Pair instructions is used to make the BC register pair point to the memory locations used for the negative sum and counter.

The first test is made with a JZ instruction.

If the data are "0" (that is, if the answer is yes), then execution is transferred back to the IN instruction. That is, we try again.

If the data are not "0," we continue. A Store Accumulator Direct instruction copies the data into memory location 0026. As you will see, this is done because later the data in the accumulator will be destroyed. When we need these data, we will be able to get a copy from the temporary register.

The next decision checks for positive data. Here, the program splits. If the answer to the JNN (Jump If Not Negative) instruction is Yes, we jump over the three decrement instructions and start the positive summation routine. If the answer to the JNN instruction's test is No, we continue without jumping. This brings us to the three decrement instructions. After the decrement instructions, both routines are the same.

If the data are negative, we decrement the BC register pair three times. Figure 10-4 shows that this leaves the BC register pair pointing to the negative counter. Now we are really ready to start the summation routine.

Since the BC register pair is pointing to the negative counter, we can use the Load Accumulator Indirect instruction. The negative counter's contents are copied into the accumulator. The INC A and STI A instructions add a binary "1" to the counter and store the *incremented* value back in memory location 0029.

We now decrement the BC register pair once more. You can see that using the BC register pair like this lets you use a series of indirect instructions to move data in and out of

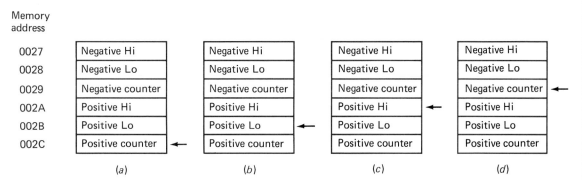

Memory address

	(a)	(b)	(c)	(d)
0027	Negative Hi	Negative Hi	Negative Hi	Negative Hi
0028	Negative Lo	Negative Lo	Negative Lo	Negative Lo
0029	Negative counter	Negative counter	Negative counter	Negative counter ←
002A	Positive Hi	Positive Hi	Positive Hi ←	Positive Hi
002B	Positive Lo	Positive Lo ←	Positive Lo	Positive Lo
002C	Positive counter ←	Positive counter	Positive counter	Positive counter

Fig. 10-4 Decrementing the BC register pair. (*a*) The original condition caused by the LRP B, 002C instruction. (*b*) The first DRP instruction. (*c*) The second DRP instruction. (*d*) The third DRP instruction.

a common memory location. This memory location (0028) contains the negative sum's low byte.

We now need the data that were in the accumulator. The data in the accumulator were overwritten with the contents of the negative counter, but we saved the data in the temporary register. An LDA A instruction puts the original data back in the accumulator. We are now ready to add these data to the negative data sum.

An Add from Memory Indirect instruction adds the data in memory location 0028 to the data already present in the accumulator. If needed, the status register's carry bit is set. The sum is then stored back in memory location 0028 when a Store Accumulator Indirect instruction is executed.

As we saw earlier, this addition may cause a result of up to 16 bits. We now have to add the second byte. One more decrement instruction points the BC register pair to the negative sum's high byte. We know that the ADC had no second (high) byte. In other words, its high byte was all "0s." Therefore, we load the accumulator with 00. An LDA A instruction does this *without* disturbing the status register's carry bit.

We now execute an Add from Memory Indirect with Carry. This instruction adds the high byte of earlier sums, the carry bit (if set), and the ADC's high byte (0). The result is placed in memory location 0027 by the Store Accumulator Indirect instruction.

The negative summation routine is now complete. We now go to a routine that decrements the D register. This is a simple routine. The D register is decremented. A JNZ instruction tests for logic "0" in the status register's zero bit. If there is a logic "0" in the status register's zero bit, the program jumps to the IN instruction at memory location 0002. If the JNZ instruction does not detect a logic "0", no jump is executed. The next instruction executed is a halt (HLT).

The program is now complete. You may want to follow it through again to be sure that you know what each instruction is doing. The program makes use of the many common techniques that you will see as you work on microprocessor-based products.

As you study this program, you will find different and better ways to solve the problem. This program, like the others in this text, was written to demonstrate certain programming principles. The program was not written to demonstrate the ultimate in compact programming. You should remember that there is always more than one way to do a job.

Self-Test

Check your understanding by answering these questions.

7. Using the program flowcharted in Fig. 10-2 and listed in Fig. 10-3, indicate the sequence of program counter contents for negative data, positive data, and data with a value of 0. List the sequence for one cycle.

8. Flowchart a program that stores data in one of three files. The file starting at memory location 0100 will contain numbers less than or equal to 0000 1000. The file starting at memory location 0200 will contain numbers between 0000 1001 and 0010 0000. The file starting at memory location 0300 will contain numbers greater than or equal to 0010 0001. Indicate what microprocessor instructions you would use to implement the various flowchart steps. The program should keep track of:
   a. The number of values not greater than 0001 0000. This is to be in memory location 00FB.
   b. The number of data values between 0001 0001 and 0010 0000. This is to be in memory location 00FC.
   c. The number of data values greater than or equal to 0010 0001. This is to be in memory location 00FD.

9. Add extra steps to the flowchart of question 8 so that you can keep track of the total number of values measured. This total is to be stored in memory location 00FE. Also, the program should halt after the total number of measurements exceeds 100.

10-3 THE SUBROUTINE INSTRUCTIONS

We have just finished looking at the jump instructions. The jump series of instructions lets us branch the program to a new set of program instructions. As we have seen, a common use for the jump instruction is to "loop" the program. But a single jump instruction will not take us back to the point at which we left the main program.

There are many times when we wish to

leave the main program but to be able to return to it on command. And we want to return *exactly* where we left off. One way to do this is to use a second jump instruction. That is, we jump to the subprogram using a jump or a Jump Conditional instruction. Once we have completed the subprogram, we use another jump instruction to go back to the exact point where we left the main program. Unfortunately, this means that we must know exactly where we did leave off.

An easier way to do this is to use the subroutine instructions. A subroutine is a subprogram that can be called from any point in the main program. When a subroutine is called, it first stores the program counter's current contents. When the execution of the subroutine ends, a single instruction tells the microprocessor to get the program counter's original contents from storage. This gives the microprocessor the information it needs to return to the original sequence in the main program.

Figure 10-5 shows a simple subroutine operation. The first five programs steps (memory locations 0000 through 0004) are executed in sequence. The fourth program step calls a subroutine. This instruction directs the program counter to the program instruction at memory location 0022. The instructions at memory locations 0022 through 0027 are executed in sequence. The program instruction at memory location 0027 is a Return instruction. The Return instruction tells the pro-

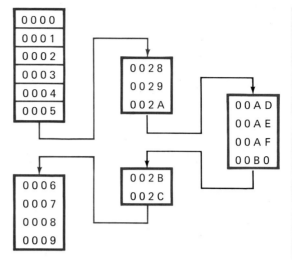

Fig. 10-6 Subroutine nesting. A subroutine can call a subroutine, causing nesting. Both the main program and the subroutine use the Subroutine Call and Return instructions.

gram counter to return to the original exit point. As a result, the program counter points to the instruction at memory location 0005. Program operation continues sequentially executing the instructions in memory locations 0005 through 0009.

Figure 10-6 shows a more complex example of subroutine operations. The first six instructions are executed in sequence. When the program counter reaches the instruction at memory location 0005, it is told that the next instruction is at memory location 0028. That is, the sixth instruction calls a subroutine starting at memory location 0028. The instructions at memory locations 0028, 0029, and 002A execute in sequence. The program counter is then told that the next instruction is at memory location 00AD.

A second subroutine call has been executed. This one, as you can see, is in the middle of the first subroutine. The instructions at memory locations 00AD, 00AE, 00AF, and 00B0 execute in sequence. The program counter is then told to return. The instruction at memory location 00B0 is a subroutine Return instruction. This causes the microprocessor's program counter to return operation to the instruction at memory location 002B. Note: The Return instruction returns the program counter to the instruction that follows *the most recent* subroutine call even though this was in the middle of a previous subroutine.

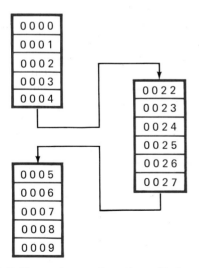

Fig. 10-5 Executing a subroutine. Each memory location has an instruction. Instruction execution begins at 0000. The subroutine call is at 0004, and the return is at 0027.

Nesting
subroutines

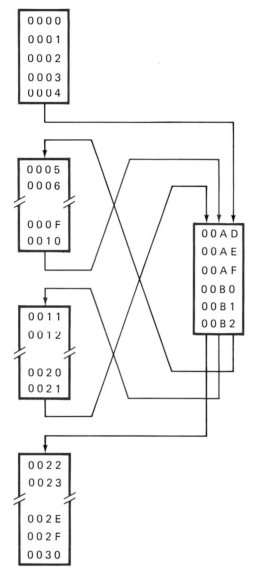

tine is called three times during the program's execution. The instructions at memory locations 0000 through 0004 execute in sequence. The subroutine call instruction at memory location 0004 calls the subroutine beginning at memory location 00AD. The subroutine executes the instructions at memory locations 00AD through 00B2 in sequence. The Return instruction at memory location 00B2 tells the program counter to return to the main program. When it does, the instructions at memory locations 0005 through 0010 execute in sequence. The Subroutine Call instruction at memory location 0010 calls the same subroutine called before. Once again, the instructions at memory locations 00AD through 00B2 execute in sequence. Again, the Return instruction at memory location 00B2 tells the program counter to return to the point at which it left the main program. This time, the point of return is the program instruction at memory location 0011. That address is where the program counter was pointing when it executed the Subroutine Call instruction at memory location 0010.

Now the program instructions at memory locations 0011 through 0021 are executed. Then the subroutine is called again. The instruction at memory location 0021 tells the program counter to go to the instruction at memory location 00AD. The instructions at memory locations 00AD through 00B2 are executed for the last time. Program execution returns to the instruction at memory location 0022. The final program instructions at memory locations 0022 through 0030 execute, completing the program.

Each of the programs outlined in Fig. 10-5, 10-6, and 10-7 shows common ways that subroutines are used. Subroutines save you from having to write common subprogram instructions over and over again. Of course, subroutines also save memory space. A commonly used routine is written only once and stored only once.

For example, suppose that you write a short program to multiply two triple-precision numbers. This program may be 30 to 50 bytes long. Instead of writing it again as many times as it is used, you write it only once. Any number of separate subroutine calls can make use of this program.

In many ways, the subroutine instructions are like the jump instructions. The conditional subroutine instructions test the status

Fig. 10-7 Multiple use of a single subroutine. While the main program in memory locations 0000 to 0030 executes, the subroutine in memory locations 00AD to 00B2 executes three times.

The instructions at memory location 002B through 002C are executed in sequence. The program counter is once again told to Return. This causes it to point to the instruction at memory location 0006. The instructions at memory location 0006 through 0009 execute in sequence.

This is called subroutine *nesting*. In nesting, the main program calls one subroutine, which in turn calls another subroutine. Most microprocessors have the ability to nest subroutines almost indefinitely.

Figure 10-7 shows another way to use a subroutine. In this example, the same subrou-

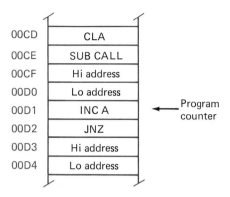

00CD	CLA
00CE	SUB CALL
00CF	Hi address
00D0	Lo address
00D1	INC A	← Program counter
00D2	JNZ
00D3	Hi address
00D4	Lo address

Fig. 10-8 The program counter during execution of a subroutine call instruction. The program counter points to memory location 00D1 because that location has the next instruction after the 3-byte subroutine call instruction.

register's bits. Depending upon how the status register's bits are set, the subroutine may or may not be called.

If the subroutine is called, the microprocessor's stack is used. The stack is a storage area that temporarily holds the information needed to return after execution of the subroutine. In some microprocessors, the stack is a series of internal registers. That is, the stack registers are located in the microprocessor. But for most microprocessors, including ours, the stack is in memory. We keep track of the stack by using a register like the BC register pair. This register is called the *stack pointer*. The stack pointer simply shows the next space to be used on the stack. In most microprocessors the stack pointer is a special register.

When a subroutine is called, the program counter's current contents are placed on the stack. Remember, the program counter will be pointing to the *next* instruction, as the example in Fig. 10-8 shows.

Each time 1 byte of information is placed on the stack, the stack pointer is *decremented*. The stack builds *down* in memory. When you call a subroutine, the program counter's current contents are stored on the stack. Then the memory location where the subroutine begins is loaded into the program counter. This address comes from the subroutine instruction's second and third bytes.

But the stack has neatly stored away the old contents of the program counter. When the subroutine ends, a Return simply reverses the stack pointer. You take the program counter's old contents off the stack.

Placing information on the microproces-

sor's stack is called *pushing* data onto the stack. Taking data from the microprocessor's stack is called *popping* data from the stack.

What happens if we are executing one subroutine and the first subroutine calls a second subroutine? You will remember that this situation was diagramed in Fig. 10-6. When the second subroutine call instruction is executed, the program counter's current contents are placed on the stack. This time, the program counter's contents designate an instruction that is in the first subroutine. These 2 bytes are put into the next two locations following the main program's current program counter values. The second subroutine's starting address is now loaded into the program counter from the subroutine instruction's second and third bytes. Program execution now begins on the second nested subroutine. The stack operation is shown in Fig. 10-9.

As you can see, this nesting can continue as long as the stack has enough memory locations. You must remember that memory for the stack *cannot* be used by other parts of the program at the same time.

In an 8-bit microprocessor, the stack pointer is usually 16 bits wide. Therefore, the stack can be the entire 65,536 bytes of memory if necessary. Usually, however, the stack and working memory will interfere with each other if the stack gets too large. If you destroy the stack, the microprocessor system will crash. The microprocessor cannot find its way back to the original program.

Once a subroutine is complete, we begin popping program counter values from the stack. When the second-level subroutine is complete, we pop the program counter value for the first-level subroutine. This value is loaded into the program counter. We can then continue executing the first-level sub-

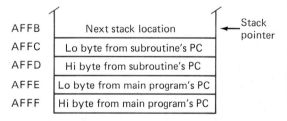

AFFB	Next stack location	← Stack pointer
AFFC	Lo byte from subroutine's PC
AFFD	Hi byte from subroutine's PC
AFFE	Lo byte from main program's PC
AFFF	Hi byte from main program's PC

Fig. 10-9 The microprocessor's stack during a two-level nested subroutine. The stack was started at memory location AFFF. If more data is to be placed on the stack, the data will go into memory location AFFB. The stack pointer is pointing to that location.

Call subroutine unconditional

Call subroutine if zero

Call subroutine if not zero

Call subroutine if carry

Call subroutine if not carry

Call subroutine if negative

Call subroutine if not negative

routine starting at the instruction following the subroutine call. When the first level subroutine is complete, we pop the original program counter value. We now begin executing the main program at the instruction following the original subroutine call.

A single instruction at the end of each subroutine directs us to return to the point of origination. This instruction is called the Return instruction. It is diagramed below with the subroutine call instructions. The Return instruction is a single-byte, 4-cycle instruction. Although our microprocessor offers only a simple Return instruction, some microprocessors offer various conditional returns. In our microprocessor, each subroutine call is a 3-byte, 5-cycle instruction. Each instruction uses direct addressing. In some more complex microprocessors, however subroutine call instructions use other addressing forms.

The subroutine call instructions are:

CALL SUBROUTINE UNCONDITIONAL
CAL,Address
PC → Stack
Hi add. → PC$_H$
Lo add. → PC$_L$

Call	1st byte
Hi address	2d byte
Lo address	3d byte

The Call Subroutine Unconditional instruction does not do any test. That is, it always calls a subroutine.

CALL SUBROUTINE IF ZERO
CZ,Address
If Z = 1, then
PC → Stack
Hi add. → PC$_H$
Lo add. → PC$_L$

CZ	1st byte
Hi address	2d byte
Lo address	3d byte

CALL SUBROUTINE IF NOT ZERO
CNZ,Address
If Z = 0, then
PC → Stack
Hi add. → PC$_H$
Lo add. → PC$_L$

CNZ	1st byte
Hi address	2d byte
Lo address	3d byte

The Call Subroutine If Zero and Call Subroutine If Not Zero instructions test the status register's zero bit. As with the similar jump instructions, these may also be referred to as Call If Equal and Call if Not Equal instructions.

CALL SUBROUTINE IF CARRY
CC,Address
If C = 1, then
PC → Stack
Hi add. → PC$_H$
Lo add. → PC$_L$

CC	1st byte
Hi address	2d byte
Lo address	3d byte

CALL SUBROUTINE IF NOT CARRY
CNC,Address
If C = 0, then
PC → Stack
Hi add. → PC$_H$
Lo add. → PC$_L$

CNC	1st byte
Hi address	2d byte
Lo address	3d byte

The Call Subroutine If Carry and Call Subroutine If Not Carry instructions test the status register's carry bit. These instructions usually follow an arithmetic operation.

CALL SUBROUTINE IF NEGATIVE
CN,Address
If N = 1, then
PC → Stack
Hi add. → PC$_H$
Lo add. → PC$_L$

CN	1st byte
Hi address	2d byte
Lo address	3d byte

CALL SUBROUTINE IF NOT NEGATIVE
CNN
If N = 0, then
PC → Stack
Hi add. → PC$_H$
Lo add. → PC$_L$

CNN	1st byte
Hi address	2d byte
Lo address	3d byte

The Call Subroutine If Negative and Call Subroutine If Not Negative instructions test the status register's negative bit. Note: The Call If Not Negative instruction can also be thought of as a Call If Positive instruction.

RETURN
RET
Stack → PC

RET

The Return instruction tells the microprocessor to pop the most recent program counter value from the stack and load that value into the program counter. Note: The Return instruction has no way of knowing what level of subroutine is being worked on or how many times the subroutine has been called. The stack pointer does not have this information either. The Return instruction simply tells the microprocessor to return to the *latest* program counter value stored on the stack.

Consequently there is no way that the microprocessor can tell if the data in the stack or

in the stack pointer are in error. This is why accidentally destroying the stack's contents will cause the microprocessor system to crash.

In Fig. 10-10, we see the program that we used in Fig. 8-25 to decrement a counter. Here, the program is rewritten to use subroutine calls instead of many inline instructions to decrement and test the counter.

The program starts by directly loading the B register with the number 03. The program then executes a number of steps called "Program" and represented here by "PGM." Once this part of the program is complete, we call a subroutine. In this example, we use the Call Subroutine Unconditional instruction. This instruction tells the program to use the subroutine shown on the right side of Fig. 10-10. When the subroutine is entered; its first instruction is executed. In this subroutine, the first instruction is the Store Indirect instruction. This stores the data from the accumulator in the memory location pointed to by the BC register pair.

The next instruction in the subroutine dec-

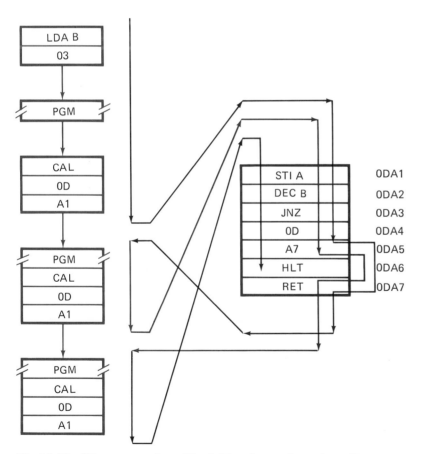

Fig. 10-10 The program from Fig. 8-25, using a subroutine call instead of inline programming, to decrement and test the counter.

rements the B register. This is followed by a Jump If Not Zero instruction. If decrementing the B register does not cause a logic "1" in the status register's zero bit, the jump instruction *is* executed. This causes the Return instruction to execute. The Return executes because the address stored in the JNZ instruction's second and third bytes points to the Return instruction. Of course, when the decrement instruction causes an accumulator of all logic "0s," the jump instruction is not executed. (Note: The jump instruction is fetched, but it is not executed.) Instead, the next instruction in sequence is executed. In this program, the Halt instruction is next.

If the Return instruction is executed, program execution restarts where it left off. That is, the next instruction executed is the one following the Call Subroutine Unconditional instruction. Program instructions are executed until the next Call Subroutine Unconditional instruction is fetched. This starts the second execution of the subroutine. The process now repeats itself until it is stopped by executing the halt instruction. When the program finally stops, it will be as a result of executing the halt instruction in the subroutine.

You can trace the operation of this program, as it runs with 03 loaded in the B register, by following the arrows in Fig. 10-10. As you can see, the subroutine is called three times. The halt in the subroutine is what stops program execution. Note that a program's halt does not have to be in the main program.

Subroutines are used to call any frequently used set of program steps. For example, the floating-point, multiple-precision math package may be called many times during the solution of a complicated mathematical problem. Delay programs are often subroutines, as are input routines, keyboard and display scans, and other frequently repeated operations.

Self-Test

Check your understanding by answering these questions.

10. One of the main reasons for using a subroutine is to save program steps. How many bytes long does a subroutine have to be to save program steps? Why?

11. How could you rewrite the subroutine in Fig. 10-10 so that the Return and halt instructions are swapped? Explain your new subroutine, showing the instructions that you used.

12. You have a 276-instruction program that calls another 25-instruction subroutine 10 times using the Call Subroutine Unconditional instruction. (*a*) Does the program execute faster or slower this way than it would without using a subroutine? (*b*) How would the program length compare with the 301-instruction length that includes the subroutine? In both cases, you may assume that the 25 instructions are fully used in a subroutine or in the straight program.

13. You are using an 8-bit microprocessor with a 16-bit program counter. You write a program that nests subroutines five levels deep. (*a*) What does this mean? (*b*) How many bytes long is the stack?

14. Most 8-bit microprocessors with 65K memory space have a 16-bit stack pointer. This means that the stack can be 65,536 bytes long. Of course, you will never use a stack of such great length. What other good reason is there to have a 16-bit stack pointer if you never use a 65,536-byte stack?

15. Assume there is a programming error in the fourth-level subroutine in question 13. The subroutine writes data into the third byte from the top of the stack. What problem, if any, will this error cause? When will the problem show up?

16. You have a microprocessor-based system that uses 2's complement arithmetic to do subtraction. The system is connected to a display that shows numbers with either a plus sign or a minus sign. To display negative results, you write a subroutine. This subroutine sets the display's minus sign and performs a 2's complement operation on the result. What subroutine call instruction will you use? Why?

17. Explain the difference between a jump instruction and a subroutine instruction.

18. Why do some programmers call the JNN instruction a Jump If Positive instruction?

19. What are the JZ and JE instructions? How does the JE instruction get its name?

Summary

1. The jump instructions let you program the microprocessor to make decisions. Sometimes jump instructions are called "branch" instructions. Most jump instructions use direct addressing. The instruction's second and third bytes contain the new program counter address. When you execute a jump instruction, the instruction does not store any information that provides a way to return to the point of origination in the main program.

2. There are two kinds of jump instructions. They are the Jump Unconditional and the Jump Conditional.

3. The Jump Unconditional instructions change the program counter every time the instruction is executed. The Jump Conditional instructions change the program counter only if the test conditions are met. The Jump Conditional instructions test the status register's zero, negative, and carry bits. The Jump Conditional instructions have two forms. There are instructions that jump when the status register's bit is set, and there are instructions that jump when the status register's bit is cleared.

4. The Jump If Zero instruction is sometimes called the Jump If Equal instruction. The Jump If Zero and Jump If Not Zero or Jump If Equal and Jump If Not Equal instructions often follow a Compare instruction.

5. The Jump If Not Negative instruction is often called the Jump If Positive instruction.

6. Two jump instructions can be used to do a three-way sort.

7. Jump instructions are usually represented in flowcharts by a diamond decision block.

8. The subroutine call instructions also change the program counter's contents, but they provide a way to return to the calling program.

9. The Return instruction restarts execution of the calling program. Calling a subroutine causes the program counter's contents to be stored on the stack. The stack can be a series of internal registers or it can be a series of memory locations.

10. A special-purpose register called the "stack pointer" always points to the next place to be used on the stack.

11. Each time an 8-bit microprocessor calls a subroutine, the stack gains 2 more bytes. These bytes are the program counter's contents.

12. Each time data are added to the stack, the stack pointer decrements.

13. Adding data to the stack is called "pushing" data onto the stack.

14. Each time data are taken from the stack, the stack pointer increments.

15. Taking data from the stack is called "popping" data from the stack.

16. If you destroy the stack's contents, the microprocessor will crash, because it cannot find its way back from the subroutine to the calling program.

17. There are both conditional and unconditional subroutine call instructions.

18. The unconditional subroutine call instructions start execution of the subroutine each time the call instruction is executed. The conditional subroutine call instructions start execution of the subroutine only when the test conditions are met. The conditional subroutine call instructions test the status register's zero, negative, and carry bits.

Chapter Review Questions

10-1. Explain why a jump to a lower memory location sets up a loop.

10-2. What makes the difference between one conditional jump instruction and another?

10-3. All of our microprocessor's jump instructions use direct addressing. What does this mean?

10-4. How can a Jump Conditional instruction be fetched but not fully executed?

10-5. What is the difference between executing a Jump Unconditional instruction and executing a Jump Conditional instruction?

10-6. The Jump If Equal instruction is really the same as the:
   a. Jump If Carry   c. Jump If Not Negative
   b. Jump If Positive   d. Jump If Zero

10-7. The Jump If Not Negative instruction is really the same as the:
   a. Jump If Carry   c. Jump If Negative
   b. Jump If Positive   d. Jump If Zero

10-8. What instructions are included in the flowchart in Fig. 10-11?

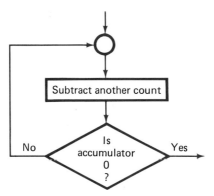

Fig. 10-11 A flowchart for review question 10-8.

10-9. What block from the flowchart in question 10-8 changes if the flowchart's Yes and No arrows are switched?

10-10. Will the program flowcharted in question 10-8 work if the process block is changed to

   Add another count

   Why?

10-11. The routine in question 10-8 is often called a "delay routine." Suppose that our microprocessor has an MPU cycle time of 1 μs. What instruction with what data must precede the routine to cause a 1-ms delay?

10-12. What is the main difference between a jump instruction and a subroutine call instruction?

10-13. A conditional subroutine call tests the:
   a. Accumulator for all "0s"
   b. Decrementing register for terminal count
   c. Status register
   d. Instruction register

10-14. A subroutine called from another subroutine causes:
   a. A JNE   c. A branch
   b. Nesting   d. A test

10-15. A Return instruction ____?____ the microprocessor's stack.
   a. Pushes data onto   c. Resets
   b. Pops data from   d. Crashes

10-16. Typically, an 8-bit microprocessor can have a stack that is ____?____ bytes long.
   a. 8   b. 16   c. 128   d. 65,536

10-17. If the microprocessors's stack is altered the program will probably ____?____ as altered data are loaded from the stack.
a. Pop data   c. Nest
b. Push data   d. Crash

10-18. The Call Subroutine If Not Negative instruction calls a subroutine if the accumulator:
a. Is positive
b. Is not positive
c. Has a logic "1" in its MSB
d. Has a logic "1" in its MSB and LSB

10-19. Explain what limits there are on memory locations that the Jump Conditional instructions can address.

10-20. One of the very early 8-bit microprocessors was the Intel 8008. Its stack consisted of seven 14-bit internal registers. Its program counter was 14 bits long. What were its nesting and memory-addressing limitations?

10-21. How would you expect the 8008 to compare with a modern 8-bit microprocessor?

10-22. The Digital Equipment Corporation LSI-11, a 16-bit microcomputer, uses one of its 16-bit general-purpose registers as a stack pointer. However, the LSB of any memory-address word selects the memory location's hi or lo byte. Therefore, the LSI-11 can address only 32,768 memory words. This limits the stack to 32,768 sixteen-bit words. Do you think that this is a serious limitation when the LSI-11 is compared with an 8-bit microprocessor that can address 65,536 memory locations and therefore can have a 65,536-byte stack?

Answers to Self-Tests

1. See Fig. 10-12. The instructions are

CPI,Data
JZ Equal
JNC Greater than

2. It is preset by using the LDA B instruction or another Load Register instruction. You test for the end of 10 counts with a Jump If Not Zero. The flowchart is in Fig. 10-13. If you use JZ, the decision block is the one shown in Fig. 10-14.

3. (*a*) 006A. (*b*) Accumulator or register. The instruction is Jump If Not Negative. Clearing the accumulator makes the MSB logic "0." The data are not negative, so the program jumps.

The program is:

0129	CLA
012A	JNN
012B	00
012C	6A

4. (*a*) 012D. (*b*) Accumulator's or register's. If the MSB is set, the Jump does not occur. The next instruction comes after the Jump's address bytes.

5. (*a*) Compare. (*b*) JZ.

6. The program to jump to the instruction 00B9. See Fig. 10-15.

7.
Negative	Positive	Zero
0000	0000	0000
0002	0002	0002
0004	0004	0004
0007	0007	0002
000A	000A	

Negative	Positive
000D	000D
0010	0013
0011	0014
0012	0015
0013	0016
0014	0017
0015	001A
0016	001B
0017	001C
001A	001D
001B	001F
001C	0020
001D	0021
001F	0022
0020	0002
0021	
0022	
0002	

8. See Fig. 10-16 (pages 215, 216). The Jump instructions in memory locations 0012, 0024, and 0032 would be Jump 0000.

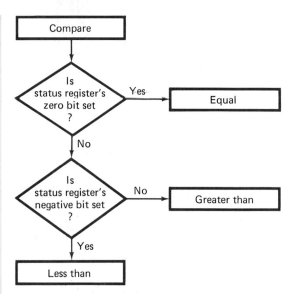

Fig. 10-12   A flowchart for self-test question 1.

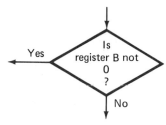

Fig. 10-14   The decision block in self-test question 2 when the JZ instruction is used.

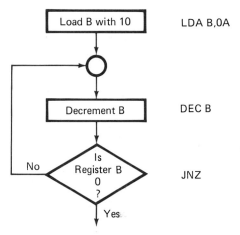

Fig. 10-13   A flowchart for self-test question 2 (see Fig. 10-14 for JZ).

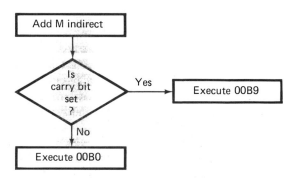

Fig. 10-15   A flowchart for the program in self-test question 6.

9. The instructions 0035 through 003B are added. The counters (pointers) at 00FB, 00FC, and 00FD keep track of the total number of low-, middle-, and high-range operations, respectively. They do a dual job.

10. At least 4 bytes long, because the subroutine call instruction takes 3 bytes and a subroutine cannot be used without a subroutine call.

11. Make the jump instruction a JZ instead of a JNZ. Halt and Return are then swapped because the program jumps to the halt when the counter decrements to 0.

12. (a) The program executes a little more slowly using the subroutine. This is because the program must execute 10 subroutine call instructions. (b) Without the subroutine, the program is 276 instructions long minus 10 subroutine call instructions plus 25 × 10 or 250 inline instructions. Therefore the program that does not use a subroutine is

$$
\begin{array}{r}
276 \\
-\ \ 10 \\
+\ 250 \\
\hline
516
\end{array}
$$

instructions long.

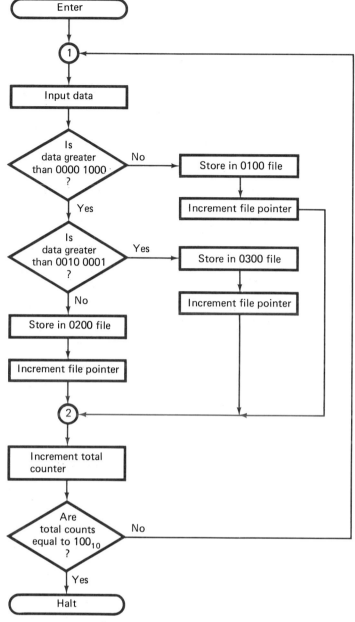

Fig. 10-16(*a*) A flowchart for self-test question 8.

13. (*a*) It means that the first subroutine calls a second subroutine that calls a third subroutine that calls a fourth subroutine that calls a fifth subroutine. (*b*) The stack must store 2 bytes for each of the first four subroutines and for the main program. That is, the stack is 10 bytes long.

14. The stack pointer needs to be 16 bits long so that it can start a stack at *any* memory location.

15. It will cause the return from the second subroutine to go to the wrong instruction. Probably the microprocessor will crash.

16. CN,Address. This instruction calls the sub-routine if the result is negative and therefore needs to be complemented and incremented before being displayed.

17. The jump instruction permanently redirects the program. The subroutine instruction stores enough information that it can return to where it left off.

Memory Address	Memory Contents	Comments
0000	LOA D	Preset register D to zero
0001	00	
0002	LOA B	Start register B at Lo file
0003	01	
0004	IN	Input data
0005	01	Is data 0000 1000?
0006	CMP I	
0007	08	
0008	JC	If greater than 0000 1000; Jump.
0009	00	
000A	17	
000B	LDDC	Get Lo file pointer's Lo byte
000C	00	
000D	FB	
000E	STI A	Put data in Lo file
000F	INC C	Increment file pointer's Lo byte
0010	MOV A, C	Move file pointer to accumulator
0011	STA A	Put incremented file pointer back
0012	00	
0013	ΓD	
0014	JMP	All done with filing. Go to finish
0015	00	
0016	37	
0017	CMP I	Is data 0010 0001?
0018	21	
0019	JC	If greater than 0010 0001; Jump.
001A	00	
001B	29	
001C	LDDC	Get Mid file pointer's Lo byte
001D	00	
001E	FC	
001F	INC B	Point register B at Mid file

Memory address	Memory contents	Comments
0020	STI A	Put data in Mid file
0021	INC C	Increment file pointer's Lo byte
0022	MOV A,C	Move file pointer to accumulator
0023	STA A	Put incremented file pointer back
0024	00	
0025	FC	
0026	JMP	All done with filing. Go to finish
0027	00	
0028	37	
0029	LDD C	Get Hi file pointer's Lo byte
002A	00	
002B	FD	
002C	INC B	Point register B at Mid file
002D	INC B	Point register B at Hi file
002E	STI A	Put data in Hi file
002F	INC C	Increment file pointer's Lo byte
0030	MOV A,C	Move file pointer to accumulator
0031	STA A	Put incremented file pointer back
0032	00	
0033	ΓD	
0034	JMP	All done with filing. Go to finish
0035	00	
0036	37	
0037	INC D	Finish. Add count to D
0038	CMP I	Does D = 100_{10}?
0039	64	
003A	JNZ	No. Get more data
003B	00	
003C	02	
003D	HLT	Yes. Quit

Fig. 10-16(*b*) Program listing for self-test question 8.

18. Because Jump If Not Negative means to jump if the number is positive.
19. They are the Jump If Zero and the Jump If Equal instructions. The Jump If Equal instruction is really a JZ used after a Compare instruction. If the compare is true, the zero bit is set.

Memory

- In earlier chapters, we looked at many microprocessor-based systems. Each of these systems has a memory. In some systems, the memory is quite small. These systems may have only enough bytes to hold the program and to store a few bytes of variable data. Other microprocessor-based systems have as much memory as their microprocessors can address.

  In this chapter, we will look at memory hardware. We will no longer think of memory simply as locations that we can write data words into or read data words from. This chapter looks at both read-write memory and read-only memory. We will also study both dynamic and static memories. We will find out why these two different types of memory exist, where each type is used, and what advantages and disadvantages each has.

  Four kinds of read-only memories (ROMs) are important in microprocessor memory systems. These four kinds are called ROMs, PROMs, EPROMs, and EAROMs. In this chapter, you will learn where each of these different read-only memories is used. Finally, we will look at a special, high-speed way of getting information into and out of memory. This process is called *direct memory access* (DMA).

11-1 RANDOM-ACCESS READ-WRITE MEMORIES

The work that we have done so far has shown us that the microprocessor must be able to read the instructions for a given program and store the data generated by that program. We have found that we must be able to read from memory and write into memory.

In today's microprocessor architecture, we often find that there is only one kind of addressable memory space. This is the microprocessor's main memory. At least some of the microprocessor's main memory must be read-write memory. We must be able to put data into the memory locations or take data from them.

Almost all of the memory in some general-purpose microcomputer systems is read-write memory. Program instructions are stored in memory by using a Memory Write process. Later, when executing the program, the microprocessor reads the instructions from memory. Data, of course, are also written into or read from memory locations. Most microprocessor memory systems are read-write memory.

Most of today's microprocessor memory systems are also *random-access*. In fact, RAM (random-access memory) is so common in microcomputer systems that we often unthinkingly call all of the microprocessor's memory RAM. As we shall see later, this is often incorrect.

The term "random-access memory" simply means a memory system in which each memory location can be accessed as easily as any other memory location.

If memory is not random-access, then it is serial-access. Serial-access memory is rarely used for microprocessor main memory. To access a memory location in a serial-access memory, you must access every memory location between the present location and the memory location that you want to read. Information recorded on a reel of magnetic tape is stored in serial-access form. Serial-access is mostly used for bulk storage. Serial-access is satisfactory for storing large quantities of data that we do not need to get at very quickly.

When we are working with memory systems, we often speak of the memory-access time and the memory-cycle time. Both of these are measures of the memory system's performance. The two measures go hand in hand. That is, the faster the memory-access time, the faster the memory cycle time.

One kind of memory-access time tells how long a memory system takes to place information on the data bus after the desired memory location is addressed. This is called the memory's *read-access time* or, simply, *read time*. Write-access time measures how long it takes the memory system to write data into the addressed location.

Memory-access time depends on the way that the memory system is built and the speed of the memory system's circuits. For example, an integrated-circuit memory system might have a 200-nanosecond (200-ns) access time. That is, the time between addressing any memory location and the placing of the data at the memory's output is 200 ns (0.2 μs).

On the other hand, the access time for magnetic tape can be quite long. In fact, access time depends on where the addressed memory location is found on the tape. If the memory location is very near the beginning of the tape, the access time is short. If the memory location is toward the end of the tape, the access time is long. Usually, we speak of the *average* access time for serial-access devices. For example, a tape that requires 40 s to run from one end to the other has an average access time of 20 s.

We also speak of the memory system's cycle time. The memory system's cycle time is the shortest possible time between two memory operations. The memory system's cycle time depends on other microcomputer-system timing factors. These other timing factors may keep the memory from being used for a set period after each memory access.

We often use two other terms when speaking of microcomputer memory systems. We speak of either *volatile* or *nonvolatile* memory. Simply, nonvolatile memory retains its data when the microcomputer system goes through a power failure. Volatile memory loses its data during a power failure.

Since the microprocessor can do nothing without instructions, it is obvious that it must have some nonvolatile memory. However, the amount of nonvolatile main memory needed does not have to be great. All that is necessary is to store a short program. This program makes the microcomputer load the rest of the instructions into main memory from a nonvolatile bulk storage device such as magnetic tape or disk. As we shall see later, this small, nonvolatile "bootstrap" program is often stored in some form of ROM.

You can also see that program instructions must be stored in some kind of nonvolatile memory. Otherwise, you would have to re-create the program each time you ran it. Writing a program on paper is one kind of nonvolatile memory storage.

Magnetic tape and disk are nonvolatile memory. *Core* memory is also nonvolatile memory. Semiconductor read-write memory is volatile unless it has a battery backup.

Many semiconductor main memory systems now have battery backup. This gives them *temporary* nonvolatility. These memory systems can last through power failures. On a large computer, the batteries may last for only 15 or 20 minutes. On a small microcomputer system, however, a power failure may be allowed to last for as long as several days. Generally speaking, battery backup does not give permanent nonvolatility. This is because the power drawn by semiconductor memories is still great enough to require an unreasonably large battery to sustain memory for long periods.

Core memory was once the most popular computer main memory. In core memory, each bit is stored in a small, doughnut-shaped permanent magnet. The permanent magnet is magnetized in one of two directions. The direction of the magnetism depends on the direction of the currents flowing through the memory wires. Core-memory systems are not often used, because they are very large and expensive and use a lot of current and generate a lot of heat. Today, computers are usually built with semiconductor memory rather than the core memory of the past. Many people still call a system's main memory "core memory" even when the main memory is actually volatile solid-state memory.

Two major semiconductor technologies are used to build integrated-circuit memories. These are the same two technologies used to make other digital integrated circuits—the bipolar and the MOS (metal-oxide-semiconductor) technologies.

Bipolar memories are seldom used with microprocessor systems. The advantage of bipolar memories is their very fast access time. However, bipolar memories have a number of disadvantages when they are compared with MOS memories. They draw a great deal of power, and there are fewer memory bits for the same-size silicon chip. The bipolar semiconductor fabrication process is much more complicated than the MOS process. This makes bipolar memory much more expensive than MOS memory. For these reasons, bipolar memory is used only for applications requiring its great speed.

MOS memory is by far the most common microcomputer memory. There are two different ways to construct MOS memory integrated circuits. MOS memory circuits are either static or dynamic. Static memory systems are simpler to build, especially for small memory systems. They are much easier to service. Dynamic memory systems use a lower-cost integrated circuit but require more support circuits. Also, dynamic memories must be refreshed regularly. They are usually used on the larger memory systems.

Both the static and the dynamic semiconductor memory technologies are steadily improving. This means that larger and larger memories are being made on the same-size silicon wafer. As a result, memory is becoming less expensive. As memory becomes less expensive, microcomputer systems will become more memory-intensive. That is, the systems will contain much more memory to do the same job. Of course, the systems will do the job in a different way.

For example, when we studied programming in Chap. 5, we learned that there are basically two different kinds of programs. There are assembly-language programs and high-level–language programs. Assembly-language programs make very compact code, but they take a great deal of programming time. High-level languages take much less development time, but they take much more memory space than assembly-language programs do.

Knowing that the cost of semiconductor memory is rapidly dropping, you can see why many manufacturers will choose to design microprocessor systems using high-level languages. When the cost of extra memory becomes less than the cost of extra engineering time for assembly-language programming, manufacturers will choose the extra memory.

Two other semiconductor-based memory systems are beginning to appear in some microprocessor systems. These are memory systems built with charge-coupled devices (CCDs) and magnetic-bubble memories (MBMs). Both of these technologies provide serial-access memory. Like other serial memory, these devices are slow. However, they give many more bits of storage than either bipolar memories or MOS memories do.

CCDs have the advantage of using very little power. They are also quite simple to use. CCD memories are volatile, but because they use such low power, battery backup will last a long time.

Magnetic-bubble memories need many more circuits than CCD memories. However, MBMs have the advantage of being truly nonvolatile. Therefore, MBMs provide large amounts of nonvolatile data storage without the complex mechanics of a tape recorder or a disk drive.

Self-Test

Check your understanding by answering these questions.

1. The main memory in a microcomputer system is usually
   a. Random-access   c. Semiconductor
   b. Read-write   d. (All of the above)

2. The performance of a memory system is often measured by the time needed to place data on the microcomputer's data bus after the memory has been addressed. This performance is measured by specifying the microcomputer system's
   a. Cycle time   c. Access time
   b. Serial access   d. Random access

3. You would expect that ___?___ is a random-access device.
   a. Magnetic tape
   b. Read-only memory
   c. A CCD shift register
   d. (All of the above)

4. Magnetic-bubble memories are used in microprocessor-based intelligent terminals. They are used to store data that are needed for the terminal to do a certain job while at a given place. You would expect magnetic-bubble memories to be chosen because of their
   a. Nonvolatility
   b. Low power consumption
   c. Volatility
   d. Ultrasmall size

Bipolar memory

MOS memory

Static memory

Dynamic memory

High-level language programs

Assembly language programs

Charge-coupled devices (CCDs)

Magnetic bubble memories (MBMs)

Bipolar memory cell

Flip-flop

5. During the late 1970s, a typical microprocessor system had about 12 kilobytes of main memory. Frequently, static MOS memory was used for this application. Even today a 65-kilobyte memory is a large system. Typically, you would expect to find ___?___ memories for a system this large.
   - a. Bubble
   - b. Dynamic
   - c. Core
   - d. Magnetic tape

6. Typically, serial-access memory devices are used on microcomputer systems to provide
   - a. Random access
   - b. Fast access time
   - c. Bulk storage
   - d. (All of the above)

7. Nonvolatility for a conventional MOS RAM is provided by
   - a. A battery backup
   - b. Core memory
   - c. Low power dissipation
   - d. CCDs

11-2 STATIC AND DYNAMIC MEMORIES

The static memory is probably one of the most popular microprocessor main memory parts. Most static memories are built using MOS technology, but some are built using bipolar technology. In this section, we will take a brief look at how both MOS and bipolar static memory devices are built. We will also look at some common integrated-circuit memory organizations.

Figure 11-1 shows a simplified schematic of a bipolar memory cell. A memory cell stores 1 bit of information. This cell is implemented by using the TTL (transistor-transistor logic) multiple-emitter technology. As you can tell by looking at this schematic, the memory cell is nothing more than a simple flip-flop. This flip-flop is either set or reset. Once it is set, it stays set until it is reset or until it loses power.

Large numbers of these memory cells are organized on a row-and-column basis. Figure 11-2 shows the row-and-column organization of a typical 4096-*bit* memory chip. This basic block diagram is the same for both bipolar and MOS static and dynamic memories.

Each chip (integrated circuit) has 12 address lines A0 through A11. These address lines are connected to the row and column address decoders. The first six address lines, A0 to A5, are connected to the column decoder. The column decoder decodes a 6-bit address to indicate one of 64 columns. The second six address lines, A6 to A11, are connected to the row decoder. The row decoder decodes a 6-bit address to indicate one of 64 rows. Where the selected row and column outputs cross, they select the desired memory cell. Simple arithmetic shows that there are 64 × 64, or 4096, crossings. Therefore, this system can address any of the memory chip's 4096 cells. Once a cell is selected, the system may either write data into the cell or read data from the cell.

Figure 11-3 shows a simplified schematic of an MOS static-memory cell. Looking at this schematic, you can see that this cell is also a simple flip-flop. Like most MOS devices, this one is implemented by using fixed-bias MOS transistors for the drain loads. Additional MOS transistors are used to couple the data into and out of the selected cell.

Like the bipolar memory cell, the MOS static-memory cell holds binary information because of the flip-flop or cross-coupled gate design. The cell retains the set or reset state as long as power is applied.

By comparison, the MOS-dynamic memory cell is much simpler. This is shown in Fig. 11-4. In this schematic, you can see that the dynamic cell does the same job with only half as many transistors. Obviously, a dynamic-memory integrated circuit can have twice as many memory bits as a static-memory circuit of the same size.

The MOS-dynamic memory cell is not built like a flip-flop. The capacitance shown in the schematic is the MOS transistor's input capacitance. This very small capacitance is

Fig. 11-1 A bipolar memory cell. The two multiple emitter transistors are cross coupled to make a simple flip-flop. The cell is set or reset by asserting the appropriate emitter. Asserting the Cell-select line makes a valid low-impedance output.

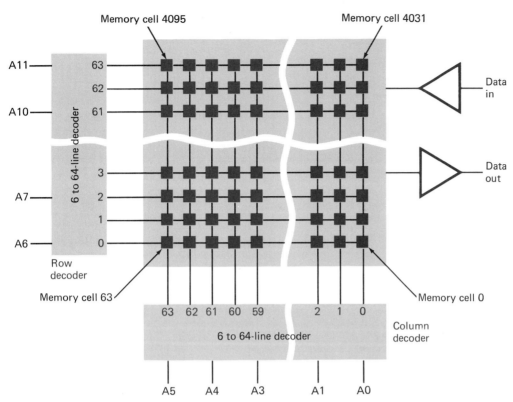

Fig. 11-2 The row-and-column addressing for a 4096-cell memory. Each cell has inputs that enable the cell when the row *and* column lines are both active. The Data in and Data out lines are connected to each cell.

used as the dynamic MOS memory cell's storage. The capacitance stores binary data by holding a charge, a logic "1" or a logic "0," for a few milliseconds. After this time, the data must be rewritten into the cell.

Rewriting the data in a dynamic MOS memory cell is called *refreshing* the data. The dynamic-memory cell is refreshed each time that it is accessed. However, there is no guar-antee that every bit will be refreshed by the microprocessor's normal memory activity. For example, the microprocessor might spend more than a few milliseconds in a simple timing loop that uses only a few memory locations. During this time, almost all the other memory words would *not* receive a Refresh cycle.

For this reason, memory systems that use

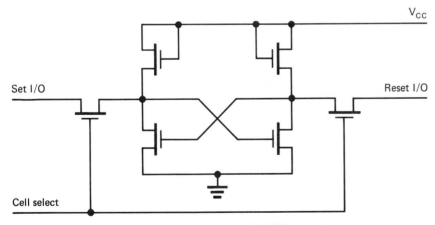

Fig. 11-3 A static-memory cell built with MOS transistors. Again note the cross-coupled design, which is a flip-flop.

221

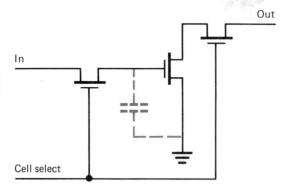

Refresh logic

Fig. 11-4 A dynamic-memory cell built with MOS transistors. The capacitor is the MOS transistor's input capacitance. A charge stored on this capacitor makes the cell hold a logic "1." No charge is a logic "0."

MOS dynamic RAMs have what is called *Refresh logic*. This logic automatically accesses each column every few tenths of a millisecond. Dynamic memories are built so that simply accessing the column refreshes all the bits in the column. The Refresh logic must be coordinated with other microprocessor activities. For example, if the microprocessor tries to access the memory while memory is being refreshed, the Refresh logic must give the microprocessor priority.

Figure 11-5 shows four different pinouts, or ways of packaging MOS integrated static memories for use in microprocessor systems. Figure 11-5(*a*) is an early 1K static RAM. This RAM stores 1024 bits. Eight of these devices are needed to store 1024 eight-bit words. Each device has 10 address lines. Ten address lines allow selection of one of the 1024 bits ($2^{10} = 1024$). The Chip Select line allows the use of an 11-bit address to selectively address one of two rows of these devices. The eleventh bit is connected directly to one row's Chip Select pins. The eleventh bit is connected to the other row's Chip Select pins through an inverter. That is, when one row of chips is selected, the other row is *not* selected.

In addition to the address lines and the Chip Select lines, the device has data input and output lines and another input line that tells the memory to be in the Read mode or in the Write mode.

Figure 11-5(*b*) shows a common 4096-bit integrated-circuit static memory. You can see this device also has address, data, Chip Select, and Read/Write lines. This chip is simply four

times larger than the one in Fig. 11-5(*a*). The chip is usually called a 4K static RAM.

Figure 11-5(*c*) shows another 4096-bit integrated-circuit memory pinout. This chip is organized as a 1024 ×4 chip. This means that there are four data input lines and four data output lines. Each time an address is selected, you either read or write on one-half of a byte. With two of these chips, you can have a 1K byte memory. This kind of memory organization is very useful for small systems.

Figure 11-5(*d*) shows a byte-oriented memory organization. This 4096-bit chip stores 512 bytes. A single chip of this kind can be used for a small microcomputer system's RAM.

Many dynamic RAMs are built to be interchangeable. That is, a printed-circuit board can be laid out so that the memory integrated-circuit positions can take either 4K, 16K, or 64K RAMs. Such a layout permits configuring the microcomputer-system memory to the customer's requirements. Often you may be asked to service a board that uses a selection of different integrated-circuit memories. You may also be asked to change the memory capacity of a microcomputer memory system.

Figure 11-6 shows the pinout of three integrated-circuit memories. Again, they are 4K, 16K, and 64K devices. As you can see, these chips are packaged in 16-pin dual inline packages (DIPs). In order to minimize the number of pins, a special memory-addressing technique is used. *Note that some* inputs are marked with an overbar, CHIP SELECT, for example. The bar means that this input is selected when the input is a *logic* "0." To explain this technique, we use the 4K example.

Figure 11-7 shows a diagram of the decoding system used. At first glance, this block diagram looks exactly like that of the 4096-bit memory shown in Fig. 11-2. The 4K memory uses a 6-line to 64-line column decoder. It also uses a 6-line to 64-line row decoder. Each decoder has a 6-bit latch. To address a memory bit in this device, you must use two cycles. First, the chip's six address pins are connected to the memory system's *lower* six address lines—lines A0 through A5. A signal then strobes the memory chip's $\overline{\text{ROW ADDRESS STROBE}}$ pin. Strobing the $\overline{\text{ROW ADDRESS STROBE}}$ pin stores the six address bits in the row-decoder latch.

Next, the microcomputer's *upper* six address bits, bits A6 through A11, are connected

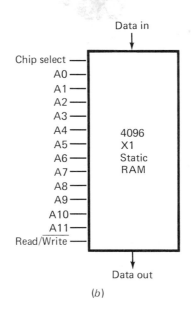

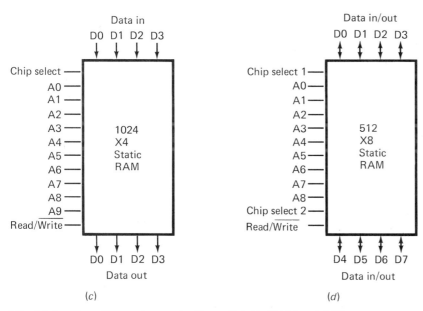

Fig. 11-5 Four different organizations of static RAMs. (a) The
1K static RAM. (b) The 4K static RAM. (c) The 1024 × 4, a half-
byte organization. (d) The 512 × 8, a full-byte organization.

to the chip's six address pins. This time the
COLUMN ADDRESS STROBE pin is
strobed. These six address bits are stored in
the column-decoder latch.

All 12 address bits are now stored in the
latches. We can now decode one of the 4096
memory cells. This technique is called *multiplexed addressing*.

Each RAM chip has a number of common
pinouts. These are shown in Fig. 11-6. Each
chip has a data input on pin 2 and a data output on pin 14. Remember, these devices

store only a single bit of information at each
memory-address location. This means that
eight devices are needed to store 1 byte of
data. You can see that these chips use separate data-input and data-output lines.

Each chip has a WRITE input. You assert
this pin to write data into the addressed memory location. If this pin is not asserted, the
chip is in the Read mode.

Each chip has a ROW ADDRESS STROBE
and a COLUMN ADDRESS STROBE. All
three chips are multiplexing addressing.

223

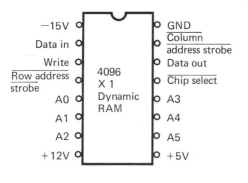

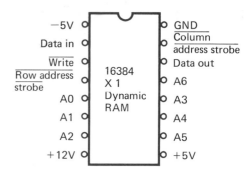

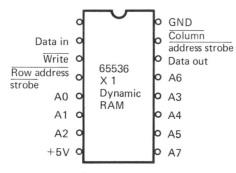

Fig. 11-6 Three dynamic RAMs that are interchangeable. To replace the 4K RAM with a 16K RAM, you change the CHIP SELECT pin to A6. To replace either the 4K or 16K RAM with a 65K RAM, the +12 V becomes +5 V, the 4K CHIP SELECT becomes A6, and the +5 V input becomes A7. The 64K RAMs only use +5 V.

The 4K dynamic RAM has six address lines: A0 through A5. The 16K dynamic RAM has seven address lines: A0 through A6. The 64K dynamic RAM has eight address lines: A0 through A7. You can see that using each one of these address lines twice gives these RAMs the address ranges that they need. These ranges are:

$$2^6 \times 2^6 = 2^{12} = 4096$$
$$2^7 \times 2^7 = 2^{14} = 16,384$$
$$2^8 \times 2^8 = 2^{16} = 65,536$$

Only the address lines A0 through A5 are common. The 16K and 64K RAMs borrow the 4K RAM's CHIP SELECT input. That input becomes address line A6. If you need the Chip Select function, then you must use external logic.

Both 4K and 16K RAMs use three supply voltages and ground. They use +12 V, +5 V, and −5 V. The 64K dynamic RAM operates from a single supply voltage (+5 V). One of the extra supply-voltage pins has been converted into A7. The single-voltage semiconnector is the newest technology. It allows a 64K RAM to be packaged in a small space. As you can see, the 64K RAM has one unused pin. If this pin is converted to A8, this package can contain a future 262,144 bit (256K) dynamic RAM.

Self-Test

Check your understanding by answering these questions.

8. The static RAM stores its information in a
   a. Capacitor   c. Bipolar circuit
   b. Flip-flop   d. MOS circuit

9. A dynamic RAM needs special circuits to perform
   a. Row decoding   c. Refreshing
   b. Column decoding   d. Addressing

10. A 4K memory can be organized as
    a. 4K × 1   c. 512 × 8
    b. 1K × 4   d. (All of the above)

11. The Chip Select lines let two chips operate with common ___?___ lines.
    a. Power   c. Address
    b. Ground   d. Inverter

12. The larger (4K, 16K, and 64K) dynamic RAMs use
    a. −5 V
    b. +12 V
    c. DIPs
    d. Multiplexed addressing

13. Asserting a memory chip's WRITE line will cause data to be:
    a. Stored in the RAM
    b. Addressed
    c. Placed on the data bus
    d. Latched

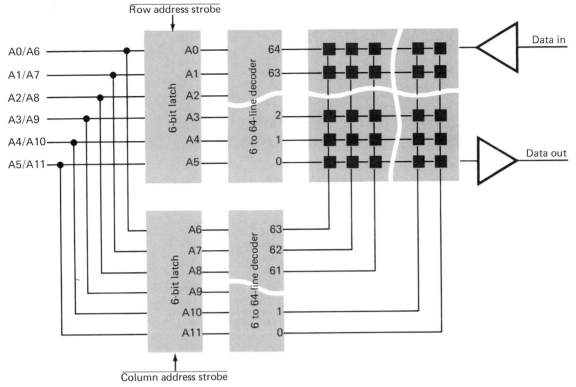

Fig. 11-7 A dynamic RAM using multiplexed row-column addressing. The ROW ADDRESS STROBE line is asserted to store address bits A0 to A5 in the row-decoder latch. The COLUMN ADDRESS STROBE line is asserted to store address bits A6 to A11 in the column-decoder latch.

14. A RAM with multiplexed addressing needs two strobe signals. What do they do? Why are these chips built with this extra complication?

15. Explain the difference between how a static RAM stores data and how a dynamic RAM stores data.

16. Why does a dynamic RAM need Refresh logic?

11-3 AN EXAMPLE OF A MEMORY CARD

In the last section, we looked at MOS static- and dynamic-memory chips. How are these actually used to build a microcomputer's memory system? What additional circuits are needed on the memory card?

Figure 11-8 shows a simplified schematic of a small microcomputer memory system. In this schematic, we use two 512×8 memory chips to build a 1-kilobyte memory system.

Keep in mind that this is a simplified schematic. Depending upon the particular microcomputer's bus structure, the exact memory chips used, and the discrete TTL devices that are available, a few more integrated circuits may be needed to build a real memory system.

The simplified bus connections are shown on the left-hand side of the schematic. Starting from the top, you can see that the first 16 connections are the memory-address lines A0 through A15. The next eight lines are the *bidirectional* data bus lines D0 through D7.

The memory system needs four more bus lines. The READ (NOT READ) line is asserted when the memory system places data on the microcomputer's data bus. The next line, WRITE (NOT WRITE), is asserted when the microcomputer writes data to a memory location. The terms READ and WRITE indicate that these lines are asserted by a low voltage level. This is done to make the electrical design of the system easier.

225

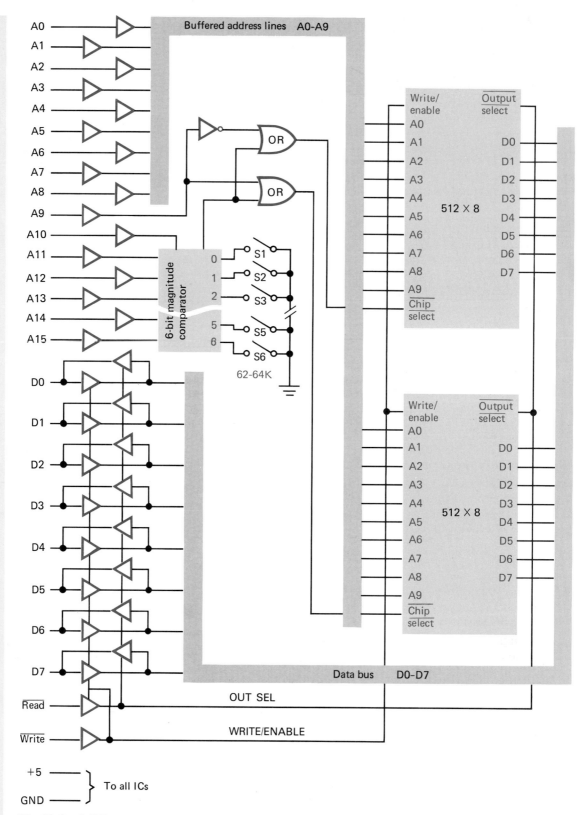

Fig. 11-8 A 1K memory system using two 512 × 8 chips. The Write/enable line is asserted when you want to write a byte into memory. The Output select line is asserted when you want the chip to place data on the data bus, otherwise the chip's D0 to D7 (Data in/out lines) are in a high-impedance state.

The last two lines supply power and ground to the integrated circuits on the memory card.

As you can see, each of the address lines is buffered. This is usually done by using small-scale integrated TTL circuits. The buffers isolate the microcomputer's bus from the integrated-circuit memory's address lines. In some small systems, these buffers may not be used.

The buffered memory-address lines A0 through A8 are connected directly to the integrated-circuit memories.

Address line A9 (remember that A9 is the tenth address line) selects either the first chip or the second chip. Memory-address lines A0 through A8 can address any location in a 512-byte range. Address line A9 selects either the first 512 bytes or the second 512 bytes.

The A9 memory signal is passed through an OR gate and is then directly connected to the first memory chip. The A9 memory signal is connected to the second memory chip through an inverter and an OR gate. Therefore, when one chip is selected, the other is not selected. The OR gates let you deselect both chips regardless of the A9 signal.

Address lines A10 through A15 are connected to a 6-bit comparator. The other six inputs come from a 6-bit switch. Usually these are in an on-board "DIP switch."* The memory-address lines A10 through A15 are compared to the switch setting by the magnitude comparator. This tells you which 1-kilobyte block of memory the microcomputer is addressing.

For example, if address lines A10 through A15 are all "0" and the switches are all logic "0" (closed), the magnitude comparator outputs logic "0" to the OR gates. If address lines A10 through A15 are all logic "1," then the magnitude comparator outputs logic "1."

In the above example, we use the all-0 switch setting. We have decided that this memory system is to respond to addresses in the 0 to 1K byte range. If, for example, the switches are set to 000010, this memory system responds to addresses in the 2K to 3K range. Figure 11-9 shows a memory map of the 1-kilobyte blocks.

The logic "0" from the magnitude comparator's output is used to enable the OR gates in series with address line A9. A logic "1" to the

* A DIP switch is a subminiature switch that looks somewhat like an integrated circuit in a dual inline package.

Buffers

Transceivers

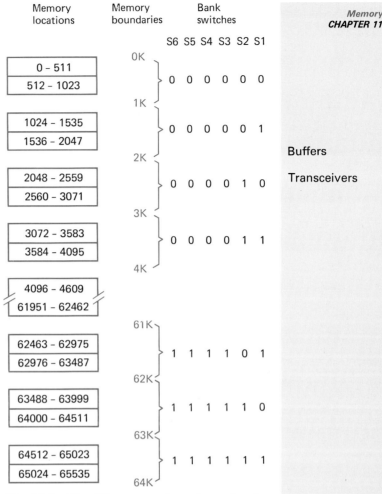

Fig. 11-9 The 1K memory boundaries for the card in Fig. 11-8. Each of the 1K (1024-byte) increments is selected by one of the bank-select switches 0 to 63.

OR gates will guarantee a logic "1" at their outputs. Because a logic "0" is needed to enable the chips, the logic "1" disables them. No Chip Select signal is permitted at all if the address is not in the range of 0 to 1K.

We have seen how the address-selection process works. Now we must look at how to get data into and out of memory. Data lines D0 through D7 are connected to integrated-circuit bus transceivers. These TTL integrated circuits perform two functions.

First, the bus transceivers buffer the microcomputer's data bus lines from the components on the memory card. Second, these transceivers can connect the card signals to the microcomputer's data bus. This lets the memory system place data on the microcomputer's data bus or receive data from the microcomputer's data bus. As you can see, the

227

input buffers and the output buffers each have a common control signal. When the input-buffer control signal is asserted, data on the microcomputer's data bus are connected to the memory chips. When the output-buffer control signal is asserted, data from the memory chips are placed on the microcomputer's data bus.

The data-buffer control signals and the memory chip's Write/enable, and Output Select signals are all controlled by the $\overline{\text{READ}}$ and $\overline{\text{WRITE}}$ bus signals.

Let us look at an example of a read operation. An address is placed on memory-address lines A0 through A15. The memory-addressing logic selects a memory location in one of the two memory chips. The memory $\overline{\text{READ}}$ line is asserted. The buffered memory $\overline{\text{READ}}$ signal asserts the chip's $\overline{\text{OUTPUT SELECT}}$ lines. The selected chip places the data at the addressed memory location on the memory card's internal data bus. The $\overline{\text{READ}}$ signal also connects the memory card's internal data bus to the microcomputer's data bus lines D0 through D7. The information from the addressed location is moved from the memory card's data bus to the microcomputer's data bus.

As you can see, the sequence of operations is as follows:

1. The microprocessor puts valid information on the memory-address lines.
2. The microprocessor's control logic generates a $\overline{\text{READ}}$ signal.
3. The addressed memory location places its data on the chip outputs.
4. The chip outputs are buffered and connected to the microcomputer's data bus.
5. The microprocessor inputs these data through the data bus port and transfers the data to the location designated.

Now let us take a look at a Memory Write operation. The sequence is the same; only the names are changed.

1. The microprocessor puts valid information on the memory-address lines.
2. The microprocessor's control logic generates a $\overline{\text{WRITE}}$ signal.
3. The microprocessor outputs data from the data bus port.
4. The microcomputer's data bus is buffered and connected to the memory-chip data inputs.

5. The data are written into the selected memory location.

The schematic shown in Fig. 11-8 uses two 4K static RAMs. To build this memory using two 4K dynamic RAMs, you would need extra circuits. These circuits are needed to refresh the dynamic-memory chips about every 300 μs. The use of dynamic memory increases the card's "overhead." Overhead refers to extra integrated circuits that do not store data but are necessary to make the memory work. In Fig. 11-8, the bus-buffering and the address-decoding integrated circuits are all overhead. They perform needed functions, but they do not store data.

Typically, a Refresh circuit might use just as many integrated circuits as the bus interface and the decoding logic use. When that is the case, the Refresh circuits double the overhead. Now you can see why dynamic memories are used only on large memory systems, and why static memories are used on small memory systems.

We can look at this memory card in detail. Adding five refresh ICs to the five ICs needed for bus interface and address decoding we have:

5	Address decoders and bus buffers	(Overhead)
5	Memory Refresh	(Overhead)
2	512 × 8 dynamic memories	(Nonoverhead)
12	Total	

The 10 overhead ICs make up 83 percent of the memory system.

However, if we build a 64-kilobyte memory using 16K dynamic RAMs, the numbers are different. Let's look at this example. We have:

5	Address decoders and bus buffers	(Overhead)
5	Memory Refresh	(Overhead)
32	16K × 1 dynamic memories	(Nonoverhead)
42	Total	

Here the overhead is only 24 percent of the memory system.

You can see from these simple examples that the overhead has dropped from 83 percent to 24 percent. Of course, there are still good reasons for using dynamic RAMs: There are no static RAMs as large as common dynamic RAMs; and the dynamic RAMs are much cheaper and faster.

Self-Test

Check your understanding by answering these questions.

17. What circuits would change if the memory system of Fig. 11-8 used eight 4K × 1 static RAMs?

18. What does the increased memory design in question 17 do to the memory card's overhead? Why?

19. Using a diagram like the one in Fig. 11-9, show how the memory "Bank Select" would divide up the memory system in question 17.

20. Why is it undesirable to use dynamic RAMs on small memory systems?

21. Often, one of the microcomputer bus signals is Valid Memory Address. If you are using a memory card with 16K dynamic RAMs, what special signals will this generate?

11-4 ROMs, PROMs, EPROMs, AND EAROMs

The ROM (Read-only memory) is a very important part of any microprocessor system. As its name tells you, the ROM is a memory device which, once set with a given bit pattern, cannot be changed. Often microprocessor systems use ROMs because the systems always execute the same program. The program instructions are stored in ROM. This storage overcomes the semiconductor RAM's volatility problem. Every microprocessor system *must have some* ROM, because every system must have at least enough built-in program to load its RAM from a mass-storage device such as magnetic tape or disk.

There are four different types of ROM. Each of the four types is used for a different application. This section looks at these four types of devices.

First we will look at the simple ROM. When we speak of a ROM, we mean a device with a bit pattern permanently fixed by the semiconductor manufacturer. Often this is called a *mask-programmed* ROM. The bit pattern is fixed by the masking part of the inte-

grated-circuit manufacturing process. The bit pattern is fixed according to the customer's specifications. ROMs are only used in fairly high-volume applications, because custom mask design is expensive.

Second we will look at PROMs (programmable read-only memories). The PROM's bit pattern can be set by the customer. Programming a PROM is a one-shot operation. That is, once the PROM's bit pattern has been fixed, that pattern cannot be changed. If you need a different bit pattern, then you must "blast" a new PROM.

Third we will look at the EPROM. The EPROM (erasable programmable read-only memory) can be programmed by the user, *erased* by the user, and *reprogrammed* by the user. Although these devices are usually much more expensive than either ROMs or PROMs, EPROMs do let the user change the bit pattern as needed. Often EPROMs are supplied with a microprocessor system whose functions will be changed as the user, by experience, decides exactly what the system should do.

Fourth we will look at the EAROM (electrically alterable read-only memory). The EAROM can be programmed and altered electrically. Unlike the EPROM, the EAROM does not need an outside device in order to be erased.

Figure 11-10 shows a schematic of a very simple ROM. This ROM could be built using only a TTL decoder and a few diodes. Since this ROM contains four 8-bit words, it is a 32-bit ROM. As you can see, this ROM has diodes at each bit that is to be a logic "0."

The 2-line to 4-line decoder places a logic "0" on the selected row. Each of the output lines goes to logic "0" *if* a diode connects the output data column to the selected row.

Most of today's ROMs use MOS technology. A few bipolar ROMs are built for use where very high-speed operation is needed. In MOS ROMs, a MOS transistor takes the place of the diode. A very simple 4-word ROM is shown in Fig. 11-11. Since each word has 4 bits, this is a 16-bit ROM.

As you can see, each data column is connected to four of the ROM's MOS transistors. A MOS transistor on each column is used as a pull-up. Some of the MOS transistors' gates are connected to the Row Select lines. When the row is selected, it is pulled high. If the row is connected to a MOS transistor's gate, the MOS transistor is turned on.

Mask programming

Programmable read only memories

Erasable programmable read only memory

Electrically alterable read only memory

Fusible link
PROM

Field
programmable
ROM

PROM blasting

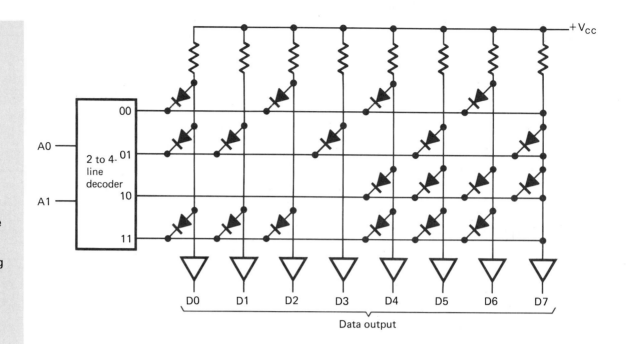

Data output

ROM contents

Word	Binary								Hexadecimal
	D0	D1	D2	D3	D4	D5	D6	D7	
00	0	1	0	1	0	1	0	1	55
01	0	0	1	0	1	0	1	0	2A
10	1	1	1	1	0	0	0	0	F0
11	0	0	0	1	0	0	0	1	11

Fig. 11-10 A simple 4-word (4-byte) ROM. This diode ROM
has a total of 32 bits. Each bit that has a diode at the matrix
cross point has a logic "0" at its output.

This pulls the row to logic "0" (ground). This
causes a logic "0" at the ROM's output. If the
gate is not connected to the Row Select line,
then the transistor is not turned on. This
causes a logic "1" at the ROM's output.

ROMs are made by mask programming.
As you know, the active parts of an integrated
circuit are interconnected by depositing very
thin layers of metal. These thin layers of
metal, like the layers of metal on a printed-circuit board, are the integrated circuit's internal
wiring. The final layer of metallization for a
mask-programmed ROM is set by the customer. It is this thin metallized layer that
connects the gates of some transistors to the
Row Select lines. The transistors are not
connected to those Row Select lines on which
a logic "1" is wanted at the output.

Mask-programmed ROMs are made by a
high-volume process. As a rule, they are not
used unless the manufacturer intends to produce a few thousand of the same ROM. The

ROMs used in microprocessor-based toys, TV
games, home computers, and other such
products use mask-programmed ROMs.

Figure 11-12 shows one way to make a user-
programmable ROM. This kind of ROM is
called a *fusible-link* PROM. As you can see,
this is really just a diode ROM like the one
shown in Fig. 11-10. When you purchase this
PROM, you find a diode and a fuse at every
bit. To program this PROM, you simply address the desired word and "blast" out the
fuses that you do not want. Once this is done
the PROM is permanently altered. If a programming mistake is made, the only way to
correct it is by throwing away this PROM and
blasting a new one. Because the bit pattern
of the fusible-link PROM can be easily set at
places other than the semiconductor factory,
this PROM is often called a *field-programmable* ROM.

The EPROM is built more like the mask-
programmed ROM. That is, it uses MOS

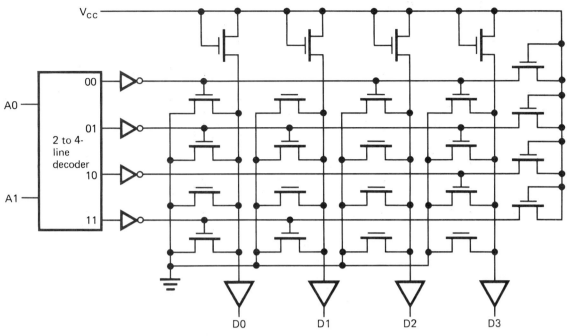

ROM contents

Word	Binary				Hexadecimal
	D0	D1	D2	D3	
00	0	1	0	0	4
10	0	0	1	0	2
01	1	1	1	0	E
11	0	0	1	1	3

Fig. 11-11 A simple 4-word (half-byte) ROM. This **ROM** shows how **MOS** transistors are used to make a mask-programmable **ROM.** The integrated-circuit process connects the MOS transistor's gate to the Row-select line if the output bit is to be a logic "0."

transistors in an array like the one shown in Fig. 11-11. However, there are a few differences between the EPROM and the ROM. First, all transistors in the EPROM are connected to the Select rows. Second, the transistors are designed so that a high voltage can be applied to the transistor's gate. This changes the transistor so that it will always be at a high impedance. Third, this characteristic can be undone by shining an intense ultraviolet light on the transistor.

The EPROM can be programmed in the field by using high-voltage pulses. Once the EPROM is programmed, it retains the program until a high-intensity ultraviolet (UV) light is shone through the EPROM's quartz window. Ultraviolet light erases the EPROM's stored bit pattern.

A fourth type of ROM is becoming popular. It is called the EAROM: the electrically alterable ROM. The EAROM is constructed very much like the EPROM. However, the EAROM has one unique characteristic. The contents of the EAROM can be altered by applying special electrical signals for a certain time. Usually the write signals must be applied for a few milliseconds, so the writing process is quite slow when compared with the Read process. The EAROM is not as permanent as the EPROM. However, it can be changed by the customer, and it is nonvolatile.

EAROMs are finding uses in such applications as channel selectors on TV sets and in storage of temporary setup information for video terminals.

To summarize, we have looked at four different ROMs. The mask-programmed ROM

231

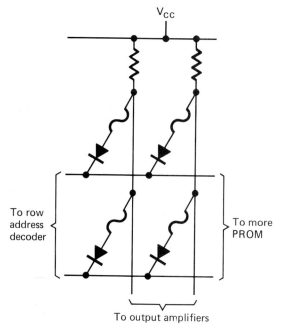

Fig. 11-12   The fusible-link PROM. A logic "1" is placed in a bit by passing enough current through the fuse to blow it. This PROM is customer-programmable, but only once. It cannot be erased or reprogrammed.

is permanent. It is also the least expensive ROM and offers the most bits. The PROM is field programmable—but only once. Its cost lies somewhere between the EPROMs and the mask programmed ROMs. The EPROM is both field-programmable and reusable. It is less dense than the first two ROMs. The EAROM is electrically alterable. It is the most expensive and the least dense kind of ROM.

Figure 11-13 shows pinouts for the popular 2716 and 2732 EPROMs. The 2716 is a 16-kilobit (2K × 8) UV-erasable PROM. The 2732 is a 32-kilobit (4K × 8) UV-erasable PROM. As you can see, both of these chips are organized in bytes. The 2732 makes double use of pin 20 so that pin 21 may be assigned to the A11 address line. A double use of one more pin permits a 64-kilobit UV-erasable PROM. The 8-, 16-, 32-, and 64-kilobit EPROMs are like the 4K, 16K, and 64K dynamic RAMs. They are built so that one device can be removed and replaced by a model with a higher bit density.

The address lines are A0 to A10 (A11), and the data are output on lines D0 to D7. Both devices use a single +5-V dc supply pin, a ground pin, and a Chip Select pin. The OUTPUT ENABLE ($\overline{OE}$) places data on the

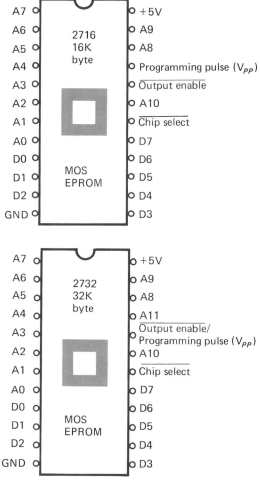

Fig. 11-13 The 2716 and the 2732 MOS EPROMs. The programming input is not used in normal operation. It is reserved for use in a special PROM programmer circuit.

output pins D0 to D7 when the enable is asserted. To program the device, address information is applied to pins A0 to A10 (A11), data are applied to pins D0 to D7, and a 50-ms pulse of 25 V is applied to V_{PP}. To erase, the EPROM is exposed through its quartz window to a special UV lamp for 15 to 20 minutes. This is the same UV energy that it would receive from three years of fluorescent lighting or one week of direct sunlight. You will see covered quartz windows in some EPROMs to prevent accidental erasure.

With four different kinds of PROMs and significant variations in density, there are many different kinds of ROMs available. There are some mask-programmed ROMs that can be directly inserted into the same socket used by an EPROM. This is very convenient, because it lets the manufacturer develop the device and place it on the market using EPROMs. Program problems can be corrected by reprogramming the EPROMs. Later, when the software design is perfected, the EPROMs can be replaced by the less expensive mask-programmed ROMs.

There are also some preprogrammed mask-programmed ROMs. These ROMs are available with certain standard tables. For example, you can find ROMs for use with CRT-based terminals. These ROMs can generate all the alphanumeric characters by using a 5×7 dot matrix.

Self-Test

Check your understanding by answering these questions.

22. The highest-cost read-only memory in the following group is
    a. Mask-programmed ROM
    b. Field-programmable ROM
    c. Erasable programmable ROM
    d. Electrically alterable ROM

23. The ____?____ uses a fusible link.
    a. Mask-programmed ROM
    b. Field-programmable ROM
    c. Erasable programmable ROM
    d. Electrically alterable ROM

24. Although you can order ROMs, PROMs, and EPROMs with your custom bit pattern already in them, the ____?____ is the only one that uses an integrated-circuit manufacturing process to set the bit pattern.
    a. Mask-programmed ROM
    b. Field-programmable ROM
    c. Erasable programmable ROM
    d. Electrically alterable ROM

25. The 2708 is the 8K version of the 2716 and 2732 family of UV EPROMs. You would expect that it has ____?____ address lines.
    a. 8   b. 9   c. 10   d. 11   e. 12

26. Why do you think the EPROM is the most popular read-only memory for development work?

27. Explain why a microcomputer must have some read-only memory.

28. Explain why it is very unlikely that a microcomputer will have EPROMs for all its memory.

11-5 DIRECT MEMORY ACCESS

So far, all our discussions of input/output data transfers have been about programmed data transfers. When we input data, the data come from the input data register to the accumulator. The data then go into memory. Programmed data transfers out of memory require the transfer of data from memory into the accumulator, and then from the accumulator into the output register.

Unfortunately, the programmed data transfer is a slow process. The fact that the data-transfer process is slow usually causes a problem only when we have to transfer large amounts of data.

For example, suppose you wish to transfer 16 kilobytes of data from a magnetic tape. The magnetic tape drive stores 800 bytes per inch of tape. The drive moves the tape at 125 inches per second (in/s). Sixteen kilobytes of data are contained on 20.5 in of tape. This means that all 16,384 bytes of data can be transferred in 0.16384 s. In other words, the data are being transferred at a rate of 100,000 bytes per second.

Figure 11-14 shows a short program that we might use to transfer data from magnetic tape by using programmed data transfers. Once the program is written, we can count the microprocessor's cycles and see how long the program will take to do the job. We will start the 16K data block at memory location 0400. The 16K data transfer will be complete at memory location 4400.

We start the programmed-data-transfer subroutine at memory location DATAIN. The subroutine is assigned symbolic addresses so that we can combine it with any program we wish. When we assemble it, the symbolic DATAIN will be assembled into an absolute address. The first two program instructions load the D register with 44 and point the BC register pair to the bottom of the memory file (0400). The D register will be compared to the B register at the end of each store. When the B register is incremented to 44, we will exit this routine. That is, the 16,384th byte will have been loaded in memory location 4400.

We begin the routine at the symbolic address INAGN. An Input instruction transfers the data from I/O port 01 to the accumulator. A Store Accumulator Indirect instruction stores the accumulator's contents in memory location 0400. We now use an IRP B instruction to increment the BC register pair.

Symbolic address	Op code		Operand	Comment
DATAIN	LDA	D	44H	; Load D with terminal counter
	LRP	B	0004H	; Point BC to memory file
INAGN	IN		01H	; Input data to accumulator
	STI	A		; Store accumulator in file
	IRP	B		; Point BC to next memory
	MOV	A,B		; Put B into A
	CMP	D		; 16K bytes yet?
	JNZ		INAGN	; No, input more data
	RET			; Yes, all Done. Exit

Fig. 11-14 A short subroutine to load 16,384 bytes of data into a memory file. This program is given in a form for use with an assembler. To assemble this program, you would need to use an ORG instruction and to specify a starting address as the ORG's operand. The "H" after the operand tells the assembler that the number is hexadecimal.

The instruction MOV A,B moves register B's contents into the accumulator. With register B's contents in the accumulator, we can now compare register D to the accumulator. We do this by using a CMP D instruction.

What we are doing is checking to see if the last increment instruction pointed the BC register pair to memory location 4400. If it did, the job is complete. If it did not, we must go back. We use the JNZ instruction to check the status register's zero bit. If the status register's zero bit is not set to logic "1," the job is not complete. We jump back to INAGN. When the job is complete, the status register's zero bit will be set to logic "1." Then the jump instruction will not execute on the 16,384th operation.

Instruction		Number of times used	μs at 1μs per MPU cycle	Total μs
LDA	D	1	3	3
LRP	B	1	5	5
IN		16384	5	81920
STI	A	16384	2	32768
IRP	B	16384	2	32768
MOV	A,B	16384	2	32768
CMP	D	16384	2	32768
JNZ		16383	5	81915
				294915

Fig. 11-15 Timing the programmed data transfer listed in Fig. 11-14. The JNZ instruction does not execute on the last operation. This instruction is used only 16,383 times.

Figure 11-15 shows this program's timing. Remember, most of the program must execute 16,384 times to fill up the file. If we assume that our microprocessor has a 1-μs instruction cycle, then we need 294,915 μs to do the job. That is almost 0.3 s! A job that should have been done in 0.16 s took almost twice as long because we used a programmed data transfer.

Even if we used a microprocessor with a 0.5-μs instruction cycle, the processor would barely be able to keep up with the data coming from the tape.

The purpose of this example is to show the need for DMA. DMA stands for "direct memory access." It is one way that we can accomplish high-speed transfers into memory. For example, we know that a good microprocessor memory has a 300- to 500-ns access time. With such a short access time, the microprocessor should be able to make 2 million or more transfers per second. However, we have seen that using a programmed data transfer sets an upper limit of about 25,000 transfers per second.

In most cases DMA is accomplished by using a separate DMA controller. The microprocessor must be disabled during the DMA process. To start the DMA process, the microprocessor loads an external register in the DMA controller with the data files' starting addresses. The microprocessor also loads a terminal-count register with the total number of bytes to be transferred. The microprocessor disables the address and data buses and gives memory-system control to the DMA controller. The DMA controller places sequential addresses on the microprocessor's memory bus and issues read-write pulses. As each byte is transferred, the terminal-count register is decremented. When this register is decremented to 0, it tells the external device that the data transfer is complete. Because this is a limited application, a special-purpose hardware controller can do it very quickly. Today DMA transfers can take place at speeds that are close to the memory-cycle time. Once the DMA controller has finished transferring data into or out of memory, the DMA controller gives control back to the microprocessor.

Integrated-circuit DMA controllers are now available. Although these may not be as fast as a discrete TTL device, they usually can keep up with memory-cycle times. The integrated-circuit DMA controllers are much easier to use than is a discrete TTL device.

Self-Test

Check your understanding by answering these questions.

29. Assume that the DMA controller and the memory system let you make 1 million transfers per second. If we transfer data from an 800 bit/in, 75 in/s tape with a DMA controller, which device will limit the data transfer's speed—the tape or the DMA system?

30. What limits the system speed if the tape transport in question 29 is a 1600 bit/in, 125 in/s drive?

31. The programmed data transfer uses only one memory transfer per byte of data. Why is it so much slower than a DMA transfer?

32. One DMA controller chip will control four different DMA channels. This controller has eight 16-bit registers. What are they for?

Summary

1. Some of the microprocessor's main memory must be read-write memory.

2. RAM stands for "random-access memory." Random-access means that you can address any memory location as quickly as any other.

3. Memory-access time tells how long a memory system takes to place information on the data bus after the desired location is addressed.

4. Memory-cycle time measures the shortest time between two successive memory-access operations.

5. Volatile memory loses its data when there is a power failure. Nonvolatile memory does not need power to keep its data.

6. Microprocessor bootstrap programs are stored in nonvolatile main memory.

7. Semiconductor read-write RAM is volatile memory. Core is nonvolatile read-write RAM.

8. Semiconductor memories are built using both the bipolar and the MOS processes. MOS is more common.

9. CCDs (charge-coupled devices) and MBM (magnetic-bubble memories) are moderately slow high-density solid-state memories.

10. Static memories store data in a flip-flop.

11. Dynamic memories store data in a capacitor. Dynamic memories have greater density and lower cost than static memories. Dynamic memories also need Refresh circuits.

12. Semiconductor read-write RAMs use row and column decoders to select the addressed bits.

13. Memory chips come in both bit- and byte-oriented packages.

14. Some dynamic RAMs are interchangeable from lower- to higher-density chips.

15. The high-density dynamic RAMs use multiplexed addressing. This is done to reduce the package pin count. Multiplexed addressing means that the chip has Row and Column Select strobe lines.

16. A memory system's overhead is made up of those devices that do not actually store data but are needed to make the system work.

17. A ROM is a read-only memory. Most ROMs are MOS devices preprogrammed during the integrated-circuit manufacturing process.

18. The PROM (programmable read-only memory) is programmed in the field by blowing fuses. Once programmed, the PROM cannot be changed.

235

19. The EPROM (erasable programmable read-only memory) can be programmed, erased, and reprogrammed in the field. EPROMs are erased by using ultraviolet light.
20. The EAROM (electrically alterable read-only memory) can be altered by an electrical signal. The EAROM is not as permanent or as dense as the EPROM.
21. Some ROMs, PROMs, EPROMs, and RAMs are pin-interchangeable.

22. Some EPROMs are pin-interchangeable with higher-density versions.
23. Direct memory access (DMA) is used for high-speed data transfers to or from a microcomputer's main memory. Often the data come from magnetic tape or a disk.
24. The DMA controller must take control of the microcomputer's data and address buses during a data transfer.

Chapter Review Questions

11-1. Which term does not apply to semiconductor read-write RAM?
    a. Dynamic   c. ROM
    b. Static   d. Volatile

11-2. Nonvolatile memory is usually used to store the microcomputer's
    a. Bootstrap program   c. Instructions
    b. Main program   d. (All of the above)

11-3. Semiconductor read-write memory is
    a. Volatile   c. Dynamic
    b. Static   d. Nonvolatile

11-4. Memory-access time is the time between
    a. Refresh cycles
    b. Addressing and Data Out
    c. Successive access operations
    d. (All of the above)

11-5. A microcomputer system must have some
    a. ROM   c. I/O ports
    b. Read-write memory   d. (All of the above)

11-6. Semiconductor memories that use the ____?____ process are the most common.
    a. Dynamic   c. MOS
    b. Bipolar   d. Static

11-7. CCDs and MBMs are ____?____ devices.
    a. Serial-access   c. Read-only
    b. Random-access   d. Older

11-8. Static RAMs store data in a
    a. ROM   c. Flip-flop
    b. RAM   d. Capacitor

11-9. A dynamic memory must be
    a. Refreshed   c. Serial-access
    b. Random-access   d. (All of the above)

11-10. A 4K × 1 and a 1K × 4 static memory are both ____?____-bit devices.
    a. 1024   c. 4096
    b. 2048   d. 8192

11-11. A dynamic memory stores its data in a
    a. ROM   c. Flip-flop
    b. RAM   d. Capacitor

11-12. Compared with a static-memory system, a dynamic-memory system with memory chips of the same density will have ___?___ overhead.
a. No c. Less
b. More d. The same

11-13. The higher-density dynamic RAMs use ___?___ addressing.
a. Multiplexed c. Binary
b. Row-column d. (All of the above)

11-14. A ROM is a ___?___ memory device.
a. Volatile c. Dynamic
b. Nonvolatile d. (All of the above)

11-15. An EPROM is a ___?___ device.
a. Mask-programmed
b. Fusible-link field-programmable
c. Random-access read-write
d. Random-access read-only

11-16. A ROM is a ___?___ device.
a. Mask-programmed
b. Fusible-link field-programmable
c. Random-access read-write
d. Random-access read-only

11-17. A fusible-link programmable read-only memory is a(n)
a. RAM c. PROM
b. ROM d. EPROM

11-18. Direct memory access is used to
a. Transfer data to memory via the accumulator
b. Transfer data out of memory via the accumulator
c. Halt the microprocessor's operation during a data transfer
d. Accomplish a high-speed data transfer

11-19. Explain the purpose of the Chip Enable input on a RAM or ROM.

11-20. How can you get some nonvolatility with semiconductor read-write RAM? Why is this only limited protection?

11-21. A DMA controller has two registers that are programmed by the microprocessor before a DMA transfer starts. What do these two registers do? Why do you suppose they are both 16-bit registers?

11-22. Why does the microprocessor go into a hold state during a DMA transfer?

Answers to Self-Tests

1. d. 6. c. 11. c.
2. c. 7. a. 12. d.
3. b. 8. b. 13. a.
4. a. 9. c.
5. b. 10. d.
14. One of the two strobe signals loads the row decoder and the other loads the column decoder. This extra complication saves address pins.

15. The static RAM stores data in a flip-flop circuit. The dynamic RAM stores data as a charge on a transistor's input capacitance.
16. If the dynamic RAM is not refreshed regularly, the capacitor discharges, losing the data.
17. The Chip Select and the address decoder.

18. It reduces the overhead because the amount of memory doubles with little or no increase in overhead chips.
19. See Fig. 11-16.
20. Because the Refresh logic adds to the memory system's overhead.
21. This will probably be used to start the row and column strobe logic.

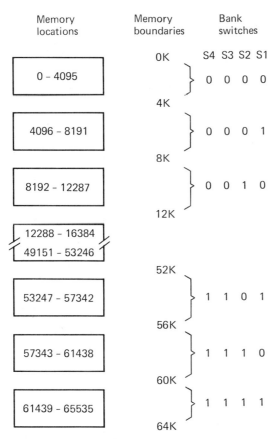

Memory locations	Memory boundaries	Bank switches

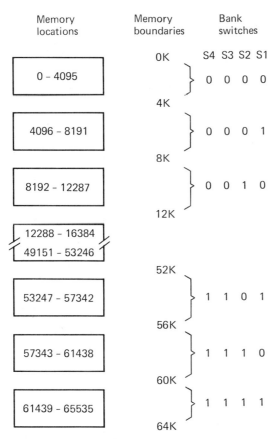

Memory locations | Memory boundaries | Bank switches S4 S3 S2 S1

0 – 4095 — 0K / 4K — 0 0 0 0

4096 – 8191 — 4K / 8K — 0 0 0 1

8192 – 12287 — 8K / 12K — 0 0 1 0

12288 – 16384
49151 – 53246 — 12K

53247 – 57342 — 52K / 56K — 1 1 0 1

57343 – 61438 — 56K / 60K — 1 1 1 0

61439 – 65535 — 60K / 64K — 1 1 1 1

Fig. 11-16 A Bank Select diagram for self-test question 19.

22. d.   23. b.   24. a.
25. c.
26. Because it can be easily changed when errors are found.

27. The microcomputer cannot do anything without instructions. There must be enough instructions in ROM that the microprocessor can read program data from an external storage device.
28. It must have some read-write memory to write data into.
29. DMA = 1,000,000 transfers per second
    Tape = 800 byte/in × 75 in/s
        = 60,000 transfers per second
    The tape is limiting.
30. Tape = 1600 bit/in × 125 in/s
        = 200,000 transfers per second
    The tape is limiting.
31. Because it also must perform an I/O read and a cycle count for each data transfer. Also, the transfer rate is limited by the microprocessor's instruction-cycle time, not just by the memory-cycle time.
32. Four are starting-address registers and four are terminal-count registers.

Microprocessor I/O

- In this chapter we will study ways of moving data into and out of the microprocessor. In earlier chapters, we used the microprocessor's In instruction to move data from an input port to the accumulator. In this chapter, you will see how to use the Out instruction. In addition, you will get to know a number of the common input and output devices that people use to communicate with microcomputer systems, and we will look at two mass-storage devices.

    We will look at an example of a parallel I/O port and see how it is controlled. We will also see how a parallel I/O port design is like a memory design. We will then look at serial communications. This is an important method that microprocessors use to communicate with remote devices. The standard code used in communicating from one serial device to another is ASCII. You will study the command signals needed to control serial hardware. You will also study the serial-to-parallel and parallel-to-serial converters.

    In previous examples, we have always worked with I/O devices by using a special Input/Output instruction. We will now look at other ways that a microprocessor can address input/output devices. When external devices are connected to a microprocessor system, sooner or later the devices require the microprocessor's attention. You will learn about the two different ways that outside devices can get the microprocessor's attention. These are the polling routines and the microprocessor's interrupt system.

12-1 INPUT/OUTPUT DEVICES

Many kinds of devices are used to move data into and out of the microprocessor. The choice of the input/output device depends on the source of the data that the microprocessor is to work on. For example, if the data are to come from magnetic media, then either a tape drive or a disk drive should be used as the I/O device. On the other hand, if *people* are to be entering and retrieving data, then a keyboard and display are probably the best choice for an I/O device. In this section we will look at a number of input/output devices to see how they connect to the microprocessor.

To start a discussion of I/O devices, we will separate them into two major groups. First, there are devices that communicate with people. Second, there are devices that communicate with machines. As you can imagine, the devices that communicate with people have some special characteristics. These devices must communicate in standard alphanumeric characters plus a few special mathematical symbols and punctuation marks. In general, communications with people must be slow. Input comes from a keyboard. Output is on a display.

On the other hand, communications between the microprocessor and machines can be in many different codes. Machines usually communicate with the microprocessor at high speeds. And in most cases, machines input data to the microprocessor in the same form as the form of the output that they accept from the microprocessor.

The most common device that enables people to input data to the microprocessor is the keyboard. Keyboards used with microprocessor systems are usually one of three different kinds. The first is the simple numeric keypad. Most electronic calculators use numeric keypads.

The second kind of keyboard is the full alphanumeric variety. Computer terminals usually have full alphanumeric keyboards.

Keyboards of this kind can transmit all the alphanumeric characters (both uppercase and lowercase), plus 20 to 30 special characters. These special characters include mathematical operators, punctuation marks, and a few control codes.

The third kind of keyboard is the dedicated, or special-purpose, keyboard. This keyboard is custom-designed for the application at hand. For example, the keyboard on a microprocessor-based environmental-control system may not have any alphanumeric input. It may simply have keys marked AIR CONDITIONING, HEATING, BLOWERS, and PUMPS, among others.

Most keyboards work in the same basic way. They are like the simplified schematic shown in Fig. 12-1. There we see the familiar row-and-column matrix. The keyboard's columns are scanned. First a signal is placed on column 1, then the signal moves to column 2, then to column 3, and then to column 4. The entire scan operation repeats itself.

Scanning can be done by the microprocessor itself, by an integrated-circuit shift register, or, as shown in Fig. 12-1, by a binary counter and a decoder. The rows are connected to the columns by the keyboard switches. In this example there are 16 switches. They are on a 4 × 4 matrix.

The column-scan and row-output lines are connected to an encoder circuit. This has two functions. First, the contact closure is scanned a number of times. This is done to make sure that it is a valid contact closure. Multiple scanning avoids false contact closures. This is called contact "debouncing." For example, after 10 scans in succession have found the same contact closed, chances are great that the particular column was in fact connected to the particular row. That is, the key at the row-column intersection was depressed.

Once we have made sure that there is a valid contact closure, we can begin the keyboard encoding process. The encoding cir-

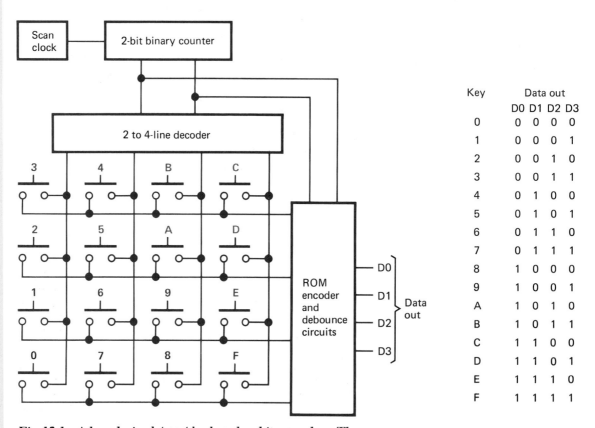

Key	Data out			
	D0	D1	D2	D3
0	0	0	0	0
1	0	0	0	1
2	0	0	1	0
3	0	0	1	1
4	0	1	0	0
5	0	1	0	1
6	0	1	1	0
7	0	1	1	1
8	1	0	0	0
9	1	0	0	1
A	1	0	1	0
B	1	0	1	1
C	1	1	0	0
D	1	1	0	1
E	1	1	1	0
F	1	1	1	1

Fig. 12-1 A hexadecimal 4 × 4 keyboard and its encoder. The binary counter is driven by a 400-Hz clock so that the keyboard is completely scanned once every 10 ms. The debounce logic waits until it detects three contact closures in a row before loading the data out.

cuit now takes over. The encoding circuit is a ROM. It takes the row and column information and generates the needed parallel or serial output signals.

Keyboard logic for microprocessor-based systems is usually made in one of two ways. First, some keyboards are made to be scanned and encoded by a microprocessor. Very simple keyboards may be scanned by the microcomputer system's own microprocessor. If so, the keyboard matrix is connected to one of the microprocessor's I/O ports. A subroutine does the scanning, the debouncing, and the encoding. On very complicated keyboards, a second microprocessor may be used only to do the scanning, the debouncing, and the encoding. The second way of making keyboard logic is custom LSI. Since keyboard communications are so common, a number of special chips for making keyboards have been developed.

Where there is a keyboard, there is usually a display. The display presents information using alphanumerics and special characters. Like the keyboard, the display can be of one of three different kinds.

First are the simple numeric-only displays. Seven-segment displays such as those shown in Fig. 12-2(a) are very often used on calculators and other products that need only a limited display. These displays can give limited alphabetic ("alpha") information. Some of the alphabetic characters are shown in Fig.

12-2(b), which shows the 16 characters used to display hexadecimal information. Using all seven segments in different combinations, the numeric-only display can spell a few words. Some examples are shown in Fig. 12-2(c).

The second kind of display uses the 5 × 7 ("five by seven") or 5 × 9 ("five by nine") dot matrix. The 5 × 7 dot matrix can form uppercase alphanumeric characters. The 5 × 9 dot matrix can form both uppercase and lowercase alphanumeric characters. Figure 12-3 shows samples of some of these characters. Figure 12-3(a) shows the 5 × 7 dot matrix and how it forms the uppercase characters "A," "B," "C," "7," and "%." Figure 12-3(b) shows the 5 × 9 dot matrix and how it forms the characters "A," "a," "(," "↑," and "*."

The 5 × 7 and 5 × 9 dot-matrix displays are available in single-character or multiple-character LCD, LED, and neon displays. One of the most common uses of dot-matrix displays is to produce characters on a cathode-ray tube. The familiar video computer terminal is a good example. A look at one of these terminals will show you that dot-matrix characters are very readable.

The third kind of display is the custom display. Custom displays usually do not display simple alphanumeric characters. Instead, they show special labels that suit the functions of the system. Returning to the example of the environmental control system, you might see panels that light up with such labels as

Seven-segment
displays

Display

Dot matrix

Custom display

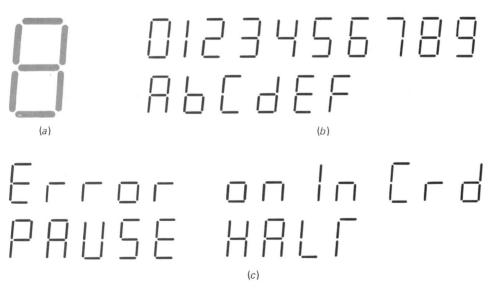

Fig. 12-2 The seven-segment display. (a) The basic seven segments. (b) The hexadecimal characters 0 through F. (c) A few words that can be spelled by a seven-segment display.

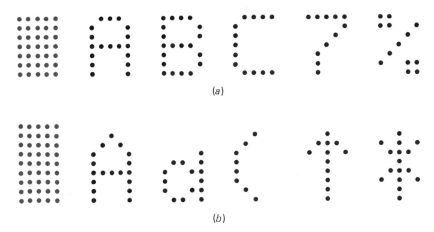

(a)

(b)

Fig. 12-3 Formation of alphanumeric characters. (a) The 5 × 7 dot matrix. (b) The 5 × 9 dot matrix.

Soft copy display

Cathode-ray tube (CRT)

Video terminal

Terminal

Smart terminal

Dumb terminal

Hard copy

Magnetic tape

Floppy disks

Philips cassette

Digital tape recorder

AIR CONDITIONING ON, MOTOR OVER-HEAT, WATER HIGH, WATER LOW, or PUMP ON.

The alphanumeric displays are called either "soft copy" or "hard copy." The video terminal is a soft-copy display. The video terminal has an alphanumeric keyboard and display built around a cathode-ray tube (CRT). Data are serially transmitted to and from the video terminal. The display can show 24 to 48 rows, each having 40, 80, or 132 columns of characters. Often, a video terminal is called either a CRT (which is actually a description of the display device, not the terminal) or simply a terminal.

As the use of microprocessors has become more widespread, "smart" terminals have appeared alongside the simpler "dumb" ones. The smart terminal's intelligence is usually a microprocessor. The smart terminal can do some data manipulating and formatting on its own. The dumb terminal simply transmits each character as it is typed on the keyboard and displays each character as it is received. Obviously, the dumb terminal has no intelligence. However, the dumb terminal's logic may be implemented by a microprocessor. What the dumb terminal lacks is smart features. For example, a smart terminal might be able to change its transmission rate, its parity check, or its print format by using special control characters.

The third common kind of alphanumeric display is the printer. The printer produces hard copy. "Hard copy" simply means output printed on paper. Most printers still use an inked ribbon. The less expensive printers use a 5 × 7 or a 5 × 9 dot matrix; the more expen-sive printers use a printing head with pre-formed characters like a typewriter's.

Microprocessors are often configured to communicate with magnetic mass-storage de-vices. Two kinds of magnetic mass storage are used most commonly. These are mag-netic tape and floppy disks. Both of these de-vices provide nonvolatile bulk storage. The magnetic tape systems offer low cost, and the floppy-disk systems offer relatively fast access time.

In most microprocessor applications, mag-netic tape recording is done with a Philips cas-sette or a somewhat larger tape cartridge. Typically, these cartridges can hold 250,000 to 1 million bytes of data. Either a serial or a parallel interface may connect the microproc-essor and the tape drive. Data are usually recorded on tape in blocks. For example, a recorder may accept 256 bytes before it ac-tually records data on tape. The recorder then records some identification called a "header." One or more blocks of data follow the header.

The technique used to record digital data is quite different from the technique used to record audio. The digital tape recorder and the home tape recorder are not nearly as simi-lar as they look. One of the biggest differ-ences is that the digital tape recorder has ex-tremely fast start and stop capability.

Figure 12-4 shows a typically formatted sec-tion of magnetic tape. Although magnetic tape offers low-cost bulk storage, tape uses se-rial access. Finding the data block that you want may require searching the entire length of a tape.

The floppy disk overcomes this problem.

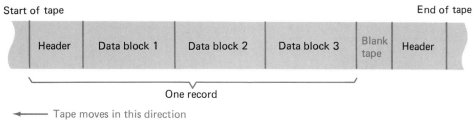

One record

Tape moves in this direction

Fig. 12-4   A length of recorded magnetic tape. The header contains information such as the name of the record, the length of the record, and the like. Each data block has 256 bytes of data. A record must be read in one continuous pass; a number of records make up a file.

Figure 12-5(a) and (b) shows the floppy disk. In Fig. 12-5(a) we see the floppy disk in its paper envelope. The floppy disk is just a disk of magnetic tape 5 or 8 in. in diameter. The slot in the envelope permits the read-write head to make contact with the magnetic material.

Figure 12-5(b) shows how the tracks are re-

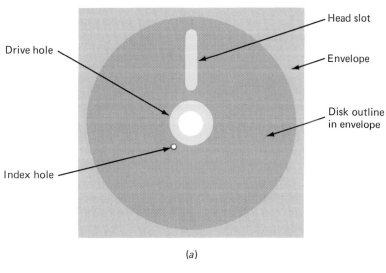

(a)

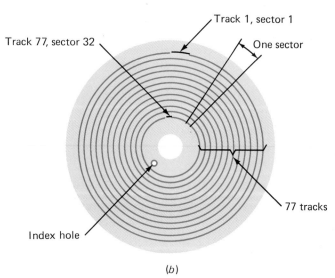

(b)

Fig. 12-5   The floppy disk. (a) The floppy disk in its envelope. (b) The disk itself with its tracks and sectors.

Controller

Drive electronics

corded on the floppy disk. An 8-in disk has 77 tracks. The tracks are recorded in concentric rings. Each track or ring is divided into 32 sectors.

When the floppy disk is in operation, the disk spins at 360 revolutions per minute (r/min). The disk takes 166 ms to make a complete revolution. The record/reproduce head can be positioned over any one of the 77 tracks. Once the head is over the desired track, all the information on the track passes under the head within 166 ms.

The average access time for data in a floppy-disk track is 83 ms ($166 \div 2 = 83$). The floppy disk's total access time depends on how fast the head can find the track and how fast the disk is spinning. Typically, data on a floppy disk can be accessed in approximately 1.25 s. This compares well with the 20- or 30-s access time of a cassette or cartridge tape system.

Each floppy-disk sector contains 128 bytes. Therefore, a 32-sector track contains 4096 bytes of information. Floppy-disk systems often access a track and write the entire track into memory.

Both floppy-disk and magnetic tape systems need special control and data-formatting circuits. These circuits are usually called the "controller" and the "drive electronics." The controller tells the drive where to find the desired information. The drive electronics operate the motor and usually contain the magnetic-head preamplifiers and drivers.

Some floppy disks and magnetic tape systems use a programmed data transfer to transfer data to and from the microcomputer's memory. Other systems use a DMA transfer, sometimes with the aid of another microprocessor.

Self-Test

Check your understanding by answering these questions.

1. The floppy disk is used as
   a. An input device
   b. An output device
   c. A mass-storage device
   d. (All of the above)

2. A video terminal displays its output on a CRT. Its local input is from
   a. A 10-digit keypad
   b. An alphanumeric keyboard
   c. A 5×7 dot matrix
   d. A 4×4 key matrix

3. A special-purpose keyboard has
   a. 10 keys
   b. 16 keys
   c. 57 keys
   d. Any number of keys

4. A video terminal uses a 5×9 dot matrix to form its character set. You would expect that it could display
   a. The seven-segment numeric characters plus A, B, C, D, E, and F
   b. All the uppercase alphanumeric characters
   c. All the uppercase and lowercase alphanumeric characters
   d. 132 columns by 48 rows

5. Why do you think keyboards use the row-column scanning circuit instead of using a ROM with one input for each key?

6. How would you use seven-segment displays to display the words:
   a. Open   e. And
   b. Run   f. Or
   c. Up   g. Pulse
   d. Off

7. (a) Why can you read the words from question 6, even though some of the characters may not be standard? (b) What would happen if some of the nonstandard characters were displayed alone?

12-2 PARALLEL INTERFACES

As discussed in earlier sections, there are two kinds of interfaces that connect data to the microprocessor. The simplest kind is a parallel interface. Using a parallel interface, an 8-bit microprocessor transfers 8-bits of information from an external device with each I/O transfer. Later, we will look at serial data transfers, which are used when data must be transmitted over distances beyond the range of parallel transmission.

Figure 12-6 shows a block diagram of an 8-bit I/O card. This card permits inputting one 8-bit data word or outputting one 8-bit data word. Some of the circuits are the same as the circuits on the memory card in Chap. 11 —specifically, the microcomputer's address bus buffers and the address-decoding logic.

The microcomputer's data bus signals are bidirectionally buffered. In this block diagram, we show a single 8-bit buffer. As you can see, the buffer is strobed by an I/O Read or Write line. Such lines are like memory

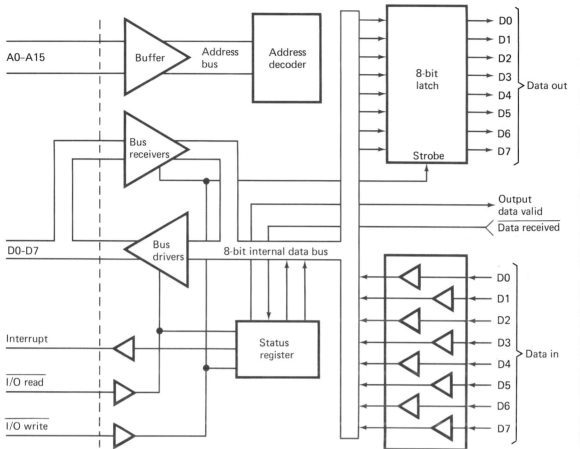

Status register

Fig. 12-6   A parallel I/O card is used to transfer 8-bits of data to or from the microcomputer's data bus. Output data is latched so that it remains stable after the transfer. The input data is the data on the input lines at the exact moment when the transfer executes.

read-write lines, but are used only during I/O operations.

The I/O READ line is asserted when the microprocessor is ready for the addressed I/O port to place data on the microcomputer's data bus. The I/O READ signal is used to let the I/O card's internal bus drive the microcomputer's data bus. The I/O WRITE line is asserted when the microprocessor is ready to write data to the addressed I/O port. The I/O WRITE line lets the microcomputer's data bus drive the I/O card's internal data bus. The I/O WRITE line also strobes data into the I/O card's output data latch.

This card also has a status register. The purpose of the status register is to allow the microprocessor to test the I/O port for certain conditions. Usually, the status register, the input register, and the output register occupy three consecutive I/O addresses. For example, the I/O status register might be addressed

as I/O port 00, the input register might be addressed as I/O port 01, and the output register might be addressed as I/O port 02.

The status register on this I/O card has only 2 bits. Asserting the card's INPUT DATA VALID line sets bit 0 in the status register. This also interrupts the microprocessor. Later, we will look at exactly what happens when a microprocessor is interrupted. For now, we will simply say that an interrupt causes the microprocessor to service the interrupting device.

Because the INPUT DATA VALID signal sets a bit in the status register, the microprocessor can get information from the status register's contents. If the INPUT DATA VALID bit is set, the microprocessor knows that there are valid data on the eight input lines. The microprocessor can then use an In instruction to transfer the data from the eight input lines to the accumulator.

245

Hand-shaking

Memory-
mapped

IEEE-488

The microprocessor's Out instruction is used to output data. Data on the microprocessor's data bus are latched into the 8-bit data latch. As a result, the status register's bit 1 is set. Bit 1 asserts the I/O port's OUTPUT DATA VALID line. This tells an external device that there are new data at the output. This status bit is reset by the external device by asserting the card's $\overline{\text{DATA RECEIVED}}$ line. If the microprocessor needs to know if the data have been received, the microprocessor can input the I/O port's status word and test bit 1.

These two signals are often called the I/O port's hand-shaking lines. They allow the external device and the microcomputer to make sure the data are transferred correctly and that no data are lost.

Some input-output cards are built using discrete devices. Other cards use special LSI circuits designed for this purpose.

Frequently a number of parallel input/output ports are included on a single-chip microprocessor or on multiple-function parts. Inclusion of ports in these ways makes possible a low-chip-count microprocessor system. For example, it is common to find two or more I/O ports combined with a mask-programmed ROM. Such a part can be used with a microprocessor chip and a RAM chip. These three chips form a powerful microprocessor-based system including multiple I/O ports and larger amounts of ROM and RAM than are available in single-chip microcomputers.

The two instructions that we have used for the I/O functions are:

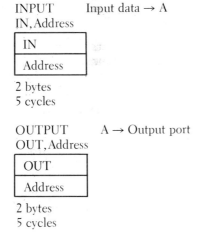

INPUT   Input data → A
IN, Address

| IN |
| Address |

2 bytes
5 cycles

OUTPUT   A → Output port
OUT, Address

| OUT |
| Address |

2 bytes
5 cycles

Both of these are 2-byte, 5-cycle instructions. It is important to note that the I/O data transfer does take some time. When many data transfers are necessary, the required

time may be long enough to cause a serious problem.

In this text, we have always referred to I/O transfers by a special address. We have kept I/O transfers completely separate from memory transfers. In some microprocessors, however, I/O transfers are the same as memory transfers. In that case, we say that the I/O devices are "memory-mapped." Memory-mapped I/O devices simply act as memory words. These devices are connected to the memory-address bus and respond to Memory Read and Memory Write signals. Memory-mapped I/O devices do not use a separate set of I/O instructions.

What is the advantage of memory mapped I/O? The disadvantage is obvious. Memory-mapped I/O reduces the memory space available by the number of I/O devices in use. Of course, this reduction is only a problem for systems that have many I/O devices or use almost all of the memory addresses. The normal five to ten I/O ports do not pose a significant problem.

Memory-mapped I/O has the advantage of simplifying the I/O process. Instead of being a different process, I/O is identical to all memory transfers. Therefore, memory-mapped I/O eliminates the need for a completely separate set of I/O instructions. It also eliminates all I/O-related signals on the microcomputer's bus. Since the I/O device is treated as if it were a word in memory, all instructions that can operate on memory can operate on the I/O device. We are no longer restricted to the simple Input and Output instructions.

For example, memory-mapped I/O makes it possible to add an input to the accumulator or to compare an input to the accumulator. In more sophisticated microprocessors that have instructions to move the contents of one memory location directly to another memory location, an input data word can be moved from the input device directly to a memory location with a single instruction.

Memory-mapped I/O can still be used on a microprocessor that has a separate set of I/O instructions. There is nothing to prevent the use of memory-mapped I/O. If it makes your system less complex, memory-mapping is the way to handle I/O.

A standard has been developed for transferring parallel data between electronic test instruments and microprocessors. The standard is the IEEE-488 bus. The concept of this bus was developed by Hewlett-Packard. The

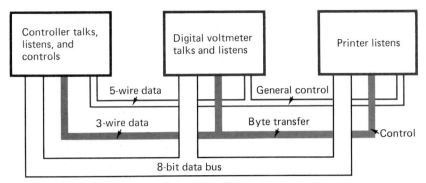

Fig. 12-7 The IEEE-488 parallel data bus. This standard has been developed for the parallel transfer of data between instruments and intelligent controllers such as microcomputers.

IEEE-488 standard has won wide acceptance in both the United States and Europe. Several microprocessor manufacturers have introduced special chips to interface their microprocessors to the IEEE-488 standard bus.

Devices attached to the IEEE-488 bus can be listeners, listener/talkers, or controllers. Each device is assigned an address. Figure 12-7 shows a simple example of a microcomputer-based IEEE-488 system. In this system, the microcomputer is in control. The microprocessor tells the voltmeter (a talker/listener) what ranges and functions to select. The microprocessor also tells the voltmeter when to put data on the bus. Both the printer (a listener) and the microcomputer (the controller) receive data. The printer simply prints data. The microcomputer puts additional data on the bus telling the printer to add calculated parameters to the raw data.

The IEEE-488 bus is capable of data-transfer rates of 1 megabyte per second or more. The bus's speed is limited only by the slowest device connected to the bus.

Self-Test

Check your understanding by answering these questions.

8. The $\overline{\text{I/O READ}}$ line is used to
   a. Read data into an I/O port
   b. Read data out of an I/O port
   c. Read a memory-mapped I/O port
   d. Load the I/O port's status register

9. A parallel I/O port's hand-shaking lines are used to
   a. Transfer data into the port
   b. Transfer data from the port
   c. Help control the transfer
   d. Enable the status register

10. Memory-mapped I/O means that the microprocessor "thinks" the I/O registers are just one more
    a. Register
    b. Accumulator
    c. I/O address
    d. Memory location

11. A parallel I/O port uses an address decoder to
    a. Select the addressed port
    b. Select the memory location for transfer
    c. Memory-map the I/O port
    d. Buffer the address lines

12. (*a*) What is the main disadvantage of using memory-mapped I/O? (*b*) What is the main advantage?

13. How can you use memory-mapped I/O on a microprocessor that has separate I/O control and addressing?

14. Does the parallel I/O port described in this section use a programmed data transfer or a DMA? Explain.

15. Below is a list of some typical kinds of instruments that have IEEE-488 interfaces. Mark the instruments as talkers, talker/listeners, or controllers.
    a. Signal generator
    b. Power meter
    c. Digital LCR meter
    d. Programmable attenuator
    e. Intelligent terminal
    f. Printer
    g. DC power supply
    h. Digital clock
    i. Thermometer
    j. Electronic counter

Parallel-to-serial conversion

Universal asynchronous receiver transmitter

Baud rate

12-3 THE SERIAL INTERFACE AND THE UART

As noted earlier, many devices are connected to the microprocessor by a serial line. The popularity of serial I/O stems largely from the limitations of parallel communication. The working distance of a parallel I/O is limited to 1 or 2 meters (m). Cable capacitance restricts high-speed parallel data transfers beyond this length. Parallel data transfer can be extended to 10 or 20 m by using special cable drivers and low speed. However, that is the limit.

With serial data transfers, distance is not a problem. Consequently, most data transfers begin by converting parallel data to serial. The serial data are then sent over dedicated lines or through the telephone network.

Parallel-to-serial conversion is done quite easily. The parallel data are loaded into a shift register. The shift register is then clocked. The data come out of the shift register's least significant bit 1 bit at a time. The first bit on the serial transmission is the data word's LSB. The second bit is the next least significant bit, the third is the third least significant bit, and so on. The last data bit transmitted is the MSB. The parallel-to-serial conversion process is shown in Fig. 12-8.

Receiving serial data and converting them to parallel data requires the reverse operation. The serial data are shifted into a shift register. After all bits have been clocked into the shift register, the data are taken out of the shift register in parallel and put into the microprocessor system.

One device that performs this parallel-to-serial and serial-to-parallel conversion is called a UART (universal asynchronous receiver-transmitter). The UART is implemented as a large-scale integrated circuit. In addition to performing the serial-to-parallel and parallel-to-serial conversions, the UART also per-

forms important control and monitoring functions.

The UART adds a Start bit and a Stop bit to the transmitted data. Transmitting an 8-bit data word actually requires sending 10 bits. The first bit tells the receiving UART that the data word is coming. The last bit tells the receiving UART that the data word is finished. Figure 12-9 shows an 8-bit data word with a Start bit and a Stop bit added. The Start bit is always a logic "0" and the Stop bit is always a logic "1."

The UART's data transmission speed is called its *baud rate*. The baud rate, or signaling rate, tells how may bits are transmitted per second. For example, a 1200-baud transmission takes place at a *rate* of 120 ten-bit characters (1 Start bit, 8 data bits, and 1 Stop bit) per second. Figure 12-10 shows a table of common UART signaling rates. It is important to understand that the baud rate is a measure of a single word's signaling rate. Later, you will see why baud rate cannot be measured for more than one word.

The 110-baud signaling rate uses a different format from the other rates. The 110-baud rate has 1 start bit and 2 stop bits. A data word is thus 11 bits long. Figure 12-11 shows an 11-bit word used for a 110-baud system. This is the signaling rate used by most mechanical teleprinters. By contrast, most video terminals can communicate at rates up to 9600 baud. Some systems use a stop that is 1½ bits long. Some UARTs can be set to generate or receive this signal.

The UART normally requires a clock that is run at 16 times the baud rate. For example, a UART operating at 1200 baud needs a 19.2-kHz clock. This signal is used to synchronize the incoming signal and to generate the outgoing signal.

Most modern UARTs are designed to be interfaced with a microprocessor's parallel I/O

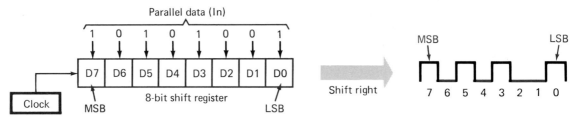

Fig. 12-8 Transmitting parallel data over a serial line. The LSB is sent first, and then the next LSB is sent. The process continues until the MSB has been sent.

Stop	D7	D6	D5	D4	D3	D2	D1	D0	Start

Fig. 12-9 An 8-bit data word with one Start bit and one Stop bit. The Start bit will always be a logic "0," and the Stop bit will always be a logic "1."

Stop	Stop	D7	D6	D5	D4	D3	D2	D1	D0	Start

Fig. 12-11 The 11-bit serial data word. Most commonly this is only used for 110-baud transmissions. The 11-bit code is very common for electromechanical teleprinters. Some serial systems also use 1½ stop bits.

American Standard Code for Information Interchange (ASCII)

Error detection code

Parity bit

Framing errors

port. Some can be directly interfaced to a microprocessor's bus. UARTs include a status register. This register indicates when the UART's receiver contains data and when the UART's transmitter has completed a transmission. Transmitting a serial signal using a UART requires use of the status bits in the UART's register. Remember that the UART's timing is completely independent of the microprocessor's timing. Therefore, once the microprocessor has placed a word in the UART to be transmitted, the microprocessor has no way of knowing when to place the next word in the UART. The microprocessor must wait for the UART to set a status bit telling the microprocessor that the UART is ready for another word.

Some UARTs also have status register bits that let the programmer control the UART's baud rate.

Often a UART is used to transmit data to or receive data from a terminal used by people to communicate with a computer. People, of course, prefer to communicate in alphanumeric characters. A special code is used to represent the alphanumeric characters in data transmissions. This code is the American Standard Code for Information Interchange. It is known as ASCII, pronounced ASK-key. A standard ASCII character has 7 bits. This permits 128 different characters, because $2^7 = 128$.

Baud rate	Bytes per second
110	10
150	15
300	30
600	60
1,200	120
2,400	240
4,800	480
9,600	960
19,200	1,920

Fig. 12-10 The common serial data-transmission rates (baud rates). Other rates are used for special situations.

Figure 12-12 is a table of the ASCII characters. Unfortunately, some of the special control codes are known by more than one name. However, the codes for the alphanumeric characters, mathematical operators, and punctuation are quite standardized. Each character, its 7-bit binary code, and hexadecimal numbers for the 7-bit binary code are given in the table. Where a character is given in mnemonic, the mnemonic is shown in the figure in black letters.

The eighth bit may be transmitted as a permanent logic "0," as a permanent logic "1," or as an error code. If an error detection code is transmitted, the eighth bit is called a "parity" bit. Most UARTs can generate or detect either odd or even parity. When we are transmitting even parity, the parity bit is set to logic "1" or to logic "0" so as to make the 8 bits of data have an even number of logic "1s." When odd parity is used, the parity bit is set to logic "0" or to logic "1" to transmit an odd number of logic "1s." In Fig. 12-12 it is assumed that the eighth bit is always logic "0."

Either odd or even parity can be used to detect transmission errors. When a data word is received, the UART tests it for either odd or even parity. If the UART detects the wrong parity, it sends an error signal to the UART's status register. The receiver can then ask for a retransmission. Parity helps catch 50 percent of the errors. Obviously, it will catch only an odd number of errors. If two bits are in error, the parity does not change.

Figure 12-13 shows how a noisy serial data transmission can cause a parity error. Bit 4 is changed by noise from logic "1" to logic "0," and therefore an incorrect message is received.

The UART can also detect framing errors. Framing errors happen when the UART misses the Start bit. The UART fails to receive the transmission with the Start and Stop bits in the correct places.

Figure 12-14 shows a received word with a framing error. You can see that the received data word is not aligned with the UART's shift

Most Significant Bits or Digit

Binary (LSB)	Hex (LSB)	0000 / 0 (Hex 0)	0001 / 1 (Hex 1)	0010 / 2 (Hex 2)	0011 / 3 (Hex 3)	0100 / 4 (Hex 4)	0101 / 5 (Hex 5)	0110 / 6 (Hex 6)	0111 / 7 (Hex 7)
0000	0	NULL NOTHING	DATA LINK ESCAPE CONTROL P	SPACE	Ø	@	P	`	p
0001	1	START OF HEADING CONTROL A	DEVICE CONT. 1 CONTROL Q*	!	1	A	Q	a	q
0010	2	START OF TEXT CONTROL B	DEVICE CONT. 2 CONTROL R	"	2	B	R	b	r
0011	3	END OF TEXT CONTROL C	DEVICE CONT. 3 CONTROL S†	#	3	C	S	c	s
0100	4	END OF TRANSMISSION CONTROL D	DEVICE CONT. 4 CONTROL T	$	4	D	T	d	t
0101	5	ENQUIRY CONTROL E	NOT ACKNOWLEDGED CONTROL U	%	5	E	U	e	u
0110	6	ACKNOWLEDGE CONTROL F	SYNCHRONIZE CONTROL V	&	6	F	V	f	v
0111	7	BELL CONTROL G	END OF TRANS. BLOCK CONTROL W	'	7	G	W	g	w
1000	8	BACK SPACE CONTROL H	CANCEL CONTROL X	(	8	H	X	h	x
1001	9	HORIZ TAB CONTROL I	END OF MEDIUM CONTROL Y	)	9	I	Y	i	y
1010	A	LINE FEED CONTROL J	SUBSTITUTE CONTROL Z	*	:	J	Z	j	z
1011	B	VERT TAB CONTROL K	ESCAPE	+	;	K	[	k	{
1100	C	FORM FEED CONTROL L	FILE SEPARATOR	,	<	L	\	l	|
1101	D	CARRIAGE RET CONTROL M	GROUP SEPARATOR	-	=	M	]	m	}
1110	E	SHIFT OUT CONTROL N	RECORD SEPARATOR	.	>	N	↑	n	~
1111	F	SHIFT IN CONTROL O	UNIT SEPARATOR	/	?	O	←	o	DELETE

Least Significant Bits or Digit

*also called XON
†also called XOFF

Fig. 12-12 A table of ASCII codes. The binary and hexadecimal codes shown here presume that the eighth bit is a logic "0." Many of the control signals are often given a mnemonic. The mnemonics are shown as the black letters in the full description. For example, start of text has **STX** as a mnemonic, and Device Control 1 has **DC1** as a mnemonic.

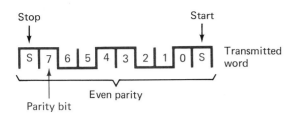

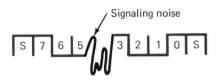

Signaling noise

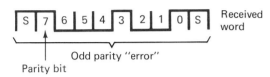

Fig. 12-13 A serial transmission with a bit error detected by the parity bit. The noise during transmission changes bit 4 from a logic "1" to a logic "0," causing incorrect data to be received.

register. Noise on the signal line is one of the most common causes of framing errors.

Figure 12-15 is a block diagram of a simple UART. The diagram shows that the UART can be divided into four major parts: the Transmit section, the Receive section, the status section, and the control logic section.

The Transmit section has two parts: the data output buffer and the Transmit register. The Transmit register shifts out the Start bit, the data bits D0 to D7, and finally the Stop bit or bits. Data in 8-bit form are loaded into the Transmit data output buffer by the trailing edge of the signal asserting the Data Input Strobe input. The leading edge of this signal causes serial data transmission to start. That is, the leading edge starts the shifting process. Figure 12-16 illustrates this action. The data are shifted out the serial output line.

The receiver is almost a mirror image of the transmitter. Data enter through the serial input. The Receive register shifts 10 or 11

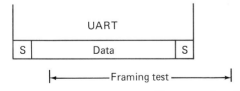

Fig. 12-14 A framing error. The incoming data does not line up with the UART's Start and Stop positions. Usually a framing error is caused by noise.

times after it detects a start bit. Once the receiver has stopped shifting, the 8 data bits can be transferred to the received-data output buffer. Asserting the Data Output Enable strobe causes the transfer.

Both the Transmit shift register and the Receive shift register are driven by a clock signal that runs at 16 times the selected baud rate. This clock rate assures that the shifting clock is never more than one thirty-second of a bit width out of synchronization with the input signal. This degree of synchronization is maintained even though the baud-rate clock and the incoming data are completely asynchronous.

Looking at Fig. 12-15, you can see that the UART's status register has two outputs. First, its five status bits are connected to individual chip pins. Second, the entire status word can also be loaded into the received-data output buffer. This loading is done by asserting the Status Output strobe input.

The status register provides the following information:

- Overrun (OR). A logic "1" in this bit indicates that the current data word overran the previous data word. That is, the previous data word was never transferred to the received-data output buffer.

- Framing Error (FE). A logic "1" in this line indicates that the UART could not find a Stop bit. The UART probably missed the real Start bit and made a false start on one of the data bits.

- Parity Error (PE). A logic "1" in this bit means that the UART detected either an odd or an even parity error. The exact parity condition is set by the UART's control logic.

- Transmit Buffer Empty (TBE). A logic "1" in this bit indicates that the next data word can be loaded into the Transmit data output buffer.

- Data Available (DA). A logic "1" in this status bit indicates that the receiver has a new data word. The word can now be outputted by asserting the Data Output strobe.

If you transfer the UART's status word to the received-data output buffer, you can transfer it to the microprocessor's accumulator by using an In instruction. There, you can use

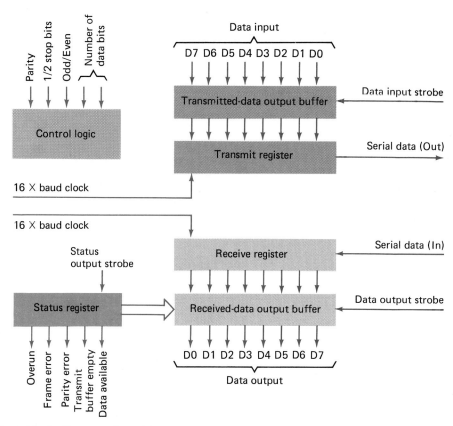

Fig. 12-15   A block diagram of a UART.

a Compare instruction to see if the proper status bits are set.

For example, a status word is shown in Fig. 12-17. If a data word has been received with no errors, the status word is:

$$0000\ 0010_2 = 02_{16}$$

You can test for this status word by using a Compare 02. The Compare instruction sets the zero bit of the microprocessor's status register to logic "1" if the only status bit set is the Data Available bit. If any other bits are set, the test fails. Failure of this test tells the microprocessor that there is a problem. Additional software can be used to tell just what the problem is.

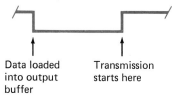

Fig. 12-16   The data input strobe signal. This signal causes one operation on the trailing edge and one on the leading edge.

The UART's control inputs let you set the UART's operating mode (again, see Fig. 12-15). The two data-bit lines let you select 5, 6, 7, or 8 *data* bits per transmitted or received word. The odd/even control line lets you select either odd or even parity. This line is used only when the No Parity line is also set to turn the parity function *on*. Again, the parity bit will be placed in the transmitted data word's last data bit. This is the eighth data bit when you are transmitting 7-bit ASCII.

The 10/11 Stop Bit line lets you select a transmission format that has either one or two Stop bits. Remember, 110-baud signaling uses two stop bits.

The above description describes a stand-alone LSI UART. Such a UART can be used either alone or with a microprocessor. If used with a microprocessor, the UART is usually connected to the microprocessor's parallel port.

There are several more complex LSI UARTs. They are designed for direct connection to a particular microprocessor's data bus and address bus. These UARTs avoid the extra interface logic needed to connect a stand-alone UART to the microprocessor.

0	0	Overrun	Frame error	Parity error	Transmit buffer empty	Data Available	0

Fig. 12-17   The UART's status word.

UARTs are also often used with a special baud-rate-generator chip. This chip generates a times-16 ($\times 16$) signal for all the standard baud rates. The basic signal comes from a crystal oscillator so that the baud rate is very stable and accurate.

As stated earlier, the UART is an asynchronous (async) device. This means that the data rate has no relation to the microprocessor's timing. In addition, the timing of one async word to the next is unknown. As an example, think of data being generated by a person at a video terminal's keyboard. Each async character is transmitted as a key is depressed. The spacing between one character and the next is unpredictable. However, once transmission of an ASCII character starts, the baud rate remains the same as long as that character is being transmitted.

What does this mean to the microprocessor? It means that the microprocessor has no way to tell when the next character will be received. The microprocessor must check the UART's status register. If the UART's status register's Data Available bit is set, the microprocessor reads the UART's data. If the Data Available bit is not set, then the microprocessor must keep checking the status register until the Data Available bit is set.

The flowchart in Fig. 12-18 shows this operation. As you can see, the microprocessor can be in this "wait loop" indefinitely. The following example uses the instructions shown in Fig. 12-18.

Suppose you are waiting for a 300-baud transmission. At 10 bits per word, the maximum data transfer rate is 30 characters per second. If the instructions (IN, ANI, JNZ) have 1-μs MPU cycles, they execute in a total of 13 μs.* (Both the IN and the JNZ instructions take 5 MPU cycles, and the ANI takes 3 MPU cycles.) With the 13-μs loop time, the microprocessor loops 2564 times waiting for the next Data Available status bit. Of course, the program loops more than 2564 times if the second ASCII character does not immediately follow the first character. More than likely the next character will not follow immediately, because few people can type at 30 characters per second. That rate is equivalent to 360 words per minute.

This wait problem is usually fixed by using the UART's Data Available output to interrupt the microprocessor. The interrupt signal causes the microprocessor to execute the In instruction followed by the input service routine. A later section covers interrupts.

Self-Test

Check your understanding by answering these questions.

16. The UART performs
    a. A serial-to-parallel conversion
    b. A parallel-to serial-conversion
    c. Control and monitoring functions
    d. (All of the above)

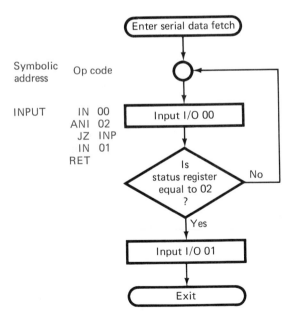

Fig. 12-18   A subroutine for handling a serial I/O port. Once the UART's status register is in the accumulator, an ANI 02 (AND Immediate 02) masks all but the Data Available bit and clears the microprocessor status register's zero bit if data is available. The instructions are also shown.

* This example uses the ANI (AND Immediate) instruction. The earlier example used the Compare instruction. Either instruction is valid, as the status word is not saved after the test and can be destroyed.

EIA RSA-232C

LED
optoisolators

17. A signaling rate of ___?___ baud is not a common speed.
   a. 300   c. 256
   b. 150   d. 1200

18. A signal of ___?___ baud has two Stop bits.
   a. 110   c. 300
   b. 150   d. 600

19. ASCII has 128 characters. Each is coded as a ___?___-bit binary word.
   a. 6   b. 7   c. 8   d. 128

20. The ___?___ is not a part of a UART.
   a. Control and logic function
   b. Transmit shift register
   c. Address decoder
   d. Receive shift register

21. Write a brief description for each of the following terms. If the term is an acronym include the expanded name.
   a. UART   *f.* Framing error
   b. Baud   *g.* Start
   c. ASCII   *h.* Parity bit
   d. ×16 Clock   *i.* JNE
   e. Overrun

22. Express the hexadecimal ASCII codes for the following characters, assuming the eighth bit is "0." Also express the hexadecimal ASCII codes when an eighth (MSB) even-parity bit is added.
   a. 6   *h.* a
   b. A   *i.* Ø
   c. ↑   *j.* Bell
   d. L   *k.* $
   e. p   *l.* b
   f. 4   *m.* Control D
   g. *   *n.* Space

12-4 SERIAL COMMUNICATION LINES

In the last section we looked at the UART. We saw that the UART is used to send and receive data over serial lines. In this section, we will look at serial lines themselves. We will see how they are used and what standards apply to them.

Serial lines are usually connected to other devices by using one of two standards. Both standards are shown in Fig. 12-19. The most common line standard is the EIA RS-232C, or simply RS-232. This is shown in Fig. 12-19(*a*). This is the Electronic Industries Association's standard RS-232C. The RS-232 standard calls for logic "1" to be a +3-V (or

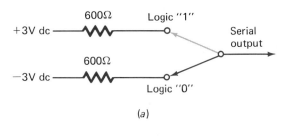

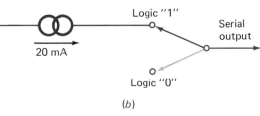

Fig. 12-19 (*a*) The EIA RS-232C and (*b*) the 20-mA standards for serial lines. The RS-232 standard calls for signaling between +3V and −3V sources. The 20-mA current loop calls for a 20-mA loop current for a logic "1" and an open circuit for a logic "0."

higher) signal. The logic "0" signal is to be −3 V (or lower). The standard also specifies a type of connector and modem "hand-shaking" signals. (We will see what modems are shortly.) The RS-232 standard is used on most video terminals and other serial devices used within a few hundred feet (a hundred meters, or so) of the transmitting device.

A 20-milliampere (20-mA) current loop is shown in Fig. 12-19(*b*). Signaling is done by making and breaking a 20-mA current source. The 20-mA loop was first used by the telephone industry, which used both 20-mA and 60-mA loops. The 20-mA loop can be used to send data over greater distances than the RS-232 can. Although the 20-mA loop can transmit much farther than RS-232 lines can, the loop also has disadvantages. The 20-mA loop has no control signals. It is also much less standardized than the RS-232. For example, the 20-mA loop has no standard connector. The 20-mA loop is often used in manufacturing plants where control lines must be run a few thousand feet. Beyond a few thousand feet (a thousand meters or so), receiving and transmitting modems must be used.

Both the EIA RS-232 and the 20-mA transmitters and receivers are often connected to the "outside" world through LED optoisolators. The optoisolators protect the UART and the microprocessor from high voltages and ground loops that might be found on the serial lines. Figure 12-20 shows a typical EIA

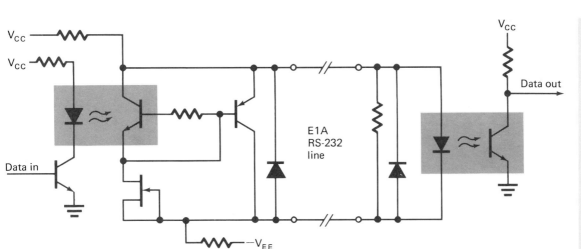

Fig. 12-20 An RS-232 line with optoisolators to keep ground loops and high voltages from damaging the microelectronics. The reverse-biased diodes serve to suppress high-voltage transient signals.

HDLC (High-level Data Link Control)

SDLC (Synchronous Data Line Control)

Modem (modulator demodulator)

Frequency shift keyed (FSK) signal

RS-232 transmitter and receiver with optoisolators.

Two other high-speed serial transmission standards are also used with microprocessor systems. These are the HDLC (high-level data link control) and SDLC (synchronous data line control) standards. The International Standards Organization established the HDLC standard. IBM established the SDLC standard. Both standards are data-independent systems. Because they are data-independent, they can be used to send a data word of any desired length. The HDLC and the SDLC standards are used for CPU-to-terminal, terminal-to-terminal, and satellite communications systems. Both standards are often used with coaxial transmission lines and at data rates exceeding 1 megabit per second. In summary, these standards provide for high-speed serial data transmission when sophisticated high-speed communications are needed.

Some UARTs also include the logic and hand-shaking signals needed to connect serial signals to a modem (modulator-demodulator). A modem, for example, might convert the transmitter's binary output into a high tone (1270 Hz) for logic "1" and a low tone (1070 Hz) for a logic "0." These tones can be transmitted over a telephone line or over any long-distance serial line. The demodulator portion of the modem converts the received tones from the telephone line into signals that can drive the UART's serial input.

Figure 12-21 shows how UARTs and modems are used to build a communications

system. The UART does the serial-to-parallel and parallel-to-serial conversions. The modem simply converts a logic-level signal to an FSK (frequency-shift-keyed) signal. The FSK signal can pass through alternating-current coupling devices, such as transformers, that are often used in long telephone circuits. Modems can also transmit data by radio as shown in Fig. 12-22. Radio transmission by modems is often done on industrial data-gathering systems that use microcomputer control. The system shown in Fig. 12-22 can also provide control signals from the parallel I/O port.

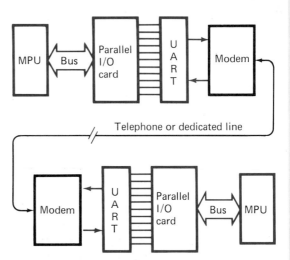

Fig. 12-21 Using modems to communicate over long distances. The modems send and receive digital signals by using different tones for logic "1"s and logic "0"s. Modems are often used on the dial op system and on dedicated lines.

255

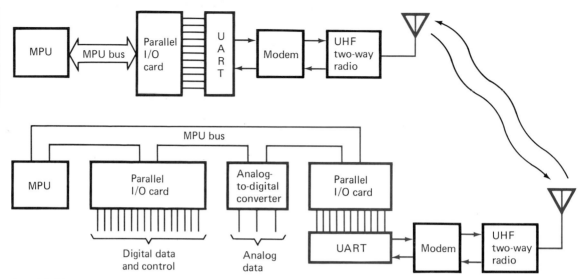

Fig. 12-22 Using microcomputers, UARTs, modems, and UHF radios to gather and analyze remote data. This system can also provide control signals from the parallel I/O port.

Figure 12-23 represents the serial transmission of an ASCII character from an asynchronous UART. The Start bit is always a logic "0." The start bit always follows a random time at logic "1." The data word D0 to D7 is a combination of logic "1s" and logic "0s" depending on the character being sent. The Stop bit is always a logic "1." The output stays at logic "1" until the next Start bit.

Figure 12-24 shows the serial transmission of four characters. You can see two important characteristics of this form of asynchronous transmission. First, the time between characters is entirely random. A Start bit can follow immediately after the previous character's Stop bit, or an interval of any length may pass before the next Start bit. Second, the interval between characters is always at the Stop level.

Self-Test

Check your understanding by answering these questions.

23. Which of the following is *not* a standard serial communications line?
   a. EIA RS-232   c. IEEE-488
   b. 20-mA loop   d. SDLC

24. A modem is used to
   a. Provide long-distance serial communications
   b. Interface a parallel I/O port
   c. Generate a UART's × 16 clock
   d. Act as a 20-mA constant-current source

25. Most video terminals are connected to the microcomputer by a(n) ___?___ serial transmission line.
   a. EIA RS-232   c. IEEE-488
   b. 20-mA loop   d. SDLC

26. The modulator part of a modem outputs ___?___ signal.
   a. A ± 3 V   c. A 20-mA
   b. An FSK   d. An HDLC

27. Rank the following data-transmission methods from 1 (the one with the shortest usable distance) to 5 (the one with the longest).

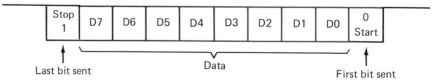

Fig. 12-23 The serial transmission of an ASCII character. Start is always a logic "0" (called a *space*), and Stop is always a logic "1" called a *mark*. When not in use, the line is *marking*.

256

4th word   3rd word   2nd word   1st word

Fig. 12-24 The serial transmission of four ASCII characters. The first three characters are randomly spaced. The fourth character starts as soon as transmission of the third is complete. The line is marking a logic "1" between characters.

a. 20-mA loop
b. EIA RS-232
c. Modem
d. Parallel I/O
e. Microcomputer bus

28. Serial transmissions from a UART always begin with a (a) ___?___ bit. The initial change from logic (b) ___?___ to logic (c) ___?___ tells the receiving UART to begin clocking in (d) ___?___ .

29. We can say that the UART's timing is asynchronous with the microcomputer. We also can say that the transmitted characters are often asynchronous with respect to each other. What does this mean?

12-5 POLLING AND INTERRUPTS

When you have one or more I/O devices connected to a microprocessor system, any one of them may demand service at any time. The microprocessor can service these devices in one of two ways. One way is to use the *polling routine*. The other way is with an *interrupt*. In this section, we look at both of these ways of servicing I/O devices.

A polling routine is very simple. The microprocessor's software simply makes a periodic check of all the I/O devices. During this check, the microprocessor tests to see if any device needs to be serviced. For example, after completing a basic calculation, the microprocessor calls the polling subroutine. The polling subroutine might look like the one shown in Fig. 12-25.

This is a simple inline program. Once we enter the polling routine, we transfer I/O port 01's status register to the accumulator. In the decision block, we test this status register to see if the service-request bit has been set. If it has, we call I/O port 01's service routine. When we return from the I/O port's service routine, we return to the polling routine.

If the service-request bit has not been set for I/O port 01, or if we have completed I/O port 01's service routine, then the microprocessor tests I/O port 02's status register to see if the service-request bit is set.

This test and service procedure continues until all the I/O status registers have been

Polling routine

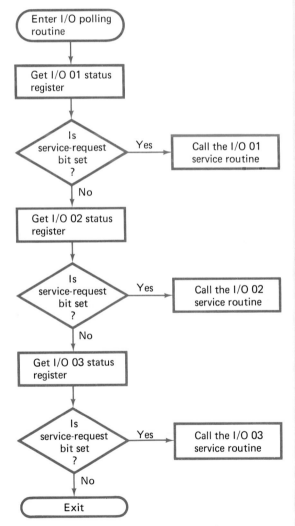

Fig. 12-25 A polling routine. This program checks the status register of each I/O device in the program's list. If the I/O device's service-routine bit is set, the program jumps to a service routine for that device.

257

tested and all the I/O ports needing service have received it.

The polling routine assigns priorities to the different I/O devices. In the routine shown, once the polling routine is started, the device at I/O port 01 is always checked first. Then ports 02 and then 03 are checked. However, the order can be changed by simply changing the polling routine. The change requires only changing the I/O port numbers in the Get Status Register instructions and changing the service subroutines' calls.

Notice that the polling routine is *not* started by the I/O devices, but by the software. When a program reaches the polling-routine subroutine call, the polling begins. Polling routines cannot be used unless the I/O devices can wait for service.

The other way to start service for an I/O device is for the I/O device to ask for service through an interrupt. The interrupt line is a special input to the microprocessor's control logic. Interrupts in different microprocessors operate in slightly different ways. However, they all have the same result.

The interrupt input is like a hardware subroutine call. When the interrupt line is asserted, a special sequence in the control logic begins. First, the microprocessor completes its current instruction. Second, the program counter's current contents are stored on the stack. Third, the program counter is loaded with the contents of two special memory locations. The next instruction is taken from the memory location pointed to by the contents of these two memory locations.

The response to an interrupt is flowcharted in Fig. 12-26. For this example (we are using the text microprocessor), the interrupt causes the program counter to fetch its new contents from memory locations FFFB and FFFA. The actual memory locations used vary from one microprocessor to another.

In Fig. 12-26, the Return instruction is used to exit from the interrupt routine. The Return instruction pops the old value of the program counter from the stack. Thus, the program can continue at the point where it was interrupted.

Sometimes more than one device must be able to interrupt the microprocessor's operation. How does the microprocessor tell which device caused the interrupt? There are two ways to solve this problem. First, we can use multiple interrupts. Some microproces-

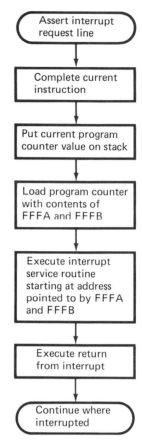

Fig. 12-26 A flowchart of the interrupt sequence from the time the interrupt line is asserted until the interrupted program starts up again.

sors have many interrupts. Each interrupt causes the microprocessor to load the program counter contents from a different memory location. We say that each interrupt has a different *vector*. Each interrupt vectors the microprocessor to a different service routine.

Some microcomputer systems use external hardware to provide different vectors for a single-interrupt microprocessor. Logic of this kind is tied to the microprocessor's bus. Figure 12-27 shows a system with eight prioritized interrupt inputs. The eight interrupts (I0 through I7) are connected to the interrupt-priority logic.

An interrupt signal on any one of these multiple inputs causes two things to happen. First, the logic asserts the microprocessor's interrupt input. Second, a unique binary number is placed in a register. This register is accessed when the microprocessor fetches data from memory location FFFB.

When the interrupt is being processed, the microprocessor takes the high address byte

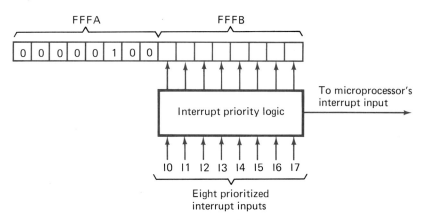

Fig. 12-27 A hardware interrupt-priority system. In this system, the microprocessor vectors to memory location FFFA and FFFB when interrupted. Asserting any one of the interrupt lines (I0 to I7) loads a different binary number into the register that the microprocessor addresses when it addresses FFFB. This logic gives a single-interrupt microprocessor eight interrupts.

from memory location FFFA. In Fig. 12-27 you see that the interrupt instruction is found at memory location 04XX. The value of XX is supplied by the interrupt priority register. The value (address) is different for each of the eight interrupts.

Figure 12-28 shows one way that the arrangement in Fig. 12-27 might set up a series of vectors (memory-location pointers). Each

interrupt is vectored to a memory location that is 8 bytes from the next vector. These memory locations might hold a short (8-byte) interrupt service routine or a 3-byte Jump Unconditional to some other, longer program.

A second, and fairly simple, way of servicing an interrupt is to use the polling routine originally described in Fig. 12-25. The interrupt starts the polling routine just as the sub-

FFFA	FFFB	Hexadecimal	Interrupt
0000 0100	0000 1000	0408	I0
0000 0100	0001 0000	0410	I1
0000 0100	0001 1000	0418	I2
0000 0100	0010 0000	0420	I3
0000 0100	0010 1000	0428	I4
0000 0100	0011 0000	0430	I5
0000 0100	0011 1000	0438	I6
0000 0100	0100 0000	0440	I7

Fig. 12-28 An interrupt vector table generated by the interrupt priority logic in Fig. 12-27. For example, if interrupt line I4 is asserted, the microprocessor will vector to memory location 0428.

"Boot-up" routine

routine call instruction did. The only difference between this use of the polling routine and the earlier one is that the device needing service starts this routine. An interrupt-started polling routine provides quicker service to the requesting device than does the simple programmed polling routine.

Our textbook microprocessor has three interrupts. These are shown on the block diagram in Fig. 12-29.

The Reset interrupt finds its vector at memory locations FFFE and FFFF. The Reset interrupt has the highest priority. The Reset is used to restart the microprocessor when all else fails. Most microprocessors are started after power-up by using the RESET instruction. Often, the RESET instruction vectors the microprocessor to the "boot-up" routine.

The boot routine brings the main program into the microprocessor's RAM from some mass-storage device.

Our microprocessor's second highest priority is a nonmaskable interrupt. The nonmaskable interrupt finds its vectors at memory locations FFFC and FFFD. This interrupt works exactly the same as the third interrupt, which is a maskable interrupt. As we have indicated before, the maskable interrupt finds its vectors at memory locations FFFA and FFFB. The only difference between these two interrupts is that the programmer can control when the microprocessor responds to the maskable interrupt. The programmer does this by setting the interrupt bit (the I bit) in the microprocessor's status register to mask the maskable interrupt.

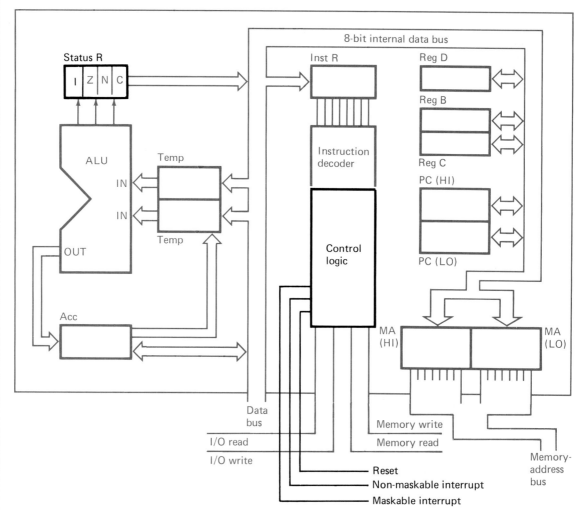

Fig. 12-29 The three interrupt inputs of the model microprocessor of this text.

Two special instructions clear or set the interrupt mask. These instructions are:

CLEAR INTERRUPT MASK $0 \rightarrow$ I bit
CLI

CLI

1 byte
2 cycles

SET INTERRUPT MASK $1 \rightarrow$ I bit
STI

STI

1 byte
2 cycles

When the interrupt mask is cleared, asserting the interrupt request line causes the microprocessor to begin interrupt processing. When the interrupt mask is set to logic "1," the microprocessor will not respond to a request on the maskable interrupt line.

Often the interrupt bit is set as the first part of an interrupt service routine. This prevents other interrupts until the service routine is complete. Once the program is far enough along to permit another interrupt, the interrupt mask can be cleared.

The status register's interrupt bit does not affect the operation of the nonmaskable interrupt input. Asserting the nonmaskable interrupt causes the microprocessor to vector immediately to the locations pointed to by FFFC and FFFD.

Clear interrupt mask

Set interrupt mask

Self-Test

Check your understanding by answering these questions.

30. If you use a simple polling technique, your I/O device must
    a. Interrupt the microprocessor
    b. Set the interrupt's priority
    c. Wait for the polling routine to start
    d. Not exceed 110 baud

31. The polling routine's priority is set by
    a. The interrupt priority
    b. The device's physical position on the bus
    c. The device's I/O speed
    d. The software

32. An interrupt is most like a
    a. Hardware subroutine call
    b. Hardware Jump Unconditional
    c. Hardware Jump Conditional
    d. RESET

33. The _____ interrupt does not work when the status register's interrupt bit is set to logic "1."
    a. Maskable   c. RESET
    b. Nonmaskable   d. Vector

34. List the three major events that happen after you assert the microprocessor interrupt line.

35. Why doesn't the RESET interrupt place the program counter's present contents on the stack?

Summary

1. Human communications require the use of alphanumeric characters and slow speeds. People input data through keyboards. Keyboards may be numeric only, alphanumeric, or custom-designed. Most keyboards use a row-and-column encoding technique. The encoding logic is either microprocessor-based or uses custom LSI.

2. Soft-copy displays usually have seven-segment characters or dot-matrix characters, on either special displays or CRTs. Hard-copy displays are usually dot-matrix or solid-character printers.

3. The two common forms of magnetic mass storage are tape and floppy disks. Magnetic tape is an inexpensive, block-formatted, slow, mass-storage device. Floppy disks hold somewhat less data, cost more, and offer much faster access.

4. A parallel interface transfers all bits of a data word between the microcomputer's data bus and the outside world.

5. To properly control a parallel I/O port, we use a status register. The status register has a separate I/O address. The In and Out instructions transfer data between the I/O port and the accumulator. I/O can be treated as special addresses or memory locations. When I/O simply occupies memory locations, we say that it is memory-mapped I/O.

261

6. The IEEE-488 bus is a standardized parallel I/O bus used to connect instruments to intelligent controllers.

7. Most microcomputers use a serial interface to communicate with remote devices.

8. A shift register may be used to do the parallel-to-serial and serial-to-parallel conversion. A more flexible device is the UART (universal asynchronous receiver-transmitter).

9. The UART adds a Start and a Stop bit to the data bits. The UART's signaling rate is called its baud rate. A UART has a transmitter, a receiver, and status and control sections. The UART's status register can detect overruns, framing errors, parity errors, an empty transmit buffer, and available data.

10. The standard 7-bit code for transmitting alphanumeric characters is ASCII. ASCII means American Standard Code for Information Interchange.

11. A parity bit makes the total number of bits at logic "1" either even or odd. The parity bit is used for error detection and is transmitted as the eighth bit.

12. A baud-rate generator is a special LSI circuit to generate a UART's ×16 clock signal for all the standard signaling rates.

13. The UART is completely asynchronous with the microprocessor. Therefore, handshaking software checks the UART's status register before commands are given.

14. The two most common serial line standards are the 20-mA loop and the EIA RS-232. The 20-mA loop uses a 20-mA constant-current source. The line uses a 20-mA signal to indicate logic "1." An open line indicates logic "0." The 20-mA loop is useful up to several thousand feet. The RS-232 standard specifies transmitting a +3-V logic "1" and a −3-V logic "0." The RS-232 standard also specifies a connector and hand-shaking lines.

15. A modem (modulator-demodulator) is used to send serial data over very long distances. A modem transmits frequency-shift-keyed signals.

16. There are two ways that a microcomputer I/O device can get service. I/O devices either can be polled or can cause an interrupt. A polled device is asked if it needs service. The device is asked each time the software reaches a certain point in the main program. An interrupt is the same as a hardware subroutine call. When servicing an interrupt, the microprocessor first completes the present instruction; second, puts the present value of the program counter on the stack; and third, vectors to the service routine.

17. Most microprocessors have maskable and nonmaskable interrupts. The maskable interrupt can be turned on or off as necessary. The nonmaskable interrupt is *always* on.

Chapter Review Questions

12-1. A full ASCII keyboard can encode ____?____ characters.
    a. 10   b. 64   c. 128   d. 256

12-2. Compared to magnetic tape, a floppy disk offers
    a. A greater amount of storage
    b. A faster access time
    c. A lower cost
    d. Serial access

12-3. A video terminal that has both uppercase and lowercase ASCII characters probably displays a ____?____ on its CRT.
    a. 5 × 7 dot-matrix character
    b. 5 × 9 dot-matrix character
    c. 4 × 4 matrix
    d. 128 × 24 character display

12-4. Hard-copy printers use
    a. Paper
    b. Dot-matrix printing
    c. Solid-character printing
    d. (All of the above)

12-5. A seven-segment display can be used to display
    a. Numbers and some letters
    b. Only the characters 0 to 9
    c. Only the hexadecimal characters 0 to F
    d. Full uppercase letters

12-6. A parallel I/O port usually has
    a. Parallel outputs
    b. Parallel inputs
    c. A status register
    d. (All of the above)

12-7. Memory-mapped I/O is a poor choice for systems with
    a. A limited amount of memory addressing
    b. A lot of I/O devices
    c. A need to add data from two I/O ports
    d. DMA

12-8. The IEEE-488 bus is a(n) _____?_____ bus.
    a. Internal memory-address bus
    b. Internal data bus
    c. External parallel bus
    d. Programmable instrument

12-9. The UART connects
    a. A modem to a parallel I/O port
    b. A serial line to a parallel I/O port
    c. A parallel I/O port to a serial line
    d. (All of the above)

12-10. The basic logic element in a UART is the
    a. Adder
    b. EXCLUSIVE OR gate
    c. Shift register
    d. Status register

12-11. The UART's baud rate is its
    a. × 16 clock input
    b. Signaling speed
    c. Data word length
    d. (All of the above)

12-12. Find the binary ASCII code for each of the following characters. Make a table showing the character, the 7-bit ASCII code, and the 8-bit code with odd parity.
    a. Control C   *g*. Space
    b. E   *h*. M
    c. F   *i*. T
    d. W   *j*. 8
    e. Line feed   *k*. 15
    f. Carriage return   *l*. Ø

12-13. Explain what a framing error is.

12-14. How can a receiving UART always tell that a Start bit has been received?

12-15. Your Transmit UART is set at 150 baud. However, your Receive UART is set to 300 baud. You send an ASCII 5 with even parity. What is received?

12-16. Which of the following is not part of a UART's status register?
    a. Overrun   c. Number of Stop bits
    b. Parity   d. Data Available

12-17. You probably would transfer the UART's status register to the UART's data-output buffer so that you could
   a. Store the data in memory
   b. Test the data in the accumulator
   c. Clear the overrun bit
   d. Check for a parity error

12-18. UARTs that are designed to connect directly to a microprocessor probably have ____?____, which a stand-alone UART does not have.
   a. A status register
   b. A clock input
   c. Address decoding
   d. Serial data out

12-19. What do the letters UART stand for? Why is each of the four words used when describing this device?

12-20. Describe a simple software routine that will synchronize the UART and the microprocessor.

12-21. Why do you think the RS-232 serial communications standard is more popular than the original 20-mA teleprinter signaling?

12-22. Why are optoisolators used with serial lines?

12-23. Briefly explain how a modem works and under what conditions it is used.

12-24. Sketch a polling routine flowchart that prioritizes the I/O ports in a 1, 3, 2 sequence.

12-25. How do you keep a UART from requesting service if it is connected to a maskable interrupt input?

12-26. What is the purpose of a hardware interrupt-priority encoder such as the one diagramed in Fig. 12-27?

12-27. Flowchart the main events from the assertion of the microprocessor's interrupt line until the return to the interrupted program.

12-28. Explain what the interrupt's vector is.

12-29. A 16-bit microprocessor is connected to a UART receiving ASCII characters with even parity. The data are being stored in a main memory file. Why would the program storing the data include many shift instructions?

12-30. You are working on a microcomputer that used 1-megabaud (1-Mbaud) SDLC communications. Would you expect this microcomputer to use a programmed data transfer or to use DMA? Why?

Answers to Self-Tests

1. d.   3. d.
2. b.   4. c.
5. A ROM input for each key would take too many inputs for a large keyboard.
6. See Fig. 12-30 for samples of word formation.

7. (a) Because you are probably looking for the word and, therefore, your mind is ready to accept anything that looks like it. (b) You might not know what they are.
8. b.   9. c.   10. d.

11. a.
12. (a) It takes up memory locations. (b) It gives you more instructions to use directly on I/O data.
13. You just use it and ignore the regular I/O lines and the I/O instructions.

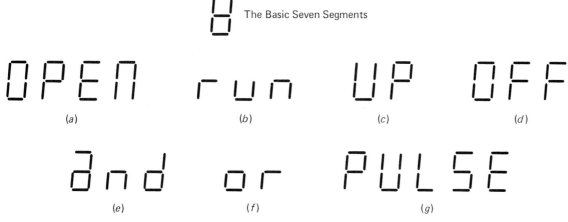

Fig. 12-30   Answer to self-test question 6.

14. It uses a programmed data transfer. The data are transferred into the microprocessor's accumulator, not directly into a memory location.

15. *a.* Listener *f.* Listener
    b. Talker/listener *g.* Listener
    c. Talker/listener *h.* Talker/listener
    d. Listener *i.* Talker/listener
    e. Controller *j.* Talker/listener

16. d.   17. c.   18. a.

19. b.   20. c.

21. *a.* Universal asynchronous transmitter-receiver. A device that transmits and receives serial data. It converts serial data to parallel and provides control and monitoring functions.
    b. The signaling rate for a single character in a serial transmission. That is, the bits-per-second rate of the character.
    c. American Standard Code for Information Interchange. The standard code used to transmit alphanumeric characters, punctuation, and mathematical operations.
    d. The timing signal used to drive a UART. This signal is 16 times faster than the baud rate.
    e. A condition in which one serial character is piled up on top of the previous character.
    f. A condition that occurs when the wrong bit starts the UART.
    g. The first bit in a serial transmission. It is indicated by a change from the logic "1" level to the logic "0" level.
    h. A bit added to the data so that the number of logic "1s" in the data and the parity bit combined will come out even or odd depending on the kind of parity desired. The parity bit is used for error detection on the receiving end.
    i. Jump If Not Equal. A jump instruction that often follows a Compare instruction. The JNE instruction tests the status register's zero bit. If the zero bit is logic "0," the jump happens.

22.

	Character	Character with Parity
a.	36	36
b.	41	41
c.	5E	DE
d.	4C	CC
e.	70	F0
f.	34	B4
g.	2A	AA
h.	61	E1
i.	30	30
j.	07	87
k.	24	24
l.	62	E2
m.	04	84
n.	20	A0

23. c.   25. a.
24. a.   26. b.

265

27. (1)e.   (2)d.   (3)b.   (4)a.
    (5)c.
28. (*a*) Start. (*b*) 1. (*c*) 0.
    (d) Data.
29. You don't know when
    the next character is
    coming. There is no
    timing relationship be-
    tween them.
30. c.   32. a.
31. d.   33. a.
34. *a.* The microprocessor
    completes its current in-
    structions.

b. The current program
counter is placed on the
stack.

c. The interrupt vector
is placed in the program
counter and the interrupt
routine begins.

35. Because there is no
    need to. The RESET is
    used when initializing
    the system after a
    power-up. The program
    counter's present value
    is a random number.

Additional Addressing Modes

- In this chapter, you will learn about three more ways that microprocessors access memory locations. Most of the instructions required to do any job are memory-address instructions. Microprocessor manufacturers have put a great deal of thought into the different ways of accessing memory.

  The three kinds of memory addressing introduced in this chapter are indexed addressing, relative addressing, and using the stack pointer. Many common microprocessors use either indexed addressing or relative addressing. Almost every microprocessor has a powerful stack pointer.

  In order to use indexed addressing, the microprocessor must have an index register. Some microprocessors have index registers and others do not. Relative addressing is also used by some microprocessors and not by others. You will learn how you would adapt a program that uses indexed addressing so that the program will run on a microprocessor that lacks an index register.

  Finally, we will also look at the stack pointer. You have already used the stack pointer for subroutine and interrupt operations. In this chapter, you will see how the stack pointer can also be used to gain access to more memory locations. You will learn about user-controlled stack instructions.

13-1 INDEXED ADDRESSING

Figure 13-1 shows a modified block diagram of our 8-bit microprocessor. In this diagram, the BC register pair has been replaced by a 16-bit index register. The index register is simpler than the BC register pair. The index register is simpler because it is a single 16-bit register, *not* a register pair.

Four index register instructions you can use are Load Index Register Immediate (similar to Load Register Pair Immediate), Increment Index Register, Decrement Index Register, and Compare Index Register Immediate. The form of these instructions is:

LOAD INDEX REGISTER IMMEDIATE
LDX,Data

| LDX | Hi data → IX_H |
| Lo data | Lo data → IX_L |

3 bytes
3 cycles

The index register instructions are just like many earlier register instructions. The Load instruction initializes the register. Loading the index register sets the status register's negative bit if the MSB is a "1" or its zero bit if data are 0. The status register's negative bit is set if the index register's bit 15 is loaded with a logic "1." The status register's zero bit is set to logic 1 if *all 16* index register bits are loaded with logic "0."

The index register is treated as a single 16-bit register. There are *no* byte operations on the index register.

INCREMENT INDEX REGISTER
INX
IX + 1 → IX

| INX |

1 byte
2 cycles

DECREMENT INDEX REGISTER
DEX
IX − 1 → IX

| DEX |

1 byte
2 cycles

From page 267:
Load index
register
immediate

Increment index
register

Decrement
index register

On this page:
Offset

Compare index
register
immediate

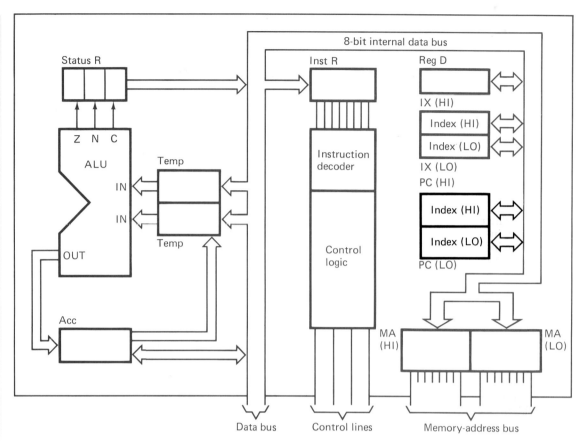

Fig. 13-1 **A microprocessor with an index register. The index register is a single 16-bit register that can be loaded, incremented, decremented, compared, or used for indexed addressing.**

The Increment and Decrement instructions let you point the index register to either a higher or a lower memory location. Incrementing or decrementing the index register affects only the status register's zero bit. This bit is set when incrementing or decrementing the index register causes logic "0s" in all 16 bits.

COMPARE INDEX REGISTER IMMEDIATE
CPX, Data
IX_H/IX_L—Hi data/Lo data

CPX
Hi data
Lo data

3 bytes
4 cycles

The Compare instruction also works on the index register as a 16-bit value. The contents of the compare instruction's *next two* immediate memory locations are subtracted from the contents of the index register. As with all other compare instructions, the result of this subtraction is never stored. The status register's zero, negative, and carry bits are set if the result causes one of these statuses *for the 16-bit operation*. Note: The Compare test works only on the complete data word. There are no byte tests for the index register.

The index register is used for indexed addressing. Indexed addressing is done by adding the contents of the instruction's second byte to the index register's current contents. The resulting sum points to a memory location.

Figure 13-2 shows what happens. You can see that this is really a "computed" register-indirect memory-address instruction. That is, you compute (by addition) a new 16-bit number. This number is made up of the sum of the 16-bit index register value and the 8-bit value in the instruction's second byte.

The 8-bit number added to the index register has a range of 00 to FF. This value is called the *offset*. You can offset the index register value from 0_{10} to 255_{10}. This means indexed addressing permits pointing to 256

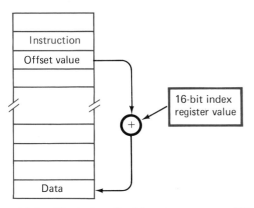

Fig. 13-2 The indexed addressing process. The offset value in the instruction's second byte is added to the index register's 16-bit value. The result (sum) is used as the memory-address word.

memory locations without changing the index register's value.

Indexed addressing is an entirely new microprocessor addressing mode. Every instruction can now use this mode. For example, a microprocessor that uses indexed addressing instead of register-indirect addressing might have Add from Memory Indexed (ADD A,X) instead of Add from Memory Indirect (ADI). The new ADD A,X instruction is a 2-byte, 5-cycle instruction. In general, indexed addressing requires a few more microprocessor cycles than register-indirect addressing.

Figure 13-3 shows a simple program that uses two instructions with indexed addressing. The two instructions are ADD A,X (Add from Memory Indexed) and STA A,X (Store Accumulator Indexed).

The first instruction (LDX) loads the index register. You must preset the index register before starting to use it. Otherwise you do not know what the index register's contents are. In this example, we preset the index register to 0100_{16}.

The CLA instruction simply makes sure that the accumulator is reset and that the status register's carry and negative bits are also reset. The zero bit is also set.

The first indexed instruction is ADD A,X 0B. This tells the microprocessor to add the contents of memory location 010B to the accumulator.

How does the microprocessor know that it is to use the contents of memory location 010B? The index mode tells the microprocessor to add the contents of the instruction's second byte to the contents of the index register. The microprocessor is to use the result as

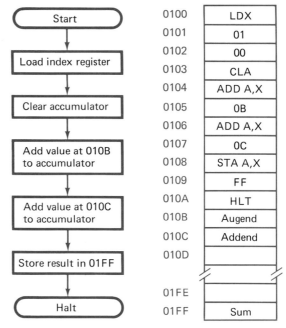

Add from memory indexed

Add from memory indirect

Store accumulator indexed

Fig. 13-3 A program to add two numbers by using indexed addressing. The LDX 0100 loads the index register with the initial value of 0100. The indexed instructions add 0B, 0C, and FF to work with memory locations 010B, 010C, and 01FF, respectively.

the memory address. In this example, we have:

	0100	Index register
+	0B	Instruction's second byte
	010B	New address

You should note that this memory-address value never appears anywhere except in the microprocessor's memory-address register. That is, both the original index register value and the original instruction offset value stay as they were.

The next instruction is also an indexed instruction. It is a repeat of the ADD A,X instruction. However, this time the offset is 0C. Therefore, when this instruction executes, the contents of memory location 010C are added to the accumulator.

The accumulator now contains the sum of the values in memory locations 010B and 010C.

The last indexed instruction is STA A,X FF. This instruction stores the accumulator's contents in memory location 01FF. The offset FF is added to the index register's value 0100. Once this instruction is executed, a HLT stops further execution.

Needless to say, there are many other ways

269

to write the same program by using indexed instructions. For example, offsets of 00 are often used. Increment and Decrement instructions are also often used to point to a new memory location.

How does indexed addressing compare with register-indirect addressing? Both addressing modes have their good and their bad points. For example, indexed addressing requires 2 bytes for each instruction, but register-indirect addressing requires only a single byte for each instruction. On the other hand, two indexed instructions can easily address two memory files separated by up to 256 memory locations. Register-indirect addressing, on the other hand, must load the two separate memory pointers either from another register or from specially reserved memory locations. Loading a memory pointer requires many more instructions.

Few microprocessors have both forms of addressing. You will also find that similar microprocessor programs using either addressing mode will be almost equally long. Some short routines, however, are much shorter using one mode than using the other.

Programming a microprocessor that uses indexed addressing requires a different approach from programming a microprocessor that uses register-indirect addressing. The algorithm for the same problem is usually somewhat different on the two types of microprocessors.

Figures 13-4 to 13-7 show a problem solved by register-indirect and by indexed addressing. This particular problem is most easily solved by using indexed addressing.

The problem is to transfer the 32 data bytes in memory locations 004F through 006E (the source file) to memory locations 00CA to 00E9 (the destination file).

Figure 13-4 shows a flowchart and a memory map. Figure 13-5 is a listing for solving this problem by using our textbook microprocessor with register-indirect addressing. The source and destination files are initialized at 004F and 00CA, respectively.

Memory locations 001A and 001B are used to store the low bytes of the source and destination pointers. As you can see, the upper byte is always the same because both the source and the destination files have an upper byte address of 00. We will use an LDD C to load register C directly. When the BC register pair's lower byte contains the value in

memory location 001A, the BC register pair points to a location in the range 004F to 006E. That is, the register pair points to the source file. When the BC register pair's lower byte is loaded with the contents of memory location 001B, the register pair points to a memory location in the range 00CA to 00E9. That is, the register pair points to the destination file.

The first instruction loads the BC register pair's upper byte with 00. The LDD C,001A instruction that follows makes the BC register pair point to memory location 004F. However, when we use the data in memory location 001A again, we want the data to point to the next higher memory location. To change the contents of location 001A as required, we move the contents of register C into register A, increment register A (the accumulator), and store the *incremented* result in memory location 001A. You can see that this operation assures that memory location 001A always points to the *next* source-file memory location.

We can now move the data. We will use register-indirect instructions to do this. Remember that moving the data from register C to register A did not destroy the original contents of register C. Register C still points to the first location in the source file.

We use a Load Indirect instruction. This instruction moves the data from the source file's first memory location into the accumulator.

A Load Register C Direct instruction is now used to put the contents of memory location 001B into register C. We are preparing to put the data into the destination file. The BC register pair now points to memory location 00CA, which is the start of the destination file.

A Store Accumulator Indirect instruction can now be used to put the data into this first memory location in the destination file.

The next time that we need the destination value from the BC register pair, the value must point to the next higher memory location. Again, we move the contents of register C into the accumulator, increment the accumulator, and store the newly incremented pointer directly in memory location 001B.

We have now transferred one byte of the source file to the destination file. This operation must be repeated 31 more times. When the last transfer is complete, we increment the accumulator from E9 to EA. We will be in-

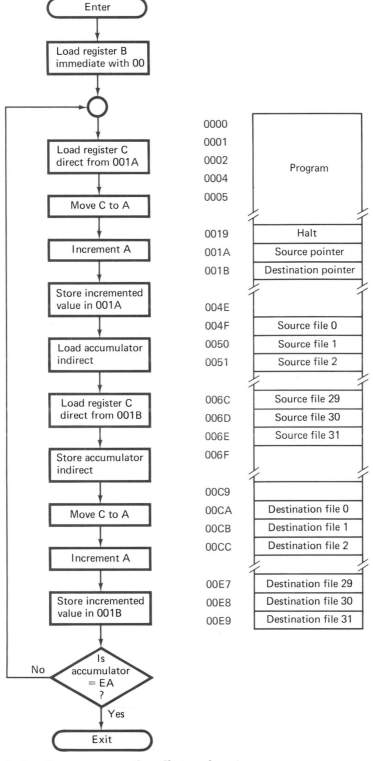

Fig. 13-4 A flowchart and a memory map for a file transfer using the microprocessor with register-indirect addressing. The 32-bit source and destination files are shown in the memory map. The program keeps a source pointer and a destination pointer in memory because there is no other storage.

Memory address	Memory contents	Comments
0000	LDA B	Make BC Hi byte 0
0001	00	
0002	LDD C	Point Lo byte to source
0003	00	
0004	1A	
0005	MOV A,C	Copy C into accumulator
0006	INC A	Increment source pointer
0007	STA A	Put in source pointer
0008	00	
0009	1A	
000A	LDI A	Load source byte into accumulator
000B	LDD C	Point Lo byte to destination
000C	00	
000D	1B	
000E	STI A	Store byte in destination file
000F	MOV A,C	Copy C to accumulator
0010	INC A	Increment destination pointer
0011	STA A	Put in destination pointer
0012	00	
0013	1B	
0014	CMP	Is destination pointer done?
0015	EA	
0016	JNZ	No, jump back to move more
0017	00	
0018	02	
0019	HLT	Yes, halt
001A	4F	Source pointer (4F initial)
001B	CA	Destination pointer (CA initial)

Fig. 13-5 A listing of the program to perform a file transfer. The source and destination pointers are initialized at 004F and 00CA, respectively.

crementing and storing the destination-file memory pointer. A Compare instruction checks for EA in the accumulator. The Compare instruction sets the status register's zero bit when the instruction finds EA in the accumulator. The status register's zero bit is tested by the jump instruction in memory location 0016. The jump either sends the program back to move more data, or it causes the program to halt.

How is this same job done by using indexed addressing? The flowchart, memory map, and listing are shown in Figs. 13-6 and 13-7.

The first instruction loads the index register. We start the program with the index reg-ister pointing to the first memory location in the source file.

A simple LDA A,X00 loads the accumulator with the contents of memory location 004F. This instruction uses a zero offset. A zero offset is used whenever the index register already points to the desired memory location.

Next, a STA A,X7B instruction stores the accumulator's contents at memory location 00CA. That is, an offset of 7B is added to the index register's base value of 004F. The result points to memory location 00CA. This is just another way of saying that the source and destination files are separated by 7B (123_{10}) memory locations.

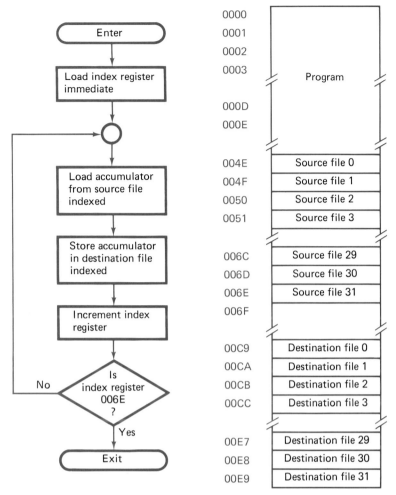

Fig. 13-6 A flowchart and memory map for a file transfer using
the microprocessor with indexed addressing. The index register
is preset to point at the source file, and the program uses an offset
value of 7B to point to the destination file.

We use an INX instruction to increment
the index register's contents. The index register now points to the next source-file location.

Throughout the program, the same 00 and
7B offsets will always point to the next higher
location.

After we have incremented the index register 32 times, its value will be 006E. That is, it
will point to the thirty-third source-file location. Each time through the program, a CPX
instruction checks the index register's value.
This time the CPX instruction sets the status
register's zero bit. The JNZ jump instruction
will not execute. This causes us to exit from
the program.

Using the index register is a much easier
way to do this particular job. However, if the
difference between the source and destination

files is greater than 256 bytes, the index register's offset will not be large enough to permit
using this method. With more than a 256-
byte separation, the job is done in the same
way for both types of addressing. You must
move the two 16-bit pointers in and out of
memory. That is, you must maintain one 16-
bit (two-memory-location) source-file pointer
and one 16-bit (two-memory-location) destination-file pointer.

Self-Test

*Check your understanding by answering these
questions.*

1. Suppose that the instruction at memory location 0100 in the program shown in Fig.
   13-3 reads LDX 010B instead of LDX

Memory address	Memory contents	Comments
0000	LDX	Point index register to source file
0001	00	
0002	4F	
0003	LDA A,X	Load accumulator from source file
0004	00	Zero offset
0005	STA A,X	Store accumulator in destination file
0006	7B	Destination file equals source file + 7B
0007	INX	Increment file pointer
0008	CPX	Is index pointer done?
0009	00	
000A	6E	
000B	JNZ	No, jump back to move more
000C	00	
000D	03	
000E	HLT	Yes, halt

Fig. 13-7   A listing of the indexed file-transfer program.   Compare this with the listing in Fig. 13-5.

0100.   What other changes to the program are needed to make it do the same job as before?   Show a new listing.

2. How could the program in Fig. 13-3 use an LDA A,X (Load Accumulator Indexed) instruction instead of the first ADD A,X instruction?   What other instruction would this change?   Show by using a new listing.

3. Write a version of the program in Fig. 13-3 for our textbook microprocessor without the index register.   Which version of the program is more efficient?   Why?

4. Given the following index register values and index-mode instructions, explain what will happen when each instruction is executed.

	Index register	Instruction
a.	01F0	ADD A,X 00
b.	0005	STA A,X 05
c.	0011	LDA A,X 00
d.	00FF	INX
e.	A1AE	SUB A,X AE
f.	A105	AND A,X A0
g.	FFFF	DEX
h.	0AEE	CLA

5. How would you change the program shown in Fig. 13-4 to make the program transfer files of any length?

6. The program in Fig. 13-7 transfers the 32-byte file from one memory location to another.   (a) What is the maximum length of file that a program like this can transfer?   (b) What is the maximum number of memory locations between file-start memory locations?   Why?

7. In the program in Fig. 13-7, why is JNZ 0003 instead of JNZ 0000 the instruction at memory location 000B?

8. How does the following program differ from that in Fig. 13-7?

0000	LDX
0001	00
0002	6E
0003	LDA A,X
0004	00
0005	STA A,X
0006	7B
0007	DEX
0008	CPX
0009	00
000A	4F
000B	JNZ
000C	00
000D	03
000E	HLT

13-2 RELATIVE ADDRESSING

In some microprocessors, mostly very powerful 16-bit microprocessors, every instruction can use a relative addressing mode.   In other microprocessors, only a few instructions use relative addressing.

Relative addressing is much like indexed addressing. However, there are differences. First, the instruction's offset is added to a different register in each of these addressing modes. *In relative addressing, the offset is relative to the program counter's current value.* Second, relative addressing usually uses a special form of 2's complement arithmetic. The use of this special arithmetic makes possible branching forward when the offset has a logic "0" in the most significant bit. The special arithmetic also permits branching backward when the offset has a logic "1" in the most significant bit. The offset is then treated as a 2's complement number.

So why do we sometimes use relative addressing instead of indexed addressing? For some microprocessors, relative addressing is the only mode provided for some instructions. Often the conditional branch instruction use only relative addressing. Furthermore, relative addressing permits the writing of *position-independent code*. Position-independent code is also called *relocatable* or *relative code*. The addressing of the programming code is written relative to the data in the microprocessor's program counter. Consequently, the same code can be used at any memory location.

Figure 13-8 shows a flowchart for a routine

that may be coded in either absolute or relative code. "Absolute code" means that the code must be used at a fixed set of memory locations. Figure 13-9(a) shows absolute code, and Fig. 13-9(b) shows relative code.

The subroutine inputs data from a UART's status register. The AND Immediate instruction masks all but the Data Available flag in the UART's status register (UART status register bit 1). If the bit is set to logic "1" (that is, if data are available) the accumulator *will not* be 0 after the ANI instruction executes. Therefore, no jump takes place. The next instruction inputs the UART's data word from I/O port 01.

If the UART's status register bit is not set, all the accumulator bits are logic "0s." A jump occurs. Here is where the two programs differ. The program in Fig. 13-9(a)

Memory address	Memory contents	Comments
0000	IN	Input status register
0001	00	
0002	ANI A	Mask all but Data Available bit. Is Data Available bit set?
0003	02	
0004	JZ	No, try status word again.
0005	00	
0006	00	
0007	IN	Yes, input data word
0008	01	
0009	RET	Leave routine

(a)

Memory address	Memory contents	Comments
0000	IN	Input status register
0001	00	
0002	ANI A	Mask all but Data Available bit. Is Data Available bit set?
0003	02	
0004	JZ R	No, jump back 6 bytes and try status word again
0005	FA	
0006	IN	Yes, input data word
0007	01	
0008	RET	Leave routine

(b)

Fig. 13-9 A program listing for the data input routine (a) using the Jump If Zero Direct instruction and (b) using the Jump If Zero Relative instruction.

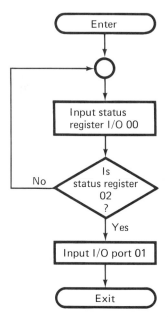

Fig. 13-8 A flowchart to test a serial input port's status register for the Data Available flag.

jumps back to memory location 0000. However, the program in Fig. 13-9(b) uses relative addressing. It jumps *back 6 memory locations* from the program counter's current value. Remember, the program counter is pointing to the In (next) instruction while the jump instruction is executing.

The jump instruction tells the microprocessor to jump back by as many steps as the 2's complement of the number in the instruction's second byte. In this case, the backward jump is six locations because FA is the 2's complement of 6. The instruction JZ R FA really just says, "Subtract 6 from the contents of the program counter." Here is the subtraction:

0000 0110	Binary 6
1111 1001	Complement of 6
0000 0001	Add binary 1
1111 1010	2's complement
F A	Hexadecimal offset

In Fig. 13-9(a) and (b) you can see that both programs occupy almost the same number of memory locations. However, the program that uses relative addressing is 1 byte shorter, because the Jump Direct instruction at memory location 0004 in Fig. 13-9(a) takes three bytes.

Figure 13-10 shows the program from Fig. 13-9(b). Here the program starts at memory location 01AE. None of the instruction mnemonics in the listing is different, and none of the op codes *or addresses* is different. Jumping back 6 locations relative to the program counter, even though the program counter now points to memory location 01B4, still

Memory address	Memory contents	Comments
01AE	IN	Input status register
01AF	00	
01B0	ANI A	Mask all but Data Available bit.
01B1	02	Is Data Available bit set?
01B2	JZ R	No, jump back 6 bytes and try
01B3	FA	status word again
01B4	IN	Yes, input data word
01B5	01	
01B6	RET	Leave routine

Fig. 13-10 The imput routine from Fig. 13-9(b) relocated to start at memory address 01AE.

takes you back to the Input Status Register instruction (now at memory location 01AE).

On the other hand, moving the program from Fig. 13-9(a) would require a code change. The JZ 0000 instruction would have to have its address changed so that the instruction reads JZ 01AE.

As you have seen, relative addressing frees the programmer from worrying about where the program's absolute address is. But the programmer must be good at hexadecimal (or octal) arithmetic to compute the relative addresses. Using an assembler relieves the programmer of the need to calculate relative addresses. The assembler does all the calculations itself.

Self-Test

Check your understanding by answering these questions.

9. Why doesn't the program in Fig. 13-9(a) use a 2-byte Jump Indexed instruction at memory location 0004 instead of the 3-byte Jump Direct instruction?

10. An instruction using relative addressing is always 2 bytes long. Relative to the instruction's memory location, what is its addressing range?

11. For the following relative address instructions, tell what will happen as each instruction is executed.

    a. | 010F | LDA A |
       |------|-------|
       | 0110 | JZ R |
       | 0111 | F1 |
       | 0112 | RET |

    b. | 00DE | JMP R |
       |------|-------|
       | 00DF | 01 |
       | 00E0 | CLA A |
       | 00E1 | CLA B |

    c. | 0021 | INX |
       |------|-------|
       | 0022 | JNZ R |
       | 0023 | 0D |
       | 0024 | DEX |

    d. | 0FAB | ADD B |
       |------|-------|
       | 0FAC | JNC R |
       | 0FAD | 8D |
       | 0FAE | RET |

12. Often, the microprocessor's single-byte addressing range (256 memory locations) is called a "page." Why do you think the relative addressing mode is said to address a "floating page"?

13-3 USER-CONTROLLED STACK INSTRUCTIONS

In this section, we will study the instructions that permit working with the microprocessor's stack. Our previous knowledge of the microprocessor's stack was related either to subroutine call instructions or to interrupts. Although each of these operations uses the stack, the user has no control. Stack operations with these instructions happen automatically.

The stack instructions in this section permit use of the microprocessor's stack for work other than subroutines and interrupts. A programmer must be very careful when using the stack. Everything done to the stack must be undone. Adding data to the stack (pushing) and not removing the data (popping) before the microprocessor executes another instruction that involves a stack operation can cause the microprocessor to crash.

Remember that the stack is a LIFO (last-in–first-out) storage device. The last data written onto the stack will *always* be the first data off the stack. Everything must be taken off the stack in reverse order from the way everything was put on.

For example, assume that you are executing a second-level subroutine (a subroutine within a subroutine). Figure 13-11 shows the stack's contents while a second-level subroutine is executing. The top byte on the stack is at memory location 0F25. This is an arbitrary memory location chosen to start this stack. This memory location must not be used by any other part of the program. The *contents* of memory locations 0F25 and 0F24 point to a memory location in the main program. They are pointing to the next instruction after the subroutine call instruction. Memory location 0F25 contains the program counter's low byte. Memory location 0F24 contains the

Memory address	Program	Stack
0F21	Next available stack	
0F22	1st subroutine PC (Hi)	02
0F23	1st subroutine PC (Lo)	01
0F24	Main program PC (Hi)	00
0F25	Main program PC (Lo)	0C

Fig. 13-11 The microprocessor's stack while a second-level subroutine is executing.

program counter's high byte. When the subroutine finishes, execution of the main program will restart with the instruction at memory location 000C. Note: As data are taken off the stack, the program counter's Hi byte comes off first, followed by the Lo byte.

You can also see that the first-level subroutine called a second-level subroutine just before the instruction at memory location 0201 was executed.

In this example, the second-level subroutine is a triple-precision Multiply subroutine. While this subroutine is executing, it needs temporary storage when performing a triple-precision Shift Left.

Figure 13-12 shows the triple-precision multiplicand as each byte is placed on the stack. In Fig. 13-12(a) the low byte is placed on the stack and the stack pointer (shown in this figure by an arrow) points to the next available stack location. In Fig. 13-12(b), the middle byte is placed on the stack and the stack pointer again points to the next stack location. In Fig. 13-12(c), the last (most significant) byte of the triple-precision multiplicand is placed on the stack. The stack pointer now points to the next stack location.

In Figs. 13-12(d), (e), and (f) you can see the information being taken off the stack. The stack pointer (shown by the arrow) follows the information, always pointing to the *next available* location. By the time we reach Fig. 13-12(f), no multiplicand information remains on the stack. The only information left on the stack is the two program counter values from Fig. 13-11. Note: We say that there is no information left on the stack because the stack pointer no longer points to those locations. Actually, memory locations 0F1E to 0F21 will contain the old information until a new stack overwrites them.

From this illustration you can see why it is so important to keep close track of what is pushed onto and popped from the stack. For example, suppose you fail to remove the multiplicand's most significant byte from the stack. That is, the multiplication problem is started with the stack looking like Fig. 13-12(a) but for some reason it is stopped with the stack looking like Fig. 13-12(e). When the multiplication subroutine ends, the stack's last two bytes are placed in the program counter. The microprocessor will then continue to execute the first-level subroutine. In this example, the stack's last two bytes would point to mem-

LIFO (Last In First Out)

Memory
address

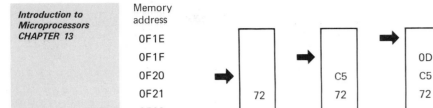
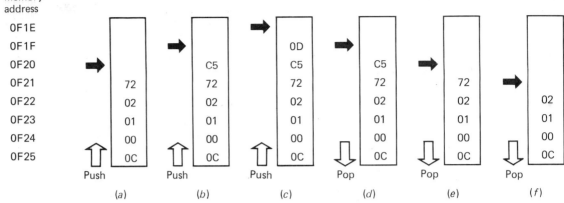

OF1E						
OF1F			0D			
OF20		C5	C5	C5		
OF21	72	72	72	72	72	
OF22	02	02	02	02	02	02
OF23	01	01	01	01	01	01
OF24	00	00	00	00	00	00
OF25	0C	0C	0C	0C	0C	0C
	Push	Push	Push	Pop	Pop	Pop
	(a)	(b)	(c)	(d)	(e)	(f)

Fig. 13-12   Adding data to the stack as a temporary storage area during a triple-precision shift. The stack pointer always points to the next available stack location.

ory location 7202. However, we know that the subroutine actually should have restarted at memory location 0201. The microcomputer system has vectored to the wrong location for subroutine restart. More than likely, the microprocessor will crash.

As noted earlier, most microprocessors have a series of instructions that permit the programmer to use the stack. For our microprocessor, these instruction are:

LOAD STACK POINTER IMMEDIATE
LDA SP,Data

LDASP	
Hi data	Hi data → SPH
Lo data	Lo data → SPL

The Load Stack Pointer Immediate instruction is a 3-byte, 3-cycle instruction used to set the stack's starting memory location. Remember, the stack is built into successively lower bytes of memory. Therefore, this instruction sets the memory location that is the "top" of the stack. This instruction's second byte contains the stack pointer's high byte. The instruction's third byte contains the stack pointer's low byte. The status register's zero and negative bit are set if the *16-bit* word being loaded is 0 or has an MSB of "1." This instruction must be used once before the stack is to be used.

Stacks *never* preset themselves! The programmer must, therefore, use the LDA SP instruction any time that the program will use either a subroutine call or an interrupt.

INCREMENT STACK POINTER
INC SP
SP + 1 → SP

INCSP

DECREMENT STACK POINTER
DEC SP
SP − 1 → SP

DECSP

The Increment Stack Pointer and Decrement Stack Pointer instructions operate on the 16-bit stack pointer register. No status register bits are affected by the increment or decrement instructions.

PUSH ACCUMULATOR ONTO STACK
PUSH
ACC → Stack
SP − 1 → SP

PUSH

The Push Accumulator onto Stack instruction places the accumulator's data onto the stack. The stack pointer is then decremented by 1. No status register bits are set by this operation.

POP ACCUMULATOR FROM STACK
POP
SP + 1 → SP
Stack → ACC

POP

The Pop Accumulator from Stack instruction loads the last data in the stack into the accumulator. The stack pointer is then incremented by 1. No status register bits are set by this operation.

Self-Test

Check your understanding by answering these questions.

13. Why isn't a Decrement Stack Pointer instruction needed immediately following a Push instruction?

14. You use a Push instruction to temporarily save a data word that you may need a few steps later in the program. If you don't Pop the data word, what instruction do you use to keep from crashing the microcomputer?

15. If you are transferring data between two memory files that are more than FF locations apart, you need to keep two index registers. Another way to do this transfer is to use the stack pointer as one pointer. How would you do this?

16. What are the dangers in question 15? What instructions would you use to make sure that there are no problems?

Summary

1. Indexed addressing is done in microprocessors with an index register. The index register in an 8-bit microprocessor is usually a single 16-bit register. Indexed addressing adds the instruction's second byte (called the "offset") to the index register's current contents. The result is a new memory address. Index registers can be loaded, incremented, or decremented. They can also be the object of a Compare instruction.

2. The offset has a range of 00 to FF.

3. The computed address is used only in the memory-address register.

4. Indexed and indirect addressing need different algorithms. Indexed addressing is very good for transferring short memory files.

5. The CPX instruction can be used to check for a file end.

6. Relative addressing addresses 255 locations (+127 to −128) around the program counter's current value. The relative offset is added to the program counter's value.

7. Offsets with a logic "1" in their MSB express the offset as a 2's complement negative number. They branch backward.

8. Relative addressing can be used to write position-independent code.

9. Subroutines and interrupts automatically keep track of the stack pointer.

10. The stack is a LIFO device. The stack pointer always points to the next available location. The stack pointer must be loaded when the microprocessor is initialized.

11. The stack pointer's Increment and Decrement instructions do not affect the status register.

12. The Push instruction puts the accumulator's current contents onto the stack and decrements the stack pointer.

13. The Pop instruction loads the last stack data into the accumulator and increments the stack pointer.

Chapter Review Questions

13-1. The memory location pointed to by indexed addressing is the result of adding the index register's current value to the instruction's
   a. Direct address   c. Offset
   b. Indirect address   d. Data

13-2. You initialize the index register with the ____?____ instructions.
   a. Reset Immediate   c. Clear Index Register
   b. Load Index Register   d. Decrement Index Register

13-3. In most 8-bit microprocessors the index register is treated as
   a. A register pair with hi and lo bytes
   b. A memory-address register
   c. A single-byte, 2-cycle instruction
   d. A single 16-bit register

13-4. The CPX instruction is used to
    a. Reset the index register
    b. Initialize the index register
    c. Check the index register's value
    d. Add the offset to the index register.

13-5. A 16-bit index register typically has offsets that range from 0 to
    a. 255_{10} c. 377_8
    b. FF_{16} d. (All of the above)

13-6. You are using two different offsets. Explain what happens to these offsets when you increment or decrement the index register.

13-7. After the offset is added to the index register's value, the result is stored in the
    a. Accumulator
    b. Index register
    c. Memory-address register
    d. Program counter

13-8. Generally you do not find indexed addressing and ___?___ addressing in the same 8-bit microprocessor.
    a. Relative   c. Immediate
    b. Direct   d. Register-indirect

13-9. Explain the difference between and ADD A,X and an ADI instruction.

13-10. At what memory location does the instruction take place when the following instructions are executed?

Index Register	Instruction		
a. 0000	JP	X	0F
b. 0100	ADD	A,X	00
c. 0100	ADD	A,X	FF
d. 1000	ADD	A,X	00
e. 1016	ADD	A,X	FA
f. FFFF	ADD	A,X	00
g. FFFF	ADD	A,X	FA

13-11. Compare indexed, relative, and register-indirect addressing. What do they have in common?

13-12. What is the maximum separation between the source and the destination files used in an index register operation?

13-13. The offset for a relative-address jump instruction is 8B. How many bytes away from the jump instruction at memory location 008F is this jump? Is this a forward or a backward jump? Why?

13-14. A Jump Conditional relative instruction depends on the status of two registers. Which two registers? How does the instruction depend on them?

13-15. What is the advantage of relocatable code?

13-16. Explain the single greatest danger when using the stack for data storage.

13-17. To get data from the stack into the accumulator, you use the ___?___ instruction.
    a. MOV A   c. Push
    b. Pop   d. STA A

13-18. The stack pointer is initialized by
    a. Pointing to the top of memory
    b. Using an LDX instruction
    c. Executing an LRP B instruction
    d. Executing an LSP instruction

13-19. What would happen if you interrupted the microprocessor soon after power-up and before initializing the stack pointer?

13-20. What precautions would you need to take in a subroutine that temporarily "borrows" the stack pointer to do file movements?

Answers to Self-Tests

1. It starts the program out with the index register pointing at the augend. Therefore, the first Add A,X instruction has an offset of 0. The next Add A,X instruction can have an offset of either 01 or 00. If you use 00, you must increment the index register before using the 00 offset. The new listings are:

		or
0100	LDX	LDX
0101	01	01
0102	0B	0C
0103	CLA	CLA
0104	ADD A,X	ADD A,X
0105	00	00
0106	ADD A,X	INX
0107	01	ADD A,X
0108	STA A,X	00
0109	F4	STA A,X
010A	HLT	F3
010B	Augend	HLT
010C	Addend	Augend
010D		Addend

2. The new use is shown in the listing. It also gets rid of the CLA instruction.

0100	LDX
0101	01
0102	00
0103	LDA A,X
0104	0A
0105	ADD A,X
0106	0B
0107	STA A,X
0108	FF
0109	HLT
010A	Augend
010B	Addend

3.
0100	LRP B
0101	00
0102	0B
0103	CLA
0104	ADI
0105	INC C
0106	ADI
0107	STA A
0108	00
0109	FF
010A	HLT
010B	Augend
010C	Addend
01FF	

Both programs use the same number of memory locations.

4. *a.* The contents of memory location 01F0 are added to the accumulator.
b. The accumulator's contents are stored at memory location 000A.
c. The contents of memory location 0011 are loaded into the accumulator.
d. The index register now contains 0100.
e. The contents of memory location A25C are subtracted from the accumulator.
f. The contents of memory location A1A5 are ANDed to the accumulator.
g. The index register now contains FFFE.
h. The accumulator is cleared. This is not an indexed instruction.

5. You would set up two 16-bit pointers, one for each file. These would be stored in memory and brought into the index or BC register each time you addressed the file. After use, they would be incremented and returned to their memory locations.

6. *a.* The maximum length of file is 255 bytes.
b. The maximum number of bytes between file-start locations is 255 (FF) bytes. This also controls the maximum file length. The maximum offset, which is FF, imposes the limit.

7. To avoid reloading the index register each time. You want it to keep the indexed value it got at memory location 0007.

8. It starts the transfer at the top (highest memory location) of the file and decrements the index register until it has worked its way to the end of the file. The program in Fig. 13-7 starts at the bottom and works its way up.

9. There is nothing to index to. That is, the index register either is not there or is not preset.

10. Using complement notation a single byte can represent −128 to

+127. Because the program counter is pointing two memory locations *higher* than the relative instruction, the relative addressing range is −126 to +129.

11. *a.* The program will jump back to memory location 0103 if a 0 is loaded by the LDA A. Otherwise the Return will be executed.

b. Register B is cleared. The CLA A is not executed.

c. If incrementing the index register does *not* cause a 0, then the program jumps to memory location 0031. If incrementing the index register causes a 0, the index register is decremented.

d. If the Add does not cause a carry, then Jump to 103D if there is a carry, then RETURN.

12. Because you can address one page (+127 to −128 bytes) around the program counter, which moves through memory as the instructions are executed.

13. Because the Push instruction automatically decrements the stack pointer.

14. The program path that does not use the Pop instruction must execute an INC SP (Increment Stack Pointer), which restores the stack pointer to where it should be.

15. You would temporarily store the stack pointer's contents in memory and load it with the new values that would point it to the top of one of the two files.

16. The danger is that you have no stack during this operation. Therefore, you must be sure that the program does not try to use the stack, and that no interrupts or subroutine calls happen unless the data files can be used as a temporary stack.

Microprocessor-Related Hardware

- This chapter introduces some of the hardware used with microprocessors. So far, we have concentrated on the microprocessor's architecture and its instruction set. However, you must always remember that a great deal of the microprocessor's versatility comes from the hardware that goes with it.

    The first section of this chapter looks at the microprocessor as a piece of hardware. This section will help you understand a typical microprocessor's control signals. You will also become familiar with the microprocessor's clock circuits, its bus signals, and its bus control signals. In the second section we look at a few of the integrated-circuit support devices that make the microprocessor more powerful. After completing this section, you will be able to recognize standard microprocessor-bus interfacing and addressing techniques. You will also study integrated-circuit timers and see how they work through the microprocessor's interrupt system.

    In the third section, we look at the single-chip microcomputer. You will be able to list the basic characteristics of the analog microcomputer and to discuss a few of its applications. Finally, we study the instruments used for development and service by the microprocessor industry. You will understand the need for a microprocessor development system. You will also understand the need and uses for a logic analyzer, a logic probe, and a signature analyzer.

14-1 THE MICROPROCESSOR AS A HARDWARE DEVICE

Most microprocessors come in 40- or 64-pin DIPs (dual inline packages). The large number of pins are needed to carry data, address, power, and control signals. We will look at some typical microprocessor signals.

Many of a microprocessor's pins are used for the data bus and memory-address lines. Usually, an 8-bit microprocessor has eight data-bus lines called D0 through D7, and 16 memory-address lines called A0 through A15 —a total of 24 of the microprocessor's 40 pins. Some microprocessors need more than 16 additional pins. In general, however, manufacturers prefer not to use the relatively expensive 64-pin packages.

To reduce the number of pins used for the data bus and memory-address lines, a technique called "multiplexed data/address" is used. Figure 14-1 shows how this technique works. The lines AD0 to AD7 are used *both* for memory addresses and for the data bus.

During the microprocessor's first clock cycle, these eight lines are used as memory-address lines. During the microprocessor's second and third clock cycles, these eight lines become bidirectional data bus lines.

The address lines A8 to A15 are always used as memory-address lines.

This technique limits the memory-address and data bus functions to 16 lines. The microprocessor must have some other outputs to communicate with devices connected to the microprocessor's multiplexed data bus. Therefore, the microprocessor must use other pins to output timing and status.

For example, the microprocessor with multiplexed address/data lines outputs an Address Strobe pulse when there are valid address data on lines AD0 to A15. This pulse is used to latch the address data at the peripheral, or external, device. After the address information is stored at the peripheral device, the microprocessor outputs a memory read-write pulse or an I/O read-write pulse. This pulse tells the peripheral device that valid *data* are now

From page 283:
Dual inline
package

Multiplexed
data/address

On this page:
Two phase

Nonoverlapping
clocks

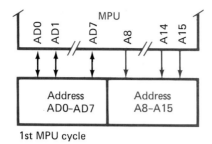

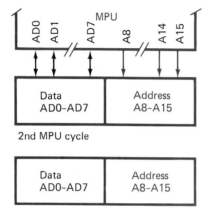

Fig. 14-1   The timing of information on a multi-plexed address/data bus. During the first cycle, the information is an address. During the second and third cycles, AD0 to AD7 are data.

cute, Memory Read, Memory Write, I/O Read, I/O Write, or Halt state.

The microprocessor's memory-address lines and data bus lines are usually capable of driving one TTL load. The data bus inputs are also TTL-compatible. That is, TTL signals can drive the data bus inputs.

Obviously the microprocessor must have a clock signal. The clock signal is used to synchronize all the data processing operations and data-transfer operations. All microprocessor operations occur in step with this clock.

Some microprocessors require a two-phase clock signal. Two-phase clock signals are nonoverlapping signals like those shown in Fig. 14-2. The $\phi1$ and $\phi2$ clock signals are derived from the main clock's waveform. The two-phase clock provides four timing points for each main-clock cycle: one on each leading edge and one on each trailing edge. Besides being nonoverlapping, these two-phase clock inputs often have one other important characteristic—they will not accept a TTL signal. This is because the input signal must be a nearly perfect ground-to-V_{cc} signal. As you know, TTL signals typically swing from 0.4 to 2.4 V.

The microprocessor's clock signals come from one of two different sources. Frequently the manufacturer provides a special integrated circuit for the microprocessor clock driver. This integrated circuit has an oscillator circuit and the logic to drive the high-level $\phi1$ and $\phi2$ signals. The integrated circuit is also frequently used to generate some other clock-synchronized signals, such as a system reset.

The second form of microprocessor clock is built into the microprocessor integrated cir-

on the data bus lines AD0 to AD7. It also tells the peripheral device what to do with these data. That is, the pulse indicates whether the data are input data, output data, data for memory, or data for I/O.

In addition to the memory-address strobe pulse, some microprocessors also have a few output pins with signals telling the status of the MPU. When decoded, these lines show when the microprocessor is in the Fetch, Exe-

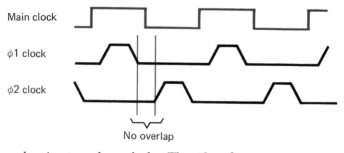

Fig. 14-2   The nonoverlapping two-phase clock. The $\phi1$ and $\phi2$ clock signals are derived from the main clock waveform. A two-phase clock provides four timing points per main-clock cycle: one on each leading edge and one on each trailing edge.

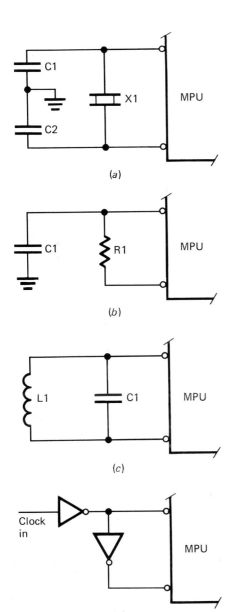

(a)

(b)

(c)

Clock in

(d)

Fig. 14-3 Four ways of controlling the frequency of a clock generator circuit. (a) The quartz crystal. (b) The RC oscillator. (c) The LC oscillator. (d) An external signal source.

cuit. This kind of clock needs only an external circuit to set the oscillator's frequency. All the different clock phases are generated within the microprocessor.

Figure 14-3 shows some typical circuits used to set the microprocessor's clock frequency. Typically, the microprocessor's oscillator must be set at 2 to 4 times the microprocessor's clock frequency. The reason is that countdown logic is used to generate the clock phases.

Figure 14-3(a) shows the most commonly used microprocessor clock-frequency control circuit. The oscillator circuit is completed by adding an external quartz crystal. Typically, microprocessor crystals resonate from 1 to 20 megahertz (MHz).

Figure 14-3(b) and (c) shows very inexpensive ways to complete the microprocessor's clock oscillator circuit. The RC oscillator in Fig. 14-3(b) offers little accuracy or stability. The LC oscillator in Fig. 14-3(c) is little better. Neither circuit can be used at much over 5 MHz. Both circuits are, therefore, used only for applications where processing speed and timing accuracy are not important.

Sometimes it is important that the microprocessor's clock signal be synchronized with an external signal. The circuit shown in Fig. 14-3(d) shows how the external signal is connected to the microprocessor's oscillator input pin.

If the microprocessor has an internal clock generator, then usually it will also have a clock output. The clock output signal can be used to drive other microcomputer-system devices that need a timing signal. Usually the microprocessor outputs the second of the two clock phases ($\phi 2$).

The microprocessor's power supply lines use a minimum of 2 and sometimes as many as 4 pins. All of the newer microprocessors are designed to operate from a single voltage supply. Usually this is +5 V dc. The microprocessor must have two power pins, one for +5 V dc (V_{CC}) and one for ground (V_{SS}). Other microprocessors may also use +12 V dc (V_{DD}) and −5 V dc (V_{BB}).

The exact power supply voltage and current requirements depend on the kind of semiconductor technology used. Microprocessors often use a substantial amount of power. Most of them draw between 0.5 watts (W) and 1.5 W. One exception to this is the complementary MOS (CMOS) microprocessor. Microprocessors are built with CMOS because of its low power and good speed characteristics. Typically, a CMOS microprocessor draws only a few milliwatts.

All microprocessors need a RESET input. This signal is a special form of interrupt. The signal is needed to start the microprocessor after power is first applied. Most microprocessor input control signals are *asserted* by grounding the input line. Grounding the input line applies a low-level logic signal to the

285

Schmitt trigger

Reset vector

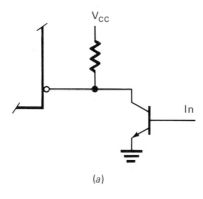

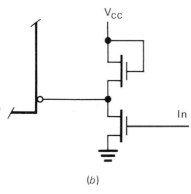

(a)

(b)

Fig. 14-4 Two solid-state drivers commonly used to assert (ground) an input. (a) A bipolar transistor. This configuration works with TTL open-collector outputs. The pull-up resistor is usually added externally. (b) A MOS transistor drive circuit. A second MOS device is used for the active load.

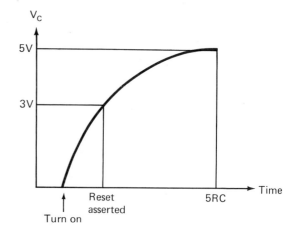

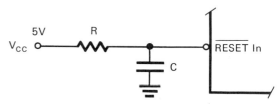

Fig. 14-5 A reset circuit. The RC time constant holds the microprocessor in a reset state until the capacitor charges to ½ V_{CC}.

input. Asserting a line in this way is called "negative true" logic. The input can be grounded by a switch or, as shown in Fig. 14-4(a) and (b), by a transistor.

The $\overline{\text{RESET}}$ input is asserted in the following way. The reset input is often called the NOT RESET input because it uses negative true logic. Resets often have a Schmitt trigger on their inputs. The Schmitt trigger allows resets to use a power-up circuit like the one shown in Fig. 14-5. The $\overline{\text{RESET}}$ input is asserted until the capacitor charges to +3 V. By choosing the right RC combination, you can assert the $\overline{\text{RESET}}$ signal until all of the circuits are stabilized.

Reset inputs that do not have a Schmitt trigger input must be buffered with an external circuit. This external circuit ensures a clean (noise-free) reset signal.

Asserting the reset line resets a number of internal registers and also the microprocessor's control logic. The program counter either is reset to 0000 or is loaded from a specific

pair of memory locations. These memory locations are called the *reset vector*.

The microprocessor may also generate a reset output signal. The reset output signal is usually used as the microcomputer's system reset signal. The signal is generated by the microprocessor's internal reset and clock circuits. The reset output signal ends at a specific time before in the microprocessor's first Fetch/Execute cycle.

Most microprocessors have at least two hardware interrupt lines. One of the interrupt lines is a nonmaskable interrupt. The other interrupt lines are usually maskable. Microprocessors with a number of maskable interrupt inputs give each input a different priority. If two interrupts happen together, the higher-priority interrupt takes over. A higher-priority interrupt can interrupt the program that is servicing a lower-priority interrupt. Each interrupt must vector to a different memory location to get the new contents for the program counter.

An interrupt may generate a microprocessor output signal. This output signal indicates that the microprocessor acknowledges an interrupt request. This Interrupt Acknowledge signal is used to control peripheral devices such as interrupt-priority logic.

If the microprocessor allows DMA (direct

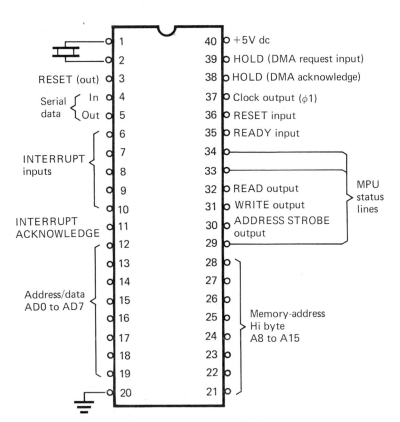

DMA request

DMA
acknowledge

Tri-state
condition

Intel 8085

Fig. 14-6 The pinout of the Intel 8085 microprocessor. It is packaged in a 40-pin DIP and uses multiplexed address/data lines AD0 to AD7 to conserve pins. The serial lines permit a simple single-bit transfer with the accumulator's MSB.

memory access), then the microprocessor must let another device take over its memory-address lines and data bus lines. Thus DMA requires two more microprocessor control signals. An input pin passes the DMA request to the microprocessor's control logic. The DMA request is acknowledged by the microprocessor on the DMA Acknowledge output pin. The Acknowledge signal is generated after the microprocessor has completed the current bus operation. Once the microprocessor acknowledges a request for the address and data buses, the microprocessor places them in a high-impedance state. This high-impedance or "tri-state" condition means that the outputs are neither logic "1" nor logic "0." The outputs are disconnected.

During a DMA operation, the microprocessor cannot execute any instructions that need either the memory-address signals or the data bus signals. The Processing operation halts until the requesting device releases the $\overline{\text{DMA}}$ $\overline{\text{INPUT}}$ line.

Figure 14-6 shows a typical 8-bit microprocessor's pinout. The microprocessor is the Intel 8085. It offers a good summary of a microprocessor's pinout. The connections are typical of those on many other common microprocessors. As you can see, this microprocessor has a few special features. The 8085 offers a very simple serial input/output port. A single bit of data is transferred between bit 7 of the accumulator and the I/O terminals. This transfer is done with a single instruction. The READY line is used to make the microprocessor wait for a slow device. Once the device is addressed, the READY line is asserted until the device is ready to place data on the microprocessor's data bus.

The 8085's other pins are similar to those that we have reviewed.

Self-Test

Check your understanding by answering these questions.

1. Why do you think most microprocessors have both a nonmaskable and a maskable interrupt input?

2. Most microprocessor control signal inputs are asserted by pulling them to a low voltage. This makes it possible for a number of different sources to easily assert a single line. Why do you think low-voltage assertion is easier than having the input asserted by a high-voltage signal? Why do you think this is called "negative true" logic?

3. What microprocessor routine might not deliver accurate results if you use an RC circuit rather than a quartz crystal as the microprocessor's clock-frequency control?

4. The microprocessor does not output ____?____ as a control signal.
   a. DMA Request Acknowledge
   b. MPU status
   c. I/O Read
   d. $\overline{RESET}$

5. One use for the Interrupt Acknowledge signal is to
   a. Indicate that the microprocessor cannot accept an interrupt
   b. Activate an interrupt controller
   c. Stop the microprocessor's clock
   d. Strobe address information into the microprocessor's peripheral devices

6. A multiplexed address/data system means that you must
   a. Have a pulse to strobe address information into peripheral devices
   b. Read data from the data lines only at certain times
   c. Connect some of the external device's address and data inputs into the same microprocessor output line
   d. (All of the above)

7. Once the microprocessor has asserted the DMA Acknowledge output, it means that
   a. The microprocessor's clock has stopped
   b. The data and address lines have gone to a high-impedance state
   c. The microprocessor has been reset
   d. (All of the above)

8. A reset signal always
   a. Is used to start the microprocessor after a power-down
   b. Gives the program counter its starting address
   c. Resets the control logic to start on a Fetch cycle
   d. (All of the above)

14-2 MICROPROCESSOR SUPPORT DEVICES

A substantial number of special-purpose integrated circuits have been developed to work with the microprocessor. Earlier, we looked at a few of these devices. We studied the UART, other serial interface devices, ROMs, and RAMs. Each of these devices can be made as a general-purpose integrated circuit. Each can also be made as a specific integrated circuit that works with a particular microprocessor or microprocessor family.

We also looked at the parallel I/O port. Parallel I/O ports are usually custom-designed to work with a particular microprocessor family. These ports have addressing logic, handshaking signals, and a status register. Such interface signals make the integrated circuit compatible with a particular microprocessor's control, address, and data signals.

Frequently, parallel I/O is included in the same chip with a ROM or an EPROM. An example of such an integrated circuit is shown in Fig. 14-7. Looking at this block diagram, you can see that the chip includes two bidirectional 8-bit I/O ports, a parallel I/O status register, and a 2048-byte ROM. The ROM may be either a mask-programmed ROM, a fusible-link ROM, or a user-reprogrammable ROM (an EPROM).

This IC directly interfaces with the microprocessor's memory-address lines, data bus lines, and control lines. The control lines include the I/O read-write, Memory Read, clock, and reset signals. The microprocessor's reset line initializes the chip's status register.

The IC's data bus lines are connected to the microprocessor's data bus lines. They carry memory data out and carry control and I/O data into and out of the IC.

The microprocessor's first 11 address lines are directly connected to the ROM's 11 address lines. These lines select one of the ROM's 2048 memory locations. The lines are also used to select one of the chip's I/O ports or its status register. If the system must have more than 2048 memory locations, then the output of an external memory-address decoder must be connected to the integrated circuit's $\overline{CHIP\ ENABLE}$ input. The external logic and the $\overline{CHIP\ ENABLE}$ input serve to select the desired device.

Another common microprocessor support device includes a timer. A timer makes it possible to start a delay sequence in hardware rather than in software. We have seen how to program a delay. Using a programmed delay, however, has a few problems. First, when the delay software is running, it keeps the mi-

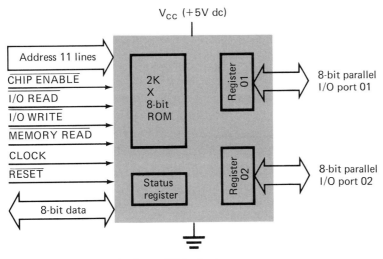

Fig. 14-7   A multifunction ROM-I/O chip.   This device connects directly to the microprocessor's data, address, and control bus lines.

croprocessor busy. The microprocessor can do nothing else while in the delay cycle. Second, the program needs a number of delay registers if the desired delay time is long.

This problem is easily solved by using a programmable hardware timer. The timer is simply a programmable down-counter. The down-counter is preset under software control. When the down-counter reaches the end of its count (0), the counter generates an output pulse. Usually this output pulse is used to interrupt the microprocessor.

The down-counter's clock input is taken from the microprocessor's system clock or any other available clock signal.

Figure 14-8 shows a typical microprocessor peripheral chip that includes a timer. This integrated circuit has three I/O ports, a status register to control and monitor the I/O ports, a 14-bit timer, and a 256-byte static RAM.

This chip, the ROM chip from Fig. 14-7, and a microprocessor could form a simple three-chip microprocessor-based system. The system would have 256 bytes of RAM,

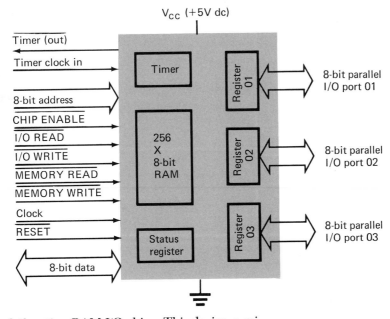

Fig. 14-8   A multifunction RAM-I/O chip.   This device, a microprocessor, and the chip in Fig. 14-7, make a minimum system with MPU, ROM, RAM, and parallel I/O.

289

One-shot mode

Tics (frequency
sources)

Bidirectional bus
transceiver

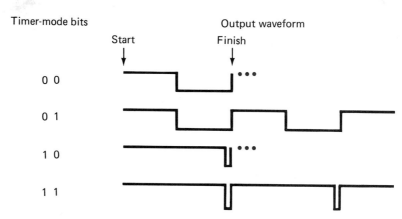

Fig. 14-9 The timer's mode selection. The timer can be either
single-shot (modes 00 and 10) or continuous (modes 01 and 11).
Either a square wave (modes 00 or 01) or a pulse (modes 10 or 11)
can be selected.

2048 bytes of ROM, a timer, and five 8-bit bi-directional I/O ports. This system would be a very powerful yet simple microprocessor system.

The timer found in the peripheral chip of Fig. 14-8 is a 14-bit programmable down-counter. The timer can be loaded with any binary number from 00000000000010 to 11111111111111. The timer's fifteenth and sixteenth bits are used to control the timer's mode. (We will look at the timer's mode a little later.) With a divisor of 2 to $16,383_{10}$, we can generate an output pulse every N clock cycles

$$\text{Delay} = \text{clock period} \times \text{N}$$

where N is any whole number from 2 to 16,383. The timer's mode-control bits permit selecting one of four combinations of output waveforms and pulse functions. All four are shown in Fig. 14-9. As you can see, the timer can be programmed to keep recycling, in modes 01 and 11. The timer will then generate an output at regular intervals. The counter can also be programmed for the "one-shot" mode, in modes 00 and 10. In the one-shot mode, the down-counter goes through one down-count cycle. When the counter reaches 0, it waits for a new count or a Restart command.

One example of a use for such a timer is a time-of-day clock. Usually, the timer's clock input is connected to the 60-Hz line. The desired rate for a time-of-day clock is one pulse every second. To achieve this rate, the down-counter is preset at 3C (60_{10}). At the end of 60 input pulses, the timer's output interrupts the microprocessor.

In this example, the timer is in the 11_2 mode shown in Fig. 14-9. In this mode, the timer immediately restarts another divide-by-60 routine. In this case, the timer outputs another interrupt pulse 1 s later. The timer's output pulse causes the microprocessor to call its interrupt routine.

In this example, the routine shown in Fig. 14-10 is called. It is typical 12-hour time-of-day clock routine. The timer's interrupt "wakes up" this routine once each second. The routine updates the seconds, minutes, and hours counters. Once the updates are complete, the routine "goes back to sleep" until the next interrupt.

There are three common "tics" (frequency sources) used to clock a timer. As we have seen in the above example, a 60-Hz signal from the power line can be used. Note: In Europe, the power-line signal is 50 Hz, but the difference can be handled by a simple software change. A 1-ms (1-kHz) tic is often used. That tic is usually derived from a high-stability 1-MHz crystal oscillator. The microprocessor's system clock may also be used.

Another common special-purpose integrated circuit for microprocessor support is the bidirectional bus transceiver. As noted earlier, the microprocessor's address bus and data bus outputs can drive a maximum of one TTL load. Typically this means that a microprocessor can drive 10 or more bus-compatible MOS devices. However, if the bus is to be extended more than 1 ft (0.3 m) or if the bus also drives TTL devices, such as decoders, the

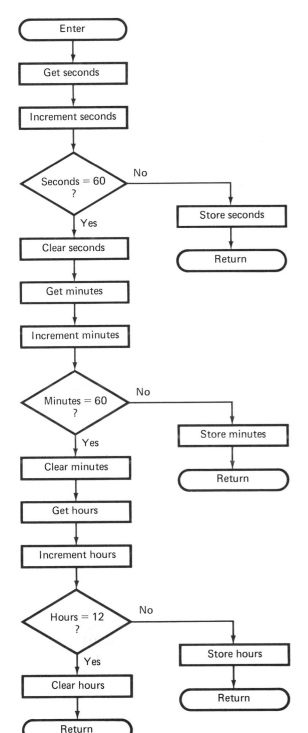

Fig. 14-10 A time-of-day clock routine. Once "woken up," this routine updates the seconds, minutes, and hours files as necessary, then "goes back to sleep."

microprocessor will run out of driving power. The bus transceiver is designed to overcome this shortage of driving power.

The typical bus transceiver schematic is shown in Fig. 14-11. This schematic shows that the transceiver bidirectionally buffers four of the eight microprocessor data bus lines.

The transceiver's common control line is connected to the input amplifiers and to the output amplifiers. This line is a tri-state control line. One set of the amplifiers (either the input amplifiers or the output amplifiers) is always active when the chip is enabled. The other set of amplifiers is in the high-impedance (off) state.

Asserting the transceiver's $\overline{\text{DATA IN}}$ line tri-states the outputs of amplifiers 1, 2, 3, and 4. Amplifiers 5, 6, 7, and 8 are turned on. This allows the microprocessor to output data to the microcomputer system. When $\overline{\text{DATA IN}}$ is not asserted, input amplifiers 5, 6, 7, and 8 are tri-stated and output amplifiers 1, 2, 3, and 4 let the microprocessor's data bus drive the microcomputer's system data bus.

Bus transceivers are designed to have a low input loading (a high input impedance). However, bus transceivers have a high output drive capability (a low output impedance). They can drive long microcomputer bus circuits, overcoming a significant bus capacitance that would otherwise reduce the bus speed and rise time. This is because the low output impedance shortens the time constant. Bus transceivers are often used at the microprocessor to buffer the MPU. These transceivers are also used on all the memory cards and I/O cards to buffer these devices. Figure 14-12 shows how a typical microcomputer system uses bus transceivers to interconnect the different modules.

There are a number of special-purpose integrated circuits built to perform complex control functions. One of these is a DMA controller. The DMA controller chip asks the microprocessor to place its memory-address and data bus lines in the tri-state mode. The DMA controller then operates the microprocessor's memory system as long as the high-speed data transfer is in process. Once the data transfer is complete, the DMA controller turns memory-system operation back to the microprocessor.

Another special-purpose integrated circuit is the interrupt-priority encoder. This chip prioritizes each of a number of interrupts. It places their correct address vectors where the microprocessor can use them as it responds to the interrupt. The interrupt-priority control-

DMA controller

Interrupt priority encoder

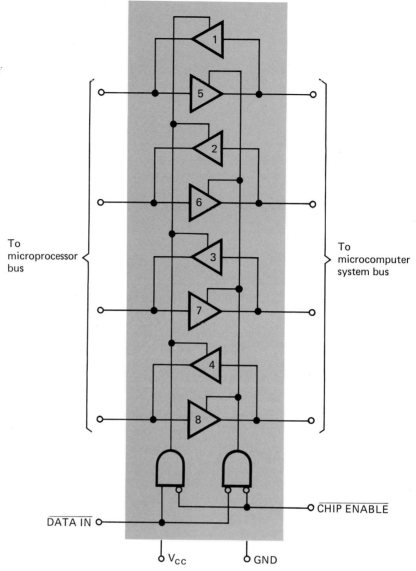

To
microprocessor
bus

To
microcomputer
system bus

CHIP ENABLE

DATA IN

V_{CC} GND

Fig. 14-11   A bidirectional bus transceiver.   This special-purpose chip can bidirectionally buffer data signals like those found on a microcomputer system.

ler also makes sure that the microprocessor services the higher-priority interrupt first.

Almost all interrupt-priority encoder chips are programmable.   A chip's function and characteristics can be controlled by loading control words into the chip's status registers.   Thus, the device's function can be changed "on the fly."   A program can change the device's characterstics or function while the device is running.

Self-Test

Check your understanding by answering these questions.

9. What value (hexadecimal) is used to program the timer in Fig. 14-8 if it is to output 1 pulse every 1.5 s when driven by a 1-ms tic?

10. You have a single-purpose microprocessor application.   Its program is only 128 bytes long and it uses 64 bytes of data storage.   Your microprocessor uses one 8-bit bidirectional I/O port.   Can a minimum microcomputer system be built using just the microprocessor and the support chip diagramed in Fig. 14-8?   If so, explain how the functions are divided between the two chips.   If not, explain why not, and indicate what additional functions are needed.

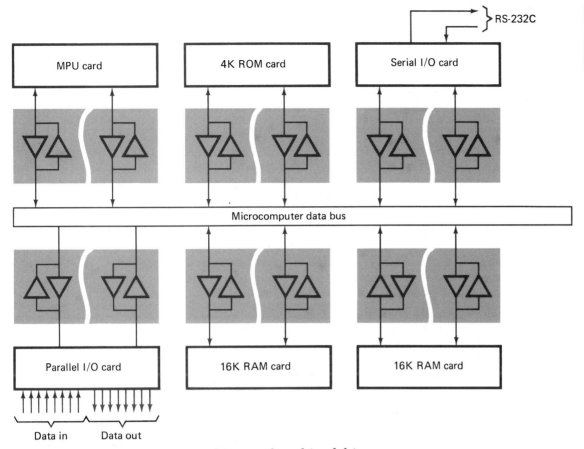

RS-232C

MPU card

4K ROM card

Serial I/O card

Microcomputer data bus

Parallel I/O card

16K RAM card

16K RAM card

Data in   Data out

Fig. 14-12 Using a bus transceiver chip on each card (module) of a microcomputer system. Each card will also have unidirectional buffers on the memory-address and control lines.

11. You have a microcomputer system with four RAM-I/O-timer chips like the one shown in Fig. 14-8. The system also has four ROM-I/O chips like the one shown in Fig. 14-7. Show how these devices can be connected to the microprocessor's data bus and memory-address bus. If any additional logic is needed, draw a block diagram of it and explain what the logic does.

12. The microcomputer system in question 11 uses a 5-MHz clock. The 5-MHz system clock is connected to the timer in one chip. Its output is connected to a second chip's timer input. The first chip is always set at the maximum divide ratio. What is the range of time between interrupt (output) pulses as the second timer is programmed from maximum to minimum?

13. You are working on a microcomputer system whose microprocessor has separate address and data pins. The system has a buffered bus. (a) How many bus transceiver chips like the one shown in Fig.

14-11 would you expect to find on the MPU board? (b) Why?

14. Why doesn't the chip in Fig. 14-7 have a Memory Write line even though it has both I/O Read and I/O Write lines?

14-3 THE SINGLE-CHIP MICROCOMPUTER

The single-chip microcomputer has made it possible to bring the power of microprocessor technology to low-cost products. A single-chip microcomputer has, at a minimum, an MPU, ROM, RAM, and I/O. These are all contained on one integrated circuit. Often the single-chip microcomputer is incorrectly referred to as a "single-chip microprocessor." The single-chip microcomputer is truly a small computer system.

In most cases, these single-chip devices look much like a microcomputer system built by using a powerful microprocessor and some

Analog
microprocessor

Analog-to-digital
converter (ADC)

Digital-to-analog
converter (DAC)

support chips from the same microprocessor family. A few single-chip microcomputers belong to no family. That is, they are designed to do a certain set of jobs but are based on no particular microprocessor family.

In many ways, a single-chip microcomputer that is related to a single-chip microprocessor is much easier to work with. The single-chip microcomputer can use many of the design and servicing aids that have been developed for the microprocessor family. Familiarity with the microprocessor also assures familiarity with the single-chip microcomputer.

Single-chip microcomputers typically have 1024 or 2048 bytes of ROM. The least expensive single-chip microcomputers are always mask-programmed. There are, however, EPROM single-chip microcomputers available. Sometimes an EPROM microcomputer will plug directly into the socket used by the mask-programmed version of the same single-chip microcomputer. The two versions are said to be pin-for-pin compatible devices. This compatibility allows easier development and initial production. The EPROM versions usually cost 25 to 50 times more.

Of course, a single-chip microcomputer must have RAM. The number of bytes of RAM provided is much less than the number of bytes of ROM. Single-chip microcomputers usually have 64, 128, or 256 bytes of RAM. Some single-chip microcomputers have the external connections needed to expand the microcomputer's memory. Other single-chip microcomputers are not expandable. In general, expansion beyond the initial design is neither necessary nor desired. Sin-

gle-chip microcomputers are often used to do a single, specific job. So long as a single-chip microcomputer can do its one job, no expansion is needed.

Many single-chip microcomputers do not permit storage of program instructions in RAM. The RAM is used only for data storage. All program storage is in ROM, because the ROM addresses are the only ones that the program counter can access. The single-chip microcomputer's program is fixed once the ROM is programmed. Again, this lack of flexibility is usually not a problem because the application of the single-chip microcomputer is limited to a single, specific function.

Most single-chip microcomputers have considerable I/O capability. Figure 14-13 shows the pinouts for two slightly different single-chip microcomputers. The single-chip microcomputer in Fig. 14-13(a) offers 16 bidirectional I/O lines and an 8 line bidirectional data bus that is used to expand memory and I/O. The single-chip microcomputer in Fig. 14-13(b) offers three 8-bit parallel ports and a serial port with full modem control. Both of these single-chip microcomputers have internal timers.

Figure 14-14 shows another type of single-chip microcomputer. Called an *analog microprocessor*, this single-chip microcomputer is dedicated to the digital processing of analog signals. The block diagram in Fig. 14-14 shows that this single-chip microcomputer has analog inputs and outputs. On the input side, an ADC (analog-to-digital converter) converts the analog input signals to a digital input word. On the output side, a DAC (digi-

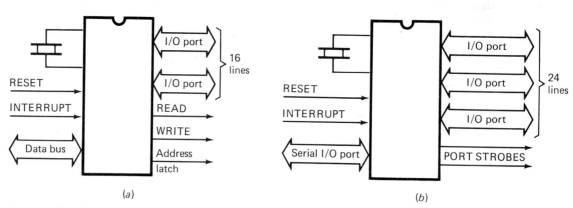

(a)   (b)

Fig. 14-13 Two single-chip microcomputers. Each package offers a somewhat different pinout, but both are I/O-intensive devices.

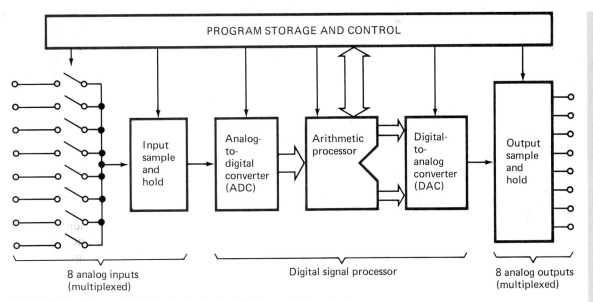

Fig. 14-14 The analog microcomputer. Eight analog input signals are digitized, processed as digital words, and then converted back into processed analog outputs. Some analog filtering is needed on both the inputs and the outputs to remove the effect of the digitizing.

tal-to-analog converter) converts the digital output word to an analog signal.

Both the input and output ports have eight lines. An eight-channel analog multiplexer may be used with a sample-and-hold circuit to convert these eight lines to a single analog channel.

A special-purpose MPU processes the digital signal. The MPU is controlled by special instructions stored in the analog microprocessor's memory.

Since the ADC uses a very fast sampling rate, the ADC can take a number of samples on each input waveform. This sampling method can even work with reasonably high-frequency signals on each input. Sampling theory tells us that to represent the input signal accurately, at least two samples must be taken for each cycle of the highest input frequency. In practice, you will find that five or more samples are the usual number taken at the highest frequency. Filters are used on the analog microcomputers inputs and outputs to assure proper representation of the original waveform and a smoothed output waveform.

Analog microcomputers find use in many areas. For example, although we can describe analog filtering very well mathematically, we cannot easily get reactive and resistive components that exactly implement the

theory. As you know, classic analog filters are implemented using resistors (R), inductors (L), and capacitors (C). Often it is hard or impossible to get real components which exactly match the theoretical requirements. For this reason analog filter design is often a compromise. Using the analog microcomputer, we can come much closer to implementing ideal filter theory. As a result, analog microcomputers sometimes make excellent digital filters. This is done by first digitizing the analog signal. The digital words that represent the analog signal are then operated on by the digital circuits in the analog microprocessor. These operations mathematically change the digital words exactly as the resistive and reactive components would, in theory, change. When the digital words are processed, they are turned back into analog signals.

The analog microcomputer is also an important part of speech recognition and synthesis. Voice recognition requires dividing the voice into its component parts. Then each part must be analyzed. This is a job for the analog microcomputer. To synthesize a voice, a signal made up to white noise is shaped in frequency, amplitude, and time. The result of proper shaping is a nearly human voice. Speech synthesis, too, is a process most easily performed by an analog microcomputer.

Self-Test

Check your understanding by answering these questions.

15. Certain single-chip microcomputers are built in both ROM and EPROM versions. Why are both types manufactured?

16. A remote monitoring system is installed at a large pumping station. It is microprocessor-based. You learn that its present status lets it monitor 32 digital inputs (points) and 8 analog inputs (points). Later, the monitoring system can be expanded to monitor another 8 digital points and 6 more analog points. Would you expect that this product is based on a single-chip microcomputer or on a multiple-chip microcomputer? Why?

17. In one application, the analog microcomputer's ADC samples at 5 times the highest analog-data rate. How many samples (conversions) per second does the ADC make if the maximum signal-data rate on any input is 5 kHz?

18. Probably the single most important feature of the single-chip microprocessor is its
    a. Interrupt structure
    b. Wide memory
    c. Low cost
    d. Positive reset

19. When the single-chip microcomputer is compared with a microprocessor, you will immediately notice the single-chip microcomputer's
    a. Crystal-controlled clock
    b. Large number of I/O ports
    c. Timer
    d. Memory-expansion provision

20. The analog microcomputer uses a sample-and-hold circuit on its inputs to
    a. Hold a sample of the input signal while the ADC converts it to a digital word
    b. Hold the DAC output for each line while the DAC is busy updating the other outputs
    c. Select the desired point on the input waveform (usually the peak) for analog-to-digital conversion
    d. Help pass the 8-bit number to the ADC

21. Most single-chip microcomputers have software-programmable or ROM mask-programmed bidirectional I/O ports. The

ports are made this way so that
    a. The user can decide if the port is to be an input or an output port
    b. The programming effort is reduced in comparison with what it would be if an EPROM were used
    c. The input lines will not be damaged during a DMA operation
    d. (All of the above)

14-4 MICROPROCESSOR SUPPORT INSTRUMENTS

Each new generation of electronic technology has introduced new measurement problems. For example, the development of ECL (emitter-coupled logic) increased the need for very-high-frequency oscilloscopes.

The microprocessor has probably demanded more new design and service instruments than any other new electronic technology.

In this section, we will take a brief look at some of the instruments that you may be expected to use when you work with microprocessor-based systems. Of course, you will also be expected to use standard instruments such as oscilloscopes, counters, voltmeters, and pulse generators.

One of the big problems that microprocessor-based systems presented was that of development and testing. How do you convert a schematic diagram and a software listing into a working microcomputer system? Of course, you can breadboard the hardware, program the ROMs, and then see if the resulting system will work. But what if it does not work? How do you find out what is wrong?

The answer lies in a special-purpose instrument called a *microprocessor development system* (MDS). The MDS plugs into hardware using the same socket that the developed microprocessor will use when it is completed. The MDS has a microprocessor at the other end of this connection. The MDS's microprocessor is connected to extra memory and special logic for capturing the microprocessor's bus data while the microprocessor being tested is running. The MDS is usually controlled by a second microprocessor.

The MDS can put your program into the target system's memory or into the MDS's own memory. The MDS is operated through commands and responses at a video terminal.

The MDS also has software-development capability. The MDS provides a powerful editor for writing assembly-language source code. The MDS also provides an assembler. The MDS's assembler assembles the source code, outputting machine code for your microprocessor.

Once you have created object code for the microprocessor under development, the object code can be loaded into the target system —your hardware. The MDS lets you "single-step" the program. That is, you can execute the program one step at a time. The MDS also lets you "breakpoint" your program. Breakpointing lets you run a few instructions at full speed and then stop. At each stop, you check to make sure that everything is going all right. The MDS will also let you run the complete program at its full speed.

Some microprocessor development systems also offer high-level languages such as BASIC and Pascal. These high-level languages also generate object code for your microprocessor.

Simply put, the microprocessor development system's job is to let you debug your hardware and software in "real time" or as close to real time as is possible. "Real time" means that the microprocessor's instructions execute at the normal operating speed. That is, execution of the instructions is now slowed down by any testing process such as single-stepping.

Real-time testing helps find problems that happen when the microprocessor is running at the system's maximum speed. Often these problems do not show up if the microprocessor is run at its slower speeds.

For example, suppose your microprocessor system is to input data through its parallel I/O port. Each time that you slowly step your microprocessor system through its instructions, they all work very well. However, when you run the system at full speed, the system goes into an endless loop.

An MDS helps you solve this problem. In this case, you will use the MDS to trace the data transfers on your microprocessor's memory-address bus and data bus for a few instructions before and a few instructions after the I/O instruction that causes the trouble.

Using the MDS, you can start tracing (storing) each bus transaction after some trigger point. The trigger point is usually when a certain instruction is executed or when a certain memory location is addressed. Later you can review all the data captured in the microprocessor development system's trace memory.

In our example, you find that at high speeds the I/O port's status register is always reset to 0 by a timing error that happens only at high speeds. An all-0 status register will prevent the microprocessor from inputting data.

Microprocessor development systems have many features other than the trace mode. For example, after each instruction is executed, the MDS can display the status of each MPU register plus a few selected memory locations. The MDS cannot do this at full speed, but the MDS still performs this operation on a limited amounts of code at fairly high speeds.

Other MDS features include sophisticated triggering to help find a fault in the tested system. Perhaps one of the microprocessor development system's strongest points is that it permits correcting software errors very quickly. When a software error is found, it can be corrected by using the editor. The program can be quickly modified, documented, and reassembled, and is soon ready for another test.

The oscilloscope is no longer the most important instrument for working with microprocessor-based systems, as the logic analyzer is a much more powerful instrument than the oscilloscope.

The logic analyzer uses a display like that of an oscilloscope. However, the logic analyzer's operation is quite different. First, the logic analyzer displays signals from a large number of inputs. Logic analyzers used for microprocessor design and service can display 16 to 32 inputs at a time. Second, the logic analyzer's inputs respond to logic levels, not to analog signals. That is, a logic analyzer displays its inputs as logic "1s" or logic "0s."

Usually, logic analyzers have very versatile and sophisticated triggering capability. For example, you can trigger on a 16- or a 32-bit word that appears in parallel on all 16 or 32 inputs. If necessary, you can also trigger on a 16- or 32-bit word that appears serially on any one of the 16 or 32 inputs.

Logic analyzers also let you trigger and then wait to display the related events until a preset number of pulses or words have passed.

The data from the logic analyzer's inputs is stored in the logic analyzer's digital memory. For example, the memory for a 32-input logic analyzer might be able to store 256 32-bit transactions. This means that such a logic analyzer stores 256 32-bit words.

Because the input data are stored in mem-

BASIC

Pascal

Real time

Logic analyzer

Timing display

State display

Logic probe

Signature
analyzer

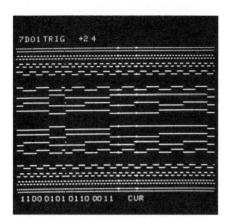

Fig. 14-15 A logic analyzer's timing display.
Much like a multiple-trace oscilloscope, the tim-
ing-display shows the timing relationships between the different logic signals in a multisignal
system. (*Courtesy of Tektronix Inc.*)

ory, you can have the logic analyzer display
data that were generated both before and after
triggering. For example, if you trigger on a
single word, there can be 255 words that came
earlier still stored in memory. The analyzer
can be told to keep these data and not accept
data after the trigger. Likewise the analyzer
can be told to store the 256 words *after* the trigger. An ordinary oscilloscope cannot do this.

Logic analyzers have two different kinds of
displays. One is called the timing display,
and the other the state display. The two different displays are shown in Figs. 14-15 and
14-16.

The timing display is shown in Fig. 14-15.
This timing display looks much like the display of an ordinary multitrace oscilloscope.

Fig. 14-16 A logic analyzer's state display. This
display shows the logic state (logic "1" or logic
"0") of each tested line in the system each time
that there is a trigger signal on the selected lines.
(*Courtesy of Tektronix Inc.*)

The data for the timing display are taken from
the logic analyzer's memory instead of directly
from the inputs. The timing display is produced by sampling the logic analyzer's inputs
at a regular interval under control of a system
clock. Usually the timing display samples the
data 5 times faster than the highest clock rate
in the system. The timing display's sampling
rate determines the display's time resolution.
For example, if the sampling period is 100 ns
you can only measure, time, and capture
events that are longer than 100 ns.

The timing display is used to measure timing relationships in a system. Looking at a
timing display, you can easily see which event
happened first. You can also use the timing
display to measure the time relationship between different events on the display.

The state display shows the binary status of
the logic analyzer's inputs. However, the
state display is updated each time the selected
inputs change state. That is, a change in the
measured system causes the input data to be
recorded. The data are usually presented in
binary, octal, or hexadecimal form. Figure
14-16 shows a typical binary state display.

State displays are very useful for watching
the data transactions on a microcomputer's
bus. You can see each data word as it occurs
on the bus. If there are no changes for a
while, the state display waits for the next
change. That is, there is no measured time
interval between the different state displays.
The state display simply stores a sequence of
changing signals.

Two other relatively simple instruments are
popular for microprocessor development and
service work. Both instruments are very important. These instruments are the logic
probe and the signature analyzer.

The logic probe is a simple logic-level detec-
tor and display. The probe shows when a circuit is at logic "1" and when it is at logic "0."
Some logic probes have a pulse-stretching circuit. The pulse stretcher makes the logic
probe's display give off a flash each time there
is a pulse in the monitored circuit. The pulse
stretcher can be used to catch very short
pulses.

The logic probe is a good instrument for
checking the microprocessor's I/O ports, status lines, and other slow-moving data points.
For example, a microprocessor can be programmed to execute a loop that repeatedly
reads one memory location. The logic probe
can then be used to make sure that the Mem-

ory Read pulse is reaching all points in the system. In some microprocessor systems, it is possible to examine the bus signals when the system is in this tight loop. In other systems, there are normally some invalid data on the bus as well as the desired data, making this kind of examination of bus signals impossible.

The signature analyzer is really just a logic probe with some memory. The memory is in the form of a 16-bit shift register. The signature analyzer is used to monitor the data on a single line. The product being tested must be preconditioned by a diagnostic program. The diagnostic program makes a repeating serial data stream on the line being tested. The signature analyzer monitors this line and displays the line's "signature" on a four-digit, seven-segment display.

The line's proper signature has been recorded earlier. When looking for faults, you compare the display signature with the previously recorded signature. If the signatures do not match, there is a very high probability of a bit error in the serial stream.

The signature analyzer lets you look for a single error in a long stream of data. This is very useful for checking systems in which you cannot stop or slow down system operation to make the system respond one bit at a time.

Figure 14-17 shows how the signature analyzer displays a signature. In this example, the microprocessor is executing a diagnostic program. The diagnostic program sends a repeating stream of logic "1s" and logic "0s" over each data line. This is caused by repetitive data being sent back and forth over the data

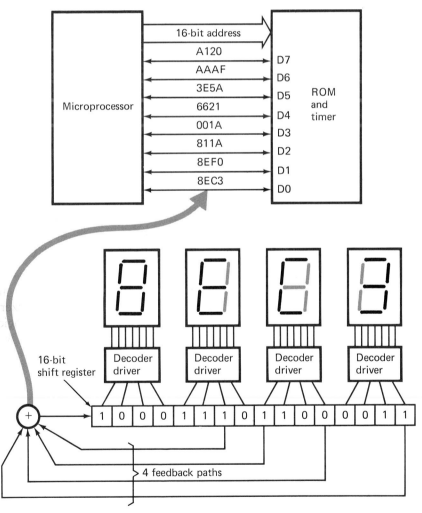

Fig. 14-17 The signature analyzer monitoring D0 on a microprocessor's D0 data bus line. On the microcomputer's schematic you can see that each line on the data bus has a characteristic signature.

bus. If the diagnostic program is working properly, each data line will have its own unique and constant signature. The stream of data on D0 is applied to the signature analyzer's input. The input stream passes through adders, which combine it with signals fed back from the shift register. The result goes into the 16-bit shift register. The shift register's parallel outputs are decoded and displayed as the stream's signature.

The display signature is compared to the signature shown on the schematic for this test. As you can see, each data bus line has its own signature. When troubleshooting this microcomputer system, you will use the signature analyzer to check each line. A single bit error in the stream will cause a different signature to be displayed, showing the location of a fault.

Self-Test

Check your understanding by answering these questions.

22. You would expect the oscilloscope not to be as useful as the logic analyzer for digital-system repair because the oscilloscope
    a. Has a slow phosphor
    b. Cannot display hexadecimal numbers
    c. Has no storage
    d. Does not have the needed frequency response

23. One feature of an MDS lets you take snapshots of all the microprocessor's registers after each instruction is executed.
    You would expect that this feature
    a. Runs in real time
    b. Runs at a somewhat slower speed
    c. Runs no faster than single-stepping
    d. Requires a logic analyzer

24. The microprocessor development system's *primary* job is to
    a. Develop microprocessor software
    b. Trace bus operations
    c. Display MPU register conditions
    d. Debug a microprocessor system's firmware in near real time

25. You would expect signature analysis not to be useful on a system that was not designed with signature analysis in mind, because
    a. The system will not have the right logic levels
    b. It requires a repeating diagnostic routine with predefined signatures
    c. The signature analyzer requires a slower operation
    d. Of the signature analyzer's shift register with feedback

26. The logic analyzer's ___?___ mode is the closest to a conventional oscilloscope's multiple-trace display.
    a. State   c. Pretriggered
    b. Timing   d. Hexadecimal

27. A logic analyzer's operation depends on having ___?___ to store many samples of the input signals.
    a. A CRT
    b. Digital memory
    c. Selective triggering
    d. Multiple inputs

Summary

1. If a microprocessor has multiplexed address/data lines, it must have timing outputs to tell peripheral devices when the address is valid and when the data are valid.

2. Most microprocessor lines are TTL-compatible. This is true of both input lines and output lines. These lines will drive a single TTL load.

3. Most microprocessors use a two-phase nonoverlapping clock.

4. Usually a 1- to 20-MHz crystal is used to control the oscillator's frequency. Some microprocessor oscillators are controlled by an RC or LC network. These oscillators also can be driven by an external signal.

5. +5 V dc is the most common microprocessor supply voltage, although older microprocessors also use +12 V dc and −5 V dc.

6. CMOS is used for low-power designs (those consuming a few milliwatts). MOS microprocessors use 0.5 to 1.5 W.

7. The microprocessor's $\overline{RESET}$ input initializes the program counter and control logic after a power-up.

8. Most microprocessors have at least a maskable and a nonmaskable interrupt in-

put. Many microprocessors have a number of maskable interrupts, each with its own priority and vector address. Once interrupted, the microprocessor outputs an Interrupt Acknowledge signal.

9. A DMA Request input causes the microprocessor to tri-state its data bus- and address bus. The microprocessor does this and then outputs a DMA Acknowledge signal after completing the current instruction.

10. Parallel I/O port logic is usually built as a custom IC for a particular microprocessor family. Parallel I/O and timers are found in family-compatible ROM and RAM chips. Timers let you initiate a delay using hardware. Initiating a delay in this way does not tie up the microprocessor, as a software delay does.

11. The bidirectional bus transceiver chip buffers the data bus. This chip boosts the microprocessor's drive capability for long lines and several TTL loads.

12. Many of the microprocessor's family of support chips are fully programmable.

13. The single-chip microcomputer has an MPU, ROM, RAM, and I/O.

14. The analog microprocessor has an ADC on its input and a DAC on its output. The analog microprocessor usually has multiple inputs and outputs controlled by an analog multiplexer. The analog microprocessor has a special set of instructions designed to perform special signal-processing functions on the digitized analog signals.

15. The logic analyzer is one of the most important digital development and servicing tools. Logic analyzers have both state displays and timing displays. The timing display shows the timing relationships of many signals. This display looks like a multiple-trace oscilloscope. The state display shows the logic state of each line at a system-transition time.

16. The logic probe lets you see the logic state of a particular line. The logic probe is very good for checking slowly changing lines.

17. The signature analyzer is used to service complex digital products that cannot be easily single-stepped.

18. In order to test a product, the signature analyzer needs to have the product put into a diagnostic loop.

19. Signatures are compared to previously recorded signatures. If the test signature and the standard signature do not match, then a bit error is likely.

Chapter Review Questions

14-1. Microprocessors are usually packaged in ____?____-pin DIPs.
a. 16 b. 24 c. 28 d. 40

14-2. Multiplexed address/data lines are used to reduce the
a. Timing-signal pin count
b. Complexity of addressing peripherals
c. Microprocessor's pin count
d. (All of the above)

14-3. A 16-bit microprocessor is packaged in a 40-pin DIP. You would expect that it has multiplexed address/data lines. This microprocessor can directly address 1,048,576 memory locations. The first (low) address and data line is AD0. List the other lines.

14-4. What additional signals are needed so that you can use the information on a multiplexed address/data bus?

14-5. When a manufacturer says the that a microprocessor is TTL-compatible, what does this probably mean?

14-6. What do the MPU status outputs tell you?

14-7. How does a microprocessor use the clock signal?

14-8. The microprocessor's clock is often internally generated. The clock circuit generates a ____?____-phase clock.

14-9. How is the clock oscillator's frequency normally controlled?

14-10. What other frequency-control techniques are sometimes used?

14-11. Most microprocessors need only a ____?____ V dc power source. Typically they draw about ____?____ to ____?____ W from this source.

14-12. Explain what the microprocessor's $\overline{\text{RESET}}$ input does and why it is needed.

14-13. Why is it called a $\overline{\text{RESET}}$ input instead of a RESET input?

14-14. The ____?____ input is not considered to be a microprocessor interrupt input.
a. $\overline{\text{RESET}}$ c. $\overline{\text{DMA Request}}$
b. Nonmaskable   d. Maskable

14-15. The Interrupt Acknowledge signal comes as the microprocessor becomes available to process the
a. DMA   c. Current instruction
b. Interrupt   d. Next instruction

14-16. The result of a DMA request is
a. A tri-stated memory-address bus
b. A DMA Acknowledge signal
c. A tri-stated data bus
d. (All of the above)

14-17. During DMA operation, the microprocessor halts operation until
a. Memory access starts
b. The data bus is accessed
c. The $\overline{\text{DMA REQUEST}}$ line is released
d. (All of the above)

14-18. The 8085's $\overline{\text{READY}}$ input is used so that a slow peripheral device can request that the processor
a. Wait a number of MPU cycles until it is ready
b. Wait until the DMA is complete
c. Interrupt its current instructions
d. Generate a Memory Read pulse

14-19. Parallel I/O devices are usually built with discrete MSI and SSI TTL logic or they use
a. All CMOS
b. Strictly parallel Data Out
c. Custom general-purpose I/O ports for a particular microprocessor family
d. Strictly parallel Data In

14-20. A family-related chip usually contains
a. Microprocessor-bus interface logic including address decoding
b. A serial I/O port with parity
c. At least 256K of RAM
d. An EPROM

14-21. A hardware timer is often used to reduce the software load on a microcomputer. Why?

14-22. Briefly explain how a hardware timer operates. What are its two basic modes of operation?

14-23. Many 8-bit microprocessors have, in their family of parts, those devices needed to make a "three-chip-minimum-part system." What are the basic functions needed and how are they likely to be split among the three chips?

14-24. Most time-of-day clocks get their tic from the 60-Hz line. What does this mean? What happens if the system is operated from a 50-Hz line?

14-25. Explain what a bus transceiver does and why it is needed.

14-26. Often a microprocessor manufacturer will indicate that a family of microprocessor support chips is fully programmable. What does this mean?

14-27. What impact would you expect a fully programmable set of peripheral chips to have on the microprocessor's start-up software?

14-28. Why do we say the term "single-chip microprocessor" is not descriptive of the actual parts? What term should be used?

14-29. Typically a single-chip microcomputer will have ____?____ bytes of ROM.
a. 64   b. 256   c. 1024   d. 16,384

14-30. Often, single-chip microcomputers offer
a. Serial I/O ports   c. MPU
b. Many parallel I/O ports   d. RAM

14-31. The analog microprocessor's input is an analog multiplexer. The multiplexer is connected to a(n)
a. DAC   c. Timer
b. ADC   d. (All of the above)

14-32. The analog microprocessor's instructions are especially designed for
a. 8-bit data   c. Signal processing
b. Wide memory   d. (All of the above)

14-33. The analog microprocessor depends on sampling theory. Sampling theory states that you must sample at a rate that is at least ____?____ times greater than the highest frequency that you wish to input.
a. 2   b. 5   c. 7   d. 32

14-34. Why can the analog microprocessor do a job that an analog RC filter might not be able to achieve?

14-35. The microprocessor has introduced a need for the
a. Microprocessor development system
b. Logic analyzer
c. Signature analyzer
d. (All of the above)

14-36. List three different functions that an MDS can perform.

14-37. What is the MDS's job?

14-38. Briefly explain what the MDS's trace feature does.

14-39. What are the two ways in which a logic analyzer can display its information? Briefly explain the difference between these two modes.

14-40. How can the logic analyzer display "pretrigger" information?

14-41. What must be done to a product before a signature analyzer can provide useful data? Why?

14-42. How does the signature analyzer differ from the logic probe in what it can measure?

Answers to Self-Tests

1. So that the microprocessor can respond predictably when simultaneous interrupts occur.

2. The negative true logic is used because a number of open-collector outputs can easily assert the line. See Fig. 14-18. It is called negative true logic because the bus line is true or asserted when it is at the lower of its two voltages.

3. A timing routine using a decrementing (or incrementing) register.

4. d.   5. b.   6. d.
7. b.   8. d.

9. You need a divide-by-1500, and so the counter is preset to 05DC.

10. No. A microprocessor plus the RAM-timer-I/O chip does not give you any ROM to store the program, nor does it give you a way to load the program into RAM. You will need to use at least an additional ROM chip and probably some address decoding.

11. See Fig. 14-19. The ROM address lines A0 to A10 and the RAM address lines A0 to A7 are all connected to the 16-bit address bus. The first address decoder decodes address lines A11, A12, and A13. The outputs 0, 1, 2, and 3 drive the ROM Chip Selects. When A13 is high, address-decoder line 4, 5, 6, or 7 is selected, indicating that a memory location of 8192 or higher is being selected. Any one of these lines enables address decoder 2, which decodes memory-address lines A8 and A9. Address decoder 2 is used to select one of the four RAM chips.

12. The first timer divides the 5-MHz 200-ns clock by 16,383 so that its output is always 1 pulse every 3.276600 ms. Therefore, the second timer's output range is 6.5532 ms (at a divide ratio of 2) to 53.680537 s (at a divide ratio of 16,383).

13. (*a*) Two. (*b*) One for data bus lines D0 to D3 and one for data bus lines D4 to D7. No other lines are bidirectional. Therefore, no others need bus transceivers.

14. Because you cannot write into a ROM.

15. The single-chip microcomputer with ROM is for high-volume, low-cost applications. The single-chip microcomputer with RAM is for low-volume or development applications.

16. Probably a multiple-chip microprocessor system, because such systems have a great deal of I/O capability.

17. 200,000. There are 5 samples per cycle and 8 channels. The highest analog data rate is 5 kHz, or 5000 cycles per second.

18. c.   19. b.   20. a.
21. a.   22. c.   23. b.
24. d.   25. b.   26. b.
27. b.

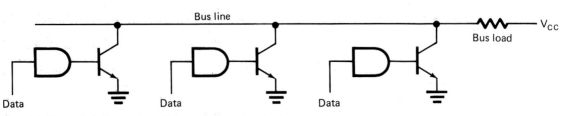

Fig. 14-18   A bus line asserted by negative true logic.

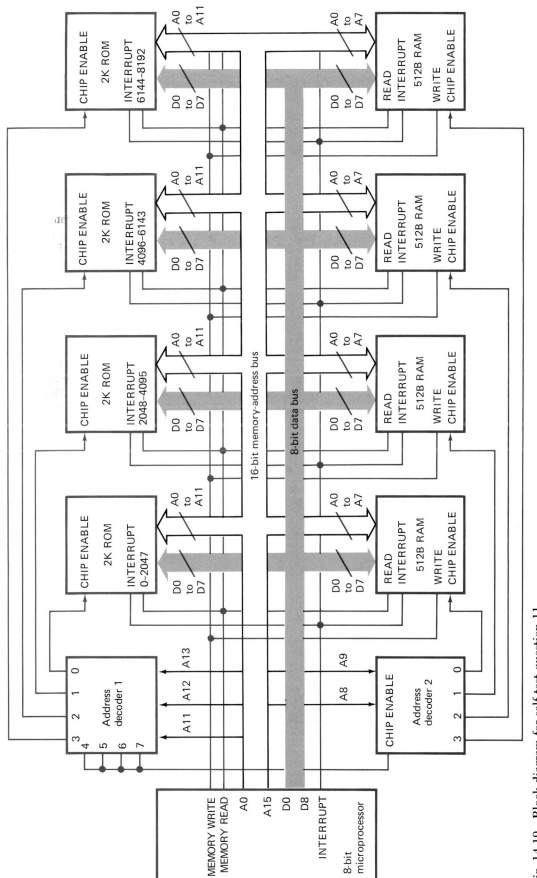

Fig. 14-19 Block diagram for self-test question 11.

Index